A Century of The Sherman Act: American Economic Opinion, 1890–1990

Edited By
Jack C. High and Wayne E. Gable

George Mason University Press
Fairfax, Virginia

Copyright © 1992 by
George Mason University Press
4400 University Drive
Fairfax, VA 22030

Distributed by arrangement with
University Publishing Associates, Inc.

4720 Boston Way
Lanham, MD 20706

3 Henrietta Street
London WC2E 8LU England

Library of Congress Cataloging-in-Publication Data

A century of the Sherman Act : American economic opinion, 1890–1990 /
edited by Jack C. High and Wayne E. Gable.
p.   cm.
Includes bibliographical references and index.
1. Antitrust law—Economic aspects—United States—History.
2. Competition—United States—History.
I. High, Jack C. II. Gable, Wayne E.
KF1652.C46   1992
343.73'0721—dc20   [347.303721]   91–38710 CIP

ISBN 0–913969–41–9 (cloth : alk. paper)
ISBN 0–913969–42–7 (paper : alk. paper)

The paper used in this publication meets the minimum requirements of
American National Standard for Information Sciences—Permanence
of Paper for Printed Library Materials, ANSI Z39.48–1984.

Acknowledgements

We gratefully acknowledge the permission to reprint the selections contained in this volume. The authors and publishers who gave permission are listed at the beginning of each article.

Albert Loan, Charles Oliver, Trudy Pearce, Mark Perry, Virginia Stouffer, and William Tulloh provided research and/or editorial assistance. Kenneth Elzinga and Charles Rowley read the manuscript and offered suggestions for improvement. Sandy Slater set the type. Mark Carroll, James Fisher, and Isabelle Gibb from George Mason University Press guided and encouraged this project at various stages. We thank everyone for his or her help.

Finally, we offer our appreciation and our gratitude to the staff and faculty of the Center for the Study of Market Processes at George Mason University. Colleen Morretta, Pamela Munkacsy, Mary Johnson, Tyler Cowen, Jerome Ellig, Don Lavoie, and Karen Vaughn have created an environment that makes research far more pleasurable than it would otherwise be.

Table of Contents

Introduction

Jack C. High and Wayne E. Gable

Congress passed the Sherman Antitrust Act on July 2, 1890 with a minimum of debate and fanfare, at least by Washington standards. The debate fills only 19 pages in the *Congressional Record,* while the McKinley tariff, which passed on September 10 of the same year, takes up 81 pages. But if the Sherman Act generated little debate at the time of its passage, it has more than made up for it in the intervening century. The number of illustrious economists who have written on antitrust law is large, too large, in fact, to be included within these pages. And the diversity of viewpoints is only slightly less pronounced than the numbers. It is not true, as the old saw has it, that two economists will produce three opinions on any one subject, but it is true that economists' opinions on the merits of antitrust are deeply divided.

For those who like easy answers—cut, dried, and served cold in a textbook—the current volume will hold little interest. But for those who want to reflect on difficult issues, who want to see some of the finest minds in the profession at work, the debate on antitrust, which has now gone on for a century, is well worth reading.

This volume lets economists of different stripes—John Bates Clark and Oliver Williamson, Joseph Bain and Harold Demsetz, John Kenneth Galbraith and Robert Bork—present their analyses of antitrust and competition.[1]

Along with discussion of antitrust's proper scope, we have included several discussions of antitrust enforcement, ranging from early recommendations that monopolists could be effectively disciplined by full financial disclosure to recent recommendations that they can be efficiently disciplined through fines.

Early Views: Competition as Rivalry

The "antitrust" laws received that name because they were originally directed against a particular form of business organization, the "trust," which placed the stock of many previously competing companies in the hands of a

---

[1]We sincerely hope that Robert Bork will forgive us for labelling him an economist. Strictly speaking, he is a distinguished legal scholar, but his writing has been sufficiently concerned with economics, and his influence has been sufficiently great, that we have included him in this volume.

single group of owners. As an economic organization, a trust centralized capital.

In common with most economists of his day, John Bates Clark does not oppose trusts *per se*.[2] He distinguishes between concentration of capital and monopoly. Concentrated capital is a part of economic progress, a business form that lowers costs and renders workers more productive. Monopoly, on the other hand, restricts output and raises prices.

Because Clark believes concentration was often efficient, he goes out of his way to attack various proposals for controlling trusts, including limits on corporate size, systematic dismantling of large corporations, maximum price controls, taxes on monopoly profits, and state ownership. All of these proposals, he believes, would stunt economic progress and deprive the public of the lower costs that large-scale enterprises can achieve. Aside from greater financial disclosure, Clark sees only two other restrictions necessary to curb monopolistic abuses: prohibition of predatory pricing and of boycotts of dealers by producers. Both of these practices place competitors and potential competitors at an unfair disadvantage. "Proper regulation," Clark avers, "will not shield an independent producer from any legitimate rivalry, though it will protect him from what is not real rivalry, but a disabling policy on the part of the big competitor."(p. 6)

Interestingly enough, Clark saw trusts as a threat to investors rather than to consumers. Clark argues that promoters usually assembled trusts, sold the shares of stock they had received as a fee, and then left the businesses in the hands of incompetent managers. The investor "...wants to have the trust make money by producing goods and selling them for more than they cost. But the manipulator often wants something so distinct from this as to draw a sharp line between his interests and all legitimate interests." (p. 3) To counter this problem, Clark essentially calls for extensive disclosure of information about the trusts' assets and prospective earnings, for otherwise, "The investor who puts money into the trust must guess as best he can what property he is getting, and the guess is apt to be a bad one for him." (p. 4)

Provided that the playing field is fair, Clark believed that potential competition exercises a powerful restraining influence upon the trusts. "If the trusts charge too much for their products, new mills are built and prices go down. Many early trusts did this, with the result that new mills were built." (p. 4) Disclosure of information about trusts' earning capacity, intended to protect investors, would also protect the general public, for predictions of high profits will likely encourage competitors to enter the industry.

Robert Liefmann retains Clark's focus on rivalry, but he shows much less sympathy for any antitrust laws. Rivalry, he believes, will frequently lead to industrial concentration because it is often least expensive for one or a small

---

[2]See Thomas DiLorenzo and Jack High, "Competition and Antitrust, Historically Considered," *Economic Inquiry*, vol. 23, July 1988.

number of firms to produce the entire industry output. This cost reduction occurs not just because of economies of scale, but because competition can lead to excessive capital investment as entrepreneurs introduce new machinery before it is socially optimal to retire the old machines owned by their competitors. Cartels and trusts help check this problem.

In Liefmann's view, the market is a process in which a few competitors may come to dominate a field, but they find themselves dethroned if they attempt to exploit their dominant position by raising prices. "Only in this sense is free competition the basic principle of our economic order; more accurately, it is not competition, but the pursuit of gain of the individual when free to develop, which organizes existing economic society..." (p. 14) Provocatively, Leifmann argues, "The climax of competition is monopoly, and all competition is nothing but a striving for monopoly." (p. 13) To ask whether competition or monopoly should prevail, therefore, is to thoroughly misunderstand how the economy actually functions: "It will appear that the question...—free competition or monopoly—is wrongly framed, that choice cannot be made between the two principles of organization; rather these inseparable principles always operate and react upon one another " (p. 10)

Liefmann has nothing good to say about U.S. anti-monopoly laws, although he favors, in principle, doing something about what modern audiences would call corporate governance issues. If the government wants an antitrust policy, Liefmann suggests, it should encourage the dissemination of financial information about trusts. He concludes, "I should suppose that, in a democratic country above all, some such means of utilizing public opinion as a remedial agent would be peculiarly adapted for combating the abuses of the trusts." (p. 18)

Allyn Young takes issue with Liefmann's central thesis. In discussing the probable scope of the Sherman Act Young says, "There is a substantial difference between competing and 'attempting to monopolize' in purpose and consequently in methods." (p. 20) In Young's view, competition occurs when the firm strives to maximize its profits under the limitations created by the existence of rival firms, where as monopoly occurs when the firm has eliminated "the limitations which competition sets upon one's ability to buy and sell at such prices and on such terms as one pleases." (p. 20) Therefore, both the Sherman Act and later antitrust legislation did indeed have a sensible basis in economic theory.

Given that "restraint of trade" had been illegal under the common law, Young addresses the question of what, if anything, the Sherman Act changed. At first glance, it might not seem that the law had changed anything; like the term "restraint of trade," the term "monopolization" was broad and would have to be given definite meaning by the courts. The Supreme Court, however, held that the Sherman Act did indeed have a wider scope than the common law. The Supreme Court's interpretations of the Sherman Act in the Standard Oil and American Tobacco cases clarified that actions taken to create a monopoly would be considered illegal even if they did not meet the old common-law definition of restraints of trade: "Whether such consolidations [the trusts] are contracts, combinations, or conspiracies in restraint of trade within the meaning of the common law terms may be a matter of doubt. But there is now no question that, if their purpose is monopoly, they come within the condemnation of the Sherman Act."(p. 21)

The Sherman Act's elastic language was both a blessing and a curse, in Young's view. It was a blessing because new, monopolistic business practices and forms of organization could inevitably be expected to spring up, and broad language gave the courts the discretion to protect the public. It was a curse because Congress failed to spell out a list of specific practices that were definitely illegal. Young saw the Clayton and Federal Trade Commission Acts as partial attempts to remedy this deficiency

The Rise of Structure-Conduct-Performance

Writing in 1937, Edward Mason documents the shift in economists' thinking about monopoly and competition. Twenty years previously, economists and lawyers had defined both terms in pretty much the same way. Freedom of entry led to competition; restrictions on entry led to monopoly. Monopoly injured the public interest because rivals were excluded from the market, while competition benefitted the public because rivals were free to enter.

Since then, however, economists had refined and redefined competition and monopoly as analytical tools. A monopolist had become a firm which had any control over price, not just a firm which benefitted from restrictions on entry. Mason states:

> The antithesis of the legal conception of monopoly is *free* competition, understood to be a situation in which the freedom of any individual or firm to engage in legitimate economic activity is not restrained by the state, by agreements between competitors or by the predatory practices of a rival...But.. the antithesis of the economic conception of monopoly is not *free* but *pure* competition, understood to be a situation in which no seller or buyer has any control over the price of his product. (p. 27)

Mason recognizes that identifying monopoly with control over the market price yields theoretical rigor, but that it also makes the economist's definition of monopoly less useful for public policy. Employing the economist's definition would make antitrust cases much more complex, and besides, "It is...by no means clear that the preservation of all the competitive elements and the suppression of all the monopolistic elements would be in the public interest, however conceived." (p. 37)

If economists' new theory of competition is to contribute to public policy, Mason suggests, extensive further economic research on monopoly and competition is necessary. He notes. "It is easy enough to present evidence of monopoly situations, which, to economics, is merely the absence of pure competition...But these practices are hardly sufficient evidence of the presence or possibility of market controls adverse to the public interest." (p. 39)

Joseph Bain took up Mason's challenge. Employing the perfectly competitive model, he identifies a class of "barriers to entry" much more extensive than those of earlier economists, whose definition of barriers encompassed state actions and predatory acts by incumbent firms. He advocates using antitrust policy to ease the conditions of entry in order to move industries closer to perfect competition. He offers the following set of policy recommendations:

1. Since high entry barriers lead to output restrictions and excess profits, these barriers should be reduced.
2. It may be advisable to leave modest entry barriers in place, since their removal could lead to "structural instability" and inefficiency.
3. Barriers based solely on economies of scale in production and distribution should not be attacked, but those based on advertising should be.
4. Barriers based on product differentiation and absolute cost differences should be attacked through "patent law reform, a policy designed to ease the supply of funds in the capital markets, attacks on resource monopolization by integrated processing firms and on unnecessary integration generally, consumer education, and grade labelling." (p. 43)
5. Policies to speed up entry are desirable. These policies, Bain argues, are likely to be more effective than dissolution or dismemberment of large companies. He bases his recommendations on an empirical study classifying industries by the extent of their entry barriers, such as "very high," "substantial," and "moderate to low." Industries with "very high" barriers had higher rates of return on equity than the others, suggesting that they were earning monopoly profits.

Bain suggests that existing antitrust laws offered broad scope to attack most barriers to entry—except those based on product differentiation. Regarding product differentiation, he writes, "Bases for action are shaky, and remedies are not apparent. In this area it would appear that a novel approach in regulatory legislation and in the assumption of functions by the government is probably required..." (p. 54) Indeed, Bain's approach to industrial economics, itself once novel, held the limelight for several decades.

Early Doubts

That is not to say that either the structure-conduct-performance approach or the antitrust laws enjoyed unanimous approval within the economics profession. H.S. Denison and John Kenneth Galbraith take the perfectly competitive ideal literally. Denison and Galbraith reject antitrust as the ultimate solution to monopoly problems because they believe that an antitrust program extensive enough to restore self-regulating competition would lead to a massive dissolution of American companies. They note, "We have seen that it is not '100% monopolies,' or even firms controlling 51% of the industry, but a growth of single producers to sizes large enough (perhaps 5%) to affect price appreciably which is the basic factor in eliminating the self-regulating character of the industry." (p. 61) Not surprisingly, they find the economy sorely lacking when compared to the perfectly competitive ideal.

Just as Bork[3] would some forty years later, Denison and Galbraith recognize that deconcentration would impose immense efficiency losses on the economy. They therefore accept large corporations as a fact of life. In place of antitrust, they propose an "exploration in the art of regulation," known to 1980s observers as industrial policy. Congress would establish a commission to study industries with "low social performance." With the input of industry representatives, the commission would establish and enforce production, price, and labor policies. Such a plan's superiority to antitrust should be clear: "Rather than blindly sub-dividing the units of an industry in the faint hope that certain desirable results will come out of the sub-division, we propose that the results be defined and a program laid out directly to achieve these socially desirable and defined results." (p. 62)

Denison and Galbraith brush aside possible constitutional objections as "objections of a purely legal sort." (p. 63) Since the purpose of the law is to serve the public, they advocate making any legal and constitutional changes necessary to put their proposal into action.

Like Denison and Galbraith, Joseph Schumpeter too accepts the existence of large firms as a fact of life. But where as Denison and Galbraith view the seemingly chaotic state of markets as a sign of failure, Schumpeter sees continual changes and upheaval as the essence of the competitive process. Indeed, innovation and change play a major role in containing monopolistic practices. The competitor who creates a new product, or a new use for an old product, or a better management structure, is much more significant than the competitor who produces the same product at some small reduction in cost.

While this notion is itself something of a challenge to structure-conduct-performance, Schumpeter goes even further, suggesting that many seemingly restrictive, monopolistic practices actually enhance welfare. Typically, he says, economists and governments equate restrictive practices with "loss of opportunities to produce." In a world dominated by the "perennial gale" of creative destruction, though, the availability of practices such as supra-competitive pricing and even predatory investment in excess capacity can encourage entrepreneurs to invest in risky new ventures. "There is no more of paradox in this than there is in saying that motorcars are traveling faster than they otherwise would *because* they are provided with brakes." (p. 66)

---

[3]Cf. Bork quotation on pp. xv.

This realization does not make a case for *laissez-faire*. However, "It does show that there is no general case for indiscriminate 'trust-busting' or for the prosecution of everything that qualifies as a restraint of trade." (p. 69)

Competition means rivalry to Schumpeter, and he also refers back to an earlier definition of monopoly. In contrast to Mason and Bain, who find elements of monopoly in the situation of any seller who does not face a flat demand curve, Schumpeter opts for what he calls the "Cournot-Marshall" theory of monopoly: A monopolist is a single seller who can "exploit at pleasure a given pattern of demand." (p. 76) So defined, long-run monopoly in capitalist economies is probably even more rare than perfect competition.

Even in this rare situation, though, the case against monopoly is hardly irrefutable. In the real world, Schumpeter notes, "[M]onopoly prices are not necessarily higher or monopoly outputs smaller than competitive prices and outputs would be at the levels of productive and organizational efficiency that are within the reach of the type of firm compatible with the competitive hypothesis." (p. 78) Such realizations "dim the halo that once surrounded perfect competition..." (p. 79) And if one rejects perfect competition as an ideal, one loses the economic rationale for criticizing many of the practices which the antitrust laws have made illegal.

Lingering Doubts

Schumpeter and Galbraith both offered fundamental criticisms of the perfectly competitive ideal. Through the 1960s, a number of other economists outside of the Chicago tradition continued to voice similar concerns. Some were more willing than others to accommodate the theory of perfect competition.

G.B. Richardson believes that economists, in studying monopolistic resource misallocation, have concentrated almost exclusively on only one possible way that market structure can influence industry performance. Market structure, he points out, can also influence the amount and type of information available to entrepreneurs, and information flows also affect industry performance. Furthermore, there is no guarantee that a perfectly competitive industry structure will also do the best job of disseminating information and prompting entrepreneurs to act upon it. A concentrated or cartelized industry may offer a more predictable investment climate, for example, encouraging investment and fostering efficiency.

In Richardson's analysis, competitors' knowledge of each others production plans is as much an opportunity for efficiency as for monopolization. "[T]he profitability of investment...in the production of a particular good will depend upon the relationship between the demand for that good and the total supply planned by competitors...[The perfectly competitive model] leaves this total volume of competitive supply quite unrestricted and therefore unpredictable." (p. 86) Richardson concludes bluntly, "It is possible for firms to undertake informed production planning, and thus promote adjustment of supply to demand, only when competition is less than perfect—a condition which the real world, fortunately, normally grants us." (p. 87)

He notes that geography, economies of scale, and product differentiation are "natural imperfections" which may be sufficient to promote efficient planning even in the absence of overt collusion. In some cases, however, collusion may be necessary. The end result is a revisionist interpretation of such seemingly inefficient practices as threatened retaliation against cartel cheaters and even legally enforceable cartel agreements. Of course, such practices also give firms monopoly power, so that, "In the final choice...we may have to seek a compromise the terms of which will vary according to the circumstances of each particular market." (p. 98)

Oliver Williamson outlines a formal theory of such a compromise, though he does not go nearly as far as Richardson in endorsing restrictive business practices. Williamson considers the case of a merger which both lowers costs and creates market power by increasing industrial concentration. Such a situation seemingly makes consumers worse off, for the new, larger firm can restrict output and raise prices.

At the same time, though, it may also help society economize on the use of scarce resources, for the industry's output can now be produced at a lower average cost. The "Williamson Tradeoff" weighs the cost savings against the deadweight loss in order to ascertain whether the merger is socially optimal. Williamson writes, "[S]ince a relatively large percentage increase in price is usually required to offset the benefits that result from a 5 to 10 percent reduction in average costs, the existence of economies of this magnitude is sufficiently important to give the antitrust authorities pause before disallowing such a merger." (p. 114)

The Williamson Tradeoff neatly captures the position taken by those who see merit in both definitions of competition, "perfect" and "rivalrous." Its assumption that a concentration-increasing merger necessarily creates market power comes straight from the structure-conduct-performance school. The resulting deadweight loss is, of course, a loss compared to what would occur under perfect competition. At the same time, Williamson's suggestion that concentration may also lower costs in many different ways refers back to an earlier era, when economists praised large-scale enterprise for its superior efficiency. The idea of *moving* from one cost curve to another, meanwhile, is hardly compatible with the concept of perfectly competitive equilibrium; it is much more synchronous with Schumpeter's "perennial gale of creative destruction." Having thus married two traditions, Williamson concludes with a plea to substitute analysis for "solemn references to early oratory" when discussing antitrust enforcement. (p. 114)

Chicago's New Learning

The Chicago school has taken issue with the structure-conduct-performance school's analysis of many different business practices, including resale price maintenance, exclusive territories, tie-in sales, and product differentiation. The most prominent manifestations of disagreement, however, concern the issues of industrial concentration and barriers to entry.

Yale Brozen provides an overview of the debate over concentration. Before World War II, he notes, economists generally believed that industries with only a few large competitors could still be competitive, partially because of incentives for collusive agreements to break down and partially because of potential competition. In the postwar era, studies by Joseph Bain and others demonstrated that high concentration tends to be correlated with high profits. Analysts drew the obvious conclusion: The presence of only a few competitors made overt or tacit collusion much more likely, leading to monopoly profits.

However, these studies were guilty of a glaring omission: "Each had provided a spot correlation showing a weak relationship between concentration and accounting rates of return at a given time. None had looked at the profitability of the same industry at a later time to determine whether the above average rates of return in concentrated industries had persisted." (pp. 120) Brozen did so, replicating Bain's and other studies for different years to see if high profits persisted in concentrated industries. They did not.

In addition, Brozen notes that the largest four firms in each of the industries in Bain's sample grew faster than average when they were making above-normal rates of return. These firms grew slower than average when they were making below-normal rates of return. This result implies that when large firms made higher profits, they did so because they were expanding and gaining market share, not restricting output to reap monopoly profits. In short, the correlation of high profits and concentration signifies efficiency rather than monopoly.

Robert Bork explains how and why the broader Chicago revolution ought to affect antitrust policy. The sole goal of antitrust, he believes, is to maximize social wealth "by requiring that any lawful products...be produced and sold under conditions most favorable to consumers." (p. 125) This dictum, however, is hardly a prescription for using antitrust policy to force the nation's industrial structure to conform to the perfectly competitive ideal. It is true that perfect competition leads to allocative efficiency, but allocative efficiency—the placing of each resource in its most highly-valued use—is only one aspect of economic efficiency. Like Mason, Bork points out that the economist's model of perfect competition is a much narrower concept than legal scholars have in mind when they speak of using the antitrust laws to promote competition. "A determined attempt to remake the American economy into a replica of the textbook model of competition," he writes, "would have roughly the same effect on national wealth as several dozen strategically placed nuclear explosions." (p. 126)

In addition to the allocative efficiency generated by perfect competition, "productive" efficiency is also crucial to maximizing output. Productive efficiency occurs whenever a firm offers something at a price that consumers are willing to pay. "Economies of scale, specialization of function, ability to obtain capital, management skill—all of these and many more are elements that contribute to the firm's ability to please consumers," Bork writes. (p. 137) Measures which enhance these factors promote productive efficiency by making it easier for firms to please their customers.

Since some practices that enhance productive efficiency, such as mergers, may also impair allocative efficiency, Bork champions the Williamson Tradeoff as a sensible guide for antitrust policy. But instead of turning antitrust proceedings into econometric battles over the proper measurement of deadweight losses and cost savings, he would use pure price theory to identify which practices can impair allocative efficiency and whether the potential damage is likely to outweigh potential gains in productive efficiency:

> We can avoid [measurement] because price theory tells us that many practices the law now views as dangerous do not contain any potential for restriction of output. In such cases there is no trade-off problem. The trade-off problem arises primarily in the context of horizontal mergers, and there we can take it into account by framing rules about allowable percentages that reflect the probable balance of efficiency and restriction of output. (p. 150)

In the rest of Bork's 1978 book, *The Antitrust Paradox,* he demonstrates why various supposedly monopolistic business practices, such as vertical restrictions, tie-in sales, and even many mergers, do not impair allocative efficiency. Frequently, his and other Chicago theorists' arguments rest on the assumption that relatively easy entry by new rivals can effectively contain possible anticompetitive abuses. However, many of the practices that Chicago theorists would cite as examples of productive efficiency, such as advertising or vertical integration, would be cited by structure-conduct-performance theorists as barriers to entry.

Harold Demsetz tackles barriers head-on, asking a fundamental question: What do economists really mean when they speak of barriers to entry? He demonstrates that common definitions of barriers, which focus on different opportunities facing entrants and incumbents, fail to identify some things which most people would intuitively recognize as barriers. A city-imposed requirement that taxicab operators must obtain "medallions," for example, is a classic example of a barrier to entry. Yet if the city requires *all* cab owners to purchase medallions at market-determined prices, incumbents face the same costs as entrants. No one earns excess profits, but few would argue that the medallion requirement is not a barrier. Even if the city does not hold a monopoly on the granting of medallions, a requirement that drivers obtain medallions will keep some resources out of the taxi industry as long as there is a cost to obtaining medallions. "Indeed,"Demsetz remarks, "medallions and licensure are not needed to keep some types of resources out of the taxi industry. Requirements to equip taxis with airbags, seatbelts, and costly

INTRODUCTION

bumpers will do." (p. 157) In fact, even the prohibition on an entrant's occupying and using an incumbent firm's factory serves as a barrier to entry.

This analysis reveals that discussions about barriers to entry are really
discussions about alternative systems of property rights. Within this framework, Demsetz proceeds to show that many common "barriers," such as higher
capital or advertising costs for entrants, actually stem from genuine scarcities—especially scarcity of information. Therefore, the fact that entrants cannot afford to surmount these barriers may simply serve as a reminder that
scarcity is always with us, not that monopoly is omnipresent. Demsetz
concludes, "The issue faced by the attempt to implement a policy toward
barriers is that of defining which costs of undertaking activities are socially
desirable and which are not." (p. 168) But since economists have not really
focused on this task, "Our utterances in this regard may be accorded the skepticism appropriate to fairly unadorned opinion." (p. 168)

Contestable Markets

The advent of contestable markets theory brought still another approach
to the topic of barriers to entry. The theory's principal insight is that no cost
constitutes a barrier to entry if the firm can fully recoup that cost upon exiting
the market. In the absence of such "sunk" costs, even a natural monopolist
may be forced to charge a competitive price, because supra-competitive prices
attract entrants who will either displace the incumbent firm or exit as soon as
the monopolist reduces its price to the competitive level. Consequently, a
monopolistic industry structure need not lead to inefficient conduct and
performance.

"In the case of contestable markets," Elizabeth Bailey writes, "potential
entry or competition *for* the market disciplines behavior almost as effectively
as would actual competition *within* the market." (p. 171) She calls upon government decision makers to alter public policy in ways that can make markets
more contestable. A major element of such a change is to promote competitive
access to facilities which involve sunk costs. Public ownership helps accomplish this goal in some cases, such as airports and highways. Shared ownership
of sunk cost facilities by all competitors can enhance contestability as well.
"Virtually any method will do as long as there are contractual or other
arrangements that are nondiscriminatory and permit easy transfer or lease or
shared use of these cost commitments," Bailey suggests. (p. 172)

Bailey cites several instances in which regulators have acted as if they have
taken contestable markets theory to heart. With the advent of airline deregulation in 1978 and trucking deregulation in 1980, the Civil Aeronautics Board
and the Interstate Commerce Commission began to grant competitors
authority to serve markets even if they had no intention of initiating service at
present. This policy, combined with the mobility of capital in both industries,
created a pool of potential competitors who could enter individual city-pair
markets easily.

William Baumol outlines contestability theory in greater detail during his presidential address to the American Economic Association in 1981. His address reveals the theory's limitations as well as its strengths. Baumol notes, "...[I]t must be made clear that perfectly contestable markets do not populate the world of reality any more than perfectly competitive markets do, though there are a number of industries which undoubtedly approximate contestability even if they are far from perfectly competitive." (p. 180) In addition, while a monopolist in a perfectly contestable market may face strong incentives to produce the competitive output and sell at the competitive price, the presence of a second firm in such a market *guarantees* that the competitive output will be produced and sold at the competitive price. Thus, industry performance need not improve as more firms enter the market; "a history of absence of entry in an industry and a high concentration index may be signs of virtue, not of vice," as long as the market is contestable. (p. 198)

Modern Rivalry

Contestability theory demonstrates a new class of cases in which markets may not perform in accord with the perfectly competitive ideal. Modern exponents of theories of rivalry go a step further, by suggesting that this welfare ideal fails to capture many aspects of economic efficiency. Some even go further than the Chicago economists, arguing that one cannot integrate notions of perfect competition and rivalry into a consistent theoretical framework. Such modern economists echo the sentiments of Edward Mason, who pointed out differences between economists' perfectly competitive model and lawyers' rivalry-based notion of "free competition." Unlike Mason, though, they see rivalry as a superior foundation upon which to build a meaningful economic theory of competition.

Dominick Armentano offers a thorough critique of the model of perfect competition. The fact that the real world deviates from this model, he suggests, offers the only economic efficiency rationale for antitrust policy. "Markets that contain large firms, locational advantages, price discrimination, differentiated products, tie-in sales, promotional advertising, collusion, and interdependent rivalry are not perfectly competitive markets, and firms in such markets are said to possess some *monopoly power*. Consistent with this perspective, such markets might require government antitrust legislation to make them more competitive and more socially efficient." (p. 206)

Unfortunately, such inferences rest upon the perfectly competitive model's assumption that firms face horizontal demand curves. Leaving aside the empirical question of whether any firm actually faces a horizontal demand curve, Armentano attacks the assumption as logically flawed. Any discrete change in quantity, he asserts, must have *some* effect on the price a firm can charge, even though that effect may be quite small. But if no demand curve can be horizontal, then we have lost the basis for distinguishing monopoly from competition: "Without perfect competition as a standard, monopoly power and monopolistic competition are indistinguishable from any selling situations where firms face a downward sloping demand curve..."(p. 212) The problem for antitrust analysis then becomes one of finding some other way of determining whether a given firm has market power.

As an alternative, Armentano opts to view competition as a dynamic process. "Competition," he writes, "is not simply a mechanical optimization within known constraints, but is seen as an exploratory process whereby opportunities for profit are discovered and exploited over time under uncertain circumstances." (p. 202) Viewed in this light, a wide variety of things thought to be monopolistic, such as industrial concentration, product differentiation, scale economies, and advertising, are actually the results of a competitive process. Monopoly, on the other hand, arises from restrictions on this information-generation and exchange process, and Armentano equates restrictions with government-imposed barriers to entry. He writes, "Government franchises, certificates of public convenience, licenses, tariffs, price-support programs, patents, and any other governmental interference with voluntary trade and production are all instances of monopoly..." (p. 231)

Unlike Armentano, Franklin Fisher, John McGowan, and Joan Greenwood see analytical value in the perfect competition model, but they warn that "A relatively superficial understanding of the competitive model—and, by contrast, its monopoly opposite—can lead to a number of errors when considering real situations." (p. 243) The principal error they point out is a tendency to overlook the fact that the real world is never in equilibrium. The careless analyst, therefore, risks attributing monopolistic motives to wholly competitive business activity which arises simply as a result of disequilibrium.

Industries facing rapid technological change pose particularly difficult analytical problems. A firm which discovers a lower-cost production method will expand its market share and earn at least some rents until competitors copy its methods. The innovator benefits in the short run, consumers benefit in the long run, and economists like to assume that the short run is very short and the long run arrives quickly. Even in this case, though, "continual improvements and continued new technical opportunities can lead to repeated 'temporary' and hence long-lasting profits." (p. 245–46) Therefore, not even persistent profits and high market share signify monopoly. The authors reach the same general conclusion when they apply this type of analysis to markets with homogeneous products, differentiated products, and substantial innovation.

Fisher, McGowan, and Greenwood emphasize, "An obvious but important lesson from this analysis of the process of competition ...is that in assessing whether a firm in such a market has monopoly power, one must be sure to examine the market over a sufficiently long period of time to be able to observe the process of innovative competition at work." (p. 259) Snapshots taken at one instant, such as measurements of market share or barriers to entry, say little about the state of competition. On the other hand, "When one can observe that the competitive process is at work and that vigorous rivalry among independent firms is creating strong pressure to push market performance toward the desired results, monopoly power cannot exist." (p. 262)

Economists who define competition as rivalry frequently fault the structure-conduct-performance school for ignoring this aspect of competition. Richard Fink's examination of Robert Bork's antitrust analysis goes further—Fink argues that perfect competition and rivalry are inconsistent, and cannot logically be combined.

Fink regards the Williamson Tradeoff as a clear attempt to mix the two views of competition. Bork explicitly advocates use of the Williamson Tradeoff to analyze business practices that impair allocative efficiency but that also enhance productive efficiency—frequently by helping firms and consumers deal with the ramifications of imperfect knowledge. But Fink points out that in order for the Williamson Tradeoff to offer valid normative assessments, its cost curves must accurately represent the opportunity costs of using resources in the industry in question. The curves only represent opportunity costs accurately if the economy is in a state of general competitive equilibrium. But one of the preconditions for general equilibrium is that all economic actors possess full relevant knowledge of demand curves and cost curves for all products. As a result, the Williamson Tradeoff cannot offer a valid normative assessment of any business practice designed to overcome problems created by imperfect information.

This quandary stems directly from the attempt by Bork and other Chicago economists to fit concepts like perfect competition and rivalry into a single model. As an alternative, Fink suggests a "market process" theory which defines competition strictly as a rivalrous process. "Incomplete knowledge, uncertainty, judgement, experiment, success and failure, spreading of information, reliance on individual knowledge for decisions—these are all characteristic of economic theory in the tradition of Knight, Hayek, Shackle, Simon, and others. It is these elements of Bork's analysis that fit in well with market process analysis, but not with equilibrium theory," he says. (p. 238) Equating competition with rivalry offers theoretical consistency as well as real-world relevance. And in response to Bork's objection that unlimited rivalry would lead to economic chaos. Fink suggests that "Equating competition with rivalry is *not* disastrous analytically, as long as we recognize the beneficial aspects of cooperation, and as long as we do not try to make rivalry the sole end of public policy." (p. 239)

Public Choice

In antitrust as in other fields, it is no longer safe to assume that policy-makers will automatically adopt the appropriate antitrust policy once economists demonstrate that it is in the public interest. Those who make and enforce the antitrust laws face costs and benefits that may prompt them to serve private rather than public interests.

William Baumol and Janusz Ordover examine one aspect of this problem as they discuss the potential for strategic abuse of the antitrust laws. Antitrust laws are susceptible to abuse because "The borderline between measures that are legitimate competitive moves and those that are destructive instruments of monopolization is often difficult to define even in principle... Moreover, whatever the criteria adopted, in practice they rarely lend themselves to clear-cut evidence and unambiguous conclusions." (p. 267) Since competitors can challenge a firm's pricing, merger, and other policies under the antitrust laws, they face strong incentives to invest resources in securing court and regulatory decisions that prohibit genuinely competitive activity. The resources expended on these efforts are a social cost with no offsetting benefit, and consumers also pay when successful strategic abuse of antitrust protects inefficient competitors.

Treble damages, vague criteria for defining offenses, and rules defining competitive behavior as anticompetitive all give inefficient firms incentives to seek protection from competition through the antitrust laws. Baumol and Ordover cite Chrysler and Ford's legal challenge to a GM-Toyota joint venture, MCI's legal challenge to AT&T's price cutting, and several antitrust challenges to tender offers as obvious examples of such behavior.

Other countries restrict this type of protectionism in a variety of ways. In Japan, the only antitrust remedy is cessation of the allegedly anticompetitive activity, and complainants cannot appeal the Japanese Federal Trade Commission's decisions. The European Economic Community does not offer triple damages, bans contingency fees in antitrust cases, concentrates some types of antitrust enforcement in government agencies, and maintains several other restrictions. To some extent, however, these restrictions are offset by the fact that EEC antitrust laws explicitly foster the protection of producer interests even in some cases when such protection harms consumers.

Baumol and Ordover tentatively offer several suggestions for curbing predatory use of the U.S. antitrust laws. In all cases, they seek to strike a balance between two evils, "excessive weakening of the deterrents to monopolization and excessive facilitation of attempts to subvert effective competition through protectionist misuse of our antitrust institutions." (p. 279)

Robert Tollison considers the relationship between public choice and antitrust, and labels the notion that "better people make better government" as "tried and true nonsense." Rather, "Government cranks along by an internal logic of its own, which in this case we do not know because we have not tried to find out what it is. If we want to have a powerful critique of antitrust, the first thing that must be done is to achieve a positive understanding of how antitrust decision makers behave." (p. 281)

Antitrust scholars of both the structure-conduct-performance and the Chicago schools, Tollison suggests, make the implicit assumption that the makers and enforcers of antitrust laws strive only to serve the public interest. In short, "The market fouls up; the government corrects." (p. 283) In contrast to this view, Tollison summarizes the small body of economic literature examining how antitrust actually works in practice. The principal implication of this literature is consistent with public choice analyses of other government activities; antitrust is at least partially a process in which interest groups secure wealth transfers.

This revelation clarifies how public choice economics can contribute to the design of antitrust policy. Before economists, or lawyers, or other policy-makers, can determine what reforms are advisable, they must understand how antitrust laws work in practice as well as in theory. The relevant policy choice "is between imperfect markets and imperfect governments." (p. 289) But when government's imperfections are recognized, the sensible scope of antitrust laws will likely decrease.

Antitrust Enforcement

At first glance, the pure mechanics of antitrust enforcement and penalties would seem to offer little scope for economic controversy. Indeed, it is true that most of the economic debate over antitrust has focused on the types of structures and conduct to be penalized rather than the penalties themselves. However, economists' conception of the nature of the monopoly problem has occasionally produced recommendations on appropriate penalties and remedies.

Writing 12 years after passage of the Sherman Act, Henry Carter Adams proposes a set of antitrust remedies based on the idea that the "trusts" can victimize investors through securities fraud as well as harm consumers through monopolistic pricing. Adams calls for "publicity," by which he means full police power to seize financial data, and to impose specific accounting procedure on corporations.

According to Adams, such disclosure carries a number of advantages. First, it would prevent promoters of trusts from misleading investors. More-over, it would rechannel capital to enterprises yielding steady dividends, which would help stabilize the economy. Publicity would also help protect the independent producer from predatory practices. With information on costs and revenues freely available, it would be easy to determine whether large companies were selling below cost.

Finally, such disclosure would also reveal when companies are charging prices in excess of costs. "[W]herever exclusive possession of the source of raw material, monopoly of the process of manufacture, or factious control of the market, enables a corporation to charge either more or less than the fair price for the service which it renders, it is incumbent upon the government to substitute the bookkeeping price for the monopoly price..." (p. 297) Adams believes that by imposing disclosure requirements on monopolistic industries, the government can avoid the need for exercising direct administrative control over business.

Kenneth Elzinga and William Breit's recommendations on antitrust remedies reflect both the ongoing debate over antitrust economics and the economic analysis of accidents, crime, and punishment. They fault the standard antitrust literature for its tendency "simply to recommend more of everything—more fines, longer jail terms, bigger government enforcement budgets, enlarged rules of standing, easier access to the courts—with little discussion of the relative efficiencies and costs of these alternatives." (p. 321)

Breit and Elzinga's concern for efficient law enforcement prompts them to reject the idea that monopolists should be forced to pay full compensation to the consumers they have injured. Such a policy attenuates consumers incentives to avoid becoming victims of monopoly. Although such a "strict liability" policy may sound fair, it does not offer the lowest-cost method of deterring monopoly. As in the case of accidents, the most efficient policy is one that forces the "least-cost avoider" to take actions which prevent the harm. Even if strict liability did not have this drawback, it raises the social cost of antitrust enforcement in another way, by giving plaintiffs an incentive to file spurious suits in the hope that judicial error will lead either to unjustified awards or to out-of-court settlement.

As an alternative, Breit and Elzinga propose that enforcement be left in the hands of government agencies rather than private plaintiffs. The government could then vary either the amount of the fine or the level of enforcement activity in order to make the expected value of the penalties for monopolization exceed the expected value of the monopoly profits.

The optimal mix of fines and enforcement activity depends on business managers' attitudes toward risk. The more risk-averse managers are, the more effective fines will be in deterring monopolistic behavior. The less risk-averse managers are, the more effective increased enforcement will be. Citing evidence that managers have become more risk-averse, Breit and Elzinga suggest that stiffer penalties would do more to discourage monopoly than would larger enforcement budgets. In order to provide a similar level of deterrence for all firms, they recommend that the fine be calculated as a percentage of the monopolist's profits, rather than its sales or assets. Such a policy, they believe, could promote much more effective antitrust enforcement at a lower social cost.

Conclusion

At the heart of the debate over antitrust lie some of the most difficult issues of modern economic enterprise. The causes and consequences of many business practices—from price fixing to exclusive dealing to holding companies to mergers—are even yet imperfectly understood. Economics has been slow to shed light on many forms of business cooperation, perhaps because business competition has compelled so much attention.

The debate over antitrust has drawn economists to consider, and reconsider, the place of competition in economic life, and the place of the State in preserving it. For better or for worse, the debate has not yet produced many settled conclusions, nor does it appear likely to in the foreseeable future. If some student of antitrust compiles a volume similar to this one in 2090, she or he will likely find the debate in full swing.

It would be a mistake to think that the debate over antitrust has been futile simply because economists have not arrived at settled conclusions. Just as consensus is no guarantee of truth, so lack of consensus is no cause for despair. The diversity of opinion merely means that we are wrestling with a particularly difficult problem, as the following pages will show.

It has been nearly ninety years since John Bates Clark wrote that the trusts are here to stay. It now appears that antitrust law is here to stay, too. As long as it remains, we may as well keep trying to understand it. The law's effects are too full of force, and too far-reaching, not to keep trying.

CHAPTER I - Early Views: Competition and Cooperation

Early Experiments and Recent Facts

John Bates Clark

This country is the especial home of trusts in their highly developed form,—that, namely, of the great corporation which has absorbed many smaller ones; and here, therefore, has been experienced, in the largest degree, the revolutionary changes which their presence is making. If the carboniferous age were to return and the earth were to repeople itself with dinosaurs, the change that would be made in animal life would scarcely seem greater than that which has been made in business life by these monster-like corporations. Their size is, however, one of the few things about them of which we can be absolutely sure. Whether in the long run they will prove to be benevolent or malevolent we cannot know more positively than we can know whether the extinct saurians were gentle or fierce. In both cases the looks imply a degree of fierceness. But we do not know definitely whether the trusts will permanently raise prices or lower them, or whether they will permanently lower wages or raise them. We do not know whether they will in the end impair investments or make them more secure. It is a singular fact that, in the face of all of these uncertainties about the character of trusts, there is one type of law which the people of many states have been able to agree upon, and that is the kind of law that aims to crush them. We propose to exterminate the monsters on uncertainties. The Montana verdict, that a man deserved hanging for shooting another by accident, inasmuch as "in such matters a man should know his own mind," seems to be applicable here; for a country should know its own mind before destroying an institution.

More general than the opinion that the trusts ought to be crushed is the conviction that they will not down. They are here to stay, and we know it. An explanation of the light-hearted way in which we put upon the statute books laws that aim to crush them is found in the fact that such laws do their principal work before they are enacted, when they are nothing but planks in political platforms. In the present temper of the public mind severe measures are at least good for the party that promises them; and, if by an experiment or two it is shown that they are not workable, there is the less danger in continuing to enact them into laws. In general, political platforms have of late required prohibitive statutes, with pains and penalties attached to them; and, though

1

such statutes have frequently been enacted, so far as large results are concerned, that has been the end of it.

Unless we can "fool all of the people all the time," we shall be forced sooner or later to change this policy; for the people will have laws that not only sound well, but work well. In order to obtain them, the first step is to get a more thorough knowledge of the facts concerning trusts and their operations. We certainly need to know more than that in its outward appearance, a trust resembles an octopus.

Not baseless, certainly, are the accusations that are universally brought against the trusts for their conduct toward their competitors. Often enough is their policy predatory. They do not literally kill men, but to a large extent they do kill competition. They often make property in the shape of rival plants very insecure. Indeed, one of the pressing questions is, whether the independent producers who have been crowded out of the field are unfortunate sufferers from natural progress, or whether they are the victims of a wrong against which society should protect them. Mere centralization means a crushing out of competitors by a process that, however hard it is for them, is in a way legitimate; for it is an incident of the process of the survival of the fittest. The large and economical establishment survives, and society gets a benefit from the fact. But centralization that goes to the length of quasi–monopoly takes a different color, for it may exterminate competitors in ways that do not benefit society. The employers who are forced out of the field are not then vicariously sacrificed for the good of the public as a whole. On the contrary, the sacrifice of them works exceedingly ill for the public; and it must be stopped, if society is to avoid graver evils than have recently come upon it from any economic cause.

How much power does great size give to one of these corporations? Can it, if it will, have the market practically to itself? Can it charge what it will for its goods? Can it shut up as many of its own mills and discharge as many of its own laborers as it pleases? Is there anything to prevent it from acting as a genuine monopoly? If there is not, the situation will soon be intolerable, so that no treatment to which the state may be forced to resort, in order to rid itself of the trust, will be unjustifiable.

I

There are two important facts to be noted before we can conclude that the trusts actually have, in a dangerous degree, the power of monopoly. The first is a weakness in the organization of the trusts themselves, and the second is the existence of a powerful restraining force in their environment. Both of these serve to curtail their monopolistic power. It might seem that, if this is so, the internal weakness of the trust ought to be fostered by the public for its own protection. May we not say that whatever weakens our enemy strengthens us? Should not a policy that would make the trust a more perfect thing, in its internal arrangements, be the last one to be adopted? Curiously enough, this is not the case. We can even help to protect the public by insuring to the trust a sounder organization. Although, as competitors, trusts are now somewhat handicapped by internal weakness, there is a method of removing that weakness which will not imperil the interests of the public, but will contribute in a certain positive way toward protecting them.

1. It should not be overlooked that at present the trust is a very imperfect thing. It is composed of a body of stockholders, a few of whom are promoters and directors. Theoretically all of its proceedings are for the benefit of the stockholders. If this were really the fact, the great issue would lie between the trust, as a whole, and the public. As it is, however, there is a more immediate and pressing issue between the manipulators and the shareholders. The investor is at present the most conspicuous of the trusts' victims; and measures for the protection of the honest and innocent investor, whose money is filched out of safe places into these perilous ones, stand first in the order of time and of immediate importance. It fortunately happens that the very things which will protect the shareholder will injure neither the body of consumers nor the excluded laborers, but will contribute toward the protection of both of these classes. There is, therefore, complete harmony between the policy that stands guard over honest capital which is lured into a position of danger and the policy that protects the public from extortionate prices and workmen from enforced idleness.

The condition of an overgrown trust often resembles that of the wolf in the Russian story. As the members of a pack were shot, one at a time, by the occupants of the sleigh that they were pursuing, each victim was devoured by his comrades; and when the number was reduced to one, this survivor had virtually eaten his thirty-nine mates. It was then seen that he wobbled somewhat in his gait and no longer kept up with the sleigh. A trust that, as the saying goes, has "swallowed" thirty-nine competitors cannot, in the nature of the case, be in an altogether healthy condition, for its power of digestion and assimilation is not unlimited. Very often the management of such a trust is inferior to that of the corporations which were absorbed by it. The promoter's purpose is attained when, having merely formed the corporation, he gets his slice of the stock and realizes on it in the market. He may have neither the energy nor the skill that is required for managing the consolidated company. He forms the combination and leaves it to its own devices—and often they are bad ones.

If this were all that the stockholder had to fear, his case would be better than it is; but unhappily a management that is bad for business may be good for speculative purposes. When profit cannot be secured by making goods and selling them, it may often be gained by "milking" the market for the stock or by wrecking the corporation. What the investor needs before all things is security. He wants to have the trust make money by producing goods and selling them for more than they cost. But the manipulator often wants something so distinct from this as to draw a sharp line between his interests and all legitimate interests. It follows, therefore, that the first thing to be done for the benefit of all parties interested is to clear out a mass of iniquity within the organization; and the means that promises to be most efficient for this end is publicity. When there are so many persons demanding the application of this principle and so few opposing it, there is little doubt that it will be practicable to get it. The trusts must stand the turning of light upon their internal affairs. The public must know what plants they own, what they gave for them, what they are worth at present, for how much they can be duplicated, what applicances they contain, whether antiquated or modern—in short, what is the substantial basis for the value of the stocks and bonds that are placed on the market. This knowledge is at present inaccessible. The investor who puts money into the trust must guess as best he can what property he is getting, and the guess is apt to be a bad one for him. The making public of such business facts as have just been specified would remove the gravest evils from stock watering. If the investor could know that there was only one dollar of property back of five dollars of stocks and bonds, he could buy the securities at a discount from par that would make him safe.

2. In the minds of the great mass of the people, however, the innocent investor is not the chief subject of thought or care. What the public chiefly wishes to know is whether the trusts are to possess and use monopolistic powers. Can they make goods dear at pleasure? Can they turn off bodies of workmen and make it hard for them to get new places? If they are genuine monopolies, they can do these things; but if much competition survives, they cannot.

As has been said, it is coming to be generally known that what it is the fashion to call "potential competition" has for a decade or two protected the public against really monopolistic extortions. If the trusts charge too much for their products, new mills are built and prices go down. Many early trusts did this, with the result that new mills were built. These facts have served as object lessons for the managers of trusts. While they have to some extent put up prices, they have usually kept them below the level at which new competitors would be called into the field.

It is commonly supposed that mere size gives corporations a competing advantage, but this is an inaccurate supposition. A concern with a capital of twenty million dollars cannot lose a million a year any more safely than one with a capital of twenty thousand dollars can lose a thousand a year. If the losses that a corporation sustains by cut-throat competition are in proportion to the amount of its capital, it is not necessarily a dangerous competitor. As a practical fact, a new mill, equipped with the newest and best machinery, is often a stronger competitor than a trust which is encumbered with antiquated plants. In so far as a legitimate rivalry in cheap production is concerned, it is safe enough to build a new mill and try to get a share of patronage for it. Wholly intolerable would be our present condition, if this were not the case. As it is, we are not greatly conscious of being under an oppressive power. We can therefore look at the situation with calmness and, before deciding upon a permanent policy with regard to trusts, we can take time for deliberation. All this is due to the fact that potential competition is working powerfully to protect us. It is not an influence of our own devising; it has set itself at work with no thought on our part; but it accomplishes indefinitely more than statutes have ever done. If it worked in perfection, there would be no need, in this connection, of our doing anything. We might protect the investor and go no further.

There is very much to be said in favor of a system in which competition of the old type shall have ceased. One can picture to himself the world as no longer filled with actual competitors engaged in an overt struggle with each other. One can imagine a department of business no longer represented by a hundred mills of one kind, working independently of each other and struggling desperately for patronage. One can imagine a condition in which it would not be necessary for rival producers to pull bewildered purchasers this way and that by the eloquence of travelling salesmen, by the enticing statements of newspaper advertisements, and by the allurements that are offered by combined art and eloquence, as these are condensed into the peculiar decorations with which American roadways are supplied. A nearly ideal condition would be that in which, in every department of industry, there should be one great corporation, working without friction and with enormous economy, and compelled to give to the public the full benefit of that economy. This last is the crucial point; for it looks far easier to secure the monopoly of the field, and even a large part of the economy that this ought to insure, than to secure the making over to the public of the benefits that accrue.

It happens, fortunately, that the degree of publicity which will protect the investor will also afford a certain help in protecting the consumer. Among the things that the public must know is the earning capacity of the plants that the trust owns. If this is large, the inducement for capital to enter the same field is proportionately large. It is clear, however, that such publicity is far from accomplishing all that the public wishes to have accomplished. It is conceivable that the investor may be made safe, while the competitor may be sacrificed, so that the consumer and the laborer may then find their interests in great danger; and the more difficult problem for the people to solve is the one which they have all along been trying to solve—that of protecting these latter classes.

II

The principle of monopoly itself is not perilous for that investor whose capital is in the monopoly, but it is intolerable for everyone else. It is safe to say that our people will ultimately find or make a way to destroy any genuine monopolistic power that is in private hands; and it is nearly safe to say that, if we do nothing beyond protecting the investor, the trusts will acquire too much of this power and will become less and less endurable. The restrictions that now hold them in check are not likely of themselves to grow more effective hereafter, while the trusts are likely to grow much stronger. Monopoly power that is increasing and restrictions that are diminishing in force point to a time when something positive will certainly have to be done in defence of property rights, if not of personal liberty. The measures that it is possible to take are not many, but we shall soon see what they are and try to make a selection from among them. Even now we can discern the principle which must dominate a sound policy in dealing with trusts. That principle is, first of all, to keep competition alive. Proper regulation will not shield an independent producer from any legitimate rivalry, though it will protect him from what is not real rivalry, but a disabling policy on the part of the big competitor.

Many a trust would now find itself in a new and strange position, if it had no power to keep down rivals save by fair competition; and recent experience seems to show that, up to the present time, goods are often produced with greatest economy, not in shops that are owned by the trusts, but in those which are owned by alert and enterprising competitors. If such producers are liable to be crushed, in spite of the economy with which they work, the public will suffer an injury that is far more serious than any which the trusts have thus far brought about. If it shall be established that economy of production, or legitimate competing power, affords no protection to an independent producer, a blight will be put upon the progress of inventions; for monopoly itself does not greatly encourage invention, and the would-be competitor of the monopoly, who would gladly introduce economical devices, will find the effort to enter the field at all very perilous. The brilliant series of industrial improvements that have been steadily raising the level of human life and have opened an inspiring vista to those who look into the future may not thus be brought wholly to an end, but it will continue under serious difficulties and with comparatively small results.

The power of trusts to crush competitors is dependent upon three kinds of unfair dealing. The first is local discrimination in prices. The trust may sell goods for less than cost in a limited section of the country, where an independent producer is operating, while it sustains itself by charging high prices in the large remaining area. Even though the competitor may greatly excel the trust in the economy with which he makes goods, he may be forced out of the business by this predatory policy. A producer, who found himself in this position, once called on the manager of the trust that was driving him to the wall and was received with a brusque admonition that he had "better get out of the business." "But do you not see," said the independent producer, "that, in my territory, I can produce more cheaply than you can?" "Do you not see," was the reply, "that, if we lose money in the twenty cities where you are operating, and make money in the two hundred other cities where we are operating, we come out ahead?" Such local discrimination is a strategic measure that is often irresistible.

Again, discriminations may be made, not between different localities, but between different grades of goods on the general price scale. The trust may make many varieties of one general kind of merchandise, while the competitor may make only one. In that case, even though he may operate in many sections of the country, the trust may pursue and destroy him. It may reduce the price of his type of goods below cost, while keeping all other prices at the original high level.

Thirdly, the trust may refuse to sell goods at all under certain conditions. It may boycott merchants who do not comply with its regulations; and one of its requirements may be that the merchants in turn shall boycott all independent producers. This is the basis of the "factors' agreement," whereby a trust which, within the wide variety of its products, has a number of things that are essential for a merchant's business, either refuses to sell him anything or refuses to give him necessary discounts, if the merchant buys goods of any description from a competing establishment.

Can these three practices be suppressed by law? Off-hand answers to this question are often in the negative; and certainly there is no blinking the difficulty of this undertaking. If a law could be made and enforced, compelling the trusts to treat all customers alike, local discriminations would, of course, have to end; but the enforcement of such a requirement would encounter difficulties. The most obvious of these arises from the fact that merchandise is not, like refined gold, of uniform quality and readily cognizable. Hence, the trust might manufacture a certain grade of goods and offer it solely in one state, for the purpose of crushing out competition showing itself there. It would thus be possible to claim that it was making no discrimination in charges, since whatever was offered elsewhere was offered at the same price in this state also. But as soon as the vital necessity for keeping home competition alive, in spite of consolidations, is fully appreciated by the public, it will be practicable to secure serious consideration of a plan of action which, if it were successful, would accomplish this.

Monopoly or Competition as the Basis of a Government Trust Policy

Robert Liefman

The question of government regulation of trusts, long an unsolved problem of American economic policy, has received renewed attention since President Wilson's inauguration, and is now leading to new trust legislation. I take pleasure, therefore, in complying with the request of the editor of this Journal for an expression of opinion upon the latest phase in the campaign against trusts in the United States. In accordance with his desire, I shall connect my discussion with the articles by Professor Durand which appeared in recent numbers of the Quarterly Journal. I do this the more willingly because the point of view from which Professor Durand proceeds to discuss the problem is the same as that which I have found necessary to adopt in preparing a third edition of my book, *Kartelle und Trusts.* Professor Durand emphasizes what has already been pointed out by others, and in my opinion is undeniably correct, that the whole Kartell and trust problem resolves itself into the general problem of the benefits and evils of free competition on the one hand and of monopoly on the other, and that the decision is a task for economic theory, and is to be obtained only by means of it. The carefully thought out articles of Durand, in which the facts are subjected to critical examination, show clearly that no conclusion as to the general significance of monopoly and competition for economic activity can be drawn from such of their effects as have been hitherto ascertained. A final judgment as to the advantages and disadvantages of the one or the other principle of organization cannot be given. Whether a system of free competition or one of monopoly would make possible the more complete satisfaction of wants can be decided with as little finality from previous experience with American trusts as from that of German Kartells. A scientific conclusion can be drawn only from theory,—from "general reasoning," as Durand says. The theoretical views can, at the most, merely be confirmed by observation of fact.

Tho I thus agree with Professor Durand concerning the point of departure from which to approach the problem, the conclusion at which I arrive as the result of theoretical consideration is rather the opposite of Durand's. Durand takes his stand for free competition and it is his endeavor, as it has been that of American trust policy at all times, to crush the trusts and to restore and maintain freedom of competition. The advantages of free competition, that supply is better adjusted to demand, that it brings about lower prices to consumers, and so on, have been pointed out so often that it appears unnecessary to enter here into detail concerning them. The whole body of economic doctrine as hitherto accepted took this standpoint; and in consequence, it seems an almost hopeless venture to wish to defend another basis theoretically. Moreover it

Reprinted by permission of The MIT Press Journals from the *Quarterly Journal of Economics,* (John Wiley & Sons, Inc.) pp. 308–325.

has never been attempted before. Much that was suggested by observation of facts has been said in favor of monopoly, and Durand also mentions certain advantages of monopoly. But in accord with prevailing theory, he is a convinced defender of the principle of free competition, and the trust policy he recommends consists in prosecuting the trusts more vigorously than has been done in the past, and in assisting free competition again to a dominating position.

It appears to me, however, that not the least reference to economic theory is to be found in Professor Durand's argument. His "general reasoning" is nothing more than a generalization, a summing up, of earlier observations. A theoretical consideration of the trust problem, on the contrary, must seek to connect it with the fundamental principles of economic theory. As yet, that has been attempted only in a very modest way. As in a measure embodying such an attempt, I may refer to the first and third chapters of my work, which appeared seventeen years ago, *Die Unternehmerverbände,* and to R. T. Ely's *Monopolies and Trusts.*[1] Both works are not out of date. Corresponding to the incomplete state which at present characterizes all economic theory, it seems to me that there still exists a great want of clearness concerning the connection between monopoly and competition. Consequently, what has been said theoretically upon the question of trusts is very inadequate. I may, therefore, be permitted, in so far as is possible within the limits of this article, to indicate my view of monopoly and competition, and at the same time the theoretical basis for my attitude upon the trust problem. It will appear that the question as put by Durand,—either free competition or monopoly,—is wrongly framed, that choice cannot be made between the two principles of organization; rather these inseparable principles always cooperate and react upon one another. When one wishes to frame the question as one of abstract theory, inquiring about the maximum satisfaction of wants, it can be proved that this is to be obtained only by means of monopoly.[2]

As a preliminary, it must be stated that according to modern principles of science, economics has the character of a science only so long as it refrains from expressing judgments. These must always be based upon some ideal which is beyond the bounds of economic consideration; and upon this basis, no propositions of general application, such as science demands, are possible.

The goal of all industry and of all economic activity is the greatest possible satisfaction of the wants of all. This satisfaction of wants extends by no means

---

[1]On Ely's book see my reviews in Conrad's Jahrbucher, 1902, III series, vol. xxiii, and in Weltwirtschaftliches Archiv, vol. ii, 1913.

[2]The following discussion supplements ideas upon the elements of economic theory which I have published in the work, Ertrag and Einkommen auf der Grundlage einer rein subjectiven Wertlehre (Jena, 1907), and in various articles, and which diverge considerably from prevailing opinion. The article upon "Die Enstehung des Preises aus subjectiven Wertschätzungen," in Archiv für Sozialwissenschaft und Sozialpolitik, 1912, and three articles in Conrad's Jahrbücher,—"Das Wesen der Wirtschaft," "Wirtschaft und Technik," and "Die ökonomische Produktivitätstheorie,"—touch the same principles.

only to the material goods which alone are usually considered by current theory, but to everything that man desires. And the essence of economics lies, consequently, not in our dependence upon external, natural objects, but in the fact that the varied needs, the sum of the desired utilities, are opposed to the costs which must be expended for them, and that the two are compared. The greatest possible utility at the smallest possible cost, in other words, the largest possible return, is the object of all industry *(Wirtschaft)*. In this connection, utility and cost are not to be understood in the sense accepted by prevailing theory, which I term quantitative-materialistic, as a quantity of goods, but as consisting of sensations of pleasure and pain, and the yield is not a quantity of goods, but is purely psychical, a surplus of the former over the latter. It can hardly be over-emphasized that all fundamental economic concepts are valuation concepts, and that valuation in terms of money turns not upon the quantity of money, but upon the individual's valuation of that quantity. To bring about the largest possible return, i.e., the largest possible surplus of pleasurable sensations, is the aim of all economic activity. Whether this object is attained, whether there is the most complete satisfaction of all wants, is a question which depends obviously upon the subjective estimates of the individuals regarding the goods offered. Upon that point no general theorems can be laid down, and hence strictly scientific, theoretical investigation seems to break down at the very first fundamental question,—when is complete satisfaction of wants present?

As I stated several years ago in my article upon the problem of productivity, and as has been conceded to me by the chief representative of those who would refrain in economic science from any formulation of judgments *(Werturteile)*, Max Weber, it is still possible to frame a question which avoids reference to these inevitably subjective judgments. One must not inquire, as does prevailing theory, about the largest possible wealth of a people, i.e., the largest possible quantity of goods, but one must ask, under what conditions, in what organization of exchange, can the greatest satisfaction of the wants of all be made possible? For this purpose it is not necessary to determine *wherein* the satisfaction of wants consists. One can investigate in a purely theoretical manner which organization of industry brings about the best provision for satisfying wants. And it is by this method also that one can reach a correct conception of the nature of monopoly and competition.

The outcome of the economic theory which I have developed,—I cannot give it here in detail,—is as follows. For the economic dealings of each individual, as well as for exchange transactions as a whole, the same law applies, which I have called the Law of the Equalization of Marginal Returns. The decisive element is the surplus of utility over cost,—the return. As already said, this must not be understood to be a material quantity, a quantity of goods. Even when we consider the industrial entities operating for exchange, in which returns appear as sums of money,—in contrast with the returns derived in self-centered domestic industry (consumers' returns),—we should regard not the pecuniary sum but the evaluation of the money, which, it must be admitted, is in turn derived from the evaluation of the goods purchased. Now, for each economic person the greatest satisfaction of wants is obtained when he expends so much effort upon each satisfaction that the marginal returns, i.e., the returns secured with the last unit of cost expended, are of the same size for the different satisfactions.

This law of the equalization of marginal returns applies in precisely the same way under developed conditions of exchange. Maximum satisfaction of the wants of all is attained when so much capital and labor flow to each branch of industry that, with due regard to the differences in risk, the marginal returns, the returns of the last and most expensive enterprises, in all branches are equal. Now it is not to be doubted that this condition will best be reached under the rule of free competition; and hence it is that the classical economists, tho unacquainted with the modern accurate theoretical formulation, found in free competition the natural regulator of exchange transactions. All capital would then, under the influence of the all–animating pursuit of gain turn to the industrial activity in which the strongest demand of consumers is still unsatisfied, and in which, therefore, the largest profit can still be realized. These needs will be so far satisfied, the supply of goods will be so adjusted, that the dearest sellers in all branches, whether they offer goods or services, still realize in the long run a certain minimum of profit. In this way the economic principle of the greatest conceivable provision for wants is fulfilled.

This theoretical premise seems at once to point to the unconditional superiority of competition as a principle of organization. But it serves only to clarify the actual relationship between competition and monopoly. One arrives in this question at a result quite different from the foregoing, if the line of thought is carried a step further. The conceivable maximum satisfaction of wants will be reached when, in each branch of industry, the cheapest sellers supply the total demand. To bring this about is, after all, the final aim of free competition. It enables new enterprises to be established as soon as some one believes that he can sell cheaper than at least a part of the sellers then in the market. But since as a rule, a single seller is the cheapest, or only a very few, who under competition secure differential gains, i.e., enterpriser's profits, competition has the tendency, when pushed to its limit, to destroy itself and to be turned into monopoly. Since the cheapest seller can often lower costs by producing the whole supply, it follows that the maximum satisfaction of wants is obtained when there is only one seller, competition remaining latent in the background, effective only when the seller does not employ the most efficient methods of production, or when as a monopolist he appropriates a profit much above the economic marginal return.

One might express it thus: economically speaking, free competition is that organization of business which effects the most complete provision for want; technically, however, the maximum is brought about by monopoly. This is the chief reason for the fact that competition, pushed to the extreme, becomes monopoly. The climax of competition is monopoly, and all competition is nothing but a striving for monopoly.

The much discussed question whether monopoly or competition is the most efficient form of organization, hitherto answered in favor of competition, is therefore, as we now see, improperly framed. Their mutual relationship is concealed when they are treated as absolute opposites. They are indeed antagonistic, yet, as may be asserted of all opposites, they not only conflict, but generate each the other. An organization of exchange based upon the principle of competition can nevertheless exhibit monopoly conditions. Monopoly and competition are special positions and strategic groupings of sellers and buyers in exchange and in price making, one of which shades imperceptibly into the other.[3]

This relation between monopoly and competition, which previous writers failed to notice, is especially clear in the Kartells and trusts. They are undoubtedly monopolistic organizations; nevertheless, competition in its most general sense, and in the sense which concerns us here, is not eliminated. It appears in the Kartells and trusts as latent competition, always in the background, and will the more surely and the more vigorously break forth, the more monopoly manifests itself not merely as monopoly state or tendency, but with monopoly effect; the more it depends, not upon the mere fact that sellers have united, but upon the influence of this union upon price making. Otherwise expressed: the problem of monopoly and competition, in common with all other problems of economic theory, is not static, but typically dynamic, a fact which current theory for the most part still fails to perceive. Competition in this sense is then not merely the presence of several sellers in the market. One might define it as the possibility of the free movement of labor and capital. Competition, latent at least, is present as long as the appearance of a new seller in a branch of industry is not precluded. An impossibility for new sellers to compete, an absolute monopoly, is present only in those cases which rest upon the law, as with patents and the administrative monopolies of public bodies, and in those of natural monopoly due to the fact that the supply of certain goods and services cannot be increased. Yet the latter are in most cases only relative monopolies, because of the possibility of employing substitutes. A person who wishes to hear Caruso sing may not care to hear any other singer, when the price of admission to the former is too high; but he will satisfy his desire for music in another way. Even Caruso cannot fix the admission prices at will, if he desires the largest possible return, but must take into account that the higher his price, the more strongly other means to satisfy the love of music compete with him.

Thus nearly all monopolies are relative monopolies, and are the more destructive to themselves, the more they lead to actual monopoly effects, as expressed in prices. It is not monopoly that kills competition, but, as was said by

---

[3]For further discussion of these views I refer to my article upon the development of price (Entstehung des Preises) in the Archiv für Sozialwissenschaft, 1911.

Proudhon in his *Contradictions économiques* seventy years ago, it is competition that kills competition. One does well, therefore, to distinguish between *free* competition, in the sense of freedom to enter any branch of industry, and the competitive *struggle,* the mutual underbidding, which has been regarded as the essential characteristic of the competitive system. The survival of the economically strongest in the competitive struggle puts an end to this, at any rate temporarily, and leads to monopoly, but at the same time gives a new impetus to free competition, so that the more an acquired monopoly position is exploited, the sooner the competitive struggle is renewed. Only in this sense is free competition the basic principle of our economic order; more accurately, it is not competition, but the pursuit of gain of the individual when free to develop, which organizes existing economic society, i.e., the provision for all through the processes of exchange.

Hence only a peculiar combination of competition and monopoly brings about the greatest possible satisfaction of wants. Free competition, i.e., the voluntary pursuit of gain, must decide, as it does not, just how much capital and labor is to flow to each branch of industry. But aside from the possibility of the appearance of new sellers, the maximum of satisfaction is effected, not by a multitude of sellers with varying costs of production, but only by the one with the lowest cost. This technical maximum, perfect monopoly of a single seller, would of course seldom be wholly realized, because in the present age of continued technical progress the position of the cheapest seller shifts very frequently. But the pursuit of gain *(Ertrag),* the dominant principle of economic activity, has the natural tendency toward monopoly, in which alone this aim can fully work itself out. The individual is simply intermingled in his efforts with the similar efforts of other individuals.

The relation between competition and monopoly is, to sum up, approximately as follows. The fundamental principle of organization in exchange is neither the one nor the other; that principle is the pursuit of gain on the part of each individual economic entity. This pursuit leads to the most effective distribution of all capital and labor among the various branches of industry. For each individual the ultimate aim is the attainment of a monopoly position; but whenever, because of external conditions, several strive for this goal, competition and the competitive struggle result.

Consequently the most rational economic organization is doubtless monopoly in each industry, but so to speak upon the basis of competition, that is, upon the basis of unfettered pursuit of gain. The competitive struggle must remain latent in the background, to become effective as soon as the monopolistic seller begins to exploit his position. Monopoly and competition, in other words, exist side by side in what may be called a state of unstable equilibrium.

Now to bring about this state is the task of an economic policy on monopolistic organizations, such as the Kartells and trusts. It appears how misdirected is the American policy, when for instance it endeavors in every way merely to maintain the competitive struggle, and to suppress every effort toward monopoly, every larger concentration of enterprises. This is simply impossible of execution, because each competitive struggle is itself an endeavor to secure monopoly, and the more violent it is the more surely does it lead to monopoly. The monopoly of Kartells and trusts is therefore nothing more than the competitive conflict pushed to its limit. A rational policy toward monopoly should endeavor to see to it that the two principles oppose each other with somewhat equal forces. On the one hand, it must endeavor to prevent individual enterprises from becoming too powerful, from approaching too closely to absolute monopoly, so as to render the rise of new competitors unduly difficult,—this is now above all the task of monopoly policy. On the other hand, it should not clumsily seek to prevent every attempt to monopolize, nor attempt to establish a state of continued competitive warfare. That is uneconomical, leads to continual upheaval, stimulates speculation, and after all is simply furthering the effort to monopolize. Not general competitive warfare, but monopoly held within bounds by the free operation of the pursuit of gain, is the best organization of industry.

If we consider more closely, from this point of view, the relation between monopoly and competition under present economic conditions, we perceive that the general tendency toward monopoly frequently attains its object, and that the competitive conflict is done away with, merely leaving free competition in latent form in the background. Many a time we observe that exploitation of monopoly position leads to resumption of the competitive struggle. The practicability of making competition effective so as to be available at the right time, is, as I have said, of the greatest importance. So to regulate it that there is not too much or too little of it, in other words, to attain the correct mixture of monopoly and competition,—here is the essence of a government policy on monopoly. Let me state in a few words what aspects of this policy should be borne in mind.

Obviously in contemporary industry the forces restricting and facilitating competition are operative side by side. All such phenomena receive their true elucidation from the standpoint from which we have considered them. In the main the effectiveness of free competition is enormously facilitated by modern economic development, and precisely upon this account the Kartells and Trusts have come to pass, as the climax of the competitive conflict. The greater volume of wealth itself facilitates new competition, still more the greater mobility of capital, resulting from the development of credit and securities, by which vast sums are put readily at the disposal of the most remunerative employment. Besides, technical factors, such as the immense improvements in transportation, which extend the circle of competing sellers and render more difficult the formation of local monopoly, make easier the rise of new competitors. The continued improvements in all branches of production render insecure the position even of the monopolist who does not exploit his position, and gives a special impetus to new enterprises in any branch not subject to monopoly.

The consequence of this development was that it was too easy to compete, there was too much competitive conflict. The opinion of the free trade school, that there can never be too much competition, has meanwhile not only been refuted by experience, which demonstrated that the competitive struggle led finally to monopoly, but can also be disproved by economic theory. I have attempted to explain this in the articles already referred to.[4] Briefly, the conclusion is the following. There is no doubt that the adoption of cheaper methods of production is under all circumstances profitable to private individuals, and that continued technical advance may therefore lead to a situation in which much more capital flows to some branch of industry than the extent of demand warrants. The capital already invested cannot simply disappear and be written off the economic balance sheet; it must be amortized. Thus the adoption of each technical improvement may not be under all circumstances rational, but may result in excessive outlay of capital, which of course must restrict consumption at some other point. In other words, the proper relation between capital formation and consumption, which theory can formulate sharply, —again through the law of the equalization of marginal returns, —and which finds also in practice its realization in the rough equalization of returns in the various forms of enterprise, can be disturbed by continued technical improvements, the adoption of which is profitable to private individuals and consequently leads to the continued establishment of new enterprises. It creates an overcapitalization; not in the sense in which one commonly uses this term in connection with the trusts, but in the sense that more capital is directed to one or another branch of industry than the increase of demand and the normal amortization warrant. Actual money income is thus converted into capital goods and into an excess of capital goods; whereas in the creation of fictitious capital on the part of many of the trusts, money merely passes from one pocket to another, and no real creation of capital, no creation of capital goods, takes place at all.

This overcapitalization, which threatens wherever numerous important technical changes are carried out under the regime of free competition, is the ultimate and most general cause of economic crises. To prevent them has been one of the chief motives for the creation of monopolies. The whole movement toward concentration, especially the rise of Kartells and trusts, is in the last analysis to be traced to this fault of construction in an industrial organization based upon competition, to the incompatibility between the individual's desire for gain and that apportionment of real capital which is most advantageous for society. The whole existing tendency toward monopoly is nothing else than a means of self-help used by the economic organism to check the growth of the anarchic state of production under the regime of competition, in other words, the uneconomic character of continually impending overcapitalization

---

[4]The article upon productivity in Conrad's Jahrbücher, and that upon the theory of saving and the creation of capital in Schmoller's Jahrbuch, 1912.

appearing as a consequence of technical advances under the influence of private pursuit of gain. Likewise the concentration of money and credit is to be classed among the phenomena which represent self-defense by the economic body against the unchecked operation of competition and the attendant danger of attracting an excess of capital.

At this point, one may perhaps object that such overcapitalization occurs not only under free competition but also under present monopolistic organizations. That is quite true. For instance, in the German potash industry, the potash syndicate supported by the government has caused the erection of new plants to be greater and production to exceed demand to a much wider extent than can be pointed out in any other industry. In the mining industries also the establishment of new enterprises and the expansion of old ones has proceeded more rapidly under the influence of Kartells than would probably have been the case under different circumstances. This simply indicates that one must not conceive of monopoly and competition as absolute opposites, and must not characterize the Kartells and trusts as really monopolistic organizations. They are not absolute monopolies, but only the results of the tendency toward monopoly, i.e., of the competitive conflict. In particular, the Kartell is merely an organization with a monopolistic purpose; but even this purpose is only monopolistic to a limited extent, since in the majority of cases it is restricted to price making. It does not extend to the creation of capital, which is quite as important economically; the establishment of new enterprises still takes place under conditions of competition, not of monopoly. Competition, in the above sense of the free mobility of capital and labor, is not eliminated in the Kartells and trusts, but remains latent, and becomes the more effective the nearer the competitive conflict reaches its culmination and actual monopoly is approached. The shifting relationship, the inseparable connection, which exists characteristically between monopoly and competition appears in these organizations, which are monopolistic in tendency but are not rightly to be entitled "monopolistic organizations." They are at once instruments to restrict competition and render it difficult, and at the same time to encourage it and give it a new impulse. Competition leads to monopoly, monopoly leads to competition; so to speak, the law of the conservation of energy is transferred to the sphere of economics. Monopoly and competition are only two manifestations of the one force which sets the economic mechanism in motion, namely, the pursuit of gain on the part of all economic subjects. If this force leads to monopoly, it produces automatically its remedy, the competitive conflict. If this later form of energy is too much developed, it has within itself the tendency to turn to the opposite, monopoly. Only a state of equilibrium between the two forms of economic energy will result in the most advantageous organization of economic activity. Such is the foundation which economic theory can give to a modern policy on monopoly.

Since the above was written, copies have reached me of the American trust acts of September 26th and October 15th. After what I have said, it need not be repeated that the principle underlying them, namely, that free competition is to be kept in effect under all circumstances, seems to me not only theoretically unsound, but in practice impossible of execution. In view of the enormous variety of the possible combinations of monopoly and competition, it will not be feasible, even after an indefinite number of judicial decisions, to lay down any general principle by which to decide when there is "substantially lessened competition" or when it is to be assumed that there is an attempt to "create a monopoly." The decisions must necessarily be arbitrary. In consequence, even tho a number of monopolistic organizations may be suppressed, others equally harmful will be left unaffected. The provision contained in Section 4 of the Anti-Trust Act of October 15th, by which every person "injured" by monopolistic action is entitled to sue for damages, may lead to great uncertainty as regards the outcome of contracts, and may lead also to a great over-burdening of the courts.

Certain provisions in Sections 8 to 10 of this act, which are designed to check financial abuses on the part of great corporations, quite apart from any monopolistic tendencies, are entitled to more favorable judgment. On principle they are to be commended. Nevertheless, in this regard also it seems to me doubtful whether a general and effective execution of the law is possible without a steady supervision and stringent control of the numberless enterprises, such as the American state, with its inadequate staff of trained officials, would seem as yet not able to carry out. The Federal Trade Commission is given tasks which may rise to such dimensions that all cannot possibly be attended to. Hence I must confess to an impression that these new enactments serve more to indicate the wish of the Administration to do something, than give promise of bringing into practical effect the principles on which they rest.

This impression is confirmed by another circumstance. The Administration has failed to turn to a weapon for combating the trusts which I regard as the most important of all, and which has been used to a much greater extent in German legislation on stock companies,—that, namely, of bringing public opinion to bear on the regulation of large corporations. The means are more stringent regulations concerning the make-up and the publication of balance sheets, especially as regards the ownership of securities, and requirements for the publication of detailed reports and prospectuses on the launching of new enterprises. Further may be mentioned the supervision of accounts and of administration by publicly authorized auditors; strict liability of directors, promoters, and financial agents for everything connected with the flotation of securities; and finally the creation of an independent financial periodical press. I should suppose that, in a democratic country above all, some such means of utilizing public opinion as a remedial agent would be peculiarly adapted for combating the abuses of the trusts.

The Sherman Act and the New Anti-trust Legislation

Allyn Young

The Sherman act is a general statute, declaratory of public policy. As such it must be judged, it seems to me, by (1) the soundness of the public policy which it declares, (2) the accuracy and completeness with which it declares that public policy, and (3) the adequacy of the mechanism which it provides for making that public policy effective. What more I have to say in this first paper will have to do with these three aspects of the statute.

1. There can be little doubt but that the public policy which the act was intended to embody is that competition should be maintained, artificial monopoly destroyed, and its growth prevented. In the congressional debates attending its enactment the great industrial combinations of the day were singled out by name as the things against which it was directed. And it is clear from the debates that the hostility toward these industrial combinations was especially directed against (1) their supposed power over prices and (2) their aggressive suppression of competition. What ever the economic advantages of monopoly *per se* may be, there will be little question of the soundness of the policy which would attempt to deprive it of its power for evil in these two particulars.[1]

But it is often urged that to attempt to maintain competition by prohibiting attempts to monopolize is illogical, since monopoly is the goal of competition, and achieved monopoly is merely the result of thoroughly successful competition.[2] The aim of each competitor is to aggrandize his own business at the expense of his rivals, and just so far as he leaves his rivals in partial possession of the field he falls short of complete success. The simplicity of this

---

Reprinted from the *Journal of Law and Economics* (1985) pp. 247–65 by permission of the University of Chicago Press.

[1]Most of the more weighty discussions of the economic advantages of monopoly have to do with the effect of monopoly upon the aggregate production of wealth measured in terms either of subjective satisfaction or of objective commodity units. Even from this point of view, the case for monopoly is exceedingly dubious and, at best, has a validity that is restricted and conditioned in many ways. Moreover, such considerations are relatively unimportant compared with matters like the effect of monopoly upon distribution, upon the scope for individual initiative, upon economic opportunity in general, and upon a host of social and political relations. In short, it is a question less of the relative "economy" of monopoly or competition than of the kind of economic organization best calculated to give us the kind of society we want. Until our general social ideals are radically changed, it will take more than economic analysis to prove that it would be sound public policy to permit monopoly in that part of the industrial field where competition is possible.

[2]Such was the opinion of a number of witnesses before the Senate Committee on Interstate Commerce, 62nd Congress. See for example the Hearings pursuant to Sen. Res. 98, pp. 1431 ff. The latest of the very few expressions of similar views by economists is to be found in Professor R. L. Liefmann's article entitled "Monopoly or Competition as the Basis of a Government Trust Policy," *Quarterly Journal of Economics*, XXIX, 308 (February, 1915). For a judicial opinion to the same effect, see Whitwell v. Continental Tobacco Co, 125 Feb. 462, where it was even held that "every sale and every transportation of an article which is the subject of interstate commerce is a successful attempt to monopolize that part of this commerce which concerns that sale or transportation." In general, however, this misuse of the word "monopolize" has no better standing in law than it has in economics.

reasoning makes it attractive, but it is too simple to fit the facts of the case. We need not discuss at this point the pertinent question as to whether a permanent industrial monopoly can be achieved by the use of permissible competitive methods by a business not enjoying any special advantage not open to its competitors aside from the possession of a larger amount of capital, for the matter can be disposed of in a simpler fashion. There is a substantial difference between competing and "attempting to monopolize" in purpose and consequently in methods. The ordinary competitor, it will be conceded, does not have the establishment of monopoly in mind as an end. He strives to increase his profits by increasing his trade, and in so doing he usually endeavors to acquire as much as he can of the custom enjoyed by his competitors. But the thing directly sought is such increase of his profits as is possible under competitive conditions. The effect of his policies on his competitors is secondary and, generally speaking, indirect. The phrase "attempting to monopolize" on the other hand is meaningless if it does not refer to conscious efforts to get rid of the limitations which competition sets upon one's ability to buy and sell at such prices and on such terms as one pleases. The elimination of competition through the absorption or crippling of competing establishments becomes the direct and primary object, and the methods used are adapted to this end. The contention that "to compete" and "to attempt to monopolize" are synonymous is clearly unsound. They are definitely antagonistic in principle.

2. Is the Sherman act an accurate expression of the public policy which it seeks to declare? If by accuracy is meant precision, it has little of it. It was, in its inception, a lawyer's statute, speaking in the language of the common law. It was drafted by the Judiciary Committee of the Senate as a substitute for the Sherman bill, which, together with a mass of proposed amendments, has been referred to that committee. These amendments included various lists of particular offenses and various delimitations of the precise field of application. It was evident that it would be difficult for Congress to come to an agreement on any one set of particularizations. Moreover, the general phrases of the Sherman act were chosen intentionally, we are told by one of its framers, in order that the responsibility of determining its exact scope might be left to the courts.[3] For seven years its interpretation was uncertain. The decisions in the lower courts were conflicting, and the Supreme Court's holdings purely negative. Nor did the Trans–Missouri decision help matters much. The words "restraint of trade" still remained to be defined, and in the next thirteen years the work of definition progressed only so far as the particular cases decided were typical of classes of possible cases. The standard of public policy announced in the Standard Oil decision was the first general criterion of the scope of the act. There is nothing in subsequent decisions which indicates any tendency on the part of the court to depart from that standard.

---

[3]George F. Edmunds, "The Interstate Trust and Commerce Act of 1890," *North American Review,* CXCIV, 801 (December, 1911). Cf. A.H.Walker, *History of the Sherman Law,* chap. i, ii; and O.W. Knauth, *The Policy of the United States towards Industrial Monopoly,* chap. i.

With restraint of trade held to be the general equivalent of monopolizing and attempting to monopolize, there is small doubt that the present interpretation of the statute is in harmony with the purposes which were in mind at the time of its enactment. The great industrial combinations against which it was hoped that the statute would be efficacious have for the most part a more thoroughly unified and compact form than they had in 1890. Whether such consolidations are contracts, combinations, or conspiracies in restraint of trade within the meaning of the common–law terms may be a matter of doubt.[4] But there is now no question that, if their purpose is monopoly, they come within the condemnation of the Sherman act. Nor does it appear that in any unimportant respects the statute has been weakened. There is no reason to think, for example, that price agreements and agreements to restrict output, whether of local or of general scope, are not as illegal now as they have been at any time.[5]

As a general expression of the public policy which it is supposed to embody, the Sherman act is adequate. The difficulty is that it goes too far. In the first place, as we have already seen, it is so worded that it is used as a weapon against strikes, boycotts, and other concerted efforts to interfere with the conduct of any business undertaking which ships its goods across state lines or to other countries. These things may be undesirable; very likely some of them are. But they are so far out of line with the other things condemned by the Sherman act, and in most instances have so little relation to "monopolizing," that the Sherman act ought to be so amended as to cut them out of the list of offenses which it condemns.[6] In some cases they clearly run counter to current conceptions of public policy. In other cases this is not so clear. At any rate, if federal law is still to condemn all or some of these things it should take the form of separate and carefully drawn statutes. Moreover, practices like those condemned in the Eastern States Lumber Association case, mentioned above, probably fall within the jurisdiction of the new Federal Trade Commission.

In the second place, the application of the Sherman act to railroads is inconsistent with the standards of public policy embodied in the Interstate

---

[4]Cf. the argument of Justice Holmes to the effect that under the common law contracts in restraint of trade are contracts with strangers to the contractor's business, and that combinations and conspiracies in restraint of trade have the purpose of keeping strangers to the agreements out of business. (*Northern Securities Co. v. United States,* 193 U.S. 404, 410.)

[5]The following extract from the opinion of the Circuit Court in the "bath–tub trust" case is directly in point: "Some men believe that price agreements should be sustained by the courts, unless they are shown to be against the public interest. Others hold that they may be permitted only when it is affirmatively shown that they promote the public interest. Still others say that a price agreement pure and simple is always illegal. That the Supreme Court has declared the last of the above–stated contentions to be the law is conclusive here." — *United States v. Standard Sanitary Mfg. Co.,* 191 Fed. 182. See also the decision of the Supreme Court in the same case, 226 U.S. 20, and *Straus and Straus v. American Publishers' Association,* 231 U.S. 222.

[6]This could be done by omitting the word "or commerce" from the first three sections of the act. Or if this should be thought to raise a doubt as to the statute's constitutionality, the words "in restraint of trade or commerce" might be changed to read "in restraint of competition in commerce."

Commerce act. We regulate railroad rates and services on the assumption that railroads are natural monopolies, and that combinations or rate agreements are inevitable. But at the same time we condemn railroad combinations and rate agreements, and (as in the New Haven case) bring criminal indictments against the men responsible for such combinations.[7] From railroads we exact the observance of two mutually inconsistent standards of morality. The real evils in railroad combinations are matters of corporation finance and of the equilibrium of the equities of various sorts of bondholders and stockholders. These evils should be dealt with by statutes appropriate to the purpose, and the Sherman act should be so amended as to be relegated to its proper field of preventable industrial "monopolizing."

Finally, there comes the question of whether even within the industrial field we want to prohibit monopoly as well as aggressive monopolizing. Probably a monopoly achieved merely by the superior efficacy of a formerly competitive business unit (if such a thing were possible) would not be condemned by the courts as a violation of the Sherman act. Monopolies achieved by the active suppression of competition are so condemned. What, then, is the status of a monopoly built up merely by the peaceful union or absorption of competitive units? Such combinations in the railroad field have already been condemned in the Northern Securities and Union Pacific cases. Should similar combinations in the industrial field likewise be broken up, or (since unfair methods are ruled out) should we put our trust in latent competition? This seems to have been in essentials the problem that was put before the District Court in the International Harvester Company case,[8] in which the decision was that the combination was condemned by the statute.[9] The decision of the Supreme Court in this case will do much to fix the boundaries of the region to which the act applies. On which side public policy properly lies is hard to determine. On grounds of economic principle there is nothing to fear from such combinations. But on the other hand there is not much to gain from them, and in practice it would prove hard to draw a line between peaceful combination and predatory combination for monopoly's sake. Probably little harm would be done, and possibly some good, if no such line were drawn except to make off one combination as illegal even in the early stages of the monopolizing process, and the other as legal except when combination has reached the full measure of monopoly.

3. Does the Sherman act provide an efficient mechanism for achieving its own ends? That its criminal features have been relatively ineffective is generally admitted. In many cases these criminal remedies could not have been enforced except at the expense of the efficiency of the proceedings for the

---

[7]This, of course, has nothing to do with the questions relating to the way in which the New Haven officers and directors discharged their trusteeship for the stockholders of that road.

[8]214 Fed. 987.

[9]This decision is criticized by Clarence E. Eldridge, "A New Interpretation of the Sherman Act," *Michigan Law Review,* November, December, 1914.

dissolution of the combination. Furthermore, it has been found in practice that it is a very difficult thing to secure a criminal conviction from a jury for an offense so general, so abstract, so little tainted with a general and customary imputation of immorality as "restraint of trade" or "monopolizing." It is often said that "restraint of trade" is no more indefinite than "fraud." This is very likely so, but there is the essential difference that fraud consists in, or is accompanied by, simple and concrete actions, while restraint of trade is, as I have suggested, general and abstract. It is significant that the few convictions obtained under the Sherman act have been in cases where the restraint of trade or of commerce consisted in, or was evidenced by, specific and objectionable acts. There is no reason to expect that it will ever be easy to secure convictions for restraint of trade or monopolizing in cases where the separate steps taken in the creation of the restraint are unobjectionable except as part of the general scheme. As it is, the statute provides merely an indirect and uncertain way of penalizing unfair competitive methods.[10] I see no reason why the criminal remedies of the Sherman act should be retained.

The proceedings in equity for the dissolution of a combination have, on the contrary, proved to be increasingly effective, in the sense that they have resulted in an increasing number of successful prosecutions. It is contended by many that the enforced dissolution of a combination means generally a mere change in form without diminution in monopoly power; that we are merely hunting the quarry from tree to tree. But in neither transportation nor industry does it clearly appear that the newer and more unified forms of consolidation would not have largely displaced the old, even if the movement had not been hastened by legislation and by decisions under the common law. Among other things tending to this end the various strategic advantages of the consolidated unit, the permanency and dependability of the newer forms of combinations, making possible the adoption of business policies based on long-time considerations, and the opportunities the single corporation, whether holding company or not, affords for the capitalization of promoters' profits may be mentioned.

But even if the Sherman act has itself been partly responsible for the change in the form of combinations (it cannot have increased their number), it does not follow that in the future its history is to repeat itself in this particular. It may be that, after a long chase, the quarry has finally been driven into a corner.

Granting all this, is it proved that the mere dissolution of industrial combinations accomplishes anything, especially in cases where the equities in the combination are made the basis of a pro rata distribution of the equities in its constituent parts? I cannot attempt here to answer so large a question. But I may suggest a few general conclusions: (1) The results must vary with the nature of the business and the degree to which the aggressive suppression of

---

[10]Neglecting its anomalous application to strikes and boycotts.

competition played a part in maintaining monopoly conditions. The results must also vary with the degree to which railway rates and other distributive conditions had been shaped for the benefit of the combination. (2) Dissolution rarely comes early enough—not until the monopolistic situation (if any exists) has become more or less crystallized. This suggests the need of emphasis upon methods rather than achieved results, upon monopolizing rather than upon monopoly. (3) The operation of the statute is intermittent. Dissolution should be carefully followed up, and every step in the process of restoring normal conditions should be carefully watched. This required administrative machinery. (4) The Sherman act needs supplementing. At certain points, at least, this is accomplished in the new anti-trust legislation which will be considered in a subsequent paper.

But in its own field the Sherman act has a value all its own. No matter how carefully drawn the rules of the game may be, no matter how high the level set by the law for competition, new business situations, new conditions are bound to arise, not covered by specific statutes, and yet contrary to the generally accepted public policy of the maintenance of competition within its own proper field. The Sherman law, as a general declaration of public policy, has an elasticity and adaptability to new situations of all kinds not possible to legislation of a more specific sort. Its declaration of public policy is general enough so that it may gradually grow in meaning and change in application through judicial decision as the common law has grown and changed. So long as the preservation of competition in that large part of the industrial field in which it is feasible is public policy, why should we not, through such a statute, continue to give to the federal courts jurisdiction in cases involving the assertion of that public policy? But, it needs amendment in the ways which have been indicated.

CHAPTER 2 - The Rise of Structure Conduct Performance

Monopoly in Law and Economics

Edward S. Mason

I.

THE TERM monopoly as used in the law is not a tool of analysis but a standard of evaluation. Not all trusts are held monopolistic but only "bad" trusts; not all restraints of trade are to be condemned but only "unreasonable" restraints. The law of monopoly has therefore been directed toward a development of public policy with respect to certain business practices. This policy has required, first, a distinction between the situations and practices which are to be approved as in the public interest and those which are to be disapproved, second, a classification of these situations as *either* competitive and consequently in the public interest *or* monopolistic and, if unregulated, contrary to the public interest, and, third, the devising and application of tests capable of demarcating the approved from the disapproved practices. But the devising of tests to distinguish monopoly from competition cannot be completely separated from the formulation of the concepts. It may be shown, on the contrary, that the difficulties of formulating tests of monopoly have definitely shaped the legal conception of monopoly.

Economics, on the other hand, has not quite decided whether its task is one of description and analysis or of evaluation and prescription, or both. With respect to the monopoly problem it is not altogether clear whether the work of economists should be oriented toward the formulation of public policy or toward the analysis of market situations. The trend, however, is definitely towards the latter. The further economics goes in this direction, the greater becomes the difference between legal and economic conceptions of the monopoly problem. Lawyers and economists are therefore rapidly ceasing to talk the same language.

Twenty years ago this was not the case. In 1915 there appeared in the JOURNAL an article on the Trust Problem which quoted the opinions of

Reprinted by permission of the author and The Yale Law Journal Company and Fred B. Rothman & Compnay from *The Yale Law Journal*, Vol. *47*, pp. 34–49.

eminent economists on the significance of a contemporary "trust" decision.[1] The point the author was trying to make, flattering indeed to the study of economics, was "that in cases of this character no decision can be legally sound that is not fundamentally correct from an economic point of view."[2] The question posed to the economists was the import in terms of monopoly of the production by the International Harvester Company of 65–85% of the national output of certain types of harvesting machinery.[3] While the answers may or may not have been helpful in the formulation of legal opinion, it is a point of peculiar interest that the economists conceived the problem in much the same way as the courts. It was not monopoly as an analytical concept but monopoly injurious to the public interest which colored their thinking. The economists' emphasis on free entry into the industry as characteristic of competition and restriction of entry as the *differentia specifica* of monopoly was in complete harmony with the judicial predilection. Monopoly was thought of as the antithesis of free competition, unregulated monopoly was always and necessarily a public evil, the nature of monopoly was to be found mainly in restrictions on trade, and its remedy was, in the Wilsonian phrase, "a fair field with no favor."

Since that time, particularly in recent years, economic thinking on the subject of monopoly has taken a radically different trend. Much more attention has been given to the shaping of the concept of monopoly as a tool of economic analysis rather than as a standard of evaluation in the judgment of public policy. Some of the consequences of this trend have been the focussing of attention on the problems of the individual firm rather than those of the industry, a recognition of monopoly elements in the practices of almost every firm, a recognition of the impossibility of using the fact of monopoly as a test of public policy, and a growing awareness of the necessity of making distinctions between market situations all of which have monopoly elements. The trend has led to a split between the approach to the monopoly problem in the law and economics which requires bridging by interpretative work of a high order. The following pages are not concerned primarily with this task but rather with an economist's impression of the divergence between the present legal and economic conceptions of the monopoly.

II.

The elements out of which both law and economics have built their ideas of monopoly are restriction of trade and control of the market. These elements are of course not independent. Restrictions of trade of various sorts are familiar devices for securing control of the market; control of the market may be used, as in predatory competition, to restrict trade and competition. Nevertheless, restraints of trade can exist without anything that the courts would be willing to call control of the market. And, control of the market, in

---

[1] Friedman, *The Trust Problem in the Light of Some Recent Decisions* (1915) 24 Yale L. J. 488.
[2] Id. at 493.
[3] Id. at 502, 503.

the economic sense, can exist independently of any practice which the law would call a restraint of trade.

It is also important at this point to understand the content of several other basic concepts. The antithesis of the legal conception of monopoly is *free* competition, understood to be a situation in which the freedom of any individual or firm to engage in legitimate economic activity is not restrained by the state, by agreements between competitors or by the predatory practices of a rival. But free competition thus understood is quite compatible with the presence of monopoly elements in the economic sense of the word monopoly. For the antithesis of the economic conception of monopoly is not free but pure competition, understood to be a situation in which no seller or buyer has any control over the price of his product. Restriction of competition is the legal content of monopoly; control of the market is its economic substance. And these realities are by no means equivalent.

An illustration of the application of these concepts is presented by the facts of the Cream of Wheat case.[4] The Cream of Wheat Company bought purified middlings, a high-grade by-product of wheat, and, "without submitting them to any process or treatment, without adding anything to them, it puts up the middlings which it selects in packages and offers its selection to the trade under the name of 'Cream of Wheat.' "[5] The court was unable to see either control of the market or restriction of trade in this practice. "The business of the defendant is not a monopoly, or even a quasi–monopoly. Really it is selling purified wheat middlings and its whole business covers only about 1 per cent. of that product. It makes its own selection of what by–products of the middling process it will put up, and sells what it puts up under marks which tell the purchaser that these middlings are its own selection. It is open to Brown, Jones and Robinson to make their selections out of the other 99% of purified middlings and put them up and sell them; possibly one or more of them may prove to be better selectors than the defendant, or may persuade the public that they are."[6]

An economist, on the other hand, would be inclined to say that the product sold is not wheat middlings but Cream of Wheat, and that the Cream of Wheat Company exercises some monopolistic control of the market unless, and this is unlikely, the number and quantity of substitute products is such as to render the price independent of the quantity sold. He would add that it does not follow that the market control incident to such a monopoly position is contrary to public policy. Furthermore he would consider monopoly of the production of Cream of Wheat as perfectly compatible with competition on the part of actual or potential producers of substitute products.

[4] Great Atlantic and Pacific Tea Company v. Cream of Wheat Company, 227 Fed. 46 (1915).
[5] *Id.* at 47.
[6] *Id.* at 48.

The economists' emphasis is on control of the supply or price of a product. And "product" is defined in terms of consumer choice, for if consumers find that the goods sold by two competing dealers are different, they are different for purposes of market analysis regardless of what the scales or calipers say. Some control of the market exists whenever a seller can, by increasing or diminishing his sales, affect the price at which his product is sold. Since, outside the sphere of agricultural and a few other products, almost every seller is in this position, it is easy to see that if monopoly is identified with control of the market, monopolistic elements are practically omnipresent. This is the logical conclusion, it is submitted, where the emphasis is laid upon control of the market and the monopoly concept is considered as a tool of analysis only, unrelated to public policy. But if monopoly is considered to be a standard of evaluation useful in the administration of public policy then other considerations must be involved.

It is so used in the law. Although the history of the term's legal usage is filled with references to control of the market as evidence of monopoly, various factors, principally the difficulties of devising tests of the reasonableness of price and output controls, have focussed the attention of courts on another element, restriction of trade, as the decisive consideration. The development of this idea may be seen in the sources of the present law of monopoly and competition, which are, according to Jervey and Deak, to be found in "(A) the Statute against Monopolies and *D'Arcy v. Allein*; (B) the old English statutes against forestalling and engrossing; (C) the judicial adaptation of the ancient law on restraint of trade to the combination acting as a unit of controlled parts; and (D) the law of conspiracy as applied to the illegal end of suppression of competition, with particular reference to labor conspiracies insofar as they were seen as restraints on the market."[7]

It is clear from the Statute of Monopolies[8] and from contemporary definitions that monopoly meant exclusion of other producers or sellers by a dispensation from the sovereign granting sole rights to some person or persons.[9] Although *D'Arcy v. Allein*[10] declared the "inseparable incidents" of monopoly to be (1) the raising of the price of the product, (2) the deterioration of its quality, and (3) the "impoverishment of divers artificers and others" because of exclusion from their accustomed trades, a monopoly was considered to exist whether or not these "incidents" followed. It was not incumbent upon the courts to show that prices had actually been raised or quality of the product

---

[7.] Hugger W. Jervey and Francis Deak, The Case of Monopoly v. Competition, (Mimeo., 1934).

[8.] 21 Jac. I, c. 3. (1623).

[9.] Coke defined monopoly in this way: "An institution, or allowance by the king, by his grant, commission, or otherwise, to any person or persons, bodies politique or corporate, of, or for the sole buying, selling, making, working, or using, of anything, whereby any person, or persons, bodies politique or corporate, are sought to be restrained of any freedom or liberty that they had before, or hindered in their lawful trade." 3 Institutes No. 181.

[10.] 11 Co. 84b, 74 Eng. Reprint 1131 (1602).

deteriorated in order to be able to hold that a monopoly existed contrary to the common law.[11] Monopoly meant exclusion from a certain trade by legal dispensation and no examination of control of the market was necessary to establish this fact.

The injuries inflicted by forestalling, regrating and engrossing were in the main conditioned and limited by an early and now obsolete system of distributing and marketing goods, principally foodstuffs. Laws were found necessary to prohibit the spreading of false reports as to the state of the market (regrating), to prohibit the purchase of victuals on the way to market for purposes of resale (forestalling), and to prohibit the cornering of the available supply of an article (engrossing).[12] It is true that engrossing in particular was an act undertaken to secure what an economist would call control of the market. But in the absence of a combination, of attempts to exclude competitors, or of other overt acts, it was difficult for the courts to find evidence of control of the market. There is no obvious answer to the question of how large a share of the available supply of an article an individual must purchase before he is guilty of engrossing. If, on the other hand, the engrossing were accomplished by a combination, particularly if the combination attempted to exclude competitors, the problem appeared to be more simple.[13] Conspiracy frequently accompanied engrossing in the early cases and was rarely absent in the later ones. In no engrossing case that has come before Anglo–Saxon courts in the last hundred and fifty years, so far as I am aware, has a court undertaken to discover the existence of engrossing by examining the control of the engrosser over the price. What cases there are, and they have been few, have been complicated by the presence of combinations or conspiracies to restrain trade. The courts have found monopoly because of conspiracy and the exclusion of others from the market rather than control of the market. It is doubtful whether the act of engrossing itself, in the absence of a conspiracy to exclude competitors, would carry any monopoly connotation in the law. Consequently it seems doubtful whether the ancient law respecting engrossing, forestalling and regrating has made much of a contribution to present legal concepts of monopoly.

[11.] As a matter of fact it is quite possible that a monopoly dispensation would not give to its holder control of the market in the sense of ability to raise price or to lower the quality of the product. Whether it did or not would depend, in economic jargon, on the elasticity of demand for that product, and this in turn would be influenced by a number of factors including the existence of effective substitutes.

[12.] See Jones, *Historical Development of The Law of Business Competition* (1926) 35 Yale L. J. 905, at 907 *et seq.*

[13.] "To gain a monopoly on a local market a common, organized action, in other words a cartel of the most powerful competitors, often became a necessity. The fact that competitors acted in agreement when engrossing the market is expressed in the English anti–monopolistic legislation by the significant term *conspiracy*. This word was first used in this connection in the Statute of 1353 [a Forestalling Statute, of 27 Edw. III], and reappears continually in the anti–monopolistic statutes. From here it passes over to the American anti–trust legislation, being thus a continuation of the old monopoly prohibitions." Pictrowski, Cartels and Trusts (1933) 148, quoted in Jervey and Deak, *op. cit. supra*, note 7.

In a somewhat different status in this respect is the law on restraint of trade. The question of restraints originally came before the courts in cases involving the sale of a business in which, as an incident to the sale, the seller contracted not to compete with the buyer. Until sometime in the 17th century the courts uniformly held such contracts unenforceable, the basis of the rule being "that public policy demands from every man the free exercise of his trade in the public interest."[14] Did public policy demand the free exercise of trade because in the absence of such free exercise there would be a control of the market?

Restrictive covenants, if enforceable, certainly may lead to control of a local market, but control of the market is not dependent on the existence of such contracts. Doctors, lawyers, or tradesmen dealing in a particular type of article may be, and frequently were in the period in which restrictive covenants were unenforceable, the sole practitioners of their profession or trade in a given locality possessing a control of the local market. Yet this fact does not appear to have led to legislative or judicial concern. It appears more consistent with the early decisions to say that restrictive covenants were feared because one who contracted himself out of a livelihood might become a public charge.

The development in the 17th and 18th century of the doctrine of "reasonable restraints," as applied to restrictive covenants in connection with the sale of a business, does not seem to have involved any closer consideration of the monopoly problem. Although it is sometimes said,[15] or implied, that the reasonableness which concerned the courts in such contracts was understood not only in relation to the interests of the contracting parties but also to the public interest in prevention of control of the market, it is difficult to substantiate this view by an appeal to the decisions.[16] The application of the doctrine of reasonableness to the interests of the contracting parties is clear. The interest of the buyer was a property interest, that the value of the purchased business not be lessened by competition from the seller in the immediate vicinity, while that of the seller was not only a property interest, since he obtained through the sale the full value of the "good will" of the business, but also an interest in safeguarding the possibility of continuing somewhere and at some time his trade or profession. The language of the courts indicates that the public interest was considered affected when the public was deprived by such a contract of a source of supply without justification, *i.e.*, when such a deprivation was unnecessary to the protection of the private interests involved in the contract. This protection of the public interest was levelled primarily not against monopolistic control of the market but against the loss to the common weal of the services of a productive agent. There is no evidence that the courts examined

---

[14.] Cooke, *Legal Rule and Economic Function* (1936) 46 Econ. J. 21.

[15.] See, e.g., Pope, *The Legal Aspects of Monopoly* (1907) 20 Harv. L. Rev. 167; Cooke, *op. cit. supra*, note 14.

[16.] Mitchel v. Reynolds, 1 P. Wms. 181 (1711).

the data relevant to the question whether such a contract might lead to control of the market. If any monopoly consideration was involved, it was monopoly in the sense of restriction of competition, not of control of the market.

If the test of reasonableness referred to the extent of competition or control of the market which would result from the restrictive contract, might we not have expected the courts to compare the market situation in the locality affected by the contract with the market situations in other localities? If the restrictive covenant reduced the number of possible competitors by one, this might have a very different effect on control of the market in a locality in which competitors were many from its effect in a locality in which only one remained. There is not much evidence, however, that the courts considered the easily available facts relative to extent of market control, and the cause seems to be that the "reasonableness" with which they were concerned in cases involving restrictive covenants was rarely, if ever, related to the monopoly problem.

The gradual relaxation of the law on restrictive covenants is easily understood with reference to the interests of the contracting parties and requires no examination of the changes in the scope of market control. With the increase in economic opportunities incident to increasing division of labor the means of gaining a livelihood open to a seller of a business expanded, and the restrictions imposed on his activities by these covenants became less serious. On the other hand, with the growth of transportation facilities the area within which the competition of the seller might lessen the value of what he has sold had increased. For both these reasons the scope permitted restraints of trade of this sort has been enlarged.[17] Moreover, whether or not the establishment of a competing enterprise in a given locality was likely to affect the value of the business sold, and whether or not a limitation in trading in a given locality was likely to deprive a man of the means of earning his livelihood and the public of the fruit of his activity were questions to which common experience might be said to provide a tolerably satisfactory answer. The question whether the elimination of one unit of competition would result in control of the market, however, could hardly be answered without an examination of the number of competitors left in the restricted area and of the behavior of prices. To such an examination the courts were hesitant to proceed.

The application of the rule of reason to contracts between competition among themselves stands on different ground. It is frequently said that, as distinguished from restrictive covenants connected with the sale of a business, the interests of the contracting parties are here not at issue since such contracts will not be entered into unless there is prospect of gain to all from the limitation.[18] While this may or may not be true, if the rule of reason is to be applied to such cases, it must be applied on different grounds, or it must be a different rule than that used in the older cases of restraint of trade. For in this

---

[17.] Handler, *Restraint of Trade*, (1934) 13 Encyc. Soc. Sciences 339.

[18.] Pope, *op. cit. supra*, note 15; Cooke, *op. cit. supra*, note 14.

type of contract the public interest in the monopoly problem is paramount, and the question of the private interests of the individual contractors is only secondary.

The disposition of American courts has been, at least until very recently, to hold all contracts for division of territory, pooling, fixing of prices, common marketing control of supply, or which restrict the freedom of the contractors to compete in other ways, unenforceable and, since the Sherman Act, illegal. The opinions of the court in these cases constantly refer to monopoly in the sense of control of the market, but little examination of evidence pertinent to the question of market control is ever undertaken. The test of monopoly, or attempt of monopoly, is here restriction of competition. American courts have in this class of cases been willing to accept the contract itself as evidence of restriction and, consequently, of an attempt to monopolize, without inquiring further into the question of how great a control of the market is secured to the contracting parties.[19] The rule of reason enunciated with much fanfare by Chief Justice White purporting to provide a standard of judgment dividing those contractual restrictions which are in the public interest from those which are not has had, at least until the Appalachian Coal case[20] in 1933, a much narrower application than might have been expected.

The British courts, confronted with the same problem of applying a rule of reason to contracts between competitors designed to limit competition, have returned a somewhat different answer. They have tended to accept every contract designed to limit competition among the contracting competitors as reasonable in the absence of intention of actual attempt to injure or destroy a competitor.[21] On the other hand, the trend of American opinion has been to regard all such contracts as unreasonable restraints of trade. In neither case has the rule of reason been given any intelligible content in terms of control of the market despite the frequency with which this phrase has graced judicial utterances.

[19.] In another class of cases, however, dealing principally with trade association activities, the Courts have drawn a distinction between limitation of competition and a regulation by business agreement of competitive methods. Nowhere is this distinction better expressed than by Justice Brandeis in Board of Trade of the City of Chicago *et. al,* v. United States, 246 U. S. 231, at p. 239. "Every agreement concerning trade, every regulation of trade, restrains. To bind, to restrain, is of the very essence. The true test of legality is whether the restraint imposed is such as merely regulates and perhaps thereby promotes competition or whether it is such as may suppress or even destroy competition."

[20.] Appalachian Coals, Inc. v. United States, 288 U. S. 344 (1933).

[21.] See the dictum of Lord Parker in the *Adelaide* case: ". . . it is clear that the onus of showing that any contract is calculated to produce a monopoly or enhance prices to an unreasonable extent will be on the party alleging it, and that if once the court is satisfied that the restraint is reasonable as between the parties the onus will be no light one." Attorney–General of Australia v. Adelaide Steamship Co., 1913 A.C. 781, 796. Such a contract *may* produce an "unreasonable" control of the market but the British courts have rarely found one. A contract which restricts competition by the destruction of a competitor's market is a different matter. Here there is an overt act, an obvious restraint of trade, partaking of the nature of conspiracy, that does not compel the courts to examine the behavior of prices and outputs which are the most obvious sources of information concerning control of the market.

Cases involving a union between competitors accomplished by amalgamation or fusion or merger have in this country most frequently involved the application of the rule of reason, and it is in these cases that the characteristic legal conception of monopoly is most evident. An amalgamation of competing firms may, and ordinarily does, take place for reasons other than to secure control of the price of the articles produced or sold by these firms. The courts could not, therefore, plausibly assume, as they did in the case of contracts to limit competition, that all amalgamations were *prima facie* evidence of an attempt to monopolize.

Since under the Sherman Act both the contract and the combination as an attempt to monopolize or restrain trade were illegal, some way had to be found of making the law on combinations equivalent to the law on contracts limiting competition. If monopoly had meant to the courts control of the market, some such equivalence might well have been found, although the problem would have been, and is, difficult. Yet the sources of evidence of control of the market are known: the behavior of prices and outputs, the relation of prices and costs, profits before and after the combination, share of the market controlled, the existence of business practices such as price discrimination, price stabilization and many others. The evidences of a control of the market established by combination would be found in the same sort of data as in control established by contract, and a rule of reason which set up as its standard control of the market would have yielded approximately the same results in both types of cases.

By monopoly, however, the courts did not mean control of the market but restriction of competition. While a contract between competitors designed to limit competition carries the evidence on its face of an attempt to monopolize, a merger between competitors does not, so that the courts had perforce to enquire, (1) into the intentions of the merging interests, and (2) into such acts of the merger as might indicate restriction of outside competition. If the intention behind a merger were control of the market it is unlikely that it would be communicated to the courts, and since the only evidences capable of indicating intention to control the market were ignored we may conclude that the courts found the presence of monopoly in other ways. If the manifestation of the intention to limit the competition of outsiders took the form of overt acts such as local price discrimination, espionage, or securing of railway rebates, the courts could find evidence of restrictions directly relevant to their conception of monopoly. As a matter of fact it is clear that this was the direction taken in the judicial application of the rule of reason. The size of the combination or its share of the total output of a product became important only when accompanied by predatory practices affecting the freedom of others to compete. In the words of one commentator it has become clear by 1918 "that the Sherman Act had evolved from an anti–trust act into an act relating to the legal control of competitive methods."[22] Since monopoly meant restriction of competition rather than control of the market, this evolution was only logical.

The decision in the Standard Oil–Vacuum merger in 1931, it is true, gave somewhat more consideration to the problem of market control than has been usual in merger cases.[23] The court took into account (1) the merged concerns' share of sales of their various products in the *local* market, (2) the state of intercompany competition in the New England market, the number and size of companies, the area of their operations, and recent changes in the market position of the various companies, and (3) potential competition. Despite the advance, the dicta of Judge Kimbrough Stone in this case cannot be said to indicate a clear conception of monopoly in terms of market control. "Competition," he declares,

"is the antithesis of monopoly. In a sense, any elimination of competition is a movement in the general direction of monopoly. But competition is, in its very essence, a contest for trade, and any progress or victory in such contest must lessen competition. . . . It is only when this lessening is with an unlawful purpose or by unlawful means, or when it proceeds to the point where it is or is threatening to become a menace to the public, that it is declared unlawful. . . . The point of danger is reached when monopoly is threatened."

We might now expect some indication of tests which the court will apply to determine when monopoly is threatened. But the opinion continues, "This threat of monopoly exists, irrespective of intent, whenever competition is lessened to the danger point." Competition is lessened to the danger point when "monopoly is threatened."[24] Judge Stone in subsequent remarks appears to be able to get no farther forward with this idea and finally falls back on a dictum of Justice Holmes that "a combination in unreasonable restraint of trade imports an attempt to override normal market conditions."[25] Since nothing is more "normal" than monopolistic market conditions, this too does not get us very far.

This summary review of the law of monopoly must lead to the conclusion that whatever are considered to be the evils resulting from monopoly — enhancement of price, deterioration of product, or the like — a monopolistic situation, or an attempt to monopolize, is evidenced to the courts primarily, if not exclusively, by a limitation of the freedom to compete. The original meaning of monopoly, an exclusion of others from the market by a sovereign dispensation in favor of one seller, has continued to mean exclusion, in the broad sense of restriction of competition. Although "undue" or "unreasonable"

[22.] McLaughlin, *Legal Control of Competitive Methods* (1936) 21 Iowa L. Rev. 280.

[23.] United States v. Standard Oil Co. of N.J., 47 F. (2d) 288 (C. C. A. 2d, 1931). For another realistic analysis of a market situation, see International Shoe Co. v. Federal Trade Commission, 29 F. (2d) 518 (C. C. A. 2d, 1931).

[24.] United States v. Standard Oil Co. of N.J., 47 F. (2d) 288, at 297 (C. C. A. 2d, 1931).

[25.] American Column Co., v. United States, 257 U. S. 377 (1921).

control of the market is constantly inserted in judicial decisions as the meaning of monopoly, the data capable of indicating this control are almost universally ignored by the courts. In this country there has been a growing tendency in the law to declare every contract between competitors which restricts competition unenforceable and, since the Sherman Act, illegal, whatever the extent of the control made possible by the contract.[26] In the case of mergers the monopoly or attempt to monopolize is discovered primarily in predatory practices designed to hamper the competition of outsiders and not in control of the market.

III.

It has been noted above that the elements on which the idea of monopoly has been built both in law and in economics have been control of the market and restriction of competition. If in their development of the law of monopoly the courts have tended to give mere lip service to the former and to identify monopoly with restriction of competition, the principal reasons are probably the following:

(1) The courts have been faced with the necessity of devising and applying to particular situations a standard of evaluation relevant to a vague concept known as the public interest. The injury to numerous private interests, and consequently to the public interest, from predatory attacks on established business enterprises, or from other attempts to restrict competition, was much more direct than that which might possibly be inflicted on buyers or sellers by a control of the market exercised independently of any attempts to restrict competition.

(2) The formulation of a standard of monopoly or monopolizing contrary to the public interest required the selection of tests capable of distinguishing competitive from monopoly situations. If monopoly were conceived as control of the market, the tests must necessarily be related to the behavior of prices, outputs and other variables indicative of control, an exceedingly difficult problem. If, on the other hand, monopoly is identified with restriction of competition, the devising of tests is comparatively simple.

[26.] There is no evidence that the courts in interpreting the Sherman Act and later anti–trust legislation in the light of common law concepts of monopoly and restraint of trade were violating legislative intention of substituting their understanding of the monopoly problem for that of the Congress. On the contrary there is every reason to believe that the principal acts which the Sherman Act sought to prevent were the predatory practices of combinations which in many cases already enjoyed a commanding control of the market. The particular practices which received special legislative attention were railway rebating, local price–discrimination and price maintenance. The sponsors of the Act announced on many occasions that it was not designed to prevent combinations either of labor or capital, and in answer to the specific question whether an enterprise would be considered a monopoly if, because of superior skill, it alone received all the orders for a particular article, Senator Hoar replied, "The word 'monopoly' is a merely technical term which has a clear and legal significance, and it is this: it is the sole engrossing to a man's self by means which prevent other men from engaging in fair competition with him." 21 Cong. Rec. 3152 (1890).

(3) There is reason to believe that in an earlier period control of the market was much more dependent upon restriction of entry and other types of restriction of competition through predatory practices and harassing tactics than at present. The law of monopoly, though directed against restrictions of competition, may once have had more relevance to control of the market than it at present possesses.

(4) Before the Sherman Act monopoly actions were brought, with but few exceptions, before the courts on the suit of private interests. These interests were more likely to be directly affected adversely by predatory practices or attempts at exclusion from the market than by control of prices.

Although these considerations may help to explain the almost complete preoccupation of the courts with restrictions on freedom of competition, it must be recognized that our modern law embraces an antiquated and inadequate conception of the monopoly problem. Attention and criticism has therefore centered around the following aspects of our public policy with respect to monopoly and competition: the tendency of the courts to find illegal every contract limiting competition among the contracting competitors regardless of the effect or probable effect of such a contract on control of the market; the tendency to judge the legality of a combination or merger primarily on the basis of its competitive practices without examination of the extent of its control of the market; the absence of a developed public policy with respect to unfair practices, in particular the unwillingness of the courts to extend the concept of unfair competition beyond injury to a competitor and to take account of the nature of the injury to the public.

The weakness of our public policy is not the result of judicial interpretation but of the inadequacy of legislation. It can only be corrected by legislation which will re-define the monopoly and trade practice problem and provide tests by means of which market situations and business practices considered to be favorable to the public interest can be separated from those that are not. Since Congress has wrestled with this problem, off and on, for fifty years without conspicuous success, it does not appear likely that a ready-made solution can be found close at hand. Certainly economics has none to provide. Nevertheless, the economic approach, which is in some ways very different from the legal, can be utilized in the shaping of a more satisfactory public policy.

For its own purposes economics has found control of the market a much more useful approach to the concept of monopoly than restriction of competition. Some control of the market may be said to exist whenever the share of the sales or purchases made by any one seller or purchaser (or group of sellers or purchasers acting by means of an agreement) is sufficiently large to influence the price of the article sold. In a market from which control is completely absent very seller and buyer, acting independently, could increase or decrease his purchases or sales without appreciable effect on the price. Such markets, which may be said to be purely competitive in the sense of being completely devoid of any element of control over price, are comparatively rare. In most markets some sellers or buyers (or both) exercise some degree of control. Of course such control is perfectly compatible with the existence of some degree of competition. A seller with complete control of the market would be able to determine his price without regard for the actions of other sellers or the prices of other products; in other words, he would have no competition. No seller or buyer has such control. All markets, practically speaking, exhibit a fusion of monopoly and competitive elements.

It follows that, if monopoly is identified with control of the market, (a) it is impossible to separate markets into those that are competitive and those that are monopolistic; (b) a public policy which attempted to eliminate all positions of monopoly would confront a problem of impossible scope and complexity. It is, furthermore, by no means clear that the preservation of all the competitive elements and the suppression of all the monopolistic elements would be in the public interest, however conceived. Consequently, the existence of some control of the market is not likely to be in itself a good indication of the necessity or wisdom of applying preventative measures.

Having identified monopoly with control of the market, economics has proceeded further to an examination of certain typical monopoly situations. But the most that can be said of the results of monopoly investigations in economics is that they cast doubts on a number of traditional legal attitudes on the question of monopoly and restraint of trade, and that they emphasize a number of relevant considerations usually neglected by the interpreters of public policy. The significance of the existence of a relatively small number of buyers or sellers is a case in point. If the number of sellers (or buyers) is small enough to induce each seller, before changing his own selling policy, to take account of the probable effect of this change upon the policies of his rivals, the results of joint action by agreement, which might well be illegal, may be accomplished without collusion of any sort. It is quite obvious from the behaviour of cigarette prices that the manufacturers of cigarettes are in something like this situation. No one can change his prices without an overwhelming probability that his rivals will immediately follow suit, and one result is that price changes are very infrequent. To produce many of the consequences of joint action no one seller has to have a preponderant share of the total output; if the number of sellers is relatively small, their individual share of the total output is of secondary importance.

Nor is control of the market to be inferred merely from the number of existing competitors. Potential competition must be considered. Indeed the dicta of many trust cases might be interpreted as indicating a judicial opinion that in the absence of legal restraints or of overt predatory acts against potential competitors, free entry to the market precludes any element of control. Free entry in this legal sense, however, is compatible under certain circumstances with a considerable degree of market control. The capital resources necessary to establish a new firm in an effective competitive position may be so large as to eliminate potential competition as a practical consideration. The fact that no new motor car company has been established in the last decade or that no new brand of cigarettes has been able since the war to capture a sizeable share of the market cannot be taken to indicate that no control of the market exists.

The legal significance attached to trade marks and trade names provides another example of the divergence between legal and economic conceptions of monopoly. Economics, primarily concerned with the fact of market control, has emphasized the control of price made possible by the exploitation of a mark or name. Extensive advertising expenditures may successfully differentiate in the minds of buyers the product of a given seller from those of his rivals. The more successful this differentiation the greater the control of the market it is possible for the seller to achieve, and, consequently, the more entrenched his monopoly position. But since there is no restriction of competition in the legal sense, the law, primarily concerned in trade mark and trade name cases with protection of intangible property interests, can see no element of monopoly. On the other hand, economic opinion does not proceed from the fact that there is a monopolistic significance in the use of a mark or name to the conclusion that this institution or practice is necessarily contrary to the public interest.[27]

It is fully consistent with the legal conception of the monopoly problem that the courts should enquire into the actual or probable results of agreements to restrain competition. But to do so would be to give up the traditional tests of monopolizing and to grapple with the problem of what is an unreasonable control of the market. The *Appalachian Coals* case[28] may indicate a tentative first step in this direction and somewhere between this and the *Sugar Institute* cases[29] is to be found the indistinct dividing line between certain types of restrictions which are and are not at present considered to be in the public interest. The ways in which competition may be restrained or "regulated," however, are many, and if the courts are now willing to delve into the problems of market control they will have to rely more and more on economic analysis of the different types of control situations. The significance of market controls established through various kinds of open price quoting, basing–point and zone price systems, agreements as to price terms and the like, are not apparent without a study of data hitherto considered by the courts to be irrelevant to the monopoly problem.

[27.] See Handler, *Unfair Competition* (1936) 21 Iowa L. Rev. 175, 185. For the views of an economist on these matters, see Chamberlin, Monopolistic Competition (1933) Appendix E.

[28.] Appalachian Coals, Inc. v. United States, 288 U. S. 344 (1933).

[29.] United States v. Sugar Institute, 297 U. S. 553 (1936), aff'g., 15 f. Suppl. 817 (S. D. N. Y. 1934). For a thorough discussion of the problems, both legal and economic, raised by these cases, see Fly, Observations on the Anti–Trust Laws, Economic Theory and the Sugar Institute Decisions (1936) 45 Yale L. J. 1339, 46 id. 228.

On the other hand, if economics is to put itself in a position to contribute to the formulation of public policy, it must conceive the monopoly problem in a more extensive way than is at present customary. It is not enough to find evidence of the existence of market controls, nor is it sufficient to conduct purely analytical and descriptive studies of various types of control situations. While this is important, the formulation of public policy requires a distinction between situations and practices which are in the public interest and those that are not. And this requirement imposes the necessity of elaborating tests which can be applied by administrative bodies and by the courts. It is easy enough to present evidence of monopoly situations, which, to economics, is merely the absence of pure competition. The existence of price discrimination, of price rigidity, advertising expenditures, price leadership and other practices are sufficient to indicate the presence of monopoly elements. But these practices are hardly sufficient evidence of the presence of possibility of market controls adverse to the public interest. A further study of different types of industrial markets and business practices and of their effects on prices, outputs, investment and employment designed to indicate means of distinguishing between socially desirable and undesirable situations and practices may or may not be fruitful. It is, in any case, the only way in which economics can contribute directly to the shaping of public policy. A simultaneous movement by legal and economic thinking away from entrenched positions might be conducive to progress on this front.

The Condition of Entry and the Public Policy

Joe S. Bain

Designed to Secure Workable Competition

Although the primary orientation of this volume is toward theoretical prediction and its implementation and testing with empirical data, some brief attention may be given to the implications of our findings for public policy.

Such implications as there are have bearing primarily on the antitrust, anti-monopoly, or pro-competitive policy of the federal government as it deals with the organization of markets and the market behavior of business firms. This policy, stemming from the Sherman Act and from later legislation in the same tradition, may undertake generally to secure or preserve market structures conducive to workable competition, and also lines of market conduct by sellers or buyers having the same tendency. Revision of market structures, and the prevention or discouragement of certain changes in them, particularly in the dimensions of horizontal seller concentration, vertical integration, and the condition of entry have all been important though perhaps not dominant aspects of past antitrust policy.

Since the condition of entry is a dimension of market structure that may have a distinct impact on the character and workability of competition, it seems reasonable that an antitrust policy, under either existing legislation or new law, might give more systematic attention than it has previously to revisions of the condition of entry which would favor more effective competition, and to the prevention of changes in the condition of entry which would adversely affect the workability of competition. Some actions along these lines are of course already a part of established policy. For example, attacks on "exclusionary tactics" designed to exclude new competitors, on exclusive dealing and typing contracts with distributors having the same effect, and on certain types of administration of patent rights designed to deny to potential entrants necessary access to techniques or product designs, are well known. What is suggested here is that a somewhat more general and comprehensive attention might be given under the law to the preservation of a socially desirable condition of entry to our industries—the preservation of an effective degree of potential competition.

Our comments here will not pretend to contain even a cursory survey of antitrust policy as a whole or any outline prescription for the future of that policy in all its aspects. They will be confined rather to suggestions as to the extent to which and the manner in which the pro-competitive policy might deal with the condition of entry in order to improve the workability of competition. Even within this restricted sphere, such suggestions as we may make are highly tentative or provisional. They are based either on tentative and only partly tested theories or on the results of an empirical study of only 20 industries. Their factual foundation is thus not overly firm, and in addition they rest on an evaluation of the condition of entry almost solely in terms of its effects on long-run tendencies in monopolistic output restriction, excess profits, efficiency in scale of firm and plant, and selling costs. The condition of entry has not been evaluated in terms of its possible effects on progressiveness in technique or product, on cyclical stability, or on other dimensions of market performance. In consequence, these policy suggestions are potentially subject to revision or qualification if the association of the condition of entry to the neglected aspects of market performance should turn out to be of a certain sort. With these disclaimers on record, let us proceed to the implications of our findings for public policy.

General indications of a priori analysis

It may as well be emphasized at the outset that a great deal of what we can say on policy could have been offered on the basis of the underlying theoretical analysis, as reviewed in Chapter 1, without undertaking the empirical study presented above. The empirical study is important mainly in offering some tentative confirmation of the assumptions and theories on which the policy recommendations rest, in giving some quantitative implementation to qualitative judgments, and in establishing findings in areas where *a priori* predictions were quite indefinite. These contributions are perhaps not inconsiderable, although they are of a provisional sort; we merely wish to emphasize that the general character of the policy suggestions now offered was apparent in suggestions developed from the theoretical analysis alone.

In 1951, the present writer sketched out the basic theory involved and included some tentative policy suggestions.[1] The recommendations for policy were roughly as follows.

First, since higher barriers to entry tend in general to be associated with higher degrees of monopolistic output restriction and larger excess profits, given the extent of seller concentration probably accompanying them, a good beginning rule for policy should be to reduce high barriers to entry wherever this is feasible—striving for "effectively impeded" rather than "blockaded" entry, and for lower absolute barriers within the "effectively impeded" range. This should in general tend to bring entry-forestalling limit prices closer to the competitive level. Second, the principal exception to this general rule would be that if "effectively impeded" entry already existed, reductions in the barrier to entry to an "ineffectively impeded" status (where entry-forestalling limit pricing policies would cease to be attractive to established sellers) might be avoided, since if concentration were to remain fairly high, structural instability

---

[1.] See J.S. Bain, "Conditions of Entry and the Emergence of Monopoly," *Monopoly and Competition and Their Regulation*, edited by E.H. Chamberlin (London, 1954), pp. 215–241, and especially pp. 237–240.

and related inefficiency might result. This suggestion is consistent with the observation that "effectively impeded" entry with barriers of moderate absolute heights may on balance be preferable to "ineffectively impeded" entry, at least in industries of fairly high seller concentration.

Third, as to the sorts of entry barriers which may be legitimately attacked, it was observed that those resting on real economies of large-scale plant and firm (whatever their importance) should not and probably could not be removed, because of the adverse effects on efficiency of such removal. On the other hand, the bases of strictly pecuniary economies of scale might be likely candidates for attack. As a result, the possibilities of reducing entry barriers based on scale economies would depend in large part on the relative importance of real and strictly pecuniary economies in the cases in question. It was added that there might be a great deal of administrative difficulty in devising a policy which would selectively eliminate strictly pecuniary economies without impairing the realization of real economies.

Fourth, it was suggested in consequence that the major part of a policy designed to reduce entry barriers would perforce be directed toward product-differentiation barriers and absolute cost barriers to entry. The techniques of policy having this aim were not discussed, but casual reference was made to patent-law reform, a policy designed to ease the supply of funds in the capital markets, attacks on resource monopolization by integrated processing firms and on unnecessary integration generally, consumer education, and grade labelling. Quantitative guesses as to the relative importance of the two sorts of entry barriers involved were not developed, but the writer must admit to an initially excessive estimate of the probable relative importance of absolute cost barriers other than those involving capital requirements.

Fifth, it was suggested that any policies tending to shorten entry lags (the interval between the emergence of an entry-attracting price and the establishment of a new producer in satisfactory operating condition) would be desirable, since the shorter the entry lag the less a barrier to entry of given height is likely to induce established sellers to follow high entry-attracting price policies as opposed to relatively low entry-forestalling limit price policies.

Sixth, it was suggested that reduction of seller concentration was by no means the sole key to a pro-competitive policy involving alterations of market structures. On the contrary, the results of fairly high seller concentration might vary widely according to the condition of entry to the industry, and alteration of the condition of entry might constitute a generally more feasible regulatory technique than dissolution and dismemberment policies aimed just at reducing seller concentration. In any event, an anti-concentration policy alone would probably prove to be insufficient.

The preceding constitutes a basic tentative outline of the suggestions for policy contained below. Let us see how much it has been elaborated, implemented, and revised in the light of our empirical study.

General reduction of entry barriers, to some limit

The leading suggestion for policy drawn from *a priori* analysis was that barriers to entry should be reduced, consistent with maintaining efficiency in production and distribution, at least to the lower end (in absolute values) of the "effectively impeded" range, as a means of lessening the incidence of monopolistic output restriction and excess profits. To this it was added that reducing barriers to the "ineffectively impeded" category might not be so desirable; very moderate barriers qualifying as effectively impeding entry might be conducive to better over-all performance in an industry.

This suggestion can be to a considerable degree reaffirmed in the light of our investigation. In effect, it appears that industries with aggregate absolute entry barriers classified as "very high" do indeed have on the average significantly higher excess profit rates than industries with only "substantial" or lower barriers to entry, and higher degrees of monopolistic output restriction. It was our guess that the "very high" barriers probably qualified either as blockading entry or as in the higher absolute range of effectively impeding it: entry could be forestalled either at industry profit–maximizing prices or at prices somewhat lower than that but still quite high relative to costs. On these assumptions, the finding in question appears to confirm in part our basic prediction. Correspondingly, we can reaffirm the suggestion that reduction of barriers to entry as high as those we have called "very high" should improve performance in the respects emphasized. Even without accompanying deconcentration actions, such a reduction might increase the workability of competition.

The light cast on our predictions and initial suggestions by a comparison of the profit rates of industries of "substantial" and "moderate to low" aggregate barriers to entry is less distinct. Given our findings in Chapter 6 as to the aggregate entry barriers in various industries, it was our guess that the "substantial" barriers would probably qualify as effectively impeding entry—that is, entry could and probably would be forestalled at prices below the monopoly level and with moderate excess profits. Further, our "moderate to low" entry barriers would probably qualify as either in the lower range of effectively impeding (adoption of relatively low entry–forestalling price, with lower excess profits than with substantial barriers, would be probable), or ineffectively impeding (with entry barriers slight enough that entry–attracting prices and at least periodic excess profits of significant size should emerge). What we found was (1) no apparently significant difference in profit rates between "substantial-barrier" and "moderate-to-low-barrier" industries; and (2) inclusion of chronic excess capacity in a part of the latter category of industries. Our difficulty is that this finding is subject to a variety of interpretations, and that we are unable to say which interpretation is valid. In consequence, the validity of our basic predictions as they affect this range of barriers to entry to industries cannot be confirmed or disconfirmed.

It is equally possible, for example, that:

(1) The "moderate to low" barriers to entry as identified ineffectively impede entry in most cases, so that entry–attracting price policies yielding moderate excess profits in the periods observed have resulted. This notion is given some support by the finding of chronic excess capacity in the cement, flour, and shoe industries, though it is uncertain in view of the general inadequacy of data on excess capacity. If this is true, the findings are potentially consistent with our theoretical hypothesis. The implication would be that though it would be desirable to reduce entry barriers to the low end of the "substantial" range as identified, it would not necessarily be desirable to drive them much lower—at any rate unless rather low seller concentration were simultaneously assured, and perhaps not even then. As this prognosis develops, perhaps the word "substantial" turns out to be a little strong as a description of entry barriers in the middle category of industries classified according to the absolute height of these barriers.

(2) Our empirical data are imprecise enough so that an invalid distinction has been drawn between the heights of entry barriers to industries classified as having, respectively, "substantial" and "moderate to low" barriers. This would make our findings potentially consistent with our theoretical hypothesis, but would confine the reaffirmation of our policy suggestions to that based on a distinction between "very high" entry barriers and others.

(3) The rates of profit on equity are sufficiently imprecise measures of price–average cost discrepancies to cast doubt on the quantitative findings in question.

(4) Sellers in general are less sensitive to the threat of entry and to the opportunities for forestalling entry than our theory assumes, and thus do not react systematically to the relatively small differences between "substantial" and "moderate to low" barriers. This would tend to undermine the basis of our predictions, as well as at least part of the policy suggestions based on them.

With the data at our disposal, we are unable to determine which of these (or other) explanations of the empirical findings is valid. In consequence, we can only affirm our earlier suggestion that a reduction (consistent with efficiency) of "very high" entry barriers down only to a "substantial" status should be good policy as far as monopolistic output restriction and related phenomena are the objects of action, and leave quite uncertain the extent to which, if at all, it would be generally desirable and worthwhile to drive entry barriers below the "substantial" and into the "moderate to low" level. One possibility is that the drawing of unattainably fine distinctions would be required to implement a policy involving these further reductions of barriers to entry.

To our general positive conclusion, moreover—i.e. reduction of the very high barriers to entry—one qualification is suggested by our detailed empirical findings. That is, lowering a high entry barrier about enough but not too much is not necessarily a simple thing in practice; it is not quite so easy as drawing a window blind halfway down but not to the bottom. Considering the techniques of revision available, it would be fairly easy inadvertently to go so far with remedies that entry barriers would be lowered enough to encourage excessive entry and structural instability. And it is not impossible that in some cases no safe technique will be available.

Our general prescription for reducing very high barriers should thus not be construed as a recommendation for every action that influences matters "in the right direction." The varying potential results of any measure should be weighed (and potentially "over-efficacious" measures placed in a doubtful category). Also, the "side effects" of any measure on efficiency should be carefully scrutinized, in the light of the full complexity of actual situations, before accepting it.

Given this amendment to our earlier judgments on policy, let us turn to the relative importance of different sorts of entry barriers, and the means of treating them.

Scale economies, and other advantages of scale

A priori speculations about the policy problem of maintaining competition frequently emphasize the possibility of probability that in a fair share of manufacturing industries economies of scale of firm are so important that highly concentrated oligopoly is a prerequisite to efficiency. Hence, it is argued, the relatively unsatisfactory competitive conduct which is associated with high concentration must be accepted unless we are to reduce efficiency or to regulate directly. In industries where this was true, it would also hold that the scale economies in question would raise considerable barriers to entry, making the dilemma of the competitive policy more acute. Therefore, a very important question in appraising the over-all policy problem is what proportion of industries are affected by scale economies of such great importance.

The general finding based on our sample of 20 manufacturing industries (mostly either highly or moderately concentrated) is that very important economies of scale are found in a rather small proportion of the industries. Economies of scale were found clearly sufficient to impede entry substantially and lead to very high concentration in only 3 or 20 industries. Of 4 more industries for which systematic scale-economy data are not available, only one seems likely to qualify for the same category. Around 20 percent of the industries in our sample thus present serious scale-economy problems. For the remainder, the economies in general probably do not require more than moderate concentration nor will they raise high barriers to entry. This is not to deny that perceptible (though moderate to small) barriers to entry are raised by scale economies in at least half of these remaining industries.

The scale economies in question that can be most definitely established are those of production and physical distribution. Such economies appear in a number of industries to be significantly reinforced, however, by advantages of large-scale sales promotion. These advantages are most evident in cases where integrated or quasi-integrated distribution has been used to advantage by manufacturers—as with autos, typewriters, farm machines and tractors, and petroleum products. In addition, there is the unproven possibility of advantages of large-scale advertising in the case of a number of consumer goods. In both cases, such promotional advantages of scale may be reinforced by some economies of physical distribution at multiplant scale, which are effective so long as nationwide or comparable distribution—required by optimal promotional techniques—must be presupposed.

The extent to which the economies in question are alternatively real and strictly pecuniary has been rather difficult to establish. The existence of strictly pecuniary economies of scale in production and distribution was frequently denied by our sources of information, and the enforcement of the Robinson-Patman law was given as a reason for the obliteration of certain strictly pecuniary economies formerly enjoyed. By and large, however, we have been unable to establish at all firmly the relative importance of the two sorts of economies in production and distribution. On the other hand, it appears that the bulk of the advantages of large-scale sales promotion are probably of a strictly pecuniary character, enhancing the revenues of the firms involved rather than actually reducing costs.

That economies of scale in production and distribution do not loom large as the basis of barriers to entry is fortunate for the policy-maker, because there is relatively little that can or should be done about them. In general, they establish entry barriers which we have to accept in order to get efficiency. To this generalization, however, there are at least two exceptions. First, it is legitimate and, from the standpoint of our problem, desirable to attack the bases of strictly pecuniary advantages of size such as are derived from monopsonistic buying power through the enforcement of legislation like the Robinson-Patman law. Second, the importance of scale economies is sometimes increased if the entrant is effectively forced to integrate backward or forward into an added stage of production in order to attain efficiency, for the reason that in the prior or succeeding stage, integrated established firms dominate the supply or the outlets. (We reserve the case of forward integration into final marketing outlets for separate consideration.) Now in this case, *if it is found that the integration is not required for real economy and does not reduce costs*, enforced disintegration of established firms, resulting in the establishment of non-integrated industries at both stages of production, may reduce the importance of scale economies at one or the other stage of production without offsetting disadvantages. Undoing of integration which is found to have neutral effects on costs may thus actually reduce barriers to entry without offsetting social loss and be conducive to more workable competition. The crucial question, of course, is whether or not in any particular industry the integration is economical. It is suggested that disintegration proposals be viewed under this added light, as well as in the light of more traditional standards.[2]

Sales–promotional advantages of scale appear in general to be private rather than social. They enhance profits without enhancing the general welfare, and at the same time they result in higher barriers to entry. Policies aimed at reducing these advantages may therefore appear virtually desirable in cases where existing entry barriers are currently excessive. The major difficulty is that such policies are not easy to devise.

In instances where the advantages of large–scale sales promotion to the manufacturer hinge on distributive integration, and where real economies of such integration are not apparent, a policy seeking distributive disintegration might be indicated (presuming entry barriers are excessive). Thus in cases like those of the automobile, farm machine, and petroleum–refining industries, the elimination of integration, and of quasi–integration through contractual exclusive–dealing arrangements, would tend to reduce the over-all advantages of large scale at the manufacturing level and to lower the barriers to entry perceptibly. If in these or other cases it were true that real economies were not realized from integration and the aggregate entry barriers were excessive, such disintegration policy might be indicated. The disintegration remedies in the recent movie antitrust cases suggest a movement along this line. (We expressly do not undertake here to pass on the question of real economies of distributive integration in the industries mentioned as examples, or to recommend any particular policy with respect to them.)

As we have argued in Chapter 4, the existence of net advantages of large–scale advertising *per se* is in doubt. As far as such advantages do exist, they could also be attacked. We defer discussion of policy measures appropriate to this phase of possibly undesirable advantages of scale until a later section.

Two qualifying provisos must be added to the preceding. First, incursions on existing promotional advantages of scale could conceivably result in some industries in a market structure wherein physical distribution would become less economical. This would be a possibility, for example, if (a) existing firms in these industries still (after the incursion) had enough advantage from nation-wide promotion and distribution to induce them to promote and distribute nationally; but (b) their advantages were reduced in such manner and degree that they could no longer maintain as efficient a distributive volume as previously through various "nodes" in the distributive system—essentially because of deconcentration consequent on the reduction of promotional advantages of scale. It follows that the ultimate impact on the organization of an industry of any regulative measure that affects promotional advantages of scale must be carefully appraised before it is approved. As indicated, certain

---

[2.] Of course, side effects of any disintegration, such as might engender distributive or other diseconomies of scale, should be watched, and compensating or correlative measures adopted, as a part of the disintegration policy, to forestall them.

"in–between" measures could lead to waste in some industries. The desirable measures there would be those which either (a) lowered barriers to entry somewhat without in effect undermining national (or comparable) sales promotion or the organization of the industry as it affects distributional economies; or (b) disrupted the processes of sales promotion enough so that firms in the industries in question would find it profitable thereafter to promote and distribute locally or regionally, thus no longer encountering those scale economies, in distribution predicted solely on nationwide promotion and distribution. Needless to say, distinguishing appropriate from inappropriate measures may be no easy task.

Second, certain distributional economies of the multiplant firm—"real" though they may be—are recognizable only "as of" the acceptance of nationwide distribution, which is in turn generally a corollary of nationwide sales promotion. Given measures affecting promotion which would thoroughly erase the advantages of nationwide promotion, these real distributional economies would drop out, and scale economies of the multiplant firm would become a less important deterrent to entry than they are, and have been represented, in the contemporary scene. The interaction between real scale economies and the institutions facilitating sales promotion is especially interesting to the serious student of anti–monopoly policies.

Absolute cost advantages of established firms

It is a commonplace in dissertations on the competitive policy that "artificial impediments" to entry should be attacked and as far as possible removed. The impediments usually cited stem from administration of patent rights and from resource monopolization via backward integration of processing firms. Such proposals are in our terms suggestions for the removal of the principal absolute cost barriers to entry.

Generally we are not inclined to disagree with these proposals. There is a serious question, however, about how far the recommended policy would take us in reducing excessive barriers to entry—in what proportion of cases these "artificial impediments" are an important source of barriers to entry. In our sample of 20 industries, such impediments do not appear to be of dominant importance. In only 3 industries—all of them involving resource control through backward integration by processors—were absolute cost barriers adjudged large; in the remainder, they were rated as slight to negligible. In none of the 20 cases was patent control found to be currently the source of a serious impediment to entry, although in two cases (gypsum products and metal containers) such impediments had been significant prior to the conclusion of antitrust actions around 1950. In a complete coverage of manufacturing industries, of course, added instances of entry barriers resulting from patent or resource control will be discovered. But it is our general impression that these "artificial impediments" are not pervasive sources of excessive barriers to entry, and that a policy directed primarily at them as the sources of such barriers would fall far short of the desired goal.

So far as these impediments are found to be strategic sources of excessive entry barriers, the appropriate public policy is fairly clear. First, regarding impediments resulting from resource monopolization by integrated established firms, disintegration movements are indicated if the integration is not essential to efficiency in production or to effectiveness in the exploration for and development of new resources. If it is essential, the resultant barrier to entry will almost have to be accepted. A considerable burden of investigation and proof would probably rest upon that public authority undertaking to implement a selective disintegration policy of the sort suggested.

In regard to patents, the sort of policy applied in the American Can and U.S. Gypsum cases (and also in the National Lead case) seems appropriate. That is, discriminatory administration of patent rights to exclude entry—either absolutely or through excessive royalties—should be attacked, and a practice of open licensing of all comers at fair and reasonable royalty rates should be secured. The developing trend in antitrust-law interpretation may suffice to secure this end; otherwise, legislative amendments of patent or antitrust laws might be required. (It is possible, though not certain, that in some cases compensating adjustments of institutions that encourage nationwide sales promotion would be required in order to forestall inefficient spreading of small or middle-sized firms over too large a market area.)

A final source of absolute cost barriers to entry is found in the size of capital requirements for efficient entry. Generally we have found that in a high proportion of the industries examined the absolute capital requirement is very large. It is suggested that large capital requirements place the potential entrant at a disadvantage, because he cannot secure the requisite funds at a rate as low as that available to established firms through the capital markets or through internal financing. What can be done about this barrier to entry?

It can hardly be removed entirely, and probably cannot be greatly reduced in the average case. Some suggestions, however, are appropriate:

(1) Disintegration and the prohibition of integration in cases where real diseconomies would not result therefrom may not only lessen the scale-economy barrier to entry but also reduce the effective absolute capital requirements for entry very significantly, thus lowering the barrier to entry.

(2) Since established firms operating in *other industries* frequently have the least disadvantage of all potential entrants to a given industry in acquiring the requisite capital, we should perhaps go slow in frowning officially on expansion of large firms via diversification to enter new fields. To discourage or prohibit this sort of diversification may well tend to raise the barriers to entry to industries generally, with adverse effects on competition. This disadvantage of an anti-diversification policy *vis-a-vis* large firms must be weighed carefully against the alleged dangers of the growth of gigantic firms *per se*.

(3) Government measures to ease the supply of capital to new firms—via loan insurance, extra-fast depreciation write offs for tax purposes, etc.—might be extended or developed, on the basis of a careful preliminary study.

In other words, something at least can probably be done to lower capital-requirement barriers to entry.

Product–differentiation barriers to entry

Perhaps the most surprising finding of our study—if previous casual comment on barriers to entry is taken as the standard—is that the most important barrier to entry discovered by detailed study is probably product differentiation. That is, the advantage to established sellers accruing from buyer preferences for their products as opposed to potential-entrant products is on the average larger and more frequent in occurrence at large values than any other barrier to entry. This is in any event apparently true in our sample of 20 industries, and the writer is by now prepared to guess that it is true in general. In 5 of 20 industries and in dominant segments of 2 others, product-differentiation barriers were found to be great; in only 6 industries, plus segments of 4 others, were they found to be slight.[3] The impact of product differentiation on entry thus appears stronger than that of either scale economies or absolute cost advantages. In some cases—e.g., cigarettes, liquor, and quality fountain pens—product differentiation almost alone is responsible for very high aggregate entry barriers. In others—automobiles, tractors, typewriters—it combines with very important economies of scale in production to produce extremely high barriers. Any general policy designed to deal with the entry problem must pay major attention to the impediments to entry raised by product differentiation.

But a feasible type of policy to deal with the problem is not easily apparent. There is an evident propensity of the profit-seeking enterprise to attempt to enhance profits through product differentiation, via the advantages it gives it over both established rivals and potential rivals. Moreover, the enterprise tends to pursue a product-differentiation policy unilaterally, and without the necessity of any sort of consensual action that might run counter to laws against collusion or concert of action by competitors. Furthermore, the psychology of consumers is very evidently such that they are frequently susceptible to the blandishments of product-differentiating sellers, so that we come at last to a presumably fairly stable characteristic of human nature as the root of the trouble. For all of these reasons, it is difficult to attack this sort of barrier to entry under laws in the anti-monopoly or anti-collusion tradition, or to legislate it away. Then too, it is difficult to organize any substantial political support for measures designed to attack extremes of product differentiation.

Given all these difficulties, we can offer no more than a few tentative comments. These all stem from the central observation that there is a good deal of institutional implementation for private policies of product differenti-

---

3. See Table XI above.

ation, and that the institutions in question are not necessarily immutable. The strategic institutions are perhaps those of distributive integration and support of entertainment and news media through advertising expenditures of commercial concerns. In addition, we may mention the lack of an institution—adequate information services (governmental or otherwise) designed to disseminate detailed product information to buyers and to improve their knowledge of what they buy.

Our comments, then, are as follows:

(1) Where product–differentiation advantages of established firms rest heavily on distributive integration, either through ownership or through contractual arrangement, disintegration and prohibition of further integration would tend to reduce product–differentiation barriers to entry. Such a policy would seem desirable provided that it did not entail perceptible real diseconomies, and provided that it did not result in a "in–between" situation whereby firms were encouraged to undertake nation–wide or comparable promotion and distribution with over–all scales inefficient for the performance of this task. The net impact of distributive disintegration on industry organization should be carefully analyzed and predicted before measures are taken along this line.

(2) Measures to restrict advertising expenditures, either absolutely or by taxation, may be considered as potentially in the public interest. But the qualification just stated applies; "in–between" outcomes are a danger to be avoided.

(3) Measures such as comprehensive grade–labelling or its equivalent, plus perhaps wide public dissemination of product information, would also be salutary, especially if they proceeded far enough to dissipate the advantages of nationwide sales promotion. The writer does not suggest that any or all of these measures is politically feasible, but they seem to embody the only apparent means of attack on excessive product–differentiation barriers to entry.

The policy toward seller concentration

We have recognized throughout that seller concentration has a concurrent influence—and probably an equally important one—with the condition of entry in determining the workability of competition in an industry. In other words, both actual competition and potential competition are important. Existing antitrust policy implicitly more or less recognizes this, although the economist commentators on that policy are inclined to give a preponderant emphasis to the effects of seller concentration, and then to append a few remarks on the problem of entry. Similarly, a great deal of attention has been given in antitrust actions of the Justice Department since 1941 to horizontal dismemberment as a proposed remedy for ineffective competition, and relatively less to the easing of entry.

Generally, this writer would subscribe to a policy of reducing very high seller concentration and keeping it from developing, subject to a freedom from diseconomies of such action and also subject to a careful interpretation of what is unduly high seller concentration. Tentative indications of studies cited above are that if we can secure situations where the first eight sellers (for example) control less than two-thirds of the market, the probabilities for effective competition are better than where the first eight firms control 80 to 90 per cent or more of the market. On the other hand, neither available evidence nor *a priori* logic support the notion that significant improvements in market performance would be likely to stem from turning a two–firm industry into a four–firm industry, into a six–firm industry (in both cases concentration remains in the very high range and alteration of behavior is improbable), or from dismembering the "big four" firms of an industry when together they control perhaps two–fifths of the market (concentration is probably already so low that further deconcentration is unnecessary or pointless). But some carefully calculated controls on concentration are probably supportable, though further study is needed to establish the character of such controls.

In devising a policy toward seller concentration, in any case, the following should be kept in mind with respect to the condition of entry, especially since dissolution and dismemberment policies may be costly and hard to secure under existing judicial interpretations of the law: The market performance of the highly concentrated industry may be much better from a social standpoint if it is not protected by very high barriers to entry. In consequence, policies designed to reduce excessive barriers to entry may be considered as *alternatives*, as well as supplements, to a policy designed to reduce seller concentration. High concentration may be a relatively innocuous phenomenon if entry barriers can be reduced to a moderate level.

Comments on the existing competitive policy

To what extent is the existing competitive policy, as embodied in our antitrust and related laws, adequate to deal with the problem of barriers to entry? No detailed analysis of this issue will be attempted here, but some suggestions may be briefly presented. The existing law has several evident applications to reducing excessive barriers to entry or to preventing their erection in the first place. These include:

(1) The application of the Sherman Act to exclusionary tactics (directed against potential entrants), as exercised unilaterally by a dominant firm or in concert by an oligopoly of leading firms. This application might conceivably extend to the prohibition of resource monopoly via backward integration and to some limits on selling expenditures (see the last *Tobacco* case), but to date we are without clear precedents for the application of positive remedies in these areas by the courts. Whether the application of the Act could be extended by interpretation is a matter for speculation.

(2) The application of the Sherman Act to a restrictive administration of patents which is designed to exclude entry. Numerous actions, some apparently effective, have been undertaken, and a considerable extension of this policy under existing law seems possible.

(3) The application of the Sherman Act to vertical integration by dominant firms, seeking disintegration under a joint monopoly charge. As in the movie cases and in the pending case involving the Pacific Coast petroleum industry, the entry–impeding effects of scale economies might be reduced by enforced disintegration. It is not as yet apparent, however, that under existing law, remedies could generally be secured for integration having noxious effects on the condition of entry.

(4) The application of the revised Section 7 of the Clayton Act, prohibiting mergers having the tendency (incipient or actual) to create monopoly or lessen competition. Although this is a new law in its revised form, its application could conceivably have a tangential effect on heading off integrations which would impede entry, and a direct effect in forestalling the establishment of large firms which would be likely to succeed in erecting more formidable product–differentiation barriers to entry.

(5) The application of Section 2 of the Clayton Act (the Robinson–Patman Amendment) to the elimination of strictly pecuniary advantages of large scale, such as inhere in the monopsonistic power of the large buyer.

(6) The application of Section 3 of the Clayton Act (involving tying and exclusive–dealing contracts) to the prohibition of quasi–integration into distribution, where that would have the effect of heightening product–differentiation barriers to entry or enhancing the advantages of large scale. Until recently, a mild policy has been followed under this section, principally as a result of conservative judicial interpretation. The Standard *Stations* and *International Salt* decision, however, suggest that a much more aggressive policy may have now become feasible.

If we view the potentialities of existing legislation as a whole, it is apparent that it might well be stretched in its application to deal fairly effectively with barriers to entry resulting from some advantages of large–scale sales promotion, from some product–differentiation advantages of large firms, and from most absolute cost advantages of large firms. But by no means can this be done with certainty, and if at all, perhaps with such crudity that losses might outweigh gains. The probability is that legislative supplementation of existing law would be required on a number of points in order to support an effective policy regarding the limitation on barriers to entry, and the precise character of desirable supplements could be specified only after detailed further study.

The principal basic deficiency of policy based on existing legislation is its substantial inability to deal (except through disintegration under joint monopoly charges, and then perhaps crudely) with the very important product–differentiation barriers to entry. Bases for action are shaky, and remedies are not apparent. In this area it would appear that a novel approach in regulatory legislation and in the assumption of functions by the government is probably required to bring serious pressure to bear on some of the most embarrassing excessive barriers to entry. But the development of an adequate policy must presuppose a fair adjudication and balancing of all interests and views, economic and otherwise, which bear on the whole matter.

Lacking or pending various sorts of legislative innovation, however, it seems probable that vigorous but careful use of existing law, within the clear orientation of the condition-of-entry problem, could go a considerable distance toward lowering excessive barriers to entry and thereby enhancing the workability of competition in American industry.

CHAPTER 3 - Early Doubts

The Alternative Courses of Action

H. S. Dennison and J. K. Galbraith

In the preceding chapters we have looked over the regulating mechanism, or rather the lack of regulating mechanism, under modern forms of competition. It is apparent that there are many faults:—faults which stand revealed when we measure the system, not against the performance of some form of collectivist society, but against the expected or supposed achievements of a competitive society. The situation we have analyzed, we may add, is integral to the present day organization of industry. It cannot be dismissed as the product of government interference, the stupidity of bankers, or the cupidity of labor leaders.

When we turn to the question of what, if anything, can be done about these weaknesses, we are faced first of all with a question of basic design. It is of considerable importance to an architect who is about to submit plans for a building that he know whether it is to be a skyscraper or a warehouse. We must know what kind of business structure we seek.

Apart from thorough–going socialization of industry, the choices in design seem to be two. On the one hand we may hope for a business organization which is self–regulating in a more or less automatic way. It happens that the only mechanism for automatic self–regulation of which we know is that of the competition of very large numbers of producers; that is to say, the sort of business structure which the nineteenth–century business man and economist assumed (and still assume) to exist. The alternative is to accept American business as it now is and to attempt to design a set of mechanisms which will do some of the work of the automatically self–regulating features which have been lost,—or which never existed.

It is useless to disguise the fact that either course of action is likely to be enormously difficult; and it is idle to attempt to say which, could it be carried out with the utmost intelligence and thoroughness, would lead to the more fruitful economic order. We do not know. But of the two possible approaches some modification of the present order of things is likely to prove more

Reprinted by permission of Oxford University Press from *Modern Competition and Business Policy*, 1938.

practical than the institution of a model radically different from the present structure.

We have already seen that the sort of competition which is automatic and self-regulating is an exceedingly special form of competition indeed. To institute this form of competition we should have to face the question of breaking up industrial units to an extent hitherto imagined by few. Our task would not be one of finding monopolies and dissolving them, nor would we be much concerned with combinations, gentlemen's agreements and price leadership. But it would be necessary to search out any scale of production which gave evidence of present or potential power to the individual producer to exercise jurisdiction over his prices. To remove this power in our important industries the individual units would have to be made small indeed. In less important industries,—where there is now 'large scale' production, also,—the individual units would be minute. Whether they could make efficient use of modern methods of production may be seriously doubted.

Half-way measures in efforts to restore self-regulative competition will not suffice; an incomplete jurisdiction of producers over prices, we have seen, may lead to consequences as unsatisfactory as more complete controls.[1] It is difficult to see how one could lessen the degree of jurisdiction one now finds in the women's garments trades, the needle trades, and the laundry trade. And it is precisely here at present that the necessity for setting prices without the power to make price control effective is at least partly responsible for price wars, low wages and cut-throat competition. Surely there is nothing that can be done to sub-divide the units further in such industries, and nothing that could be accomplished were they sub-divided. At the other extreme there are industries where it is hopeless to expect that self-regulative competition can be made effective. This is already recognized in the case of railroads and communications, light and power utilities and milk distribution. It is not so generally recognized, but is, nevertheless, true of such industries as ship-building, locomotive construction, and others. It is fantastic to suppose that we would ever take actual steps to reduce to anywhere near 'atomistic' proportions the unit scale of operations in the manufacture of automobiles or farm implements, or steel; unit costs would certainly go to impossible levels. We have seen, also, that there are lines of activity, notably retailing and the distributive trades generally, where mere numbers of operations give no assurance of optimum output at low cost,—in fact, numbers are more likely to mean diluted business and inefficient operation.

The most dubious aspect of an effort to restore regulative competition is that it seeks to 'restore' something which has never existed in most modern industry. When most human activity was devoted to the production of food and to the handicraft manufacture of clothing, a degree of regulative competition among many small producing units somewhat similar to modern staple agricul-

---

[1.] See pp. 36–43.

ture may have existed, although even then it was limited by the royal monopolies in raw materials and the regulations of the guilds. But, as the standard of living has become higher and more varied in content, production of food and clothing has become less important relative to the production of all goods. Farm production, and some of the subsequent manufacture of food and clothing, still show characteristics of self–regulating competition. But of the wide variety of other industries which produce for modern needs many were cast from their beginning in a different mold, and in many of the remainder the competition of large numbers disappeared before the industry grew out of the stage of experimental adolescence.[2] To attempt to re–institute regulative competition would be to impose upon much of American industry a wholly new and untried form of organization. To achieve self–regulative competition American industry would have to undergo major surgery.

If we do not or cannot return to the regulation of 'atomistic' competition, how are we to re–design and supplement the organization of modern industry to provide that degree of regulation which is so obviously essential? How, in other words, is it to be made to operate more nearly at capacity or optimum output with less unemployment, with freedom from price warfare at the expense of employee groups and, most important of all, with a lessened susceptibility to booms and depressions? Further, what changes are to be made in the corporation, the unit in modern industrial organization, so that a management which responds to the individual profit motive will, by so doing, contribute to the welfare of the community?

We would not expect to find any one formula for achieving these objectives; in any case we have not sought for one. The attack we propose is a frankly piecemeal affair which works upon not one but several fronts. We do not pretend that our suggestions on each of the several fronts are the best possible, or that in total they would eliminate all the weaknesses in our present industrial organization. We shall be content if they do two things,—if they demonstrate that practical steps can be taken, and point the way to further progress.

Regulation

The crux of the subject of public regulation of business has never been whether or not there should be regulation. It has always been a question of the kind of regulation there should be and of its objectives. The businessman who pleads for freedom from government regulation does not desire the repeal of all public supervision and control of economic life. Patent laws, laws of contract and their enforcement, and tariffs are government controls which businessmen would not care to abolish.

We have been speaking much in the preceding pages of regulative competition. The term suggests that the form of regulation which accompanies such competition is of a special sort, and this is indeed the case. Where regulative or

---

[2.] For example, the automobile industry had many times the present number of individual manufacturers in the pre–war years, but nowhere near enough for regulative competition.

'pure' competition obtains and industry is so organized (or is presumed to be so organized) that it tends toward a moving equilibrium of optimum or high efficiency output, full employment, and constant search for greater efficiency and technological improvement, then any regulation by the state must follow a special design. Broadly it must be the kind of regulation and only the kind that promotes the condition of equilibrium or balance. Or, to change the metaphor, it must be the sort of regulation which oils the machinery, meshes unmeshed gears, and which, perhaps, reinforces certain structurally weak parts. The regulation must not, however, alter the machine itself, attempt to change its speed, or interfere with new departures in design.

In nineteenth century England and late nineteenth and early twentieth century America, the theory, if not the fact, of self-regulative competition held general sway. In England and America there was a fairly consistent adherence to the kind of public regulation appropriate to this competition. The state oiled the machinery in various ways. It protected property, enforced contracts, adjusted disputes between employers, and insisted on minimum standards of business honesty. These functions were regarded by many as the greatest permissible range of public activity. Competition was assumed to do the remainder of the regulating.

The state, however, was gradually forced to accept a larger measure of responsibility. Yielding to the view that the private individual is structurally weak as the unit for doing business, it fostered and protected the joint stock company or corporation. Certain labor groups (notably women and children), seemed likely to be squeezed or mangled by the machine. The state came to their aid. In America the design of the machine was altered to a considerable extent by tariff protection. In both England and America there came gradually to be marked out an area where self-regulating, self-adjusting competition could not work or could not be trusted. Into this breach, likewise, the state stepped. Railroads and light and water utilities were either necessarily monopolies, or else competition, if it did exist, took on a peculiarly violent and uncertain form. The state found it necessary in the interest of the railroads and utilities, and the users of their services, to set and enforce prices. In the case of banks, fiduciaries and the professions, the occasional debauches which characterized all self-regulative competition were so dangerous to the community that some regulation there was necessary.

In America there was a Frankenstein complex, also, which gave rise to another and quite distinct form of regulation. It was feared that some part of the machine would one day get out of control and presently rise up and devour the rest of it. Drive shafts, pistons, bolts, nuts, and buzz saws and even consumers would all go down the hungry maw of this monster. The monster, of course, was monopoly—monopoly in the absolute sense—and once out of hand it was feared that monopoly would be more likely to control the country than be controlled by it. Since the very existence of a self-regulating machine depended on keeping monopoly under control, it was safe to do some redesigning of parts to keep it down. The Sherman Act in the eighties, followed by the Federal Trade Commission Act, the Clayton Act, and last of all the Robinson–Patman Act, were all aimed in varying degree at monopoly. But we have seen that it is not '100% monopolies,' or even firms controlling 51% of the industry, but a growth of single producers to sizes large enough (perhaps 5%) to affect price appreciably which is the basic factor in eliminating the self-regulating character of industry. This mis–direction of legislative emphasis is understandable, however, because attention was inevitably centered on the well-known power of the monopoly to engage in exploitative price practices.

It is plain that even when self–regulative competition was assumed to exist, a considerable amount of regulation was necessary, including regulation that sought to maintain competition. Naturally, however, the disappearance from modern industry of so much self–regulative competition has made this type of regulation inadequate. The present task, therefore, is not to improve the machinery for doing an old and familiar job. It is to invent new machinery for a new job.

We can conveniently break our suggestions on public regulation into two parts. First we consider the problem of regulation where competition has been and is by some still assumed to be the regulative force, but where in fact the characteristics of competition which might make it self–regulative are gone forever. Next we survey in a brief and general way the regulation which has long been applied to railroads, utilities, and like industries where it was early recognized that competition was not a satisfactory regulator in itself.

General Industrial Regulation

In suggesting a program for industrial regulation we are faced at the outset with the fact that we do not yet know with any degree of precision the form which that regulation should take or the techniques it should employ. There has been no lack of discussion of regulation; perhaps one difficulty is that there has been so much discussion which lacked a careful definition of terms and a rigorous scrutiny of the issues of principle and practice which regulation involves. In addition, we had for two years in the N.R.A. the beginnings of a large scale experiment in at least one phase of industrial regulation. But none of this is enough as yet to justify any one attempting to draw a detailed blueprint. For a business structure as varied and complex as that of the United States there can be no simple formula, no easy rule which can be laid down for all. Indeed, in our forty years of floundering anti–trust policy, and in the N.R.A. ineffectiveness and difficulties may be attributed to over–simple formulae and to the effort to apply fixed rules over too wide a variety of industrial conditions.

On the other hand, we are faced with a structure of economy which, if our analysis or our common sense is correct, does not have the power of self–regulation. If industry cannot regulate itself, and if regulation, as we have shown, is necessary in the interest of the community, then the responsibility rests with the state. There is no place else for this responsibility to rest; either the state must make the attempt or we must content ourselves with a policy of drift.

If, therefore, we must regulate and don't yet know how to, we must start as sensibly and safely as possible and learn as we go along. The device we recommend is not regulation *per se*, but exploration of the art of technique of regulation. We must do some rational experimental work in the art of industrial regulation. The first steps might be taken in the case of those industries which have shown in recent years extreme under–utilization or extreme fluctuation in use of plant and labor resources; or which have had strikingly high profits combined with unreasonably high or inflexible prices; or which have undergone competitive reduction of labor standards; or which have shown excessively wasteful distributive methods. Exploration in the art of regulation should begin where a lack of regulation at present is producing the most unsatisfactory results.

For practical machinery we suggest that a Commission be empowered by Congress to identify and make the necessary study of industries with a low social performance. On the basis of such study, the Commission would be authorized to invite representatives of the industry to co–operate in formulating a plan for such industrial policies, e.g., such level and such regularity of production and such price and labor policies, as conform to the public interest. If co–operation proves impossible, the Commission should be empowered to prepare such a plan itself.

Upon completion of a plan we think its submission to a technically qualified semi–judicial Board of Review would be desirable. This Board would pass on any disputed points of equity in connection with the plan. When approved by it the Commission would be empowered to put the plan into effect for the industry. Changes in the plain initiated by the Commission and approved by the Board of Review could be made at any time. Changes in or perhaps even discontinuance of the plan could be ordered, also, by the Board of Review at any time.

We do not propose that industry plans be draw up for all industry within any short space of time. We repeat that this program is an exploration in the art of regulation where regulation appears to be most needed. We do not conceive of the initiative in the adoption of the plan as coming from industry, but rather from the regulating commission. In this sense we look upon the program as a substitute for anti–trust prosecution. Rather than blindly sub–dividing the units in an industry in the faint hope that certain desirable results will come out of the sub–division, we propose that the results be defined and a program be laid out directly to achieve these socially desirable and defined results. It would be hoped that the co–operation of each industry would be obtained in achieving the objectives which the community has the right to expect of it. In the absence of full industry co–operation, however, there would be no choice but to proceed with as much of it as can be gained, or as a last resort without it.

The objectives of the industry plans, like the objectives of regulation itself, are, of course, enlarged and regularized output and the maintenance of such price policies, labor standards, and earnings as would place the industry in the best relation to the welfare of the community. But even these are not matters to which we would care to give *a priori* definition. A major task in the development of the art of regulation is the appraisal of specific industrial policies in their relation to the general welfare.

For effecting its objectives it is important that the Commission be provided with the widest practical variety of tools. It should not be bound by an narrow concept of order-giving in the regulation which it undertakes. In certain instances tariff adjustment might well be an appropriate and effective means to do the desired ends; in certain cases yardstick competition would be a desirable tool; subsidy as a means of directing economic resources should certainly be one of the tools of the Commission. It is possible that with Congressional consent taxation might be used. That it have such a variety of measures at hand is essential; for, a always granting the need of proper safeguards, it would be through working with a goodly assortment of tools that the Commission would develop its techniques of regulation.

Certain interpretations of the constitution doubtless stand in the way of this program although we do not pretend to say whether or not these interpretations are likely to be the ruling ones. But since the only function of the law is to serve man we do not believe in being stopped by objections of a purely legal sort—at least so long as we have means for revising laws to meet the ends we seek.

While a Commission is studying the industries which society most needs to have regulated and is making its first experiments, there should be thrown open to the rest of the business world the chance to develop the technique of self-regulation under government supervision. This could take several of the forms which in recent years have been discussed as fair-trade practice agreements. They make legal such agreements as a significant majority—say two-thirds or three-fourths—of a trade or industry may work out and such as may be approved by a department of the government as of net value to the country as a whole.

These self-regulatory experiments could not be expected to go very far,—certainly not at first. For without any plan to coerce the ten per cent or more who would surely stay out no tackling of the more important wasteful abuses in present trade practices would be possible. But much underbrush might be cleared away; and in any case work under such agreements would be an education in the realities of business.

Monopolistic Practices

Joseph A. Schumpeter

What has been said so far is really sufficient to enable the reader to deal with the large majority of the practical cases he is likely to meet and to realize the inadequacy of most of those criticisms of the profit economy which, directly or indirectly, rely on the absence of perfect competition. Since, however, the bearing of our argument on some of those criticisms may not be obvious at a glance, it will be worth our while to elaborate a little in order to make a few points more explicit.

1. We have just seen that, both as a fact and as a threat, the impact of new things—new technologies for instance—on the existing structure of an industry considerably reduces the long–run scope and importance of practices that aim, through restricting output, at conserving established positions and at maximizing the profits accruing from them. We must now recognize the further fact that restrictive practices of this kind, as far as they are effective, acquire a new significance in the perennial gale of creative destruction, a significance which they would not have in a stationary state or in a state of slow and balanced growth. In either of these cases restrictive strategy would produce no result other than an increase in profits at the expense of buyers except that, in the case of balanced advance, it might still prove to be the easiest and most effective way of collecting the means by which to finance additional investment.[1] But in the process of creative destruction, restrictive practices may do much to steady the ship and to alleviate temporary difficulties. This is in fact a very familiar argument which always turns up in times of depression and, as everyone knows, has become very popular with governments and their economic advisers—witness the NRA. While it has been so much misused and so faultily acted upon that most economists heartily despise it, those same advisers who are responsible for this[2] invariably fail to see its much more general rationale.

[1.] Theorists are apt to look upon anyone who admits this possibility as guilty of gross error, and to prove immediately that financing by borrowing from banks or from private savers or, in the case of public enterprise, financing from the proceeds of an income tax is much more rational than is financing from surplus profits collected through a restrictive policy. For some patterns of behavior they are quite right. For others they are quite wrong. I believe that both capitalism and communism of the Russian type belong in the latter category. But the point is that theoretical considerations, especially theoretical considerations of the short–run kind, cannot solve, although they contribute to the solution of, the problem which we shall meet again in the next part.

[2.] In particular, it is easy to show that there is no sense, and plenty of harm, in a policy that aims at preserving "price parities."

Practically any investment entails, as a necessary complement of entrepreneurial action, certain safeguarding activities such as insuring or hedging. Long-range investing under rapidly changing conditions, especially under conditions that change or may change at any moment under the impact of new commodities and technologies, is like shooting at a target that is not only indistinct but moving—and moving jerkily at that. Hence it becomes necessary to resort to such protecting devices as patents or temporary secrecy of processes or, in some cases, long-period contracts secured in advance. But these protecting devices which most economists accept as normal elements of rational management[3] are only special cases of a larger class comprising many others which most economists condemn although they do not differ fundamentally from the recognized ones.

If for instance a war risk is insurable, nobody objects to a firm's collecting the cost of this insurance from the buyers of its products. But that risk is no less an element in long-run costs, if there are no facilities for insuring against it, in which case a price strategy aiming at the same end will seem to involve unnecessary restriction and to be productive of excess profits. Similarly, if a patent cannot be secured or would not, if secured, effectively protect, other means may have to be used in order to justify the investment. Among them are a price policy that will make it possible to write off more quickly than would otherwise be rational, or additional investment in order to provide excess capacity to be used only for aggression or defense. Again, if long-period contracts cannot be entered into in advance, other means may have to be devised in order to tie prospective customers to the investing firm.

In analyzing such business strategy *ex visu* of a given point of time, the investigating economist or government agent sees price policies that seem to him predatory and restrictions of output that seem to him synonymous with loss of opportunities to produce. He does not see that restrictions of this type are, in the conditions of the perennial gale, incidents, often unavoidable incidents, of a long-run process of expansion which they protect rather than impede. There is no more of paradox in this than there is in saying that motorcars are traveling faster than they otherwise would *because* they are provided with brakes.

2. This stands out most clearly in the case of those sectors of the economy which at any time happen to embody the impact of new things and methods on the existing industrial structure. The best way of getting a vivid and realistic idea of industrial strategy is indeed to visualize the behavior of new concerns or industries that introduce new commodities or processes (such as the alumi-

---

[3.] Some economists, however, consider that even those devices are obstructions to progress which, though perhaps necessary in capitalist society, would be absent in a socialist one. There is some truth in this. But that does not affect the proposition that the protection afforded by patents and so on is, in the conditions of a profit economy, on balance a propelling and not an inhibiting factor.

num industry) or else reorganize a part or the whole of an industry (such as, for instance, the old Standard Oil Company).

As we have seen, such concerns are aggressors by nature and wield the really effective weapon of competition. Their intrusion can only in the rarest of cases fail to improve total output in quantity or quality, both through the new method itself—even if at no time used to full advantage—and through the pressure it exerts on the preexisting firms. But these aggressors are so circumstanced as to require, for purposes of attack and defense, also pieces of armor other than price and quality of their product which, moreover, must be strategically manipulated all along so that at any point of time they seem to be doing nothing but restricting their output and keeping prices high.

On the one hand, largest-scale plans could in many cases not materialize at all if it were not known from the outset that competition will be discouraged by heavy capital requirements or lack of experience, or that means are available to discourage or checkmate it so as to gain the time and space for further developments. Even the conquest of financial control over competing concerns in otherwise unassailable positions or the securing of advantages that run counter to the public's sense of fair play—railroad rebates—move, as far as long-run effects on total output alone are envisaged, into a different light;[4] they may be methods for removing obstacles that the institution of private property puts in the path of progress. In a socialist society that time and space would be no less necessary. They would have to be secured by order of the central authority.

On the other hand, enterprise would in most cases be impossible if it were not known from the outset that exceptionally favorable situations are likely to arise which if exploited by price, quality and quantity manipulation will produce profits adequate to tide over exceptionally unfavorable situations provided these are similarly managed. Again this requires strategy that in the short run is often restrictive. In the majority of successful cases this strategy just manages to serve its purpose. In some cases, however, it is so successful as to yield profits far above what is necessary in order to induce the corresponding investment. These cases then provide the baits that lure capital on to untried trails. Their presence explains in part how it is possible for so large a

---

[4.] The qualification added removes, I think, any just cause for offense that the above proposition might conceivably cause. In case that qualification is not explicit enough, I beg leave to repeat that the moral aspect is in this case, as it must be in every case, entirely unaffected by an economic argument. For the rest, let the reader reflect that even in dealing with indubitably criminal actions every civilized judge and every civilized jury take account of the ulterior purpose in pursuit of which a crime has occurred and of the difference it makes whether an action that is a crime has or has not also effects they consider socially desirable.

Another objection would be more to the point. If an enterprise can succeed only by such means, does not that prove in itself that it cannot spell social gain? A very simple argument can be framed in support of this view. But it is subject to a severe *ceteris paribus* proviso. That is to say, it holds for conditions which are just about equivalent to excluding the process of creative destruction—capitalist reality. On reflection, it will be seen that the analogy of the practices under discussion with patents is sufficient to show this.

section of the capitalist world to work for nothing: in the midst of the prosperous twenties just about half of the business corporations in the United States were run at a loss, at zero profits, or at profits which, if they had been foreseen, would have been inadequate to call forth the effort and expenditure involved.

Our arguments however extends beyond the cases of new concerns, methods and industries. Old concerns and established industries, whether or not directly attacked, still live in the perennial gale. Situations emerge in the process of creative destruction in which many firms may have to perish that nevertheless would be able to live on vigorously and usefully if they could weather a particular storm. Short of such general crises or depressions, sectional situations arise in which the rapid change of data that is characteristic of that process so disorganizes an industry for the time being as to inflict functionless losses and to create avoidable unemployment. Finally, there is certainly no point in trying to conserve obsolescent industries indefinitely; but there is point in trying to avoid their coming down with a crash and in attempting to turn a rout, which may become a center of cumulative depressive effects, into orderly retreat. Correspondingly there is, in the case of industries that have sown their wild oats but are still gaining and not losing ground, such a thing as orderly advance.[5]

All this is of course nothing but the tritest common sense. But it is being overlooked with a persistence so stubborn as sometimes to raise the question of sincerity. And it follows that, within the process of creative destruction, all the realities of which theorists are in the habit of relegating to books and courses on business cycles, there is another side to industrial self–organization than that which these theorists are contemplating. "Restraints of trade" of the cartel type as well as those which merely consist in tacit understandings about price competition may be effective remedies under conditions of depression.

[5.] A good example illustrative of this point — in fact of much of our general argument — is the postwar history of the automobile and the rayon industry. The first illustrates very well the nature and value of what we might call "edited" competition. The bonanza time was over by about 1916. A host of firms nevertheless crowded into the industry afterwards, most of which were eliminated by 1925. From a fierce life and death struggle three concerns emerged that by now account of over 80 per cent of total sales. They are under competitive pressure inasmuch as, in spite of the advantages of an established position, an elaborate sales and service organization and so on, any failure to keep up and improve the quality of their products or any attempt at monopolistic combination would call in new competitors. Among themselves, the three concerns behave in a way which should be called corespective rather than competitive: they refrain from certain aggressive devices (which, by the way, would also be absent in perfect competition); they keep up with each other and in doing so play for points at the frontiers. This has gone on for upwards of fifteen years and it is not obvious that if conditions of theoretically perfect competition had prevailed during that period, better or cheaper cars would now be offered to the public, or higher wages and more or steadier employment to the workmen. The rayon industry had its bonanza time in the twenties. It presents the features incident to introducing a commodity into fields fully occupied before and the policies that impose themselves in such conditions still more clearly than does the automobile industry. And there are a number of other differences. But fundamentally the case is similar. The expansion in quantity and quality of rayon output is common knowledge. Yet restrictive policy presided over this expansion at each individual point of time.

As far as they are, they may in the end produce not only steadier but also greater expansion of total output than could be secured by an entirely uncontrolled onward rush that cannot fail to be studded with catastrophes. Nor can it be argued that these catastrophes occur in any case. We know what has happened in each historical case. We have a very imperfect idea of what might have happened, considering the tremendous pace of the process, if such pegs had been entirely absent.

Even as now extended however, our argument does not cover all cases of restrictive or regulating strategy, many of which no doubt have that injurious effect on the long–run development of output which is uncritically attributed to all of them. And even in the cases our argument does cover, the net effect is a question of the circumstances and of the way in which and the degree to which industry regulates itself in each individual case. It is certainly as conceivable that an all–pervading cartel system might sabotage all progress as it is that it might realize, with smaller social and private costs, all it is that it might realize, with smaller social and private costs, all that perfect competition is supposed to realize. This is why our argument does not amount to a case against state regulation. It does show that there is no general case for indiscriminate "trust–busting" or for the prosecution of everything that qualifies as a restraint of trade. Rational as distinguished from vindictive regulation by public authority turns out to be an extremely delicate problem which not every government agency, particularly when in full cry against big business, can be trusted to solve.[6] But our argument, framed to refute a prevalent theory and the inferences drawn therefrom about the relation between modern capitalism and the development of total output, only yields another theory, i.e., another outlook on facts and another principle by which to interpret them. For our purpose that is enough. For the rest, the facts themselves have the floor.

3. Next, a few words on the subject of Rigid Prices which has been receiving so much attention of late. It really is but a particular aspect of the problem we have been discussing. We shall define rigidity as follows: a price is rigid if it is less sensitive to changes in the conditions of demand and supply than it would be if perfect competition prevailed.[7]

Quantitatively, the extent to which prices are rigid in that sense depends on the material and the method of measurement we select and is hence a

---

[6.] Unfortunately, this statement is almost as effective a bar to agreement on policy as the most thoroughgoing denial of any case for government regulation could be. In fact it may embitter discussion. Politicians, public officers and economists can stand what I may politely term the whole–hog opposition of "economic royalists." Doubts about their competence, such as crowd upon us particularly when we see the legal mind at work, are much more difficult for them to stand.

[7.] This definition suffices for our purposes but would not be satisfactory for others. See D.D. Humphrey's article in the *Journal of Political Economy*, October 1937, and E.S. Mason's article in the *Review of Economic Statistics*, May 1938. Professor Mason has shown, among other things, that contrary to a widespread belief price rigidity is not increasing or, at all events, that it is no greater than it was forty years ago, a result which in itself suffices to invalidate some of the implications of the current doctrine of rigidity.

doubtful matter. But whatever the material or method, it is certain that prices are not nearly as rigid as they seem to be. There are many reasons why what in effect is a change in price should not show in the statistical picture; in other words, why there should be much spurious rigidity. I shall mention only one class of them which is closely connected with the facts stressed by our analysis.

I have adverted to the importance, for the capitalist process in general and for its competitive mechanism in particular, of the intrusion of new commodities. Now a new commodity may effectively bring down the preexisting structure and satisfy a given want at much lower prices per unit of service (transportation service for instance), and yet not a single recorded price need change in the process; flexibility in the relevant sense may be accompanied by rigidity in a formal sense. There are other cases, not of this type, in which price reduction is the sole motive for bringing out a new brand while the old one is left at the previous quotation—again a price reduction that does not show. Moreover, the great majority of new consumers' goods—particularly all the gadgets of modern life—are at first introduced in an experimental and unsatisfactory form in which they could never conquer their potential markets. Improvement in the quality of products is hence a practically universal feature of the development of individual concerns and of industries. Whether or not this improvement involves additional costs, a constant price per unit of an improving commodity should not be called rigid without further investigation.

Of course, plenty of cases of genuine price rigidity remain—of prices which are being kept constant as a matter of business policy or which remain unchanged because it is difficult to change, say, a price set by a cartel after laborious negotiations. In order to appraise the influence of this fact on the long–run development of output, it is first of all necessary to realize that this rigidity is essentially a short–run phenomenon. There are no major instances of long–run rigidity of prices. Whichever manufacturing industry or group of manufactured articles of any importance we choose to investigate over a period of time, we practically always find that in the long run prices do not fail to adapt themselves to technological progress—frequently they fall spectacularly in response to it[8]—less prevented from doing so by monetary events and policies or, in some cases, by autonomous changes in wage rates which of course should be taken into account by appropriate corrections exactly as should changes in quality of products.[9] And our previous analysis shows sufficiently why in the process of capitalist evolution this must be so.

[8.] They do not as a rule fall as they would under conditions of perfect competition. But this is true only *ceteris paribus*, and this proviso robs the proposition of all practical importance. I have adverted to this point before and shall return to it below (5).

[9.] From a welfare standpoint, it is proper to adopt a definition different from ours, and to measure price changes in terms of the hours of labor that are currently necessary to earn the dollars which will buy given quantities of manufactured consumers' goods, taking account of changes of quality. We have already done this in the course of a previous argument. A long–run downward flexibility is then revealed that is truly impressive. Changes in price level raise another problem. So far as they reflect monetary influences they should be eliminated for most of the purposes of an investigation into rigidity. But so far as they reflect the combined effect of increasing efficiencies in all lines of production they should not.

What the business strategy in question really aims at—all, in any case, that it can achieve—is to avoid seasonal, random and cyclical fluctuations in prices and to move only in response to the more fundamental changes in the conditions that underlie those fluctuations. Since these more fundamental changes take time in declaring themselves, this involves moving slowly by discrete steps—keeping to a price until new relatively durable contours have emerged into view. In technical language, this strategy aims at moving along a step function that will approximate trends. And that is what genuine and voluntary price rigidity in most cases amounts to. In fact, most economists do admit this, at least by implication. For though some of their arguments about rigidity would hold true only if the phenomenon were a long-run one—for instance most of the arguments averring that price rigidity keeps the fruits of technological progress from consumers—in practice they measure and discuss primarily cyclical rigidity and especially the fact that many prices do not, or do not promptly, fall in recessions and depressions. The real question is therefore how this short-run rigidity[10] may affect the long-run development of total output. Within this question, the only really important issue is this: prices that stay up in recession or depression no doubt influence the business situation in those phases of the cycles; if that influence is strongly injurious—making matters much worse than they would be with perfect flexibility all round—the destruction wrought each time might also affect output in the subsequent recoveries and prosperities and thus permanently reduce the rate of increase in total output below what it would be in the absence of those rigidities. Two arguments have been put forth in favor of this view.

In order to put the first into the strongest possible light, let us assume that an industry which refuses to reduce prices in recession goes on selling exactly the same quantity of product which it would sell if it had reduced them. Buyers are therefore out of pocket by the amount to which the industry profits from the rigidity. If these buyers are the kind of people who spend all they can and if the industry or those to whom its net returns go does not spend the increment it gets but either keeps it idle or repays bank loans, then total expenditure in the economy may be reduced thereby. If this happens, other industries or firms may suffer and if there upon they restrict in turn, we may get a cumulation of depressive effects. In other words, rigidity may so influence the amount and distribution of national income as to decrease balances or to increase idle balances or, if we adopt a popular misnomer, savings. Such a case is

---

[10.] It should, however, be observed that this short run may last longer than the term "short run" usually implies—sometimes ten years and even longer. There is not one cycle, but there are many simultaneous ones of varying duration. One of the most important ones lasts on the average about nine years and a half. Structural changes requiring price adjustments do in important cases occur in periods of about that length. The full extent of the spectacular changes reveals itself only in periods much longer than this. To do justice to aluminum, rayon, or motorcar prices one must survey a period of about forty-five years.

conceivable. But the reader should have little difficulty in satisfying himself[11] that its practical importance, if any, is very small.

The second argument turns on the dislocating effects price rigidity may exert if, in the individual industry itself or elsewhere, it leads to an additional restriction of output, i.e., to a restriction greater than that which must in any case occur during depression. Since the most important conductor of those effects is the incident increase in unemployment—unstabilization of employment is in fact the indictment most commonly directed against price rigidity—and the consequent decrease in total expenditure, this argument then follows in the tracks of the first one. Its practical weight is considerably reduced, although economists greatly differ as to the extent, by the consideration that in the most conspicuous cases price rigidity is motivated precisely by the low sensitiveness of demand to short-run price changes within the practicable range. People who in depression worry about their future are not likely to buy a new car even if the price were reduced by 25 per cent, especially if the purchase is easily postponable and if the reduction induces expectations of further reductions.

Quite irrespective of this however, the argument is in conclusive because it is again vitiated by a *ceteris paribus* clause that is inadmissible in dealing with our process of creative destruction. From the fact, so far as it is a fact, that at more flexible prices greater quantities could *ceteris paribus* be sold, it does not follow that either the output of the commodities in question, or total output and hence employment, would actually be greater. For inasmuch as we may assume that the refusal to lower prices strengthens the position of the industries which adopt that policy either by increasing their revenue or simply by avoiding chaos in their markets—that is to say, so far as this policy is something more than a mistake on their part—it may make fortresses out of what otherwise might be centers of devastation. As we have seen before, from a more general standpoint, total output and employment may well keep on a higher level with the restrictions incidents to that policy than they would if depression were allowed to play havoc with the price structure.[12] In other words, under the conditions created by capitalist evolution, perfect and universal flexibility of prices might in depression further unstabilize the system, instead of stabilizing it as it no doubt would under the conditions envisaged by general theory. Again this is to a large extent recognized in those cases in which the economist is in sympathy with the interests immediately concerned, for

---

11. The best method of doing this is to work out carefully all the assumptions involved, not only in the strong case imagined but also in the weaker cases that are less unlikely to occur in practice. Moreover, it should not be forgotten that the profit due to keeping prices up may be the means of avoiding bankruptcy or at least the necessity of discontinuing operations, both of which might be much more effective in starting a downward "vicious spiral" than is a possible reduction in total expenditure. See the comments on the second argument.

12. The theorist's way to put the point is that in depression demand curves might shift downwards much more violently if all pegs were withdrawn from under all prices.

instance in the case of labor and of agriculture; in those cases he admits readily enough that what looks like rigidity may be no more than regulated adaptation.

Perhaps the reader feels some surprise that so little remains of a doctrine of which so much has been made in the last few years. The rigidity of prices has become, with some people, the outstanding defect of the capitalist engine and—almost—the fundamental factor in the explanation of depressions. But there is nothing to wonder at in this. Individuals and groups snatch at anything that will qualify as a discovery lending support to the political tendencies of the hour. The doctrine of price rigidity, with a modicum of truth to its credit, is not the worst case of this kind by a long way.

4. Another doctrine has crystallized into a slogan, viz., that in the era of big business the maintenance of the value of existing investment—conservation of capital—becomes the chief aim of entrepreneurial activity and bids fair to put a stop to all cost-reducing improvement. Hence the capitalist order becomes incompatible with progress.

Progress entails, as we have seen, destruction of capital values in the strata with which the new commodity or method of production competes. In perfect competition the old investments must be adapted at a sacrifice or abandoned; but when there is no perfect competition and when each industrial field is controlled by a few big concerns, these can in various ways fight the threatening attack on their capital structure and try to avoid losses on their capital accounts; that is to say, they can and will fight progress itself.

So far as this doctrine merely formulates a particular aspect of restrictive business strategy, there is no need to add anything to the argument already sketched in this chapter. Both as to the limits of that strategy and as to its functions in the process of creative destruction, we should only be repeating what has been said before. This becomes still more obvious if we observe that conserving capital values is the same thing as conserving profits. Modern theory tends in fact to use the concept Present Net Value of Assets (= capital values) in place of the concept of Profits. Both asset values and profits are of course not being simply conserved but maximized.

But the point about the sabotage of cost-reducing improvement still calls for comment in passing. As a little reflection will show, it is sufficient to consider the case of a concern that controls a technological device—some patent, say—the use of which would involve scrapping some or all of its plant and equipment. Will it, in order to conserve its capital values, refrain from using this device when a management not fettered by capitalist interests such as a socialist management could and would use it to the advantage of all?

Again it is tempting to raise the question of fact. The first thing a modern concern does as soon as it feels that it can afford it is to establish a research department every member of which knows that his bread and butter depends on his success in devising improvements. This practice does not obviously suggest aversion to technological progress. Nor can we in reply be referred to the cases in which patents acquired by business concerns have not been used promptly or not been used at all. For there may be perfectly good reasons for this; for example, the patented process may turn out to be no good or at least not to be in shape to warrant application on a commercial basis. Neither the inventors themselves nor the investigating economists or government officials are unbiased judges of this, and from their remonstrances or reports we may easily get a very distorted picture.[13]

But we are concerned with a question of theory. Everyone agrees that private and socialist managements will introduce improvements if, with the new method of production, the total cost per unit of product is expected to be smaller than the prime cost per unit of product with the method actually in use. If this condition is not fulfilled, then it is held that private management will not adopt a cost–reducing method until the existing plant and equipment is entirely written off, whereas socialist management would, to the social advantage, replace the old by any new cost–reducing method as soon as such a method becomes available, i.e., without regard to capital values. This however is not so.[14]

Private management, if actuated by the profit motive, cannot be interested in maintaining the values of any given building or machine any more than a socialist management would be. All that private management tries to do is to maximize the present net value of total assets which is equal to the discounted value of expected net returns. The amounts to saying that it will always adopt a new method of production which it believes will yield a larger stream of future income per unit of the corresponding stream of future outlay, both discounted to the present, than does the method actually in use. The value of past investment, whether or not paralleled by a bonded debt that has to be amortized, does not enter at all except in the sense and to the extent that it would also have to enter into the calculation underlying the decisions of a socialist management. So far as the use of the old machines saves future costs as compared with the immediate introduction of the new methods, the remainder of their service value is of course an element of the decision for both the capitalist and the socialist manager; otherwise bygones are bygones for both of them and any attempt to conserve the value of past investment would conflict as much with the rules following from the profit motive as it would conflict with the rules set for the behavior of the socialist manager.

[13.] Incidentally, it should be noticed that the kind of restrictive practice under discussion, granted that it exists to a significant extent, would not be without compensatory effects on social welfare. In fact, the same critics who talk about sabotage of progress at the same time emphasize the social losses incident to the pace of capitalist progress, particularly the unemployment which that pace entails and which slower advance might mitigate to some extent. Well, is technological progress too quick or too slow for them? They had better make up their minds.

[14.] It should be observed that even if the argument were correct, it would still be inadequate to support the thesis that capitalism is, under the conditions envisaged, "incompatible with technological process." All that it would prove is, for some cases, the presence of a lag of ordinarily moderate length in the introduction of new methods.

It is however not true that private firms owning equipment the value of which is endangered by a new method which they also control—if they do not control it, there is no problem and no indictment—will adopt the new method only if total unit cost with it is smaller than prime unit cost with the old one, or if the old investment has been completely written off *according to the schedule decided on before the new method presented itself.* For is the new machines when installed are expected to outlive the rest of the period previously set for the use of the old machines, their discounted remainder value as of that date is another asset to be taken account of. Nor is it true, for analogous reasons, that a socialist management, if acting rationally, would always and immediately adopt any new method which promises to produce at smaller total unit costs or that this would be to the social advantage.

There is however another element[15] which profoundly affects behavior in this matter and which is being invariably overlooked. This is what might be called ex ante conservation of capital in expectation of further improvement. Frequently, if not in most cases, a going concern does not simply face the question whether or not to adopt a definite new method of production that is the best thing out and, in the form immediately available, can be expected to retain that position for some length of time. A new type of machine is in general but a link in a chain of improvements and may presently become obsolete. In a case like this would obviously not be rational to follow the chain link by link regardless of the capital loss to be suffered each time. The real question then is at which link the concern should take action. The answer must be in the nature of a compromise between considerations that rest largely on guesses. But it will as a rule involve some waiting in order to see how the chain behaves. And to the outsider this may well look like trying to stifle improvement in order to conserve existing capital values. Yet even the most patient of comrades would revolt if a socialist management were so foolish as to follow the advice of the theorist and to keep on scrapping plant and equipment every year.

5. I have entitled this chapter as I did because most of it deals with the facts and problems that common parlance associates with monopoly or monopolistic practice. So far I have as much as possible refrained from using those terms in order to reserve for a separate section some comments on a few topics specifically connected with them. Nothing will be said however that we have not already met in one form or another.

(a) To begin with, there is the term itself. Monopolist means Single Seller. Literally therefore anyone is a monopolist who sells anything that is not in every respect, wrapping and location and service included, exactly like what other people sell: every grocer, or every haberdasher, or every seller of "Good Humors" on a road that is not simply lined with sellers of the same brand of ice

---

[15.] There are of course many other elements. The reader will please understand that in dealing with a few questions of principles it is impossible to do full justice to any of the topics touched upon.

cream. This however is not what we mean when talking about monopolists. We mean only those single sellers whose markets are not open to the intrusion of would-be producers of the same commodity and of actual producers of similar ones or, speaking slightly more technically, only those single sellers who face a given demand schedule that is severely independent of their own action as well as of any reactions to their action by other concerns. The traditional Cournot-Marshall theory of monopoly as extended and amended by later authors holds only if we define it in this way and there is, so it seems, no point in calling anything a monopoly to which that theory does not apply.

But if accordingly we do define it like this, then it becomes evident immediately that pure cases of long-run monopoly must be of the rarest occurrence and that even tolerable approximations to the requirements of the concept must be still rarer than are cases of perfect competition. The power to exploit at pleasure a given pattern of demand—or one that changes independently of the monopolist's action and of the reaction it provokes—can under the conditions of intact capitalism hardly persist for a period long enough to matter for the analysis of total output, unless buttressed by public authority, for instance, in the case of fiscal monopolies. A modern business concern not so protected—i.e., even if protected by import duties or import prohibitions—and yet wielding that power (except temporarily) is not easy to find or even to imagine. Even railroads and power and light concerns had first to create the demand for their services and, when they had done so, to defend their market against competition. Outside the field of public utilities, the position of a single seller can in general be conquered—and retained for decades—only on the condition that he does not behave like a monopolist. Short-run monopoly will be touched upon presently.

Why then all this talk about monopoly? The answer is not without interest for the student of the psychology of political discussion. Of course, the concept of monopoly is being loosely used just like any other. People speak of a country's having a monopoly of something or other[16] even if the industry in question is highly competitive and so on. But this is not all. Economists, government agents, journalists and politicians in this country obviously love the word because it has come to be a term of opprobrium which is sure to rouse the public's hostility against any interest so labeled. In the Anglo-American world monopoly has been cursed and associated with functionless exploitation ever since, in the sixteenth and seventeenth centuries, it was English administrative practice to create monopoly positions in large numbers which, on the one

---

16. These so-called monopolies have of late come to the fore in connection with the proposal to withhold certain materials from aggressor nations. The lessons this discussion have some bearing upon our problem by way of analogy. At first, much was thought of the possibilities of that weapon. Then, on looking more closely at it, people found their lists of such materials to be shrinking, because it became increasingly clear that there are very few things that cannot be either produced or substituted for in the areas in question. And finally a suspicion began to dawn to the effect that even though some pressure can be exerted on them in the short run, long-run developments might eventually destroy practically all that was left on the lists.

hand, answered fairly well to the theoretical pattern of monopolist behavior and, on the other hand, fully justified the wave of indignation that impressed even the great Elizabeth.

Nothing is so retentive as a nation's memory. Our time offers other and more important instances of a nation's reaction to what happened centuries ago. That practice made the English–speaking public so monopoly–conscious that it acquired a habit of attributing to that sinister power practically everything it disliked about business. To the typical liberal bourgeois in particular, monopoly became the father of almost all abuses—in fact, it became his pet bogey. Adam Smith,[17] thinking primarily of monopolies of the Tudor and Stuart type, frowned on them in awful dignity. Sir Robert Peel—who like most conservatives occasionally knew how to borrow from the arsenal of the demagogue—in his famous epilogue to his last period of office that gave so much offense to his associates, spoke of a monopoly of bread or wheat, though English grain production was of course perfectly competitive in spite of protection.[18] And in this country monopoly is being made practically synonymous with any large–scale business.

(b) The theory of simple and discriminating monopoly teaches that, excepting a limiting case, monopoly price is higher and monopoly output smaller than competitive price and competitive output. This is true provided that the method and organization of production—and everything else—are exactly the same in both cases. Actually however there are superior methods available to the monopolist which either are not available at all to a crowd of competitors or are not available to them so readily: for there are advantages which, though not strictly unattainable on the competitive level of enterprise, are as a matter of fact secured only on the monopoly level, for instance, because monopolization may increase the sphere of influence of the better, and decrease the sphere of influence of the inferior, brains,[19] or because the monopoly enjoys a disproportionately higher financial standing. Whenever

---

[17.] There was more excuse for that uncritical attitude in the case of Adam Smith and the classics in general than there is in the case of their successors because big business in our sense had not then emerged. But even so they went too far. In part this was due to the fact that they had no satisfactory theory of monopoly which induced them not only to apply the term rather promiscuously (Adam Smith and even Senior interpreted for instance the rent of land as a monopoly gain) but also to look upon the monopolists' power of exploitation as practically unlimited which is of course wrong even for the most extreme cases.

[18.] This instance illustrates the way in which the term keeps on creeping into illegitimate uses. Protection of agriculture and a monopoly of agrarian products are entirely different things. The struggle was over protection and not over a non–existent cartel of either landowners or farmers. But in fighting protection it was just as well to beat up for applause. And there was evidently no simpler means of doing so than by calling protectionists monopolists.

[19.] The reader should observe that while, as a broad rule, that particular type of superiority is simply indisputable, the inferior brains, especially if their owners are entirely eliminated, are not likely to admit it and that the public's and the recording economists' hearts go out to them and not to the others. This may have something to do with a tendency to discount the cost or quality advantages of quasi–monopolist combination that is at present as pronounced as was the exaggeration of them in the typical prospectus or announcement of sponsors of such combinations.

this is so, then that proposition is no longer true. In other words, this element of the case for competition may fail completely because monopoly prices are not necessarily higher or monopoly outputs smaller than competitive prices and outputs would be at the levels of productive and organizational efficiency that are within the reach of the type of firm compatible with the competitive hypothesis.

There cannot be any reasonable doubt that under the conditions of our epoch such superiority is as a matter of fact the outstanding feature of the typical large-scale unit of control, though mere size is neither necessary nor sufficient for it. These units not only arise in the process of creative destruction and function in a way entirely different from the static schema, but in many cases of decisive importance they provide the necessary form for the achievement. They largely create what they exploit. Hence the usual conclusion about their influence on long-run output would be invalid even if they were genuine monopolies in the technical sense of the term.

Motivation is quite immaterial. Even if the opportunity to set monopolist prices were the sole object, the pressure of the improved methods or of a huge apparatus would in general tend to shift the point of the monopolist's optimum toward or beyond the competitive cost price in the above sense, thus doing the work—partly, wholly, or more than wholly—of the competitive mechanism,[20] *even if restriction is practiced and excess capacity is in evidence all along*. Of course if the methods of production, organization and so on are not improved by or in connection with monopolization as is the case with an ordinary cartel, the classical theorem about monopoly price and output comes into its own again.[21] So does another popular idea, viz., that monopolization has a soporific effect. For this, too, it is not difficult to find examples. But no general theory should be built upon it. For, especially in manufacturing industry, a monopoly position is in general no cushion to sleep on. As it can be gained, so it can be retained only by alertness and energy. What soporific influence there is in modern business is due to another cause that will be mentioned later.

(c) In the short run, genuine monopoly positions or positions approximating monopoly are much more frequent. The grocer in a village on the Ohio may be a true monopolist for hours or even days during an inundation. Every

---

[20.] The Aluminum Company of America is not a monopoly in the technical sense as defined above, among other reasons because it had to build up its demand schedule, which fact suffices to exclude a behavior conforming to the Cournot–Marshall schema. But most economists call it so and in the dearth of genuine cases we will for the purposes of this note do the same. From 1890 to 1929 the price of the basic product of this single seller fell to about 12 per cent or, correcting for the change in price level (B.L.S. index of wholesale prices), to about 8.8 per cent. Output rose from 30 metric tons to 103,400. Protection by patent ceased in 1909. Argument from costs and profits in criticism of this "monopoly" must take it for granted that a multitude of competing firms would have been about equally successful in cost–reducing research, in the economical development of the productive apparatus, in teaching new uses for the product and in avoiding wasteful breakdowns. This is, in fact, being assumed by criticism of this kind; i.e., the propelling factor of modern capitalism is being assumed away.

[21.] See however *supra*, 1.

successful corner may spell monopoly for the moment. A firm specializing in paper labels for beer bottles may be so circumstanced—potential competitors realizing that what seem to be good profits would be immediately destroyed by their entering the field—that it can move at pleasure on a moderate but still finite stretch of the demand curve, at least until the metal label smashes that demand curve to pieces.

New methods of production or new commodities, especially the latter, do not *per se* confer monopoly, even if used or produced by a single firm. The product of the new method has to compete with the products of the old ones and the new commodity has to be introduced, i.e., its demand schedule has to be built up. As a rule neither patents nor monopolistic practices avail against that. But they may in cases of spectacular superiority of the new device, particularly if it can be leased like shoe machinery; or in cases of new commodities, the permanent demand schedule for which has been established before the patent has expired.

Thus it is true that there is or may be an element of genuine monopoly gain in those entrepreneurial profits which are the prizes offered by capitalist society to the successful innovator. But the quantitative importance of that element, its volatile nature and its function in the process in which it emerges put it in a class by itself. The main value to a concern of a single seller position that is secured by patent or monopolistic strategy does not consist so much in the opportunity to behave temporarily according to the monopolist schema, as in the protection it affords against temporary disorganization of the market and the space it secures for long-range planning. Here however the argument merges into the analysis submitted before.

6. Glancing back we realize that most of the facts and arguments touched upon in this chapter tend to dim the halo that once surrounded perfect competition as much as they suggest a more favorable view of its alternative. I will now briefly restate our argument from this angle.

Traditional theory itself, even within its chosen precincts of a stationary or steadily growing economy, has since the time of Marshall and Edgeworth been discovering an increasing number of exceptions to the old propositions about perfect competition and, incidentally, free trade, that have shaken that unqualified belief in its virtues cherished by the generation which flourished between Ricardo and Marshall—roughly, J.S. Mill's generation in England and Francesco Ferrara's on the Continent. Especially the propositions that a perfectly competitive system is ideally economical of resources and allocates them in a way that is optimal with respect to a given distribution of income—propositions very relevant to the question of the behavior of output—cannot now be held with the old confidence.[22]

Much more serious is the breach made by more recent where in the field of dynamic theory (Frisch, Tinbergen, Roos, Hicks and others). Dynamic

---

[22.] Since we cannot enter into the subject, I will refer the reader to Mr. R.F. Kahn's paper entitled "Some Notes on Ideal Output" (*Economic Journal* for March 1935), which covers much of this ground.

analysis is the analysis of sequences in time. In explaining why a certain economic quantity, for instance a price, is what we find it to be at a given moment, it takes into consideration not only the state of other economic quantities at the same moment, as static theory does, but also their state at preceding points of time, and the expectations about their future values. Now the first thing we discover in working out the propositions that thus relate quantities belonging to different points of time[23] is the fact that, once equilibrium has been destroyed by some disturbance, the process of establishing a new one is not so sure and prompt and economical as the old theory of perfect competition made it out to be; and the possibility that the very struggle for adjustment might lead such a system farther away from instead of nearer to a new equilibrium. This will happen in most cases unless the disturbance is small. In many cases, lagged adjustment is sufficient to produce this result.

All I can do here is to illustrate by the oldest, simplest and most familiar example. Suppose that demand and intended supply are in equilibrium in a perfectly competitive market for wheat, but that bad weather reduces the crop below what farmers intended to supply. If price rises accordingly and the farmers there upon produce that quantity of wheat which it would pay them to produce if that new price were the equilibrium price, then a slump in the wheat market will ensue in the following year. If now the farmers correspondingly restrict production, a price still higher than in the first year may result to induce a still greater expansion of production than occurred in the second year. And so on (as far as the pure logic of the process is concerned) indefinitely. The reader will readily perceive, from a survey of the assumptions involved, that no great fear need be entertained of ever higher prices' and ever greater outputs' alternating till doomsday. But even if reduced to its proper proportions, the phenomenon suffices to show up glaring weaknesses in the mechanism of perfect competition. As soon as this is realized much of the optimism that used to grace the practical implications of the theory of this mechanism passes out through the ivory gate.

But from our standpoint we must go further than that.[24] If we try to visualize how perfect competition works or would work in the process of creative destruction, we arrive at a still more discouraging result. This will not surprise us, considering that all the essential facts of that process are absent

---

[23.] The term dynamics is loosely used and carrier many different meanings. The above definition was formulated by Ragnar Frisch.

[24.] It should be observed that the defining feature of dynamic theory has nothing to do with the nature of the economic reality to which it is applied. It is a general method of analysis rather than a study of a particular process. We can use it in order to analyze a stationary economy, just as an evolving one can be analyzed by means of the methods of statics ("comparative statics"). Hence dynamic theory need not take, and as a matter of fact has not taken, any special cognizance of the process of creative destruction which we have taken to be the essence of capitalism. It is no doubt better equipped than is static theory to deal with many questions of mechanism that arise in the analysis of that process. But it is not an analysis of that process itself, and it treats the resulting individual disturbances of given states and structures just as it treats other disturbances. To judge the functioning of perfect competition from the standpoint of capitalist evolution is therefore not the same thing as judging it from the standpoint of dynamic theory.

from the general schema of economic life that yields the traditional propositions about perfect competition. At the risk of repetition I will illustrate the
point once more.

Perfect competition implies free entry into every industry. It is quite true,
within that general theory, that free entry into all industries is a condition for
optimal allocation of resources and hence for maximizing output. If our
economic world consisted of a number of established industries producing
familiar commodities by established and substantially invariant methods and if
nothing happened except that additional men and additional savings combine
in order to set up new firms of the existing type, then impediments to their
entry into any industry they wish to enter would spell loss to the community.
But perfectly free entry into a new field may make it impossible to enter it at
all. The introduction of new methods of production and new commodities is
hardly conceivable with perfect—and perfectly prompt—competition from
the start. And this means that the bulk of what we call economic progress is
incompatible with it. As a matter of fact, perfect competition is and always has
been temporarily suspended whenever anything new is being introduced—automatically or by measures devised for the purpose—even in otherwise perfectly competitive conditions.

Similarly, within the traditional system the usual indictment of rigid prices
stands all right. Rigidity is a type of resistance to adaptation that perfect and
prompt competition excludes. And for the kind of adaptation and for those
conditions which have been treated by traditional theory, it is again quite true
that such resistance spells loss and reduced output. But we have seen that in
the spurts and vicissitudes of the process of creative destruction the opposite
may be true: perfect and instantaneous flexibility may even produce functionless catastrophes. This of course can also be established by the general
dynamic theory which, as mentioned above, shows that there are attempts at
adaptation that intensify disequilibrium.

Again, under its own assumptions, traditional theory is correct in holding
that profits above what is necessary in each individual case to call forth the
equilibrium amount of means of production, entrepreneurial ability included,
both indicate and in themselves imply net social loss and that business strategy
that aims at keeping them alive is inimical to the growth of total output.
Perfect competition would prevent or immediately eliminate such surplus
profits and leave no room for that strategy. But since in the process of
capitalist evolution these profits acquire new organic functions—I do not want
to repeat what they are—that fact cannot any longer be unconditionally credited to the account of the perfectly competitive model, so far as the secular
rate of increase in total output is concerned.

Finally, it can indeed be shown that, under the same assumptions which
amount to excluding the most characteristic features of capitalist reality, a
perfectly competitive economy is comparatively free from waste and in particular from those kinds of waste which we most readily associate with its counterpart. But this does not tell us anything about how its account looks under
the conditions set by the process of creative destruction.

On the one hand, much of what without reference to those conditions would appear to be unrelieved waste ceases to qualify as such when duly related to them. The type of excess capacity for example that owes its existence to the practice of "building ahead of demand" or to the practice of providing capacity for the cyclical peaks of demand would in a regime of perfect competition be much reduced. But when all the facts of the case are taken into consideration, it is no longer correct to say that perfect competition wins out on that score. For though a concern that has to accept and cannot set prices would, in fact, use all of its capacity that can produce at marginal costs covered by the ruling prices, it does not follow that it would ever have the quantity and quality of capacity that big business has created and was able to create precisely because it is in a position to use it "strategically." Excess capacity of this type may—it does in some and does not in other cases—constitute a reason for claiming superiority for a socialist economy. But it should not without qualification be listed as a claim to superiority of the perfectly competitive species of capitalist economy as compared with the "monopoloid" species.

On the other hand, working in the conditions of capitalist evolution, the perfectly competitive arrangement displays wastes of its own. The firm of the type that is compatible with perfect competition is in many cases inferior in internal, especially technological, efficiency. If it is, then it wastes opportunities. It may also in its endeavors to improve its methods of production waste capital because it is in a less favorable position to evolve and to judge new possibilities. And, as we have seen before, a perfectly competitive industry is much more apt to be routed—and to scatter the bacilli of depression—under the impact of progress or of external disturbance than is big business. In the last resort, American agriculture, English coal mining, the English textile industry are costing consumers much more and are affecting *total* output much more injuriously than they would if controlled, each of them, by a dozen good brains.

Thus it is not sufficient to argue that because perfect competition is impossible under modern industrial conditions—or because it always has been impossible—the large-scale establishment or unit of control must be accepted as a necessary evil inseparable from the economic progress which it is prevented from sabotaging by the forces inherent in its productive apparatus. What we have got to accept is that it has come to be the most powerful engine of that progress and in particular of the long-run expansion of total output not only in spite of, but to a considerable extent through, this strategy which looks so restrictive when viewed in the individual case and from the individual point of time. In this respect, perfect competition is not only impossible but inferior, and has no title to being set up as a model of ideal efficiency. It is hence a mistake to base the theory of government regulation of industry on the principle that big business should be made to work as the respective industry would work in perfect competition. And socialists should rely for their criticisms on the virtues of a socialist economy rather than on those of the competitive model.

CHAPTER 4 - Lingering Doubts

The Theory of Restrictive Trade Practices

G. B. Richardson

We are here concerned with that branch of economic theory which seeks to establish connexions between market structure and economic performance. This theory begins by postulating hypothetical forms, or models, of market organization and then examines the nature of the opportunities available to entrepreneurs within them; it then proceeds to predict the kinds of behaviour that entrepreneurs will adopt and the properties of the patterns of resource allocation that will thereby come to be established. Formal welfare theory provides us with the criteria of optimum allocation to serve as a standard of comparison and thus it becomes possible to judge whether particular restrictions on competition, as an element of market structure, either promote or impede economic efficiency.[1]

Private property will be the common feature of all the models of economic structure with which we are concerned, so that resources will come to be allocated as a result of decisions taken by individual businesses seeking profit. In these conditions one can distinguish at least four distinct ways in which the organization of a market can influence economic efficiency.

First, to the extent that a market provides producers with monopoly power, it will give them an incentive to fix the volumes of their outputs below the socially ideal levels; prices, that is to say, will diverge from marginal costs in varying degrees, thus indicating a departure from optimum allocation either in the proportions in which products feature in final output or in the proportions in which factors are combined in production. This is the influence of market

---

©Oxford University Press 1965. Reprinted from *Oxford Economic Papers,* vol. 17 (1965) pp. 432–449 by permission of Oxford University Press.

[1]There is also a macro–economic aspect to our subject. We may wish to know how restraints on competition might effect the distribution of income or an economy's liability to suffer unemployment or inflation. I propose to exclude these matters from consideration in order to have space to concentrate upon what seems to me the most important issue the effect if restrictive practices on economic efficiency. I have also decided, in order to reduce the subject to manageable proportions, to confine myself to the relationship between manufacturing firms and to ignore the relationships between manufacturers and distributors or between distributors themselves.

structure that has been given most attention by economic theorists and least attention by the man in the street.

Misallocation of the kind caused by monopolistic restriction can equally well result simply from the fact that entrepreneurs, if they are inadequately informed of the circumstances relevant to their decisions, make mistakes. I shall argue that market structure affects the information available to them and therefore influences, in this second way also, the pattern of resource allocation that will emerge.

The efficiency with which resources are made use of will also depend on the quality of entrepreneurship. This in turn will vary will market structure in its roles as a provider of incentives, positive and negative, and as a mechanism of selection causing the control over resources to pass to those who can employ them profitably from those who fail to do so. Here then we have a third and fourth way in which structure can influence performance.

Our formal theory of markets tends to concentrate our attention on the first of these four influences—on the distortions, that is to say caused by monopolistic exactions—although I much doubt if it is the most important. In strong contrast to this, little heed has been paid to the way in which market organization, by influencing the predictability of the business environment, determines the availability of information to entrepreneurs. I shall therefore feel justified in giving prominence to this aspect in the discussion that is to follow. The effect of economic organization on the quality of entrepreneurship is of the highest importance but difficult to handle in theoretical terms.

Before turning to a systematic consideration of the analysis of market forms, and of restrictive agreements in particular, I wish to make mention, in passing, of one general limitation to which this analysis is subject. By and large, our standard theory is founded on the assumption of profit maximization, an assumption that is, for two reasons, exceedingly *simpliste*. In the first place, the alternative opportunities before entrepreneurs cannot be ranked unequivocally in order of profitability, as they are normally associated with a range of possible outcomes. Secondly, money–making is not the only motive; business men may also value, for example, independence or a quiet life.

The relevance of these considerations to any analysis of the effects of restrictive agreements can be seen from two examples. Let us suppose that the operation of a restriction reduces the uncertainty attaching to the yield from an investment, but at the same time provides greater scope for monopolistic exaction. Will the net effect of the restriction be to increase or to diminish the volume of output planned? The reduction of uncertainty should strengthen the willingness to invest, whereas the protection from competition should provide an incentive deliberately to restrict supply. Clearly, the net result cannot be predicted without some knowledge of the magnitude of the factors at work; we require some quantitive assessment of the degree to which the restriction will reduce uncertainty and of the significance that the entrepreneur in question will attach to this. As these magnitudes will vary according to circumstances, we will be able to assess them as best we can only in the context of particular cases or groups of similar cases.

Consider, as a second example, an industry in which the firms are too small to exploit all the available economies of scale; and suppose, further, that the firms agree prices. Now it is evident that the existence of the agreement does not eliminate the gains to be had, in the form of cost reductions, from amalgamation between two or more firms. It may be, however, that so long as the common price level is high enough to provide reasonable profits, the firms will not consider the gain from amalgamation sufficient to compensate for the associated loss of independence. The proscription of the agreement, were this to cause prices to fall to unremunerative levels, might provide the jolt required to induce managements to sacrifice their independence and overcome that inertia which takes the form of a settled preference for the *status quo*. Nevertheless, it is possible, at the same time, that the price agreement does fulfil useful functions; about this I shall have more to say at a later stage. Once again therefore we are forced back to an exercise of judgement to be made only with a full knowledge of the circumstances of the case; and judgement is made the more difficult by the fact that the quality of business enterprise is itself a function of market organization. Entrepreneurs' desire for independence has been represented as a barrier to realizing economies of scale. Independence, however, may provide positive benefits; a manager may show more enterprise as his own master than when obliged to account for all his decisions to higher authority. Concentration in an industry, or even the subjection of the firms within it to restrictive regulations, may be bought at the price of some loss in freshness and variety of decision.

In mentioning, at the outset, these several limitations, my aim is to stress the need for a proper modesty, on behalf of economists, when they endeavour to apply their theoretical constructions to the questions that here concern us. Our formal models of market organization do not readily accommodate many factors that practical judgement must take into account; nor can we often assess the relative magnitude—which may be crucial—of the elements that these models help us to identify. These reservations made, we must proceed; although an appraisal of restrictive practices may be difficult even with the help of economic theory, it is certainly not possible without it.

Let us adopt the traditional procedure and begin our analysis of the effects of restraints on competition by considering the model in which such restraints are wholly absent. Perfect competition has been regarded, for about a century, as of key importance by virtue of the fact that it is supposed to result in a determinate pattern of resource allocation the relevant properties of which are those of a Pareto optimum. From this many economists have deemed it an easy leap to conclude that the market structure defined by the model is an ideal, deviations from which produce misallocation. Thus a market structure is made to appear defective if the number of firms is small, if there exist understandings between them and if output is not homogeneous. Each of these circumstances is seen as capable as affording a firm some control over price and thereby an incentive to restrict output below the optimum level. I believe this analysis—set out here, albeit, in crudely simplified form—to be radically defective.[1]

We may begin by observing that no one has ever been able to explain satisfactorily how the equilibrium configuration associated with perfect competition might in practice be attained. The earlier writers on the subject did at least realize the existence of a problem; thus Edgeworth had recourse to the process of 'recontracting' and Walras to his prices *crié,s au hazard*. But these are not genuine solutions, if only for the reason that they require the mediation of very special arrangements to be found neither in the real world nor in the conditions of the model.

In order to explain how equilibrium is reached we need to provide an account of how entrepreneurs are able to identify investment opportunities the exploitation of which will cause resources to be distributed in the required way. The crucial difficulty is to show how, in perfectly competitive conditions, investment opportunities could ever be identified. I have endeavoured to set out elsewhere[2] reasons for believing that it is impossible, within the context of the model, for entrepreneurs to acquire the information on which to base investment and current output decisions. At the same time, I sought to show that investment decisions not based on the relevant information, but simply on projections of current prices, would not lead to equilibrium. This is not the place to recapitulate all the argument; suffice it to say that the profitability of investment by an entrepreneur in the production of a particular good will depend upon the relationship between the demand for that good and the total supply planned by competitors. The model we are dealing with, by postulating an indefinite number of firms ready and willing to set up in the production of any good, leaves this total volume of competitive supply quite unrestricted and therefore unpredictable.

Progress beyond this point can only be made, it seems to me, by giving explicit recognition to this most important principle; the *availability to entrepreneurs of the information on which to base investment decisions is a function of the structure of the model in which they are presumed to operate*. Alternative market forms may be compared, in other words, according to the predictability of the environment that they afford entrepreneurs. Perfect competition represents an environment in which predictability (of the appropriate kind) is zero;[3] only by postulating some restriction on the freedom of individual entrepreneurs

---

[1]There seems no need to discuss the ways in which the analysis has to be qualified to take into account indivisibilities or divergences between private and social cost; that such qualifications are required is agreed by everyone.

[2]*Information and Investment*, Oxford University Press, 1960.

[3]It is for this reason absurd to postulate the existence of both perfect competition and perfect knowledge. Yet this is often done.

can this predictability be increased. Once this is admitted, practices in restraint of competition no longer appear as so much sand in the works.[4]

It is possible for firms to undertake informed production planning, and thus promote the adjustment of supply to demand, only when competition is less than perfect—a condition which the real world, fortunately, normally grants us. But this is not to say that the restrictions on trade, such as would concern the Registrar, are always, or indeed normally, required. Sufficient stability in the business environment may be provided by natural imperfections in competition or by the adoption by entrepreneurs of codes of behaviour that regulate the relationship between rivals without the need for agreements or understandings in the ordinary sense.

The natural imperfections take the form of geographical barriers, of product differentiation in the widest sense, and of economies of scale such as leave room, in any one market, for only a few competing firms. It is not difficult to see how each of these facilitate foresight of the kind required by entrepreneurs. Geography and product differentiation reduce the dependence of the profitability of investment by one firm on the investments being planned by others; they give natural advantages to particular producers that may suffice to permit them, so long as they remain efficient, to presume that the whole of a limited market is their own to develop. The existence of only a few firms in an industry, if these are in possession of some advantage over outsiders, likewise works towards more predictable markets. The restriction in numbers makes it much easier for each entrepreneur to know what his rivals plan to do.

Although natural imperfections of the kind described will usually increase the predictability of business environment, it is clear that they need not do so, at all times and in all markets, to the extent required to permit informed investment and production planning. Their strength will vary from market to market; and according to the scale and irreversibility of investment decisions, so will the need for them. Circumstances will therefore arise in which entrepreneurs, in the absence of deliberately contrived restrictions on competition, are unable to make any capable estimates of the likely volume of supply being planned by their rivals.

The most objectionable feature of this situation, from the firms' point of view, is the risk of excess supply and negative returns on investment. They will therefore be led to modify their relationships in such a way as reduces the risk of excess supply or mitigates the effects of excess supply on profits.

The forms of behaviour adopted, though various, have for the most part this in common; each firm does something (or refrains from doing something)

---

[4]I am inclined to think that many economists, rather than give full recognition to the relationship between information and market structure, will prefer to endeavour to salvage perfect competition through the introduction of additional special assumptions. Not only industrialists may be reluctant to scrap obsolete equipment. That the model may be patched up to some extent I do not deny, although the changes that have to be imposed upon it will probably be equivalent to some kind of restriction on competition.

on the expectation that its rivals will do likewise. In this limited sense, at any rate, the behaviour in question is co–operative; the reciprocal expectations or understandings that form its content may be set out in express agreement or may be merely the silent premiss of actual conduct. The motive at work is self–interest, but self–interest enlightened by the sense that the interests of each member of the group coincide, at least partially, with the interests of the group as a whole. (Thus, for example, a firm may refrain from an apparently advantageous price reduction in the realization that if all competitors were to reduce prices, all of them would lose.) The sanctions available are of three kinds. The first is the threat of retaliation; each entrepreneur may appreciate that if he breaks the code others will do so also, with the result that any gains will be illusory or short–lived. But transgression may not always be easily detected and retaliation may take place, if at all, only after some delay. Further sanctions may therefore be provided by means of an express agreement; if it is legally enforceable, the sanction in force is the law of the country, if not, it is the fact that promises have been exchanged. The parties to these undertakings may regard their promises as binding, either from a sense of moral obligation or in the realization that others will not enter into future undertakings with those who have acquired a bad reputation. The forms of behaviour in question may perform the same function irrespective of whether the sanction is provided by the fear of retaliation or by the existence of an agreement, although it is only in the latter case that legal control or prohibition can easily be applied.

I have maintained that firms may act so as to restrict competition in the hope of thereby reducing the risk of excess supply. Were this the only aim and effect of their co–operation, then, provided excess supply were defined appropriately, the co–operation would always be in the general interest. Not only would wasteful gluts be rendered less likely; to the extent that fear of gluts inhibit investment, the incidence of scarcity would also, paradoxically, be diminished. That there is a problem of policy arises from the fact that the power to prevent excess supply may be used to limit supply unduly, just as the power to reduce uncertainty may be used to provide an easy life.

In considering in more detail the various forms of restrictive behaviour adopted by entrepreneurs, it will be convenient to distinguish investment decisions, relating to the installation of fixed plant, and output decisions, relating to the amount to be produced from fixed plant already in existence. Let us first consider investment decisions.

In the endeavour to prevent a wasteful duplication of capacity, firms might decide, with or without express agreement, to maintain constant shares of their common market. But the practical difficulties in working such an arrangement are formidable. In surprisingly many markets firms lack accurate information as to the shares they currently enjoy and are therefore unable to know whether or not they are maintaining them. And even if actual shares are known, firms may entertain different ideas about how total demand for the product will change. This being so, it would be difficult to judge from the observed investment policies of firms whether they were observing the code, in the sense that they were just maintaining their share of the increment of demand they expected, or whether they were seeking to encroach on the markets of rivals. If a firm lacked assurance that others were observing the code, however, it would not feel bound to do so itself. It is evident therefore that strict market sharing would require formal agreement, quotas being negotiated and some common forecast made of demand. Given inevitable differences of interest between the parties, these arrangements are not easy to make—quite apart from the attention they are likely to receive from the appropriate governmental authorities. And it can scarcely be denied that formal market sharing can be operated in such a way as to exploit the purchaser or retard the differential growth of the more efficient firms.

Theory cannot of course determine, in any general way, whether it is better to prohibit firms from co–ordinating their investment plans, and thus run the risk of some maladjustment of capacity to demand, or to permit such co–ordination subject, perhaps, to some form of control. Much will depend on the circumstances of the market. Maladjustment may develop more easily, and involve more waste, when much fixed and durable capital is employed in production and when this capital is installed in large and indivisible units. Where investment decisions are on a small scale and easily reversible, and when demand is on a strong upward trend, maladjustment may be less severe and less persistent.[5]

Where the losses from the maladjustment of capacity to demand a likely to be serious, then it may be desirable to permit firms (or oblige them) to coor-

---

[5]It is worth noting that industrial organization can often be improved, in the relevant respects, without recourse to systematic co–ordination of investment plans. Arrangements can be made, for example, to ensure that firms are informed of the total sales in their market and therefore of their share of them. Decisions to install additional capacity, once taken, can be made known to competitors. A system of accounting may also be introduced sufficiently sophisticated for firms to know the true costs of what they are producing. Surprisingly, this quite often does not exist. (There have been firms that first estimated the return from capital on particular products when required to do so by the Restrictive Practices Court.) An efficient allocation of resources, in the full sense, requires that the manufacture of particular products is undertaken by those firms best suited to that manufacture; but unless management knows the costs attributable to each of the firm's products, this specialization according to comparative advantage will not come about. Firms may fail to relinquish the production of articles which they are ill suited to manufacture simply because it is not apparent to them that these lines are unprofitable. Ideally, it is desirable for management to know (at least approximately) both its own costs of manufacture, for each of its products, and the corresponding costs of competitors either individually or, in the form of a weighted average, as a body. In the long run, no doubt, a firm that continues in too many unprofitable lines will lose ground. In this way competition works automatically so as to withdraw control of resources over those unable to make efficient use of them; but if it is to provide all its benefits it should also act as a signalling mechanism able to tell managements, in time to take remedial action, where their weaknesses lie. I make these points, in this theoretical article, to show that the efficiency of a market structure depends on factors other than those commonly taken into account. The information made available to entrepreneurs, by a particular market organization, will influence not only the process of adjustment of supply to demand, but also the effectiveness of competition in stimulating firms to reduce costs and specialize according to their comparative advantages.

dinate their investment plans, subject to some control designed to ensure both that aggregate capacity is planned in accordance with the best estimate of future demand and that the more efficient firms have an opportunity to expand their share of the total market. If prices are fixed so as to yield only normal profits to a firm of normal efficiency, the less efficient firms may in any case be willing to give ground to their lower cost rivals. The danger, of course, is that too great respect will be given to vested interests, small firms or potential entrants having little or no influence on the arrangements made. State supervision may prevent some abuses but there is not guarantee that it will do so; even governments have been known to favour the industrial establishment.

It is perhaps curious that indicative planning, of the kind now in vogue in France and in England, stresses the need for the inter-industry coordination of investment plans while apparently accepting the absence of coordination between the investment plans of firms in the same industry. The coordination of plans within an industry seems the logical extension of coordination between industries; indeed if the former is not realized the latter is unlikely to be realized. Presumably the doctrine must be that the coordination of investments within an industry can usually come about spontaneously, by virtue of the existence of the natural restrictions on competition referred to earlier and without measures designed to this end. Theory, however, lends no support to the view that such spontaneous adjustment can always be relied upon.

Let us now turn to the way in which market structure may affect economic efficiency through its influence on entrepreneurs' decisions about how much to produce from given equipment. We know from welfare theory that, for the prices of products and factors to be consistent with optimum allocation, the output that ought to be produced from given equipment is that just saleable at a price equal to the short-run marginal costs of its production, these being the same for all firms if production is distributed efficiently among them. Many writers appear to believe that, if perfect competition were to exist, this is precisely what would happen, profits being maximized—the demand for the firms' output being perfectly elastic—where price equals marginal costs. But this would be true only if entrepreneurs were able to obtain the information with which to predict future prices, this being something, I have argued, the conditions of the model will not permit them to do. We must therefore banish from our minds the widespread but erroneous belief that allocation will be efficient if competition is perfect and inefficient if it is not.

Let us begin by noting that, in the real world, manufacturing businesses are not characteristically concerned in their short-run output decisions with the prediction of future prices. Prices do not generally move so as to equate demand and supply at every point of time. In practice, therefore, firms are normally engaged in predicting the volume of demand on the assumption that prices are steady in the short run. These predictions, which will be based on trends in sales, on stock movements and the state of orders, will not be perfectly accurate, but they are feasible and permit tolerably informed output decisions to be taken. The feasibility of the prediction, moreover, depends upon the short-run stability of prices. If the price level of an article moves continuously to equate demand to current supply, then it will no longer be possible to use changes in stocks and order books as indicators of the trend in demand. In addition, and equally important, if the relative prices quoted by different manufacturers of an article vary in the short run, then no seller will be able to assume that his share of the total demand will remain roughly constant, with the result that even if he can predict the total future demand for the article he will nevertheless be unable to decide how much to produce.

Short-run price stability, we must now recognize, is maintained by a certain code of behaviour among entrepreneurs.[6] Let us suppose that there are several producers of a particular commodity the demand for which begins to fall relative to the available capacity with the result that the price previously charged now exceeds marginal costs. In these circumstances each entrepreneur is under temptation to adopt a policy which, if he alone were to adopt it, would greatly increase his profits, but which, if all were to adopt it, would bring losses to all sellers and a net loss to society as a whole. This policy would consist in lowering price so as to divert trade from rivals and thereby ensure that the firm was working at full capacity. If the cross elasticity of demand for the firms' outputs were very high, only a very small price cut would be required; a great increase in profits would then be obtained, the actual magnitude of which would depend on the proportion that fixed costs bore to the total costs of production.

Competition in this form, if practised by all concerned, could lead to heavy excess supply. If all firms acted in this way then none of them would succeed in increasing its share of total sales. Each would find that the increased output it had produced and hoped to sell at a price only slightly below its previous level could not in fact be sold at that price. It would then have either to reconcile itself to holding an undesirably large volume of stocks or to endeavour to sell the goods it had available by a further price cut. Each producer might in fact be able to sell all his increased volume of output provided price fell to a sufficiently low level, but this level might be well below the marginal costs at which the output was manufactured. The losses sustained by the producers, as a result of the competitive policies they pursued, might be very great, their actual magnitude depending on elasticity of demand for the product and upon how great an increase in market share each of them had hoped to achieve. The consumers of the product would gain, by virtue of the fall in price, but it is important to note that there may be a net loss to society as a whole. Economists are prone to assume that competitive price-cutting in a situation of the kind we are considering will cause prices to fall only to the level of marginal costs; this then entitles them to conclude that competitive price-cutting secures the

---

[6]The remainder of this paper draws on my article 'Les Relations entre Firmes' in *Economie Appliquée*, 1965.

optimum supply. But we have no right to make this assumption; that economists so often do so derives from their belief (or need to believe) that the equilibrium solutions of competitive theory are somehow always realized. There is no reason to believe that, as a result of competitive striving by which each firm endeavours to increase its share of the total market, the aggregate supply produced will clear the market at a price just equal to the marginal costs of each producer. In fact, if each producer expected a small price–cut to produce a substantial increase in market share, the total supply forthcoming would be in excess of the amount that could be sold at a price sufficient to cover marginal costs and constitute, for that reason, a misallocation of resources.

Competitive activity of this particular kind (which we may term short–run price competition) is so obviously destructive that entrepreneurs have a very strong incentive to develop codes of behaviour capable of preventing it. The simplest of such codes would consist in each firm maintaining the price of its product when capacity exceeds demand, in the expectation that its rivals would act likewise. Firms would refrain, as Marshall pointed out some time ago, from 'spoiling the market.' This restraint would have as its motive the fear of retaliation, a sense of common interest with rival sellers or even a vague feeling, almost of a moral kind, that this was 'the right thing to do.'

Very often, however, this simple form of co–operative action would give way to the pressure of individual interests. An individual seller may be tempted to reduce his price in the hope that he will enjoy a large increase in sales before his rivals discover what he has done. He may be able, for example, to offer rebates to large customers which he hopes will be kept secret, at least for some time, from competitors. If the size of an individual order is large compared to total annual turnover, the incentive to acquire it, by slightly reducing price, will be strong. If the seller also carries large surplus stocks, and is in great need of cash, the incentive will be even stronger. Once prices begin to be cut it will only be a matter of time before this becomes known to all concerned; the code of behaviour will soon be undermined and the market, in business men's terms, be 'demoralised.' Even if there is a strong fear of price–cutting, as distinct from its actual practice, the situation will be highly precarious.

In many markets therefore one will expect more formal co–operation to develop. The next step in this direction is an agreement to exchange information about the prices actually being charged or the price changes that firms plan to make in the future. In this way firms voluntarily give up the advantages of surprise attack in return for similar assurances from their rivals. In these circumstances, when retaliation can be immediate, a firm will only cut price when it believes that it is in its long–run interest to do so; when it believes, that is to say, either that other firms will not act like–wise or that it will benefit even if they do. Information agreements of this kind are very common, especially in countries where agreements on price itself are illegal, and they undoubtedly help to check short–run price competition of the kind we have been discussing. They are subject, nevertheless, to important limitations.

Complete price stability would be as undesirable as it would be impracticable. Prices ought to change when costs change and it may be desirable to change them also, to some extent, in response to changes in demand. There is then a problem of how these changes are to be brought about without at the same time causing the prices charged by different manufacturers to alter, in relation to each other, in unpredictable ways. One seller may wish to raise price but be afraid to do so in case others do not raise their prices also. Alternatively, a seller may think that conditions justify a lower level of price but may not wish to initiate a process of continuous and irregular price reductions. A solution to this problem, providing for uniform price changes, is given by the system of price leadership in which one firm announces in advance that it proposes to alter its price list and other firms then make similar announcements. Once again, however, there are limitations. The interests of all the firms in the industry will not be identical and it may therefore happen that the price chosen by the leader is unsuitable for some of them. In this case either the system may break down or it may be replaced by an agreement on prices themselves.

Of all the methods arranged to prevent short-run price competition an agreement of prices is probably the most effective. So long as it operates, firms' market shares will be relatively constant in the short run, being determined essentially by traditional connexions with buyers, reputation, quality differences, and the like. Each firm will have given up its freedom to endeavour to gain a temporary increase in market share by secret or unexpected price changes and will have obtained, in exchange, a more predictable demand than it would have had otherwise. From the point of view of the short-run planning of output—i.e., decisions about how much to produce from given plant—this is a substantial gain; the costs of the arrangement, from the community's point of view, will concern us shortly. Although less fragile than collusion based merely on the exchange of information, associated with price leadership, agreements on prices are nevertheless, as is well known, liable to break down. Being voluntary, they cannot survive without each of the parties believing that they are in their own long-run interest; given the likely disparity of firms in terms of costs, size, and ambition, this is a condition that may often fail to be met.

Let us now endeavour to draw up a balance of the gains and losses associated with the business behaviour we have been examining. On the credit side we have the fact that this behaviour may prevent such forms of competition as may result in excessive supply or may deter investment through fear of the losses that such excess supply may bring. This end is achieved by making the environment of entrepreneurs more stable and thus permitting more informed planning of output. On the debit side, there may be losses of three kinds. First, co-operation of the kinds we have described may give the firms concerned the power to restrict output unduly; secondly, it may retard the differential growth of the more efficient firm, and, thirdly, it may make profits too easy to obtain so that entrepreneurs lack the stimulus to develop their energies and inventiveness to the full.

It will be convenient to consider the effects of a price agreement—or those related forms of behaviour that perform roughly the same function—in two stages. I shall examine first the welfare implications of the fact that the volume of output from given equipment will be different when a price agreement is operated than when it is not. The long-run consequences of such an agreement—on investment, efficiency, and incentives—will be discussed later.

Ideally, we noted, existing equipment should be used to produce just that volume of output that will sell at a price equal to marginal cost. We have seen that where there is short-run price competition this is unlikely to come about, for the reason that entrepreneurs will be unable to predict the demand for their own output. If, however, price is kept wholly unresponsive to short-run demand changes, then, in these circumstances also, even if there is perfect predictability, a divergence between price and marginal cost is to be expected. This follows obviously from the fact that marginal cost is likely to be different for different volumes of output whereas price remains the same. The resultant social loss will depend on the shapes of the demand schedule and of the curve relating marginal cost to output. It will be greatest when the elasticity of demand of great and when marginal costs fall sharply when output is reduced. The extent to which these two circumstances obtain will depend on the market in question and there is therefore little that can usefully be said in general terms about the magnitude of the social loss to be expected. It would seem, however, that the range of possible divergence between price and marginal cost is greater when the divergence is the result of uninformed output decisions than when it is merely the consequence of an inflexible price. If the fluctuations in the total demand for the product, moreover, are modest, then the misallocation resulting from an inflexible price will itself be slight. (We leave until later the question of whether the level of price is too high.) Even modest demand fluctuations, however, if they lead producers to seek a larger market share by short–run price cutting, can lead to large variations in supply and therefore to more substantial waste.

If then a choice has to be made, in any particular market, between price stability resulting from price agreements and price flexibility resulting from the promotion of short–run price competition, the factors that ought to govern the choice are clear; price agreements, or some equivalent code of behaviour, are the more likely to be necessary the lower the elasticity of demand for the product, the higher the proportion of fixed to variable costs, and the larger the fluctuations in demand to be expected.

Our argument has tacitly assumed, until now, that the only alternatives were complete price stability, on the one hand, and short–run price competition on the other. But there is of course no reason why firms should not co–operate in quoting a common price which was varied uniformly according to demand conditions. This would be achieved most readily where all firms were committed to formal discussion and agreement in prices, less readily by a system of price leadership, and very doubtfully where firms felt obliged only not to spoil the market. In principle it would even be possible for a cartel to adjust supply so as to maintain equality continuously between expected price and marginal cost although, as this would not maximize profits, it is not the policy one would expect it to adopt.

A little reflection, moreover, leads one to doubt whether this policy would be practicable even if cartels had the public interest rather than profits as their objective. There is a good deal of evidence, that cannot be reviewed here, to the effect that most firms operate for most of the time under conditions of excess capacity—in the sense that marginal costs are less than average costs of production. If this is indeed the case, then it follows that under marginal cost pricing, firms would normally be making a loss, so that, for production to be profitable over the long period, they would have to make, occasionally, a level of profits that was very abnormally high. This could be done if the volume of manufacturing capacity were kept small enough to cause acute scarcities in times of peak demand and if prices were raised so as to clear the market at these times. Whether such an arrangement would be superior, on welfare grounds, to the usual practice of maintaining a steady level of price high enough to yield normal profits over the long period is, at least, open to doubt. It consists, in fact, of creating occasional bottlenecks and exploiting them, by raising price, to an extent sufficient to make profits high enough to offset the losses that firms would make normally. Would purchasers welcome such a policy? Would not the social loss produced by the bottlenecks, which might spread to other industries using the product in question, normally outweigh the social loss occasioned by a normal divergence between price and marginal costs? These are questions that can be answered with confidence only in relation to a particular, specified industry, but one might be prepared to guess that the answer would usually be in the negative.

Let us now turn again to the long–run effects of restrictions of the kind we have been examining. We may begin by inquiring whether these restrictions will result in the level of an industry's investment being less than optimal. It may be that the behaviour adopted merely serves to maintain prices in response to a temporary fall of demand below capacity, while leaving each entrepreneur prepared—and expecting others to be prepared—to endeavour to increase his share of the market by means of price reductions that his unit costs enable him to make permanent. If there is so there is no reason to expect a sub-optimal level of investment; on the contrary, the greater security offered by the absence of short–run prices competition, may make investment in the industry more attractive. Inter–firm co–operation, however, may have less modest aims. Prices may be not only stabilized, but maintained at a level that yields abnormal profits and implies a sub-optimal supply. A tightly organized cartel is clearly well placed to aim at this objective, which may be also pursued, without formal arrangements, by a group of firms small enough for each to appreciate that high prices are in its long–run interest. The obstacles in the way of this restrictive policy are, as is well known, dissension between the parties and the threat of outside competition.

If the entry into the industry is somehow blocked, then it is clear that those already in it, taken as a whole, can be made better off by the restriction of supply. It does not follow, however, that the restriction will operate so as to benefit each firm individually. The gain from it will accrue to firms according to their size and the smaller among them may not wish to perpetuate their disadvantage. Some firms, moreover, having the capital and the managerial resources that permit both expansion and the reduction of costs, will be eager to extend the market; others, with high costs and little growth potential, will oppose any reduction in price. Restriction may not therefore make every firm better off than it would be in the absence of restriction; generally, however, it would be possible in principle to arrange this, in that there will be some redistribution of the gains from restriction that would make every firm benefit from its operation. Whether firms succeed in acquiring monopoly profits will often depend, therefore, on whether they can agree on how these should be shared. In order to reach agreement and to put the terms into effect, fairly formal arrangements for consultation and for compensation may be required. Loose, informal co–operation, such as might escape legal prohibition, may be unable to resolve substantial differences of interest between the parties concerned.

No system of compensation is likely to be able to bribe the potential entrants into an industry to stay out; it is for this reason that the threat of entry is likely to be a more powerful check on monopolistic restriction than is internal dissension. What we require is that conditions of entry be such that existing firms need not fear invasion by newcomers only so long as they maintain normal efficiency and cater for all demands at prices offering only normal profits. It might at first seem that these conditions are met provided only that newcomers are at some very slight disadvantage in terms of experience, market contacts, &c. Unfortunately, however, matters are not quite so simple. Let us suppose that the firms already in the industry pursue the policy, discussed above, of maintaining prices stable in response to short–run demand fluctuations. In these circumstances it will be profitable for an outsider to enter the market even though firms already in it earn no more than normal profits in the long term. All the entrant need do is charge rather less than the established firms when capacity exceeds demand and as much as or more than they do when demand exceeds capacity. By acting in this way it will be able to operate at full capacity and therefore to flourish at the expense of the firms that continue to maintain stable prices.

The entry of new firms into the industry, in response to these opportunities, would lead to the installation of excessive capacity and, in most cases, to the breakdown of the codes of behaviour by which price stability was maintained. The chief deterrent to entry under the circumstances we are postulating is, of course, the fact that the firms already established may abandon their policy of price stability in order to match the prices of the intruder. It is this same threat that may dissuade firms tempted to leave the association from doing so. It may prove effective or it may not. If the potential entrant, or potential defector is small, then it may be prepared to take the risk that the rest of the firms in the industry may tolerate some incursion into their markets rather than give up the advantages of a stable and agreed price. If the new firm is located abroad, and protected in its home market, then it will be strongly inclined to quote lower prices for its exports. For these reasons, as is well known, inter–firm co–operation in prices setting may frequently break down.

To what extent does the restrictive behaviour we have been examining make it more difficult for the more efficient firms to grow at the expense of their less efficient rivals? If a low–cost firm believes that it would gain from larger sales at a lower price, then it is difficult to believe that the restrictive arrangements that we have been considering are likely to prove a strong barrier to the firm acting accordingly. In order to obtain the agreement of other firms to a price reduction, it can threaten to act independently; high–cost firms will have good reasons to accept a uniformly lower price, while maintaining whatever form of co–operation is practised, rather than face an irregular fall in prices brought about through competitive warfare. The situation is otherwise when the low–cost firm already possesses a large share of the market and considers that its interests are best served by keeping its present volume of sales at a high margin of profit rather than to increase them at the cost of a cut in this margin. In these circumstances, price competition, by means of secret rebates and the like, may bring prices down and the restrictive forms of behaviour that inhibit it—whatever their benefits in other ways—can act so as to shelter the inefficient.

There remains the question of whether restrictive arrangements, despite their useful functions, make life too easy for all the firms concerned, with the result that the general level of efficiency in the industry suffers. I can see no reason why short–run price stability need make producers lazy; it would do so only if prices were set so as to give profits higher than normal to firms of no more than normal efficiency. Provided price is low enough, the high–cost producers will be under pressure to improve their performance. If short–run price competition were practised, then no doubt entrepreneurs would have an incentive to exert themselves in a particular way—in concealing their own price reductions, in predicting competitors' moves, and in endeavouring to deduce from price changes the likely shift in consumers' demand. But there is little reason to believe that skill in this particular game deserves to be rewarded and encouraged; it is not at all evident that it is in the public interest for each entrepreneur to devote much of his time and energies to guessing what the others are going to do. It would seem in general preferable for entrepreneurs to eliminate or reduce the uncertainties that are generated by certain forms of competitive behaviour and thereby release more of their attention for directly useful activities such as improving products and processes of production.

The abuses to which the restraint of competition may lead are very well known. Both popular and academic opinion on this matter (which is subject to a good deal of fluctuation) is reluctant to accept that restrictions of certain kinds and in certain circumstances, can be to the general advantage. In considering the best forms of economic organization we are faced with a genuine dilemma and nothing is to be gained from pretending that it does not exist. If firms have the power to make their environment more favourable to informed planning they may also have the power to act against the public interest, either by the restriction of supply or by the protection of high-cost production. In the final choice, therefore, we may have to seek a compromise the terms of which will vary according to the circumstances of each particular market. Any maladjustment of supply to demand will be the more serious the lower the elasticity of demand for the product and the higher the proportion of fixed costs employed in its manufacture. The likelihood that unrestrained competition will produce misallocation depends on a variety of factors. It will be greater the higher the elasticity of substitution between the outputs of rival manufacturers, for this will determine the gains to be had from short-run price competition. It will be greater the longer the period of production in that this will make overproduction take longer to become recognized. The more frequent the periods of deficiency of demand relative to capacity, and the higher the ratio of fixed to variable costs, the stronger will be the incentive for each firm to endeavour to enlarge its share of the market by a price reduction. The codes of behaviour necessary to check short-run price competition will need to be less formal the smaller the number of firms, the longer the tradition of co-operation between them, and the easier it is to find out the prices that competitors are actually charging. At one extreme, prices may be maintained without any arrangements between the firms concerned simply by virtue of the fact that each recognizes that price reductions would be immediately noted and matched. At the other a complex agreement may be necessary. In the former situation, there will be little or nothing that legislation can do to make firms behave differently; in the latter, co-operation on prices can be prevented, or made very difficult, by a prohibition of agreements in restraint of trade. Thus anti-trust policy is likely to have much more impact in some industries than in others even though the economic effects of interfirm co-operation, as distinct from the forms in which it is practised, are much the same.

These considerations lead us, however, to questions of public policy with which this article does not directly deal. I have been concerned with the general theoretical ideas that ought to guide us in reaching a decision for or against the restraint of competition in any particular case.

St. Joseph's College, Oxford

Economies as An Antitrust Defense:
The Welfare Tradeoffs

Oliver E. Williamson

Suppose that a merger (or other combination) is proposed that yields economies but at the same time increases market power. Can the courts and antitrust agencies safely rely, in these circumstances, on a literal reading of the law
which prohibits mergers "where in any line commerce or any section of the
country, the effect of such acquisition may be substantially to lessen competition, or to tend to create a monopoly,"[1] or does this run the risk of serious
economic loss? In the usual merger where both effects are insubstantial this
problem is absent.[2] But in the occasional case where efficiency and market
power consequences exist, can economies be dismissed on the grounds that
market power effects invariably dominate? If they cannot, then a rational
treatment of the merger question requires that an effort be made to establish
the allocative implications of the scale economy and market power effects
associated with the merger.

The initial indication of the Supreme Court's view on this question came
on the occasion of the first merger case to come before it under the 1950
amendment to Section 7 of the Clayton Act. In a unanimous opinion, the
Court took the position in *Brown Shoe* that not only were efficiencies no

---

Reprinted from *American Economic Review* (1968) pp. 18–36 with permission of the
American Economic Association.

[1]Public Law 899, Sec. 7, 38 Stat. 731, as amended; 15 U.S.C. 18.

[2]Donald Dewey has observed in this connection that most mergers "have virtually nothing to
do with either the creation of market power or the realization of scale economies" [9, p. 257].
Jesse Markham agrees that since 1930 monopolization has not been a principal merger objective, but finds that "some mergers have undoubtedly come about as adjustments to major innovations...: the first great wave of mergers followed a period of rapid railroad building, and the wave
of the 1920s came with the rise of the motor car and motor truck transportation and a new advertising medium, the home radio" [22, pp. 181–82]. It might be useful briefly to summarize some
of the ways in which efficiencies might result from combination. These would include miscalculation, shifts in demand, technological developments, displacement of ineffective managements,
and mixtures thereof.

As an example of miscalculation consider two firms that have entered a market at an efficient
plant scale but have incorrectly estimated the volume necessary to support an efficient distribution system. Combination here could lead to efficiencies but might also have some market power
effects (reducing competition between the two but possibly enhancing their competitive position
with respect to their rivals). A significant, persistent decline in demand might produce a condition of excess capacity in which combination would permit economies but would also have
market power consequences. As discussed in Section III, an increase in demand might induce a
change from job shop to assembly line type operations with vertical integration consequences.
Technological developments may similarly provide opportunities for a significant reorganization
of resources into more efficient configurations — the electronic digital computer being a recent
example. Finally, merger may be the most expeditious way of displacing an inefficient by a more
efficient management — but the benefits here may only be of a short-run variety. A manifestly
inefficient management would, hopefully, be displaced by other means if, by reason of the
market power consequences of a combination, the merger route were closed.

A merger can, of course, produce diseconomies as well. What I have previously characterized
as the "control loss" phenomenon appears to be an increasing function of firm size [31]. See also
Parts 7 and 8, section II, infra.

defense, but a showing that a merger resulted in efficiencies could be used affirmatively in attacking the merger since small rivals could be disadvantaged thereby [6, p. 374]. Opportunities to reconsider this position have presented themselves since, *Procter & Gamble* being the most recent.

Justice Douglas, in delivering the opinion of the Court, observed that Procter & Gamble "would be able to use its volume discounts to advantage in advertising Clorox," and went on to state that "economies cannot be used as a defense to illegality. Congress was aware that some mergers which lessen competition may also result in economies but it struck the balance in favor of protecting competition" [10, pp.1230–31]. Although reference to congressional intent may relieve the Court of the responsibility for making tradeoff valuations, this does not fully dispose of the issue. What tradeoff calculus did Congress employ that produced this result?

In a concurring opinion to the Clorox decision, Justice Harlan provides the first hint that efficiencies may deserve greater standing. At least with respect to conglomerate or product–extension mergers "where the case against the merger rests on the probability [as contrasted, apparently, with a certainty] of increased market power, the merging companies may attempt to prove that there are countervailing economies reasonably probable which should be weighed against the adverse effects" [10, pp. 1240–41]. But inasmuch as the economies in Clorox were in his opinion merely pecuniary rather than real, which distinction is of course appropriate, he concluded that Procter's efficiency defense was defective [10, p. 1243].

Even if Justice Harlan's position were the prevailing one, it is clear that economies would be an acceptable antitrust defense for only a restricted set of structural conditions. Since the relevant economic theory, although widely available, has never been developed explicitly on this issue, such a result is not unexpected. Indeed, lacking a basis for evaluating net effects, for the Court to hold that the anticompetitive consequences of a merger outweight any immediate efficiency advantages is only to be expected. An institution acting as a caretaker for the enterprise system does not easily exchange what it regards as long–term competitive consequences for short–term efficiency gains.

The merits of the Supreme Court's position on mergers are at the heart of the recent Bork and Bowman v. Blake and Jones debate [2, 3, 4, 5]. Although this dialogue deals directly with the critical issues, its failure to produce a consensus is at least partly due to the fact that essential aspects of the relevant economic model were not supplied. Lacking a tradeoff relation, Bork is forced to assert that "Economic analysis does away with the need to measure efficiencies directly. It is enough to know in what sorts of transactions efficiencies are likely to be present and in what sorts anticompetitive effects are likely to be present. The law can then develop objective criteria, such as market shares, to divide transactions [into those predominantly one type or other]" [5, p. 411]. But this obviously leaves the mixed cases which are the hard ones, unresolved. Blake and Jones, by contrast, conclude that "claims of economic efficiency will not justify a course of conduct conferring excessive market power. The objective of maintaining a system of self–policing markets requires that all such claims be rejected" [3, p. 427]. But what are the standards for "excessive" market power and "self–policing" markets? And are these really absolute or do they reflect an implicit tradeoff calculation? And if it is the latter, should we (if we can) make this tradeoff explicit?

Indeed, there is no way in which the tradeoff issue can be avoided. To disallow tradeoffs altogether merely reflects a particularly severe a priori judgment as to net benefits. Moreover, it is doubtful that a goal hierarchy scheme of the sort proposed by Carl Kaysen and Donald Turner has acceptable properties. As they formulate the problem, higher level goals strictly dominate lower level goals, so that only when the latter are available without sacrifice in the former is lower level goal pursuit allowed [16, pp. 44–45]. Inasmuch as they rank efficiency and progressiveness above reductions in market power, an absolute defense would appear to obtain when, for any structural condition present or prospective, it could be shown either tha economies have not yet been exhausted or that discreteness conditions (indivisibilities) would not efficiently permit a separation [16, pp. 44–46, 58, 78]. But this may be to construe their intentions too narrowly; for it is with antitrust actions that result in *substantial* efficiency losses [16, pp. 44, 133] and involve *too great* a sacrifice in performance [16, p. 58] that they are especially concerned. Although these distinctions are important, they are not ones for which goal hierarchy analysis is well suited to deal. Tradeoff analysis, by contrast, is designed to cope with precisely these types of issues.

The relevant partial equilibrium model with which to characterize the tradeoffs between efficiency and price effects together with a representative set of indifference relations are developed in Section I of this paper. A variety of essential qualifications to this naive model are then presented in Section II. Extensions of the argument, which is developed initially in horizontal merger terms, to deal with questions of dissolution as well as vertical and conglomerate mergers, are given in Section III. The conclusions follow in Section IV.

I. The Naive Tradeoff Model

The effects on resource allocation of a merger that yields economies but extends market power can be investigated in a partial equilibrium context with the help of Figure 1. The horizontal line labeled AC_1 represents the level of average costs of the two (or more) firms before combination, while AC_2 shows the level of average costs after the merger. The price before the merger is given by P_1 and is equal to k (AC_1), where k is an index of pre–merger market power and is greater than or equal to unity. The price after the merger is given by P_2 and is assumed to exceed P_1 (if it were less than P_1 the economic effects of the merger would be strictly positive).[3]

---

[3]This is a simple but basic point. It reveals that market power is only a necessary and not a sufficient condition for undesirable price effects to exist. It would be wholly irrational to regard an increase in the price to average cost ratio $(P_2/AC_2 > P_1AC_1)$ as grounds for opposing a merger if, at the same time, the post–merger price were less than the pre–merger level $(P_2 < P_1)$.

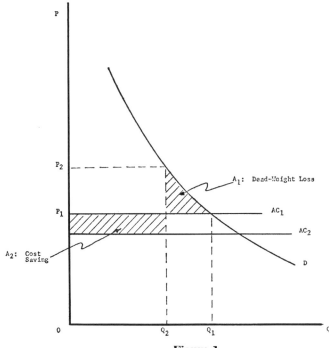

Figure 1.

The net welfare effects of the merger are given (approximately) by the two shaded areas in the Figure. The area designated A_1 is the familiar deadweight loss that would result if price were increased from P_1 to P_2, assuming that costs remain constant. But since average costs are actually reduced by the merger, the area designated A_2, which represents cost savings, must also be taken into account. The net allocative effect is given by the difference, $A_2 - A_1$, of these two areas.[4]

The area A_2 is given by $(AC_2 - AC_1)Q_2$, or $[\Delta(AC)]Q_2$, while A_1 is given approximately by ½ $(P_2 - P_1)$ $(Q_1 - Q_2)$, or ½ (ΔP) (ΔQ). The net economic effect will be positive if the following inequality holds:

(1) $[\Delta(AC)]Q_2 - 1/2(\Delta P)(\Delta Q) > 0.$

Dividing through by Q_2 and substituting for $\Delta Q/Q$ the expression $\eta(\Delta P/P)$, where η is the elasticity of demand, we obtain:

---

[4]My use of dead–weight loss is somewhat restrictive. Inefficiency is also a dead–weight loss. For convenience of exposition, however, I refer to the Marshallian triangle as the dead–weight loss and compare this to the cost saving (efficiency) aspects of a merger. Estimating the value of consumers' surplus by the Marshallian triangle follows the common (and broadly defensible) practice of suppressing the income effects associated with a price change. The net social benefit associated with a particular cost–price configuration is defined as total revenue plus consumers' surplus less social cost, where social and private costs are assumed to be identical (externalities and producers' surplus are both assumed to be zero).

(2)
$$\Delta(AC) - 1/2(\Delta P)\eta\frac{\Delta P}{P} > 0.$$

Finally, dividing through by $P_1 = k(AC_1)$ we have as our criterion:

(3)
$$\frac{\Delta(AC)}{AC} - \frac{k}{2}\eta\left(\frac{\Delta P}{P}\right)^2 > 0.$$

If this inequality holds, the net allocative effect of the merger is positive. If the difference is equal to zero the merger is neutral. If the inequality is reversed the merger is negative.

In words, the inequality shown in (3) says that if the decimal fraction reduction in average costs exceeds the square of the decimal fraction increase in price multiplied by one-half k times the elasticity of demand, the allocative effect of the merger is positive. Setting k equal to one (which it will be if the pre-merger market power is negligible), the cost reductions necessary to offset price increases for various values of the elasticity of demand are shown in Table 1.

For example, if price were to increase by 20 per cent, then running across the row $[(\Delta P/P)\text{x}100] = 20$ we observe that if η is 2 a cost reduction of 4 per cent will be sufficient to offset the price increase, while if η is 1 only a 2 per cent cost decrease is needed to neutralize the price effect, and if η is ½, a cost reduction of 1 per cent is sufficient. More generally it is evident that a relatively modest cost reduction is usually sufficient to offset relatively large price increases even if the elasticity of demand is as high as 2, which is probably a reasonable upper bound. Indeed, if a reduction in average costs on the order of 5 to 10 per cent is available through merger, the merger must give rise to price increases in excess of 20 per cent if $\eta \cong 2$, and in excess of 40 percent if $\eta \cong$ ½, for the net allocative effects to be negative. Moreover, it should be noted, if the merger reduces average costs by x per cent and the post-merger price increases by y per cent, the post-merger price to average cost differential slightly exceeds $x + y$ per cent. Thus, expressing price with respect to the post-merger level of average costs yields an even greater differential than is reflected by the relations stated above. The naive model thus supports the following proposition: a merger which yields non-trivial real economies must produce substantial market power and result in relatively large price increases for the net allocative effects to be negative.

Table 1—Percentage Cost Reductions [(Δ(AC)/AC)x100] Sufficient to Offset Percentage Price Increases (ΔP/Px100) for Selected Values of η

[(ΔP/P)x100] \ η	2	1	1/2
5	.25	.12	.06
10	1.00	.50	.25
20	4.00	2.00	1.00
30	9.00	4.50	2.25

II. Qualifications

Our partial equilibrium analysis suffers from a defect common to all partial equilibrium constructions. By isolating one sector from the rest of the economy it fails to examine interactions between sectors. Certain economic effects may therefore go undetected, and occasionally behavior which appears to yield net economic benefits in a partial equilibrium analysis will result in net losses when investigated in a general equilibrium context. Such a condition has been shown to exist in an economy in which monopoly exists in many sectors. Thus, whereas partial equilibrium analysis indicates that an increase in the monopoly price in any one sector invariably yields a loss, viewed more generally such an isolated price increase may actually lead to a desirable real-location of resources.[5] Conceivably, therefore, a merger that has monopoly power and cost-saving consequences could yield benefits in *both* respects— although it is probably rare that operational content can be supplied to this qualification. But were there no other considerations, such bias as our partial equilibrium construction produces would be to under-estimate the net economic gains of combination.

This does not, however, exhaust the range of qualifications. Among the other factors that can or should be taken into account are inference and enforcement expense, timing, incipiency, weighting, income distribution, extra-economic political objectives, technological progress, and the effects of monopoly power on managerial discretion.

A. Inference and Enforcement Expense

The relevant effects are those which take the form of real rather than pecuniary economies. Also, since evaluating a claim that economies exist will itself absorb real resources, it seems reasonable to impose a requirement that the net gain exceed some threshold value before such a defense will even be entertained. This, in conjunction with qualifications B through D below, would appear to meet Donald Turner's point that if economies are to be

---

[5]This is the familiar "second-best" argument. For a discussion of second-best qualifications in treating the monopoly problem, and references to this literature, see Ferguson [11, pp. 16–17, 49–51].

invoked as a defense "the law might well require clear and convincing evidence that the particular merger would produce substantial economies that could not be achieved in other ways" [27, p. 1328]. As the tools for assessing economies are progressively refined (and the incentive to make such improvements is obvious once an efficiency defense—even in principle—is granted), this threshold level should be reduced accordingly.

Operationally it may be essential to express the value of the threshold as a function of the ease with which economies can be established. Economies that have a highly speculative aspect should be required to reach a higher minimum level than those which are more objectively specified. (Thus if economies in both production and distribution expenses are claimed, and if the former are better specified than the latter, distribution economies would have to reach a higher threshold than would production economies to be admissible.) Since the ease with which exaggerated claims are detected varies directly with the degree of distortion attempted, and since evidence of distortion seriously debilitate a defense, adjusting the threshold in this way will tend to protect the enforcement agencies against grievously inflated efficiency claims.

Bork, apparently, would resist the argument that the defendants should bear the burden of proof on efficiencies since many efficiencies may be difficult to establish [5, p. 410]. But if efficiencies are to be a defense at all, it is clear that the companies—which are, presumably, sensitive to the relevant economies in proposing the merger in the first place—must be prepared to make the case for them in court. They have the data and these must be supplied. Otherwise the mixed cases which involves both scale economy and market power effects can only be handled arbitrarily—and this is satisfactory to no one.

B. Timing

Significant economies will ordinarily be realized eventually through internal expansion if not by merger. Growth of demand can facilitate this internal adjustment process; the necessity for part of the industry to be displaced in order that efficient size be achieved is relieved in a growing market. Thus, although a merger may have net positive effects immediately (cost savings exceed the dead–weight loss), when allowance is made for the possibility of internal expansion these effects can become negative eventually (the cost savings persist, but these could be realized anyway, and the deadweight loss could be avoided by prohibiting the merger).

Designating the dead–weight loss effects of the merger by $L(t)$ and the cost savings by $S(t)$, the argument would be that the value of $S(t)$ falls while $L(t)$ persists over time. Thus, taking the discounted value of net benefits (V) we have:

(4) $$V = \int_0^T [S(t) - L(t)e^{-rt}dt,$$

and if initially $S(t)/L(t) > 1$, but eventually $S(t)/L(t) < 1$, this can easily become negative. Consider, for example, the case where $S(t) = \overline{S}$ for a period of length T' and then becomes zero, while $L(t) = \overline{L}$ indefinitely. Using a social discount rate of 10 per cent, what initial combinations of $\overline{S}/\overline{L}$ and T' would leave us just indifferent over the allocative effects of a merger? For $\overline{S}/\overline{L}$ of 3, indifference occurs at a value of T' of 4 years; any value of T' less than 4 years would reveal that the scale economies can be realized by internal expansion in a sufficiently short interval that the merger should be dis allowed, while any value of T' that exceeds 4 years would show that net gains are available by approving the merger. For $\overline{S}/\overline{L}$ of 2, the corresponding value of T' is 7 years, while for $\overline{S}/\overline{L}$ of 1.5, the value of T' increases to 11 years. The necessary qualifications to our earlier results are thus obvious: only if $\overline{S}/\overline{L}$ is relatively large, or T' reasonably long, should a merger which results in eventual net losses be approved.

By contrast with a growing market, to force economies to be realized by internal expansion in a static market is generally without merit. The market power effects will occur here anyway, and the internal expansion route merely delays and may upset the market adjustment.

The above results are merely illustrative. More generally, equation (4) calls attention to the importance of considering the shape of the time stream of benefits and costs that a merger produces. Thus it is not sufficient to justify a merger on the basis of merely potential economies. Not only is it relevant to consider whether the merger would produce net benefits, but whether the timing is such as to maximize these gains. If a merger is proposed that promises potential economies, but these will not be realized for some time, it may be better to delay the combination. Such might be the case in circumstances where the existing plant has not exhausted its useful life and has limited value in other uses; in this situation investment in the new facilities may not be economical immediately. For the merger to occur much earlier than the indicated economies will be realized would permit whatever market power effects as the merger produces to take effect at an earlier time than is clearly most beneficial.

Plausible as this last argument may appear, it raises a serious question of how extensive a "management" function the enforcement agencies should play in merger matters. It is an easy step from the suggestion that a proposed merger should be delayed until maximum net gains are realized to the proposition that the enforcement agencies should "arrange" optimal firm pairings. Both of these, however, are much more ambitious tasks than merely testing whether the net gain associated with a proposed combination is positive. Subject possibly to occasional exceptions where the social net benefit calculus identifies a distinctly superior timing or combination from that which has been proposed privately (and assuming that the change can be implemented), the simple requirement that discounted net gains be positive is probably a sufficient test. Otherwise, mergers are too complex to postpone casually; and the enforcement agencies are not designed (nor should they be redesigned) to function in a brokerage capacity.

C. Incipiency

It is likewise vital to consider not merely the market power effects of any single merger taken in isolation, but whether the merger is representative of a trend. If a series of such mergers can reasonably be expected, the judgment of whether to permit any given combination should properly be cast in an industry context—in which case the anticipated economy and market power effects throughout the industry should be examined. Since, *if* economies are available by combining one pair of firms they will often be available more generally, this may frequently be an important consideration. The notion of incipiency thus has special relevance in administering the law on mergers where economies are claimed.

This propositon might usefully be contrasted with that of Bork and Bowman [2, p. 594]:

> The difficulty with stopping a trend toward a more concentrated condition at a very early stage is that the existence of the trend is prima facie evidence that greater concentration is socially desirable. The trend indicates that there are emerging efficiencies or economies of scale—whether due to engineering and production developments or to new control and management techniques—which make larger size more efficient. This increased efficiency is valuable to the society at large, for it means that fewer of our available resources are being used to accomplish the same amount of production and distribution. By striking at such trends in their very earliest stages the concept of incipiency prevents the realization of those very efficiencies that competition is supposed to encourage.

Their evaluation of the social desirability of a trend suggests a certain insensitivity to the relevant scale economy-market power tradeoff considerations, and they appear to read the significance of a trend somewhat too loosely. That a trend necessarily implies emerging efficiencies is incorrect: it may also indicate an emerging awareness that market power advantages might be realized through a series of combinations.[6] Moreover, whereas they seem to suggest that to disallow a merger is to prevent the realization of scale economies altogether, ordinarily it is not a question of whether economies will be realized but when and with what market power effects. Thus, while Bork and Bowman may be correct in charging that scale economy justifications have not been given sufficient weight in the recent enforcement of the merger law, they are also guilty of a certain heavy-handedness in their own treatment of the incipiency question.

------

[6]This is George Stiger's point in his treatment of "Monopoly and Oligopoly by Merger" [25]. Bork concedes this possibility in his response to Blake and Jones [5, p. 412]; but his principal emphasis, which is probably correct, is that a trend signals emerging economies.

D. Weighting

The economies that a merger produces are usually limited strictly to the combining firms. But the market power effects of a merger may sometimes result in a price increase across a wider class of firms. Where this occurs, a weighting factor should be introduced into expression (3) to reflect this condition. The criterion becomes:

$$(3') \qquad \left(\frac{(Q_2)}{(Q_T)}\right) \frac{\Delta(AC)}{AC} - \frac{k}{2}\,\eta\left(\frac{\Delta P}{P}\right)^2 > 0.$$

where Q_2 is the output of the merging firms and Q_T is the total quantity of industry sales for which the price increase becomes effective.

E. Income Distribution

An additional qualification to our analysis involves income distribution effects. The rectangle in Figure 1 bounded by P_2 and P_1 at the top and bottom respectively and O and Q_2 on the sides represents a loss of consumers' surplus (gain in monopoly profits) that the merger produces. On the resource allocation criteria for judging welfare effects advanced above, the distribution of these profits becomes a matter of indifference. For specific welfare valuations, however, we might not always wish to regard consumer and producer interests symmetrically—although since, arguably, antitrust is an activity better suited to promote allocative efficiency than income distribution objectives (the latter falling more clearly within the province of taxation, expenditure, and transfer payment activities), such income distribution adjustments might routinely be suppressed. If they are not, the tradeoff between efficiency gains and distributive losses needs explicitly to be expressed. Thus, while economies would remain a defense, any undesirable income distribution effects associated with market power would be counted against the merger rather than enter neutrally as the naive model implies.

Inasmuch as the income redistribution which occurs is usually large relative to the size of the dead–weight loss, attaching even a slight weight to income distribution effects can sometimes influence the overall valuation significantly. Thus, expressing the dead–weight loss ($L = \frac{1}{2}\,(\Delta P)\,(\Delta Q)$) as a ratio of the income distribution effect ($I = (\Delta P)Q$), and substituting into this ratio the expression for the elasticity of demand (η) the fraction ($L/I = \frac{1}{2}\,(\Delta P/P)\,\eta$) obtains. It is therefore obvious that, except where the elasticity of demand is "high," the dead–weight loss as a fraction of the income distribution effect is relatively small—certainly less than unity. Hence if, as is probably common, the income redistribution which results when market power is increased is regarded unfavorably, an appropriate weighting of this factor will, at least occasionally, upset a net valuation which on resource allocation grounds is positive.

Note in this connection that the transfer involved could be regarded unfavorably not merely because it redistributes income in an undesirable way (increases the degree of inequality in the size distribution of income), but also because it produces social discontent. This latter has serious efficiency implications that the above analysis does not take explicitly into account. This same point also appears to have gone unnoticed in the entire Bork and Bowman v. Blake and Jones exchange [2] [3] [4] [5]. Distinguishing social from private costs in this respect may, however, be the most fundamental reason for treating claims of private efficiency gains skeptically.

F. Political Considerations

Combinations which involve firms that are already very large in absolute terms might be resisted on grounds that these raise extra-economic problems of political significance. There is not, however, any obvious way in which to integrate these into the analysis. Rather, although the political implications of control over wealth are a matter for serious concern, these are separable from the economic problems posed by control over markets; a different calculus is required to deal with each. The necessary political judgment, ideally, is one for Congress to make. Possibly, as Carl Kaysen has suggested, this would take the form of a prohibition against expansion by merger of the largest 50 or 100 corporations [17, p. 37].

The issue here reaches beyond the social discontent matter raised above. Thus, whereas social discontent can be reduced, in principle at least, to efficiency-equivalent (net value product) terms, the political implications of the control over wealth involve a judgment of how the quality of life in a democracy is affected by size disparities. The latter is less easily (or even appropriately) expressed in efficiency terms. The issue is nevertheless important, and failure to deal with it may be unresponsive to the position taken by Blake and Jones. Inasmuch as several of the counterexamples that they pose in their critique of Bork and Bowman appear deliberately to have been selected from the giant firm universe [5, pp. 425–27], possibly it is mergers within this subset that concerns them most. Should economies be allowed as a defense, therefore, the rule proposed by Kaysen would limit such a defense in a way which would presumably relieve this aspect of their concern.

G. Technological Progress; and
H. Managerial Discretion

The highly conjectural nature of qualifications G and H makes it unclear at this time what weight ought to be assigned to them. It is at least arguable that the prevailing uncertainties are too great to give any effect to these two factors at this time. They are, nevertheless, potentially of such significance that to dismiss them may run the risk of serious error. In consideration of this potential importance, additional research which would permit us better to evaluate their actual significance would seem warranted. The manner in which each would influence the estimate of net effects is sketched out below.

Consider technological progress first. Such increases in market power that result in predictable effects on technological progress should, if they can easily, be taken into account. The present evidence, while hardly abundant, suggests that, as a general rule, the research and development expenditures of the four largest firms in an industry are neither as large proportionately nor as productive as those of their immediately smaller rivals.[7] But this fails to answer the question of what market structures most enhance progressiveness. The evidence on this latter is somewhat mixed.[8] It seems unlikely, however, that subsequent investigation will upset the basic proposition that progressiveness is promoted by at least some elements of competition at virtually every stage of an industry's development—if for no other reason than that competition tends to assure that variety in research approaches will be employed. Local or regional monopolies may provide partial exceptions (since here the requisite variety will be available nationally, although the rate at which innovations are implemented may nevertheless lag if competitive pressures are lacking), but monopoly, or near–monopoly, would not seem to be the perfect instrument for technical progress in industries for which the relevant market is national.

Lacking additional evidence, it would not seem injudicious to assume that mergers between relatively small–sized firms rarely have negative (and may frequently have positive) effects on progressiveness, whatever the condition of concentration. This judgment probably holds for most mergers involving lower–middle sized firms as well. Thus it is mainly in the relatively large firms, particularly those in moderately to highly concentrated national markets (which, of course, are also ones where market power effects may be important), that the effects of a merger on technological progress deserve special attention.

---

[7]With respect to size, Mansfield found that the ratio of innovations to firm size reached a maximum at about the sixth largest firm for the petroleum and coal industries, and at a much lower rank for steel [20, p. 566]. Elsewhere Mansfield reports that the largest firms in petroleum, drugs, and glass spent somewhat less on R&D, relative to sales, than did somewhat smaller firms; in chemicals they spent somewhat more; in steel they spent less, but the difference was not statistically significant [21, p. 334]. Scherer concludes from his study of patent behavior in a group of 448 firms selected from the Fortune list of the largest 500 industrial corporations in 1955 that "the evidence does not support the hypothesis that corporate bigness is especially favorable to high inventive output" [23, p. 1114]. Turning to productivity, Mansfield concludes that "in most industries, the productivity of an R&D program of given scale seems to be lower in the largest firms" [21, p. 338]. Comanor found that diseconomies of scale in the pharmaceutical industry were encountered at even moderate firm sizes [8, p. 190]. For a recent review of this literature, see Johnson [15, pp. 169–71].

[8]Hamburg [13, Ch.4] and Horowitz [14, pp. 330–01] report a positive correlation between R&D expenditures and industrial concentration. Scherer finds a much weaker but slightly positive association [23, pp. 1119–21]. Kendrick concludes from an examination of Terleckyj's data that there is no significant correlation between productivity changes and industrial concentration [18, p. 179]. Stigler found in an earlier study "hints that industries with lower concentration had higher rates of technological progress" [26, p. 278], while I using Mansfield's data, found a negative correlation between the proportion of innovations introduced by the four largest firms and industrial concentration [30].

Whether the effects be positive or negative, the necessary extension to the model is identical. Assume therefore that a merger is proposed involving a large firm in a concentrated industry, and that while it yields economies it also predictably decreases the rate of progressiveness. Holding constant for the moment the effects on price, how large a change in the rate of technical progress would be required to offset the available economy of scale advantage? To obtain a crude estimate of this, let θ be the ratio of the immediate post–merger average costs (so that $1-\theta$ is the immediate decimal fraction reduction in average costs), g_1 be the rate of productivity increase in the absence of the merger and g_2 the rate if the merger is approved (where $g_1 \geq g_2$), $Q(t)$ be the output in period t, and let r be the social discount rate. Then the merger will have neutral effects if the discounted value of costs under each condition is the same. This requires that the equality given below should hold:

$$(5) \qquad \int_0^\infty [(AC)Q(t)e^{-g_1 t}]e^{-g r t}dt = \int_0^\infty [\theta(AC)Q(t)e^{-g_2 t}]e^{-r t}dt$$

Assuming that output increases exponentially at the rate α the critical value of g_2 is given by:

$$(6) \qquad g_2 = \theta g_1 - (1 - \theta)(r - \alpha)$$

If, for example, the values of θg_1 and $r-\alpha$ were .90, .03, and .07 respectively, the critical value of g_2 would be .02. Were g_2 to fall below this value, an indicated economy of 10 percent would not be sufficient to offset the cumulative productivity loss associated with the merger, to say nothing of the market power effects that the merger produces. If indeed the selected values of g_1 and $r-\alpha$ are at all representative, a predictable decrease in the rate of productivity advance by one–third or more would thus be sufficient to disallow a merger for which an efficiency advantage as large as 10 per cent could be expected.[9]

Consider now the managerial discretion argument. Here the direction of the effect is not so much a matter for dispute as is its quantitative significance. The argument is that market power provides a firm with the opportunity to pursue a variety of other–than–profit objectives. Although this is an "old" argument, its persistence at least suggests the possibility that it may not be without merit.[10] Whether qualitatively there is anything to it turns essentially on the behavioral proposition that where competition in the product market presents no significant threat to survival, the resources of the firm are

---

[9]If the beneficial economies of scale are available only to the combining firms, while the negative progressiveness effects are felt throughout the industry, the above results underestimate the extent of economies necessary to produce indifference.

[10]As Arthur Hadley observed in 1897, "The tendency of monopoly to retard the introduction of industrial improvement is ...a more serious thing than its tendency to allow unfair rates. This aspect of the matter has hardly received proper attention. We have been so accustomed to think of competition as a regulator of prices that we have lost sight of its equally important function as a stimulus to efficiency. Wherever competition is absent, there is a disposition to rest content with old methods, not to say slack ones. In spite of notable exceptions this is clearly the rule" [12, p. 383].

absorbed in part as corporate consumption activities by those members of the firm who are knowledgeable of discretionary opportunities, powerfully situated, and disposed to be assertive [29, 32]. Its quantitative significance rests on a judgment over whether the conspicuous evidence is sufficiently strong.[11]

If indeed a predictable relaxation in the least–cost posture of a firm which has acquired market power through merger can be made, the estimated cost savings that appear in equation (4) should be adjusted accordingly. Economies which are available in theory but, by reason of market power, are not sustainable are inadmissible.

III. Extensions

Although the foregoing analysis has been concerned exclusively with horizontal mergers, the argument applies generally to problems in which market power–efficiency tradeoffs exist. Dissolution, vertical mergers, and conglomerate mergers can all be treated within this general frame-work.

A. Dissolution

The argument here is perfectly straightforward. It is simply not sufficient in a monopolization case for which dissolution is the indicated relief that (1) a persistent monopoly conditon $(P_1 > AC_1)$ exist, and (2) a reduction in price following dissolution $(P_2 < P_1)$ be expected. It is necessary in addition that the gains realized by the price reduction be sufficient to offset any losses in economies that result. The relevant test is that shown in equation (3)—modified, as may be necessary, by the qualifications discussed in Section II above.

B. Vertical Mergers

It is important to note in dealing with vertical mergers that the conventional analysis of vertical integration, which takes a historical definition of an industry as given, often leads to incorrect results. The logical boundaries of a firm are not necessarily those which have been inherited but rather are defined by the condition that the firm be unable to arrange a transaction internally more cheaply than the market.[12] This is not something which is given once–for–all but depends both on technology and the extent of the market. Thus what may be regarded as "vertical integration" under a historical definition of an industry might, in many instances, more accurately be characterized as a reorganization into a more efficient configuration. For example, as technology evolves processes that are more fully automated or as demand for a commodity increases sufficiently to warrant continuous processing techniques, combinatorial economies may result by serially linking activities within

---

[11]This presently is the weakest part of the argument. For a recent survey of the data, see [19].

[12]As Ronald Coase has pointed out, "a firm will tend to expand until the costs of organizing an extra transaction within the firm become equal to the costs of carrying out the same transaction by means of an exchange on the open market or the costs of organizing in another firm" [7, p. 341].

a single firm that had previously been done in separate specialty firms.[13] A transformation of this sort accomplished in part through vertical mergers is probably common in the production of commodities which shift from sequential job shop to continuous assembly line type operations.

That vertical integration can produce real economies is a result of the fact that the market does not perform its exchanges costlessly. Going to the market involves search costs, contracting costs, misinformation costs, delay costs, transfer costs, interface costs, etc.,[14] and these must be balanced against the costs of organizing a transaction internally. Where the former exceed the latter, "vertical integration" is indicated. But of course this is vertical integration in only an apparent sense: in fact it represents a rationalization of the firm into an optimum economic unit.

The historical organization of an industry can ordinarily be presumed to reflect adequately basic efficiencies where significant market or techno logical developments have been lacking. And even where such recent changes have occurred, an efficiency defense is not automatic. Furthermore, if an efficiency defense can be supplied, any market power consequences that a vertical merger produces need also to be considered.[15] Again the basic tradeoff calculation is that given by equation (3)—modified as necessary by the qualifications discussed in Section II.

C. Conglomerate Mergers

The principal ways in which conglomerate mergers can produce efficiencies have been given previously by M.A. Adelman [1, pp. 241–42] and Turner [27, pp. 1323–39, 1358–61]. The ways in which conglomerate mergers may produce market power are also discussed by Turner. All that remains, essentially, is to deal with the tradeoff question. Again the rules for estimating net benefits are substantially those given above.

IV. Conclusions

Most mergers produce neither significant price nor efficiency consequences, and where this is true the analysis of this paper has limited relevance. Where both occur, however, and if without merger the transition to an efficient industrial configuration is apt to be both painful and delayed, an efficiency defense deserves consideration. This does not of course mean that

---

[13]Stigler argues that increasing the extent of the market will often lead to dis–integration of manufacturing processes since now the market will be sufficient to support a specialized firm [25, pp. 188– 90]. Although this may often occur, there is also the countervailing tendency to maintain or extend integration where coordination among the parts in the face of market uncertainties is critical—as it often is where assembly line operations are employed. See Coase [7, p. 337].

[14]Coase discusses some of these [7, pp. 336–37]. (For an early example in which the costs going to the market were examined in a common law proceeding, see Hadley v. Baxendale.) In addition, if suppliers possess market power, going to the market may involve pecuniary expenses that could be avoided by integrating backward into supply activities.

[15]Stigler identifies barriers to entry that take the form of increased capital and/or knowledge requirements as potential anticompetitive consequences of a vertical merger [25, p. 191].

the mere existence of economies is sufficient to justify a merger. But since a relatively large percentage increase in price is usually required to offset the benefits that result from a 5 to 10 per cent reduction in average costs, the existence of economies of this magnitude is sufficiently important to give the antitrust authorities pause before disallowing such a merger. There are, as indicated in Section II, a variety of qualifications that they may upset this general conclusion in any particular case, but absent these and the result clearly holds.

It might be objected that the courts do not possess the expertise to make the types of judgments described. This is typically true. But that does not mean that an analysis of these effects should be not performed by the Antitrust Division or Federal Trade Commission before deciding to challenge a merger. The enforcement agencies can obtain, at reasonable cost, the necessary expertise to make these evaluations.[16]

Only after they are convinced that such economies as may exist are not sufficient to justify a merger should a case go forward. Although possibly this extends the responsibility of the enforcement agencies beyond those that are clearly intended, the alternative is scarcely acceptable. For if neither the courts nor the enforcement agencies are sensitive to these considerations, the system fails to meet a basic test of economic rationality. And without this the whole enforcement system lacks for defensible standards and becomes suspect.

Once economies are admitted as a defense, the tools for assessing these effects can be expected progressively to be refined. Since such refinements will permit both the courts and the enforcement agencies to make more precise evaluations, the threshold value under which an economies defense will be allowed can be reduced accordingly. Thus even if initially only a few mergers for which mixed effects are present are able to pass an appropriately qualified tradeoff test because of high threshold requirements, this proportion can be expected to increase as research results and analytical aids for evaluating scale economies accumulate. As an interim gain, solemn references to early oratory might finally be displaced in favor of analysis in the continuing dialogue on antitrust enforcement.

---

[16]That the enforcement agencies are sensitive to scale economy considerations is evidenced by the recent Federal Trade Commission merger guidelines "Enforcement Policy with Respect to Mergers in the Food Distribution Industries," issued January 3, 1967. See especially pages 6–9.

Justice Brennan observed in the Philadelphia National Bank merger that "a merger the effect of which 'may be substantially to lessen competition' is not saved because, on some ultimate reckoning of social or economic debits and credits, it may be deemed beneficial....[Such] is beyond the ordinary limits of judicial competence" [28, p. 371]. My point is that, at least with respect to efficiencies, such reckoning need not and indeed should not be beyond the competence of the antitrust agencies. It is here that the first critical decision of whether to file suit is made.

References

1. M.A. Adelman, "The Antimerger Act, 1950–60," *Am. Econ. Rev., Proc.*, May 1961, 51, 236–44.

2. H.M. Blake and W.K. Jones, "In Defense of Antitrust," *Columbia Law Rev.*, March 1965, 65, 377–400.

3. _____, "Toward a Three-Dimensional Antitrust Policy," *Columbia Law Rev.*, March 1965, 65, 422–66.

4. R.H. Bork and W.S. Bowman, "The Crisis in Antitrust," *Columbia Law Rev.*, March 1965, 65, 363–76.

5. R.H. Bork, "Contrasts in Antitrust Theory: I," *Columbia Law Rev.* March 1965, 65, 401–16.

6. *Brown Shoe v. United States*, 370 U.S. 294 (1962).

7. R.H. Coase, "The Nature of the Firm," *Economica*, N.S., IV, 1937, 386–485. Reprinted in G.J. Stigler and K.E. Boulding, Eds., *Readings in Price Theory*, Homewood, Ill., 1952, pp. 331–51.

8. W.S. Comanor, "Research and Technical Change in the Pharmaceutical Industry," *Rev. Econ. and Stat.*, May 1965, 47, 182–90.

9. D. Dewey, "Mergers and Cartels: Some Reservations about Policy," *Am. Econ. Rev., Proc.*, May 1961, 51, 255–62.

10. *Federal Trade Commission v. Procter & Gamble Co.*, 87 S. Ct. 1224 (1967).

11. C.E. Ferguson, *A Macroeconomic Theory of Workable Competition*. Durham, N.C., 1964.

12. A.T. Hadley, "The Good and Evil of Industrial Combination," *Atlantic Monthly*, March 1897, 79, 377–85.

13. D. Hamburg, R&D: *Essays on the Economics of Research and Development*. New York 1966.

14. I. Horowitz, "Firm Size and Research Activity," *So. Econ. Jour.*, Jan. 1962, 28, 298–301.

15. R.E. Johnson, "Technical Progress and Innovation," *Oxford Econ. Papers*, July 1966, 18, 158–76.

16. C. Kaysen and D.F. Turner, *Antitrust Policy: An Economic and Legal Analysis*, Cambridge, Mass., 1959.

17. C. Kaysen, "The Present War on Bigness: I," in *The Impact of Antitrust on Economic Growth*, Fourth National Industrial Conference Board Conference on Antitrust in an Expanding Economy, New York 1965, pp. 31–38.

18. J.W. Kendrick, *Productivity Trends in the United States*. Princeton, N.J., 1961.

19. H. Leibenstein, "Allocative Efficiency versus 'X-Efficiency'," *Am. Econ. Rev.*, June 1966, 56, 392–415.

20. E. Mansfield, "Size of Firms, Market Structure, and Innovation," *Jour. Pol. Econ.*, Dec. 1963, 71, 556–76.

21. _____, "Industrial Research and Development Expenditures: Determinants, Prospects, and Relation to Size of Firm and Inventive Output," *Jour. Pol. Econ.*, Aug. 1964, 72, 319–40.

22. J.W. Markham, "Survey of the Evidence and Findings on Megers," in *Business Concentration and Price Policy*, Princeton, N.J., 1955, pp. 141–82.

23. F.M. Scherer, "Firm Size, Market Structure, Opportunity, and the Output of Patented Invention," *Am. Econ. Rev.*, Dec. 1965, 55, 1097–1125.

24. G.J. Stigler, "Monopoly and Oligopoly by Merger," *Am. Econ. Rev., Proc.*, May 1950, *40*, 23–24, reprinted in R.B. Helfebower and G.W. Stocking, eds., *Readings in Industrial Organization,* Homewood, Il., 1958, pp. 69–80.

25. _____, "The Division of Labor is Limited by the Extent of the Market," *Jour. Pol. Econ.*, June 1951, *59*, 185–93.

26. _____, "Industrial Organization and Economic Program," in L.D. White, ed., *The State of the Social Sciences,* Chicago 1956, pp. 269–82.

27. D.F. Turner, "Conglomerate Mergers and Section 7 of the Clayton Act," *Harvard Law Review,* May 1965, *78,* 1313–95.

28. *United States v. Philadelphia Nat'l Bank,* 374 U.S. 312 (1963).

29. O.E. Williamson, *The Economics of Discretionary Behavior: Managerial Objectives in a Theory of the Firm.* Englewood Cliffs, N.J. 1964.

30. _____, "Innovation and Market Structure," *Jour. Pol. Econ.,* Feb. 1965, *73,* 67–73.

31. _____, "Hierarchical Control and Optimum Firm Size," *Jour. Pol. Econ.,* April 1967, *75,* 123–38.

32. _____, "A Dynamic–Stochastic Theory of Managerial Behavior," in A. Phillips and O.E. Williamson, eds., *Prices: Issues in Theory, Practice and Public Policy,* Philadelphia (forthcoming).

CHAPTER 5 - Chicago's New Learning

Concentration and Profits:
Does Concentration Matter?

Yale Brozen

In the post–World War II period, the economics profession made a 180–degree turn from its pre–Great Depression position in its view of concentration. In the late nineteenth and early twentieth centuries, the prevailing view seemed to have been that even with only a few firms in an industry, price competition would be persistent and collusion difficult. There was little concern with any probability of successful collusion (shared monopoly or oligopoly) in industries where four firms had, say, 70 percent or more of an industry's capacity or sales. Three or four firms were felt to be sufficient for competitive behavior.[1] What concern was concerned was expressed was in terms of "trusts" combining most of an industry's capacity under a single management.

Even where more than 70 percent of an industry's capacity had been combined to form a single firm, no fear was felt by many economists that a monopoly result would ensue.[2] (Some expressed approval of such combinations in terms of the economies that would be realized.)[3] J.B. Clark, for example, pointed to the power of potential competition to produce the same competitive result as a larger number of firms or noncolluding behavior of a few, saying:

> Let any combination of producers raise the prices beyond a certain limit, and it will encounter this difficulty. The new mills that will spring into

Reprinted by permission from *Antitrust Bulletin,* Summer 1974, pp. 381–399.

[1]Eliot Jones, for example, remarks that, "In 1904 there were some seventy–five independent refiners all told. . . . Had the total independent output been concentrated in a few large refineries, competition with the Standard Oil Company would have been much more vigorous and successful." *The Trust Problem in the United States* 59(1929). George Stigler has pointed out that, "When the Sherman Act...was passed in 1890, most economists and most non–economists believed that an industry with a modest number of firms could be tolerably competitive." "The Changing Problem of Oligopoly," *Proceedings of the Mont Pelerin Society* 3 (1966).

[2]"The key to the situation is the position of the consumers, rather than that of the producers. Has every consumer a choice of efficient and independent producers to buy from? If so, there is no monopoly, even if one combination should control three quarters of the output." J.B. Clark and J.M. Clark, *The Control of Trusts* 184–5 (1912).

[3]H.R. Seager, Introduction to Economics 150 (1905); C.J. Bullock, *Introduction to the Study of Economics* 178 (1908); F.W. Taussig, *Principles of Economics i,* 53–55 (1915); E.R.A. Seligman, *Principles of Economics* 345 (1921).

existence will break down prices; and the fear of these new mills, without their actual coming, is often enough to keep prices from rising to an extortionate height. The mill that has never been built is already a power in the market: for it will surely be built under certain conditions, the effect of this certainly is to keep prices down.[4]

Even Professor Jones, who believed in the necessity of active government intervention to break up trusts because they would seek to maintain unfairly high prices, provides evidence of the failure of the trusts to accomplish their objective. He lists a number which failed financially and were voluntarily dissolved. In addition, he mentions others which were unable to keep the dominant position required to maintain prices above the competitive level when they attempted to do so.[5]

Professor A.S. Dewing undertook an empirical analysis to determine whether or not any advantages accrued to "large scale enterprises brought about through combination—the so-called 'trusts.' "[6] Choosing "a random selection of thirty-five industrial combinations" where "at least five separate, independent and competing plants" were merged, he examined profits of the independent companies in the year preceding consolidation. These he compared with the profits in the year following consolidation, in the tenth year following consolidation, and average profits in the ten years following. He found no evidence, showing, on the average, that combinations of 40 to 95 percent of an industry's capacity produced any enhancement of profits either through economies of scale or combination or through monopoly.

Roughly, the promoters of the consolidations believed that the mere act of combination would increase the earnings by about a half. But in actual results the earnings before the consolidation were nearly a fifth *greater* (18%) than the earnings of the first year after consolidation. The promoters expected the earnings to be a half greater than the aggregate of the competing plants; instead they were about a sixth less. Nor were the sustained earnings an improvement, for the earnings before the consolidation were between a fifth and a sixth greater than the average for the ten years following the consolidation. In brief, the earnings of the separate plants before consolidation were greater than the earnings of the same plants after consolidation.[7]

As late as the 1930's, after the discussion of administered (rigid) prices in concentrated industries had begun, Professor Henry Simons said

---

[4]J.B. Clark, *The Control of Trusts* 13 (1901).

[5]Eliot Jones, *supra* note 1, at 538–540.

[6]A.S. Dewing, "A Statistical Test of the Success of Consolidations," 36 *Quarterly Journal of Economics* 84 (1921–22).

[7]*Id*. at 90–91. Inasmuch as no failures were included in the thirty–five consolidations examined since only those with a ten–year history of earnings were included in the sample, the decline in earnings is underestimated.

I am, indeed, not much distressed about private monopoly power. . . . serious exploitation could be prevented by suppression of lawless violence. . . . The ways of competition are devious, and its vengeance—government intervention apart—will generally be adequate and admirable.[8]

In the post–World War II era, in contrast to this earlier view, "most practitioners assumed that successful (tacit or explicit) collusion [among oligopolists] would approach joint maximization and that the ability to collude increases with concentration."[9] A major exception to this post–World War II view appeared in a book by Paul MacAvoy, describing competition among the few in transportation "between the Mississippi River Valley and the East Coast."[10]

Discussing the observed behavior of these few firms, MacAvoy found that collusion was not effective despite being *explicitly* agreed upon among them. He observes that ". . . there seems to have been persistent 'cheating' on the rates set in conference, so that the level of rates declined markedly as one agreement after another broke down."[11] He goes on to point out that collusively determined rates became the actual rates only after governmental support was provided in 1887 under the Act to Regulate Interstate Commerce. As he says, "The effect of regulation seems to have been to establish the cartel rates as the actual rates."[12]

The question, "Why did economists' views shift from the earlier outlook to the opposite view characteristic of the post–World War II period?" may well be raised. The answer appears to be that the data relating concentration and profits first provided by Bain and later by other students in industrial organization convinced economists they had been wrong. The groundwork for acceptance had been laid by various discussions of administered pricing beginning in the thirties.[13]

This view that successful tacit or explicit collusion was probable in concentrated industries reached a culmination in the recommendation of the White House Antitrust Task Force that a deconcentration act be added to the antitrust arsenal.[14] The Task Force stated that there was some evidence for the view that underlay the recommendation, although it cited none. When the Staff Director of the Antitrust Task Force was asked for the evidence used, he referred to the articles by Bain, Mann, Stigler and others showing correlations

[8]Henry C. Simons, "The Requisites of Free Competition," 26 *American Economic Review*, *Supplement* 68 (1936). Simons spoke out strongly against concentration largely to offset the drive in government and the press at that time to force independent firms into cartels (as under NRA) and combinations. *ID.* at 72.

[9]Leonard Weiss, "Quantitative Studies in Industrial Organization," in *Frontiers of Quantitative Economics* at 363, ed. M.D. Intriligator (1971).

[10]Paul w. MacAvoy, *The Economic Effects of Regulation* v (1965).

[11]*Id.* at v.

[12]*Id.* at v.

[13]*Industrial Prices and Their Relative Inflexibility*, Senate Document No. 13 (January 1935).

[14]White House Task force on Antitrust Policy, Report 1 (in Trade Regulation Reports, Supplement to No. 415, May 26, 1969) at I–8.

between concentration and profitability and to the price selected cost margin studies of Collins and Preston.[15]

The Task Force had stated that the evidence showed "a close association between high levels of concentration and persistently high rates of return."[16] None of the studies cited by the Staff Director, however, had examined the *persistence* of high rates of return in concentrated industries. Each had provided a spot correlation showing a weak relationship between concentration and accounting rates of return at a given time. None had looked at the profitability of the same industries at a later time to determine whether the above average rates of return in concentrated industries had persisted.

Since there was no evidence on persistence (or lack of persistence) of above average ("high") rates of return in concentrated industries, I compiled accounting rates of return at a later time in the industries used in the studies cited by the Task Force staff. For each of the samples of industries used by Bain, Mann, and Stigler, later rates of return in concentrated industries turned out to be insignificantly different from those in less concentrated industries.[17]

The correlations between concentration and accounting profits, which were weak in the original studies, deteriorated to insignificance with the passage of time. In the seventeen Bain industries which were more than 60 percent concentrated (four firm), the coefficient of determination dropped from 40 percent for 1936–40 profitability on 1935 concentration ratios to a non–significant 18 percent for 1953–57 profitability. It deteriorated further to 11 percent for 1962–66 profitability. (Bain's 42–industry sample coefficient was 8 percent for 1936–40 profitability on 1935 concentration declining to 1 percent for 1953–57 profitability.) Similarly, Stigler's seventeen–industries' (eleven of which were in the Bain seventeen) coefficient of determination declined from 34 percent for 1953–57 profitability on 1954 concentration to 1 percent for 1962–66 profitability (and a non–significant 17 percent for 1962–66 profitability on 1963 concentration).[18]

The Task Force economists replied saying that the wrong industries had been selected.[19] They thoughtfully provided a list of the appropriate

[15]Joe Bain, "Relation of Profit Rate to Industry Concentration: American Manufacturing, 1936–1940," 65 *Quarterly Journal of Economics* 293 (1951); H. Michael Mann, "Seller Concentration, Barriers to Entry, and Rates of Return in Thirty Industries, 1950–1960," 48 *Review of Economics and Statistics* 296 (1966); George J. Stigler, "A Theory of Oligopoly," 72 *Journal of Political Economy* 44 (1964); Norman R. Collins and Lee Preston, *Concentration and Price–Cost Margins in Manufacturing Industries* (1968).

[16]White House Task Force on Antitrust Policy, Report 1 (in Trade Regulation Report, Supplement to No. 415, May 26, 1969) at I–8.

[17]Yale Brozen, "The Antitrust Task Force Deconcentration Recommendation," 13 *Journal of Law and Economics* 279 (1970).

[18]*Id.* at 287, 289.

[19]P.W. MacAvoy, J.W. McKie and L. Preston, "High and Stable Concentration Levels, Profitability, and Public Policy: A Response," 14 Journal of Law and Economics 493 (1971).

industries where concentration had been persistently high and said persistently high returns would be found in those industries. Examining rates of return for the industries they specified, it was found that rates of return were not even high (significantly above average), much less persistently high.[20]

There was still the puzzling fact that any correlation had been found between concentration and rates of return at any given time in some studies. Since there had been convergence on mean rates of return, it seemed that what had been found was a disequilibrium phenomenon. That is, concentrated industries happened to be earning above equilibrium rates of return which disappeared with the passage of time, as would occur under competitive circumstances. But why had a disproportionate number of concentrated industries been earning above equilibrium rates of return while a disproportionate number of less concentrated industries had been earning below equilibrium returns?

Since Bain had used only forty-two out of 340 industries in the 1935 Census of Manufacturers to test for differences in rates of return between more and less concentrated industries, it was possible that his result was the consequence of the non-representativeness of his sample. Also, each of his industries was represented by only a few firms (three or more). Those he chose might have been non-representative of their industries.

In order to test whether Bain's forty-two industries are representative, an enlarged sample of ninety-eight industries (including Bain's forty-two) has been assembled (Appendix Tables 1 and 2). Industries for which less than three firms could be found were omitted (Appendix Tables 1A and 2A). In a few instances, rates of return computed by Bain have been recomputed using a larger number of firms (Appendix Table 3).

The results are strikingly opposed to those found in Bain's smaller sample. Where he found that the accounting profitability of concentrated industries was 4.4 percentage points *greater* than that of the less concentrated industries, the ninety-eight industry sample shows profitability to be *less* (insignificantly) in the concentrated industries (Table 1). There is no greater proportion of concentrated industries at above equilibrium rates of return than of less concentrated industries (see Appendix). No disequilibrium explanation is needed to account for a higher average rate of return in concentrated industries. There is no higher average rate of return in concentrated industries.

There remain the Mann and Stigler findings using post-World War II data, to be explained. If competition is prevalent in concentrated industries, as is indicated by the convergence of rates of return on the average, why did Professors Mann and Stigler find a correlation at any given point in time between accounting profitability and concentration? Again, the nonrepresentativeness of their small samples apparently accounts for their findings.

[20]Yale Brozen, "The Persistence of 'High Rates of Return' in High Stable Concentration Industries," 14 *Journal of Law and Economics* 501 (1971).

TABLE 1

Average of Industry Average Profit Rates Within Concentration Deciles
(42 and 98 Industries)

1936–1940

Concentration Range Per cent of Value Product Supplied by Eight Firms (1935)	42 Industry Sample		98 Industry Sample	
	Number of Industries	Avg. of Industry Profit Rates[a] 1936–1940	Number of Industries	Avg. of Industry Profit Rates[a] 1936–1940
a	b	c	d	e
90–100	8	12.7%	14	10.0%
80–89.9	10	9.8	14	9.7
70–79.9	3	16.3	10	11.9
60–69.9	5	5.8	11	8.2
50–59.9	4	5.8	6	14.8
40–49.9	3	8.6	10	9.5
30–39.9	5	6.3	16	10.4
20–29.9	2	10.4	9	12.0
10–19.9	1	17.0	5	13.4
0–9.9	1	9.1	3	7.6
0–100	42	9.6	98	10.5
70–100	21	11.8	38	10.4
0–70	21	7.5	60	10.6
Difference		4.4		–0.2

Sources: Columns a, b, and c from Joe S. Bain, "Relation of Profit Rate to Industry Concentration: American Manufacturing, 1936–40," 64 *Q.J. Econ.* 313 (1951), is corrected in Corrigendum, 64 *Q.J. Econ.* 602 (1951). Columns d and e from Appendix Tables 1 and 2.

[a] Average of net profits after income taxes as percentage of net worth.

Professor James Ellert has examined the post–World War II data using larger samples of industries. He is unable to find a dichotomous relationship. Using 141 industries with 565 firms he finds no significant difference between more and less concentrated industries in any post–war period. What differences there are frequently have the wrong sign.[21]

Professor Ellert also examined the high stable concentration group of industries. His findings agree with mine. That is, the rate of return in the high stable group is not high, much less persistently high.

A most interesting finding that emerged from a study of Bain's data was the relationship between rates of return in the Big 4 in the industries he

---

[21] James Ellert, "Industrial Concentration, Market Disequilibrium and the Convergence Pattern in Industry Rates of Return." Unpublished paper presented before the Industrial Organization Workshop, University of Chicago, January 27, 1972.

selected for his book on barriers to competition[22] and other firms in those industries. Where the Big 4 showed higher accounting rates of return than smaller firms, they tended to grow more rapidly than their industries. Such behavior is to be expected if the Big 4 behave competitively and we can take intra-industry comparisons of accounting rates of return seriously. Where the Big 4 showed lower accounting rates of return than smaller firms, they tended to grow less rapidly than their industries and concentration tended to decrease.[23]

This would seem to indicate that relatively high rates of return in manufacturing are manifestations of relative efficiency, if we can generalize from the inadequate sample of industries and firms provided by Bain. Resources flow from less efficient to more efficient firms. Manufacturing industry structure moves over time toward that dictated by an efficient allocation of resources.[24] Persistent high concentration, where it is found, is a consequence of the economies of scale or the relative efficiency of specific managerial groups.[25] Mandatory deconcentration would cause a loss of efficiency with no gain in the competitiveness of the economy.[26]

---

[22]J.S. Bain, *Barriers to New Competition* 195 (1956).

[23]Y. Brozen, "Concentration and Structural and Market Disequilibrium," 16 *Antitrust Bulletin* 241 (1971).

[24]Harold Demsetz, "Industry Structure, Market Rivalry, and Public Policy," 16 *Journal of Law and Economics* 1 (1973). H. Demsetz, The Market Concentration Doctrine (1973).

[25]Horizontal mergers of large groups of firms may overconcentrate an industry for efficient operation, as appears to have been the ease in the turn of the century merger wave. However, such overconcentration appears to be a *temporary* phenomenon, judging by the experience of these amalgamations. Of those merging a majority of the capacity in their industries, 40.4 percent failed and 6.4 percent went through voluntary financial reorganization. [Shaw Livermore, "The Success of Industrial Mergers," 50 *Quarterly Journal of Economics* 75 (1935–36).]

Of those which escaped this fate, most appear to have lost market share rather quickly. Of the few who lost market share slowly, some were broken up by dissolution decrees. However, even these were dropping in share before they were dissolved. American Tobacco, formed in 1890 with 91 percent of the cigarette market, declined to 83.6 percent in 1893. It acquired additional companies in 1894 and 1895 which brought it back to 85.6 percent of the market, but then dropped to 80.9 percent in 1896. Continued acquisitions brought it back to 93 percent in 1899. This position faded rather quickly to 75.9 percent in 1903. [U.S. Bureau of Corporations, *Report of the Commissioner on the Tobacco Industries* 329 (1909).] Similarly, Standard Oil's share of market declined from 88.15 percent in 1899 to 83.88 percent in 1904 to 67.10 percent in 1909 despite acquisitions during this period [Ralph W. and Muriel E. Hidy, *Pioneering in Big Business* (1955) for data on Standard's crude runs to stills. U.S. Census of Manufactures, 1919, 757, cited in H.F. Williamson, R.L. Andreano, A.R. Daum, and G.C. Klose, *The American Petroleum Industry* 111 (1963) for data on U.S. crude runs to stills.]

[26]Richard Posner indicates that limits on market share above which mandatory deconcentration would be applied would result in *less* competitive behavior. "The threat of dissolution may. . . have a serious disincentive effect. Firms may hold back from expanding sales to the point at which they would become subject to dissolution under the statute, even if they are more efficient than their competitors." "Oligopoly and the Antitrust Laws: A Suggested Approach," 21 *Stanford Law Review* 1562 (1969).

Appendix

Bain's 42–Industry Sample and the 98–Industry Sample

Bain's sample contained fourteen concentrated industries (out of twenty-one) showing an accounting return greater than the sample average. The majority (67 percent) of his concentrated industries were earning above equilibrium (sample average) rates of return (if we can assume that accounting biases did not differentially affect rates of return). The ninety–eight–industry sample contains seventeen concentrated industries (out of thirty–eight) showing an accounting rate of return greater than the sample average (Appendix Table 1). In contrast to Bain's 67 percent, only 45 percent of the concentrated industries in the enlarged sample earned above equilibrium (sample average) rates of return. This is in the range we can expect by chance. It is the same proportion (43 percent) as that found in the less concentrated portion of the ninety–eight–industry sample (Appendix Table 2). In Bain's sample of less concentrated industries, only three (14 percent) earned above sample average rates of return.

In the ninety-eight-industry sample, there is not a disproportionate number of concentrated industries earning more than the sample average. Neither is there a disproportionate number of less concentrated industries earning less than the sample average. There are no differences to explain. The distribution is about as might be expected under competitive circumstances, confirming the finding that the behavior of rates of return in Bain's sample of industries over time indicates competitive circumstances in both concentrated and less concentrated industries.

Business Behavior and the Consumer Interest: Some Rudiments of Theory

Robert H. Bork

Antitrust is about the effects of business behavior on consumers. An understanding of the relationship of that behavior to consumer well–being can be gained only through basic economic theory. The economic models involved are essential to all antitrust analysis, but they are simple and require no previous acquaintance with economics to be comprehended. Indeed, since we can hardly expect legislators, judges, and lawyers to be sophisticated economists as well, it is only the fact that the simple ideas of economics are powerful and entirely adequate to this field that makes it conceivable for the law to frame and implement useful policy.

Consumer welfare is greatest when society's economic resources are allocated so that consumers are able to satisfy their wants as fully as technological constraints permit. Consumer welfare, in this sense, is merely another term for the wealth of the nation. Antitrust thus has a built–in preference for material prosperity, but it has nothing to say about the ways prosperity is distributed or used. Those are matters for other laws. Consumer welfare, as the term is used in antitrust, has no sumptuary or ethical component, but permits consumers to define by their expression of wants in the marketplace what things they regard as wealth. Antitrust litigation is not a process for deciding who should be rich or poor, nor can it decide how much wealth should be expanded to reduce pollution or undertake to mitigate the anguish of the cross–country skier at the desecration wrought by snowmobiles. It can only increase collective wealth by requiring that any lawful products, whether skis or snowmobiles, be produced and sold under conditions most favorable to consumers.

The role of the antitrust laws, then, lies at that stage of the economic process in which production and distribution of goods and services are organized in accordance with the scale of values that consumers choose by their relative willingness to purchase. The law's mission is to preserve, improve, and reinforce the powerful economic mechanisms that compel businesses to respond to consumers. "From a social point of view," as Frank H. Knight puts it, "this process may be viewed under two aspects, (a) the assignment or *allocation* of the available productive forces and materials among the various lines of industry, and (b) the effective *coordination* of the various means of production in each industry into such groupings as will produce the greatest result."[1]

From the Antitrust Paradox *A Policy At War With Itself,* by Robert H. Bork. Copyright ©1978 by Basic Books, Inc. Reprinted by permission of Basic Books, Inc., publishers, New York.
[1]Knight, The Economic Organization (University of Chicago Press, 1933), p. 9.

These two factors may conveniently be called *allocative* efficiency and *productive efficiency*.* (When, for convenience, the word "efficiency" alone is used, productive efficiency is meant). These two types of efficiency make up the overall efficiency that determines the level of our society's wealth, or consumer welfare. The whole task of antitrust can be summed up as the effort to improve allocative efficiency without impairing productive efficiency so greatly as to produce either no gain or a net loss in consumer welfare. The task must be guided by basic economic analysis, otherwise the law acts blindly upon forces it does not understand and produces results it does not intend.

The Nature of Allocative Efficiency

Both economics and law generally link business behavior to consumer welfare through the concepts of "competition" and "monopoly." But the two disciplines mean quite different things by those terms, and when the differences go unremarked—or, worse, when various common-speech meanings are inserted without notice—debate grows more and more heated and less and less illuminating. The economist's models of competition and monopoly are descriptive. The lawyer's, if he thinks of antitrust as designed to preserve competition and destroy monopoly, must be normative. There is a wide gap in practical consequences. The economist builds a pure model in order to clarify thought; such models are indispensable starting places for policy analysis, but they are not prescriptions for policy. They leave out too much. A determined attempt to remake the American economy into a replica of the textbook model of competition would have roughly the same effect on national wealth as several dozen strategically placed nuclear explosions. To say that is not to denigrate the models but to warn against their misuse.

An understanding of the efficient allocation of resources, and hence of the evils of misallocation, is best attained through simple models of firm behavior under differing market structures. I will sketch the most basic aspects of the conventional theories of competition, monopoly, and oligopoly. Each of these terms describes an industry structure. Economic theory attempts to relate structure to performance, and performance to the goal of consumer welfare. The theories are listed in descending order or rigor. The theory of competition states the way in which firms *must* behave if they are to survive when the market is competitively structured. The theory of monopoly states the way in which a firm possessing control of a market *can* behave in order to maximize profits. Conventional oligopoly theory, however, is little more than a guess about the ways in which firms might be able to behave in a market composed of a few sellers.

---

*It is important that the distinction be very clear. Allocative efficiency, as used here, refers to the placement of resources in the economy, the question of whether resources are employed in tasks where consumers value their output most. Productive efficiency refers to the effective use of resources by particular firms. The idea of effective use, as we shall see, encompasses much more than mere technical or plant-level efficiency.

Competition

The operation of pure competition may be illustrated by an imaginary widget industry (widgets are the customary product of hypothetical industries) composed of 100 firms of equal size making a uniform product, which is sold to 1,000 well-informed purchasers. Under these conditions—as under a wide range of conditions we need not stop to argue about now—no company would have power significantly to affect the market price for widgets because both its output and the variations in its output would be trivial with respect to total industry output. The demand for the output of any individual manufacturer would then be perfectly elastic, which is just a way of saying that any manufacturer who quoted a price above the prevailing market price would make zero sales, since every purchaser would turn to another supplier. Any manufacturer who quoted a price below market would be offered all the business, but for reasons that will become apparent, he would not want it and could not afford to take it.

The demand faced by the individual manufacturer in a completely competitive industry is reflected in Figure 1 by a price line drawn flat to indicate that he will face the same market price no matter how he adjusts his own rate of output. Another way of saying this is that in a completely competitive industry the individual firm's marginal revenue (the revenue added by selling one more unit) is always the same as the market price. This is an extreme statement, since it may be that all sellers can affect market price somewhat, but it is conventional to ignore very small effects and to draw the individual firm's demand curve flat in fragmented markets.

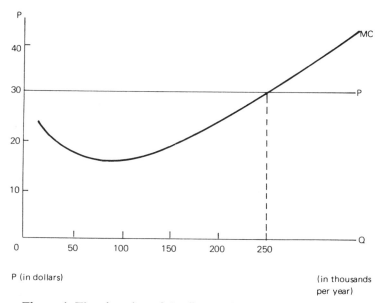

P (in dollars)

(in thousands per year)

Figure 1. The situation of the firm under pure competition.

Our hypothetical widget manufacturer also lacks short-run control over the costs of making his product. Costs are presented to him as brute facts of life in the prices of labor, raw materials, machinery, electricity, and so forth. His existing method of coordinating these factors of production determines his costs, and he cannot alter costs until he finds a better method of coordination, that is, a better method of production or distribution. He does, however, have power to affect one species of costs, those that vary with his rate of output. By changing his rate of output he can change his marginal cost (the cost, starting at any specified rate of output, of producing one more widget in the period of time under discussion). Thus, if he is producing 5,000 widgets per week, his marginal cost is the additional cost he would incur by increasing the rate to 5,001. This is important to the manufacturer, for though he cannot change market price or basic cost determinants, he can alter his rate of output and so choose the marginal cost associated with the new rate.

The manufacturer may or may not be completely aware of these facts, but in adjusting his rate of output until he arrives at the profit-maximizing solution, he will, whether he thinks of it that way or not, be working up and down his marginal cost curve.* The profit-maximizing solution may be described for all sellers, whether competitors or monopolists, as the rate of output at which marginal cost is equal to marginal revenue. For the competitor alone, however, marginal revenue is equal to market price.

That profits are maximized by equating marginal cost and marginal revenue (or price) is simply shown: if the firm produces one more widget, the marginal cost will be greater than the marginal revenue and the extra widget is sold at a loss; if it produces one less, marginal cost is less than marginal revenue, and the firm is failing to pick up profitable business. (Marginal cost includes normal return, so there is a profit when marginal cost equals marginal revenue.) In the explanation that follows, the distinction between the state of affairs in the short run and in the long run is not made, both because it is unnecessary to the analysis and because, given the dynamism of the market process, it is quite unlikely that the long-run result of the textbooks is often approached.

Let us assume that the individual widget manufacturer equates marginal costs and marginal revenue (price) at an output of 250,000 units per year, and that market price is $30 per widget. The firm's position may then be represented as in Figure 1. The graph makes it easy to see why marginal costs are always rising at the rate of output chosen by any competitive firm. We infer a

---

*Costs are, of course, affected by factors other than the rate of output. Absolute volume of output has important effects. See Armen A. Alchian, "Costs and Outputs," in *The Allocation of Economic Resources*, by Moses Abramovitz et al. (Stanford University Press, 1959). Increasing the rate of output tends to increase costs, while an increase of absolute volume, without an increase in rate, tends to decrease costs. Such complications are not, however, essential at the moment. The important fact is that marginal costs do rise at some point and that the firm operates at a point where they are rising. It is convenient here to speak of output rate as the determining factor, though the existence of other factors will become relevant in particular contexts.

rising cost curve from the existence of more than one firm, since if marginal costs were level or declining, the firm would continually increase its rate of output until it occupied the entire industry.

All of this has a clarity and precision that is spurious in one sense and quite real and useful in another. The clarity and precision are spurious if one is so misled as to conclude that the widget maker has a chart like this on the wall and has only to read off the correct output to earn his profit for the week. He has no such exact information and cannot, for a variety of reasons, including the imprecise nature of cost information and constant changes in both costs and demand. In fact, the analysis here is not even intended to represent the mental processes of businessmen.

The chart may mislead in other ways as well. It focuses attention exclusively on the price and cost aspects of competition, though competition in product characteristics is equally important. Moreover, the chart suggests a static situation, while the reality is one of shifting prices and costs, changing technologies and organizational structures, and attempts to alter and improve products, so that it is most unlikely that price equals marginal cost for long in most industries. Market rivalry is a much more complex and progressive process than can be represented on any chart. Fatal errors in analysis are easily made when the limitations of the diagram are forgotten.

The clarity and precision of the analysis are both valid and useful, however, when the model is understood to be a statement of the limiting condition of tendencies we know to be at work. Regardless of the ways in which management may choose to think about or to explain its decision making (and the explanations can be marvels of empty, public–relations–style prose), the model represents the ultimate situation toward which economic forces tend to drive the firm. The model, that is to say, resembles an equation showing how chemicals tend to combine, not a statement of the psychological predisposition of chemicals or an assertion that there are never factors that impede the reaction. Firms that achieve a poorer approximation of the ideal will have a lower rate of return and will, sooner or later, run short of capital: they must improve or die. This mechanism would work even if management decisions were made by flipping coins, though we do have the additional reassuring factor that men, unlike chemicals, generally prefer to succeed and will seek the solution to the economic equation that ensures their prosperity. Under the conditions hypothesized for the widget industry, we could predict with confidence that firms would arrive precisely at the solution shown here. Under more realistic conditions, with continual change and incomplete information built into the model, no firm might ever reach the ideal solution; firms would then thrive or decline according to the nearness of their approach. The model predicts the tendencies of business behavior, which is all that is possible and all that we need.

Public policy, however, is interested in the performance of the widget industry as a whole. For this analysis we require a new graph (see Figure 2).

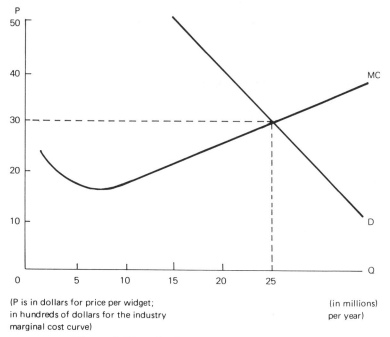

(P is in dollars for price per widget;   (in millions)
in hundreds of dollars for the industry   per year)
marginal cost curve)

**Figure 2. Hypothetical output and price for an
entire industry under pure competition.**

The demand curve facing the individual manufacturer is flat (perfectly elastic) because the widgets of 99 other manufacturers are perfect substitutes for his. There are no perfect substitutes for widgets as a commodity, however, and the demand curve for all widgets will display some inelasticity, sloping down and to the right to indicate that as price declines more widgets are demanded. It is an axiom of price theory that, other things being held constant, more units of a product can be sold only by lowering the price; conversely, if fewer units are offered, the price will be bid up. That is the relationship symbolized by the sloping demand curve D. (The demand curve is drawn as a straight line only to simplify the arithmetic.) The industry marginal cost curve is arrived at by summing the marginal costs of the 100 identical firms that constitute the industry. (This ignores, as an unnecessary complication, the possibility that changes in industry output may affect the prices of input factors and so give an industry supply curve different from the sum of the individual firms' marginal cost curves.) The graph reflects the fact that the efforts of all firms to maximize their profits result in an industry output of 25 million widgets per year at a price of $30 each.

This solution is not merely "correct" for the industry but also for consumers. The forces of competition have balanced social desires and costs through the intermediary of the widget industry. The demand curve expresses the amounts that consumers are willing to pay for widgets as against all other uses of their purchasing power; it expresses, at all prices shown, their desire for widgets at different prices relative to their desire for all other things the market has to offer: automobiles, bubble gum, education, sweet potatoes, whiskey, medical services, ski lessons, or what have you. The demand curve thus expresses a social ranking of wants. Similarly, the marginal cost curve expresses the cost not merely to the firm or the industry but to the society of producing widgets. We are talking here about real costs, not historical costs or bookkeeping costs, and the cost of using a unit of a resource is the maximum amount that unit could earn elsewhere. Real costs are thus forgone alternatives or opportunities, and so they are often called alternative or opportunity costs. These are brought home to the widget maker through the price he must pay for factors of production. If he must pay $50 for a ton of steel, that is the price of bidding that ton away from alternative uses. And his cost is also the real cost to society, because the ton of steel was valued in the alternative use at $50. Thus, when the widget firm and the widget industry equate demand and marginal cost, they also equate social desire and social cost. The closer the members of the industry come to maximizing their profits, the closer they come to maximizing the welfare of consumers.

This process goes on not only within firms and industries but also between industries. Should the automobile industry experience an increased demand and bid up the price for steel, that higher price will be reflected in the marginal cost of the widget industry. In Figure 2 a higher marginal cost curve would mean a new intersection with demand to the left of and higher than the old intersection, hence a lower rate of output and a higher price. This situation represents a new equilibrium in which production has adjusted to take account of a change in competing consumer desires.

Processes of this sort go on endlessly in the economy. Resources are combined and separated, shuffled and reshuffled, in the endless pursuit of greater net revenues by persons who own resources and persons who employ them. Each productive resource tends to move to that employment where the value of its marginal product (the sum of money added to the firm's net receipts by the employment of an additional unit of the input or resource per unit of time), and hence the return paid to it, is greatest. If equilibrium were ever reached, the value of marginal product would be the same in all employments—which is the same as saying that the price put upon the resource by consumers would be the same in all its possible uses—and the distribution of resources would be ideal. Output, as measured by consumer valuation, would then be maximized, since there would be no possible rearrangement of resources that could increase the value to consumers of the economy's total output.

This condition has never been and can never be achieved. Changing wants and technologies are in themselves sufficient to prevent the attainment of such an equilibrium. But the forces of competition in open markets cause the actual allocation of resources to be ever shifting in pursuit of the constantly moving equilibrium point. And the more closely the economy approximates this limiting condition, the more closely do we approach the maximization of consumer welfare. Indeed, the best practicable approximation to the limiting condition can realistically be called the maximization of consumer welfare.

Monopoly

We are now in a position to understand the case against monopoly. As we shall see, it is not an absolute case, for though monopoly may interfere with allocative efficiency, it may also rest upon productive efficiency. Whether a particular monopoly is, on balance, beneficial or detrimental to consumer welfare must take both types of efficiency into account. Later on, we shall see how that is done. For the moment, remember that the case made here is entirely in terms of allocative efficiency and is therefore one-sided.

Suppose that our hypothetical 100 widget manufacturers either merge into a single corporation or simply meet and agree to place the power to make output decisions for all firms in a central industry committee. Let us suppose also that neither course of action produces any change in costs. We would have, in one case, a monopolistic horizontal merger or, in the other, a cartel. In either case, the new management would have control of 100 percent of widget output. The new monopolist, whether corporation or committee (I will no longer distinguish, the principles being the same), will perceive at once that its output decisions do affect market price. Since the monopolist is the entire industry, it faces the sloping industry demand curve rather than the competitive firm's flat demand curve. More important, the monopolist does not maximize profits by continuing to run along at the old output rate of 25 million widgets annually. The reason is simple. For the competitor, marginal revenue was always the same at any output rate and always equaled market price. But for the monopolist, marginal revenue is always less than market price because his demand curve slopes. Should he decide to offer an additional 1 million widgets per year, the demand curve shows that he would have to accept a lower price, and the crucial point is that the lower price would apply not just to the additional million but to all his output. He would get less for the first 25 million widgets as well as for the additional million. The additional output has a drag effect upon his marginal revenues all the way along the line. The difference that a sloping demand curve makes is a matter of simple arithmetic, as shown by Table 1.

TABLE 1
Effect of Monopoly on Total and Marginal Revenues

Rate of output (Q) (in millions)	Price (P)	Total revenue (in millions)	Marginal revenue (in millions)
10	60	600	—
11	58	638	38
12	56	672	34
13	54	702	30
14	52	728	26
15	50	750	22
16	48	768	18
17	46	782	14
18	44	792	10
19	42	798	6
20	40	800	2
21	38	798	-2
22	36	792	-6
23	34	782	-10
24	32	768	-14
25	30	750	-18

Now the widget monopolist, like the widget competitor and all business-men under any circumstances, maximizes profits by producing at a rate where marginal cost equals marginal revenue. As may be seen from Figure 3, the intersection of marginal cost and marginal revenue is well to the left of the intersection of marginal cost and demand.

This means that the monopolist will find it profitable to produce fewer widgets annually than did the same industry when competitively structured. This cutback in the rate of production and sale is what economists call a "restriction of output." Here, the lowered rate is 15 million widgets annually. Fewer widgets on the market, the demand curve informs us, means that purchasers will bid a higher price for what is available, in this case $50 each. (Perhaps it should be stressed again that these graphs and the table are not intended to be typical except in the sense that they show the directions, though not the magnitudes, of movements in price and output when competition is converted to monopoly.)

But the higher price is not the root of the problem, nor is the lower output. Many unobjectionable developments could produce these. An increased demand for housing, and hence for steel, could have made the raw material for widgets more expensive, raising the marginal cost curve, so that even a competitive widget industry might have cut back to an annual production of 15 million, with a resulting $50 widget price. The distinctive feature of the monopoly situation is that the monopolist has created a gap between marginal cost and price, which means that social costs and social desires are no longer equated. Indeed, the monopolist has made his monopoly profit by creating an imbalance between cost and desire. With the restriction in output, moreover, the widget industry no longer needs as many resources as before. The unneeded resources must either lie idle, an obvious social waste, or migrate to other industries where the value of their marginal product will be less than it would be in the monopolized widget industry. The result, of course, is that they contribute less wealth as consumers define wealth, so that consumers would be better off if these resources could return to making widgets.

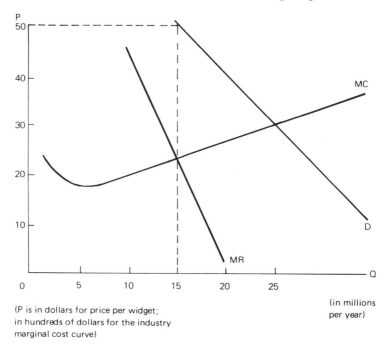

(P is in dollars for price per widget; in hundreds of dollars for the industry marginal cost curve)

(in millions per year)

Figure 3. Hypothetical marginal cost, marginal revenue, and demand curves for a monopoly.

This is the mechanism by which restriction of output, made possible by monopolistic merger or cartel or any other means of controlling the market, creates a misallocation of resources and thereby makes society poorer. The evil of monopoly, then, is not higher prices or smaller production (though these are its concomitants) but misallocated resources, or allocation inefficiency.

It is a common misconception that a monopolist's increased efficiency redounds only to the monopolist's benefit. Figure 3 should dispel that notion. If marginal cost is lowered, the intersection with marginal revenue moves to the right, indicating a larger output and a lowered price. That benefits consumers as well as the monopolist.

One important caveat should be stated here. As the monopolist pushes the price of widgets higher, consumers may suddenly switch to a product that was not considered a substitute at lower prices. That is to say, the demand curve may suddenly approach the horizontal at some point. If this occurred at a price of $40 per widget, for example, the monopolist would not misallocate resources to the same extent as supposed here. This limitation may often be important and, as will be discussed, is probably important in the case of monopoly gained by superior efficiency.

Oligopoly

Almost none of the markets with which antitrust law must deal resemble the atomized or monopolistic models just outlined. For the vast majority of actual markets, therefore, we may not automatically assume that business behavior has the effect upon resource allocation predicted by either model. To this intermediate range of market structures has been applied the theory of oligopoly, which attempts to predict the behavior of firms in markets where rivals are "few." The lack of rigor in that theory may be suggested by the observation that there appear to be about as many oligopoly theories as there are economists who have written on the subject. In fact, it is a most unsatisfactory branch of economic theory, and as I will attempt to show in Chapter 8, there is no very good reason to think that so-called "concentrated" markets behave in a less satisfactory manner than more fragmented ones.

The dominant, but by no means universal, opinion among economists and antitrust commentators holds that markets with few rivals (there is very little agreement as to how many firms may still be "few" enough for the theory to apply) will perform poorly because the firms will, without overt agreement, recognize their mutual self-interest and restrict output in order to behave, so far as possible, as if they had formed an actual cartel.

Now in their desire to achieve cartel results, though without collusion, the firms in a concentrated industry differ not at all from those in a fragmented industry. Rather, it is their ability that differs; this, the theory holds, is chiefly a matter of numbers and the effect of individual firm behavior on the market. The 100 widget manufacturers of our hypothetical competitive industry know as well as any economist that they would make more money if they could all restrict output and take higher prices. If businessmen did not know this principle, they would not form cartels. Being barred by law from agreeing explicitly, they would like to get the same results by each behaving as if he were in a cartel. That is, mutual forbearance in rivalry could approach a situation in which industry marginal cost and industry marginal revenue are equated, so that each firm takes 1 percent of a monopoly profit instead of 1 percent of a lower competitive return. No one thinks that will happen in a fragmented industry, for a variety of reasons: each firm will be severely tempted to take more sales at the higher price, letting the others make the sacrifice of holding price up by holding back on sales; costs will differ, so that the firms will not arrive at the same judgment as to the most profitable price; costs and demand will change, increasing the probability of differing responses; and so on.

But the situation is thought by many persons to be different if the industry becomes concentrated. Suppose that in the fragmented widget industry, over time, some firms grow and others decline, many leaving the industry altogether, so that eventually there remain only four firms. One of these has 50 percent of actual sales, another 30, a third 15, and the fourth is struggling somewhat at 5 percent. Almost all economists would describe such an industry as "oligopolistic" or "concentrated," and perhaps most would predict that its structure would cause it to behave noncompetitively. The basis for that prediction is the concept of *oligopolistic interdependence*. Each firm is aware that its price and output decisions are no longer insignificant with respect to total industry price and output. Sellers no longer face an impersonal market price but one they can, to a greater or lesser degree, affect.

This much is true. If the 50 percent firm, which, let us suppose, now makes 12,500,000 widgets annually, expanded its output by 10 percent, perhaps because it lowered its costs, to 13,750,000 widgets per year, the market price would drop initially from $30 to under $28 per widget. If the other firms adjusted by reducing output to equate marginal cost with the new price, the price would rise somewhat and after a series of adjustments would settle down perhaps above $28 but below $30. The point of all this is that the widget makers would be aware of their power over price and might separately decide to try raising it. The 50 percent firm might begin by announcing a new $35 widget price. If the others did not follow, the higher price would not last long. The theory supposes, however, that the 30 percent firm's management will realize that undercutting the largest firm is short-sighted, since that firm will drop its price and all firms will be back where they began. Why not follow the price up? If the other two firms reason similarly, all will be getting $35, a price above the competitive level, though not at the monopoly level. By such a process the rivals may work themselves up to the monopoly price (and the restricted output necessary to raise the price), jointly maximizing their profits, without ever once meeting surreptitiously at a country club or leaving the tell tale evidence of long-distance calls to one another in the telephone company's records.

Devotees of oligopoly theory rarely claim that businesses' maneuvers and reactions will be adroit enough for the oligopolists to arrive at the monopoly output and price that a single firm occupying the entire industry would choose. Changing conditions of demand and technology will continually alter the profit–maximizing solution, and four firms are most unlikely to read an uncertain and fluid situation in an identical way. When costs differ, as they always do, the best price and degree of restriction will differ for each firm, making tacit cooperation still more difficult. When products are not identical, and particularly when product descriptions change, so that prices must vary, yet another unsettling factor is introduced. Moreover, there will always be a temptation to "cheat," to pick up a very profitable piece of extra business with a small price cut. Purchasers can play sellers against each other to break down the oligopoly price.

It will be urged, however, that the theory does not demand perfect formation flying. If oligopolists cannot achieve the complete monopoly solution, that does not mean they will necessarily arrive at the complete competitive solution with prices at marginal cost. No, it does not. But nothing in the theory compels the conclusion that oligopolists do not behave as competitors. The whole thing is speculation about how firms may or may not be able to behave. The theory has nothing like the definiteness and rigor of the theories of competition and monopoly. We will examine it more closely and attempt to gauge its usefulness for antitrust policy in Chapter 8.

The models described so far constitute the rudiments of the theory of allocative efficiency. So far as consumer welfare is concerned, they are only half the story. We turn next to the other half.

The Nature of Productive Efficiency

Productive efficiency is a simple, indispensable, and thoroughly misunderstood concept. Not one antitrust lawyer in ten has a remotely satisfactory idea of the subject, and the proportion of economists who do, though surely higher, is perhaps not dramatically so. The situation has deteriorated so badly that one can hear it hotly denied that efficiency has anything to do with antitrust. There even appears to be an impression among the more zealous antitrust enforcers that efficiency does not exist but is some sort of trick thought up by unscrupulous defense attorneys. Yet, as Frank Knight points out, this form of efficiency is one of the two that enter into the organization of production to meet consumer preferences, and it follows that antitrust policy cannot be rational unless productive efficiency is understood and weighed in the law's processes.

Productive efficiency is any activity by a business firm that creates wealth. The concept is symmetrical with that of allocative efficiency. Productive efficiency, like allocative efficiency, is a normative concept and is defined and measured in terms of consumer welfare. Since a free market system assumes that consumers define their own welfare, it follows that productive efficiency consists in offering anything, whether products or services, that consumers are willing to pay for. (The caveat that the goods or services concerned must not be ones that society outlaws for other reasons—addictive drugs or prostitution, for example, is obvious.) The relative efficiency of firms is therefore measured by their relative success in the market.*

Attention must be focused on this definition of productive efficiency rather than on the wide variety of factors that contribute to it. Economies of scale, specialization of function, ability to obtain capital, management skill—all of these and many more are elements that contribute to the firm's ability to please consumers, but they are causes rather than manifestations of efficiency. Efficiency is at bottom a value concept, not a description of mechanical or engineering operation. As Knight points out:

---

*Exceptions to this will be discussed later, particularly in connection with the theory of predatory practices in Chapter 7.

There is a common misconception that it is possible to measure or discuss efficiency in purely physical terms. The first principles of physics or engineering science teach that this is not true, that the term efficiency involves the idea of value, and some measure of value as well. It is perhaps the most important principle of physical science that neither matter nor energy can be created or destroyed, that whatever goes into any process must come out in some form, and hence as a mere matter of physical quantity, the efficiency of all operations would equal one hundred per cent. The correct definition of efficiency is the ratio, not between "output" and "input" but between useful output and total output or input. Hence efficiency, even in the simplest energy transformation, is meaningless without a measure of usefullness or value. In any attempt to understand economic efficiency, the notion of value is more obviously crucial since most economic problems are concerned with a number of kinds both of outlay and of return, and there is no conceivable way of making comparisons without first reducing all the factors to terms of a common measure.[2]

In antitrust the required common denominator is provided by the goal or value of consumer welfare. In a system which permits consumers to define their own welfare by their purchases, it follows, that, with an important reservation to be mentioned shortly, a firm's efficiency is shown by its success. It is useless, for antitrust purposes, to study the minimum efficient size of the firm by studying the engineering efficiencies of the plant and production line because the important factor is consumer response to what comes off the production line. (This subject is taken up at greater length in Chapter 6 in connection with proposals to make efficiency an explicit defense in antitrust litigation.)

Considerations such as these, perhaps, led George Stigler to define efficiency simply as "competitive effectiveness." That will do as well as any other brief definition, but it must be remembered that competitive effectiveness or productive efficiency is not a concept coterminous with profitability. A firm may be profitable because it forms a cartel, merges to monopolistic size, or employs predatory tactics successfully. Profitability based upon such tactics is not evidence of productive efficiency because consumer welfare is lessened rather than increased. Profitability in such cases is based upon the disruption of allocative efficiency rather than the enhancement of productive efficiency. The methods of distinguishing efficiency from mere profitability are discussed in Chapter 6, and their application takes up much of the remainder of this book.

It may be objected that I have created a false dichotomy by assuming that the effects of business behavior are always classifiable with respect to allocative efficiency or productive efficiency. There are other problems in the world; among them are income distribution, externalities, and the purchase of goods

---

[2]*Id.* at 8.

that society does not want consumers to have. Quite right. If it were asserted that all of society's concerns with business behavior can be summed up as the effect on allocative and productive efficiency, the dichotomy would be false. The claim, however, is only that the dichotomy is proper for the specialized purposes of antitrust law. The classification is not merely proper, for we shall see in Chapter 6 that it is essential to reasoning about antitrust.

This definition of productive efficiency—competitive effectiveness— must necessarily be left without more content at this stage. As we go along we shall see in a variety of contexts some of the elements that go to produce efficiency.

THE METHOD OF ANTITRUST ANALYSIS

To read antitrust literature or to participate in the numerous conferences convened to discuss policy is to become convinced that antitrust is less a discipline than a buzzing confusion of unrelated opinion. Even agreement on conclusions is usually superficial, papering over fundamental disagreement about reasons. One cause of this eminently unsatisfactory state of affairs lies in a failure to focus and settle the question of the form of reasoning, or argument, proper to the subject matter.

The mode of correct antitrust analysis is determined by the strengths and weaknesses of price theory. Once these are understood and respected, we should achieve greater agreement on substantive issues.

This chapter will advance several related propositions.

First, price theory assures us that economic behavior is not random but is primarily directed toward the maximization of profits.

Second, attempts to maximize profits can stand in only three relationships with respect to consumer welfare. Economic behavior is primarily efficiency creating, primarily output restricting, or neutral in its consumer welfare impact.

Third, price theory enables us to identify, with acceptable degree of accuracy, those activities whose primary effect is output restricting, leading to the inference that all other activity is either efficiency creating or neutral.

Fourth, antitrust must avoid any standards that require direct measurement and quantification of either restriction of output or efficiency. Such tasks are impossible.

Finally, in all cases in which behavior is neutral or in which analysis does not provide a basis for predicting effects upon consumer welfare, tie-breaking considerations indicate that the law should not intervene.

The Relation between Price Theory and Antitrust

The basic assumptions and doctrines of conventional price theory will be used throughout this book. To those who object that economics is not a sufficiently certain discipline upon which to rest major policy conclusions, the answer given here is not (though it could be) that they misunderstand the nature and strength of the theory, but rather that such reliance is inevitable. There is no body of knowledge other than conventional price theory that can serve as a guide to the effects of business behavior upon consumer welfare. To abandon economic theory is to abandon the possibility of a rational antitrust law.

Since the argument of this book will disagree rather strongly with some economists, it had better be explained that such disagreement does not of itself contradict my claim to rely upon basic economic postulates. The layman is likely to think that economic theory is what any economist theorizes, but of course it is not. If it were, we should have to believe that there are dozens or hundreds of mutually incompatible versions of economic theory, each as good as any other. Basic economic theory is an intensely logical subject, and much of it consists of a drawing out of the implications of a few empirically supported postulates. When I speak of economic theory, therefore, I mean those statements which, judged by the evidence available and the quality of the argument which supports them, appear to be the most probably correct statements at the moment. That way of stating the matter may make some theory appear more tentative than it really is. In many cases the theory is so well grounded that we can be certain, or virtually so, of its reliability. Economists differ on particular subjects for a variety of reasons, some of which it would be invidious to discuss. To mention a few of the others, it is quite easy to make mistakes in the process of creating and applying a detailed logical system, and it is particularly easy in fields where emotions and political and social attitudes vie with reason to control men's beliefs. There are, moreover, special difficulties in applying theory to business practices. It is easy to overlook the existence of alternative theoretical explanations for a single practice, or to neglect a seemingly minor aspect of behavior that will not fit the theory being imposed.

All of this means that the judge, legislator, or lawyer cannot simply take the word of an economist in dealing with antitrust, for the economists will certainly disagree. Unless we would be driven to a sterile agnosticism, therefore, we must work through the arguments and make up our own minds. And we will find that on most subjects there is a better view which we ought to accept until fresh analysis provides yet a superior position.

Several of the first principles of antitrust methodology derive from an aspect of the market system that has often been expressed in the analogy to the Darwinian theory of natural selection and physical evolution. The familiarity of that parallel, and the overboard inferences sometimes drawn from it, should not blind us to its important truths. The environment to which the business firm must adapt is defined, ultimately, by social wants and the social costs of meeting them. The firm that adapts to the environment better than its rivals tends to expand. The less successful firm tends to contract—perhaps, eventually, to become extinct. The Stanley Steamer and the celluloid collar have gone the way of the pterodactyl and the great ground sloth, basically for the same reasons. Since coping successfully with the economic environment also forwards consumer welfare (except in those cases that are the legitimate concern of antitrust), economic natural selection has normative implications that physical natural selection does not have. At least there seems to me more reason for enthusiasm about the efficient firm than about the most successful physical organisms, the rat and the cockroach, though this view is, no doubt, parochial.

A key factor in evolution is death, and that holds true in economic as in physical evolution. The firm has an advantage over the animal because it can consciously change not just its behavior but its structure and so avoid or postpone death, but the threat is there and it becomes an actuality for many firms every year. There is in the literature much loose talk by people who should know better to the effect that the large modern corporation can escape the forces of the market through internal financing. Internal financing may often be a means of lowering the costs of acquiring capital, but it does not insulate the firm from the demands of the market. To expand, or even to survive, every firm requires a constant flow of capital for employees' wages, raw material, capital investment, repairs, advertising and the like. When the firm is relatively inefficient over a significant time period, it represents a poorer investment and greater credit risk than innumerable alternatives. If the firm is dependent upon outside capital, the firm must shrink and, if no revival in its fortunes occurs, die. That fate cannot be averted by financing out of retained earnings. There is, in the first place, no reason for a firm to throw its own money into a losing proposition rather than invest elsewhere. Even if one postulated a management that did so, and also postulated an ability to escape stockholder revolts, takeover bids, and so forth, internal financing could only delay the end. The firm would be incurring expenses that were not recovered, and it could continue only so long as it was willing and able to go on giving away its capital to consumers. There is no theoretical, empirical, or intuitive reason to suppose that such conduct is at all common.

The need to make profit produces the search for it. Profit motivation is patently ubiquitous and overwhelming, and it matters little whether we view it as entirely a conscious motivation, merely the type of behavior selected for survival by the economic environment from random forms of behavior, or, perhaps most realistically, as something of each. It is a common observation of biologists that whenever the physical environment provides a niche capable of sustaining life, an organism will evolve or adapt to occupy the place. The same is true of economic organisms, hence the fantastic proliferation of forms of business organization, products, and services in our society. We turn out everything from the most sophisticated electronic equipment to chartreuse compact cars to hair sprays, from business executives to field goal specialists to psychiatrists for disturbed household pets to rentable conversationalists for sagging dinner parties. The yellow pages of the telephone book do not begin to tell the story. The strength of the driving force that sends persons and firms into every crevice capable or even just possibly capable of sustaining profitable economic activity can hardly be overestimated.

This assumption of price theory is so crucial—and yet so insistently misunderstood by, among others, businessmen and antitrust lawyers—that elaboration may not be amiss. It is commonly objected that businessmen are not purely, or perhaps even primarily, rational profit seekers, that they could not in any case master and apply the complex calculations that such a goal requires, and that they employ guidelines to behavior that are inconsistent with profit maximization. None of these is a valid objection. Though if required I should not hesitate to impute conscious profit maximizing to businessmen—experience with businessmen and, even more, with antitrust lawyers and consulting economists should convince anyone that profit is a goal not only consciously but constantly borne in mind—price theory requires no such assumption. The validity of its tenets depends upon their success in predicting behavior, and the basic tenet of price theory, as Milton Friedman points out, states that businessmen generally behave *as if* they were engaged in maximization, just as a theory of physical science might state that leaves position themselves on trees "as if each leaf deliberately sought to maximize the amount of sunlight it receives."[3]

Thus, "firms behave *as if* they were seeking rationally to maximize their expected returns . . . and had full knowledge of the data required . . .; *as if*, that is, they knew the relevant cost and demand functions, calculated marginal cost and marginal revenue from all actions open to them, and pushed each line of action to the point at which the relevant marginal cost and marginal revenue were equal."[4]

Friedman uses an analogy that effectively disposes of the objections both that profit maximization is too complicated a goal and that businessmen often do not talk like profit maximizers:

> Consider the problem of predicting the shots made by an expert billiard player. It seems not at all unreasonable that excellent predictions would be yielded by the hypothesis that the billiard player made his shots as if he knew the complicated mathematical formulas that would give the optimum directions of travel, could estimate accurately by eye the angles, etc., describing the location of the balls, could make lightning calculations from the formulas, and could then make the balls travel in the direction indicated by the formulas. Our confidence in this hypothesis is not based on the belief that billiard players, even expert ones, can or do go through the process described; it derives rather from the belief that, unless in some

---

[3]Friedman, "The Methodology of Positive Economics," in *Readings In Microeconomics,* edited by Breit and Hochman (New York: Holt, Rinehart and Winston, 1968), p. 33; reprinted from Friedman, *Essays in Positive Economics* (Chicago: University of Chicago Press, 1953).

[4]*Id.* at 34–35.

way or other they were capable of reaching the same result, they would not in fact be *expert* billiard players.

. . . Now, of course, businessmen do not actually and literally solve the system of simultaneous equations in terms of which the mathematical economist finds it convenient to express this hypothesis, any more than leaves or billiard players explicitly go through the complicated mathematical calculations or falling bodies decide to create a vacuum. The billiard player, if asked how he decides where to hit the ball, may say that he "just figures it out" but then also rubs a rabbit's foot just to make sure; and the businessman may well say that he prices at average cost, with of course some minor deviations when the market makes it necessary. The one statement is about as helpful as the other, and neither is a relevant test of the associated hypothesis.[5]

Friedman's point is not that firms maximize perfectly, any more than expert billiard players plan and execute every shot correctly. Perfection is the limiting condition to which the more successful come closer than their rivals. As Armen Alchian observes, business success is measured against rivals rather than the ideal: "Realized positive profits, not *maximum* profits, are the mark of success and viability . . . Positive profits accrue to those who are better than their actual competitors, even if the participants are ignorant, intelligent, skillful, etc. The crucial element is one's aggregate position relative to actual competitors, not some hypothetical perfect competitors."[6] Profit maximization is the limiting point toward which success tends.

The fact that businessmen talk in terms not always equatable with profit maximization is of no particular importance, though it does mislead those who look no further. There are a variety of explanations: the simplest is that businessmen are no more self-conscious and articulate than the rest of the human race about their real motivations and conduct. Moreover, in a society whose intellectual leaders seem often not to understand the social value of self–seeking business behavior, the ability to talk vaguely about broad "social responsibility" while actually engaged in profit maximizing may be an important adaptive technique. Besides, many businessmen are as confused as other people about the morality of profits. Stigler reports that "in one field study, when [businessmen] were asked whether they maximized profits, they indignantly rejected the suggestion and pointed out that they were sincerely religious, public–spirited, and so on—as if these traits were inconsistent with profit-maximizing. But when the question was reformulated as: would a higher or lower price of the product yield larger profits?, the answer was usually, no."[7]

[5]*Ibid.*

[6]Alchian, "Uncertainty, Evolution, and Economic Theory," in *Readings In Industrial Organization and Public Policy* (Homewood, Ill.: Richard D. Irwin, 1958), p. 210; reprinted from 58 *J. of Pol. Econ.* 211 (1950).
[7]Stigler, *The Theory of Price,* 3d ed. (New York: Macmillan, 1966), p. 177, n.1.

The unsophisticated observer may also mistake for irrationality, or as indicating a goal other than profits, those rules of thumb that businessmen use to cope with uncertainty or to avoid the impossible task of rethinking every problem every time it arises. "Thus," according to Alchian, "the urge for 'rough-and-ready' imitative rules of behavior is accounted for. What would otherwise appear to be merely customary, 'orthodox,' nonrational rules of behavior turn out to be codified imitations of observed success, e.g., 'conventional' markup, price 'followship,' 'orthodox' accounting and operating ratios, 'proper' advertising policy, etc."[8] Such rules serve the function that habit and custom perform in other areas of life. Without them, moment-to-moment behavior would pose insuperable complexities. The firm will do better or worse as its rules of thumb prove to have survival value or not, and as it has or lacks the ability to alter them to meet circumstances.

We come now to a crucial point. To carry out its mission, antitrust must classify varieties of profit-maximizing behavior with respect to their probable impacts upon consumer welfare. Obviously, only three relationships are possible, and these correspond to three quite different ways of making money. A business firm may seek to increase its profits by achieving new efficiency (beneficial), by gaining monopoly power and restricting output (detrimental), or by some device not related to either productive or allocative efficiency, such as taking a bookkeeping advantage of some wrinkle in the tax laws (neutral).

The task of antitrust is to identify and prohibit those forms of behavior whose net effect is output restricting and hence detrimental. It should, of course, leave untouched behavior that is beneficial or neutral. The available resources of price theory dictate the manner in which this task must be accomplished. The best-developed branch of price theory is the theory of the ways in which firms may profit by interfering with allocative efficiency. Though we know something of the subject, there is no comparably clear, reliable, and general theory of the ways in which they may create productive efficiency. It follows, therefore, that antitrust analysis, if it is to be successful, must proceed primarily by elimination. We must appraise any questioned practice—say, a merger or a requirements contract—in order to determine whether it contains any likelihood of creating output restriction. If it does, and if it also contains the possibility of efficiency, we have a mixed case, which raises problems that will be discussed in a moment. If a practice does not raise a question of output restriction, however, we must assume that its purpose and therefore its effect are either the creation of efficiency or some neutral goal. In that case the practice should be held lawful.

It makes some people uneasy to have to rely entirely upon theory to infer the nature of a reality that is not directly observed. Yet I am convinced both that the theory is good enough to make the task doable and, equally important, that there is no other possible way to proceed. An economist once called this

---

[8]Alchian, supra n. 4, at 215.

the "Philo Vance approach to antitrust"; he was not, one gathered, one of that detective's greatest admirers. (As a matter of fact, he was probably thinking of Sherlock Holmes's dictum: "When you have eliminated the impossible, whatever remains, *however improbable*, must be the truth.")[9] The characterization is not without justice, but the objection it implies is wide of the mark. Philo (or Sherlock) did not have the advantage of the tight, logical system provided by price theory. If he had, his method of deduction would have been perfectly practical.

This is not by any means to suggest that it is not possible and desirable to go further and to specify the nature of the efficiencies created or intended by various forms of business behavior. Such an effort may serve as a valuable double-check upon conclusions arrived at by the process of elimination, and it is certainly likely to be more persuasive. But it is not logically necessary.

The application of this technique to particular situations will not be completely error free. But that is not a fatal objection. No system of laws is error free. The legal system makes mistakes in perceiving reality in the decision of every kind of case, from torts and contract disputes to homicide prosecutions. To demand perfection is to demand the abolition of law. The question is whether a method of applying the law can give an acceptable degree of accuracy and whether this method is better than any alternative method. The method of reasoning by elimination in antitrust cases passes both these tests. Indeed, no other method of antitrust analysis is even possible, since the only alternative, that of quantifying both efficiency and restriction of output, is well beyond the present powers of economic analysis and is likely forever to remain so.

Before we turn to the question of alternative modes of analysis, a possible misunderstanding should be cleared up. A moment ago it was said that when a practice does not have the capacity to restrict output, we should assume that its purpose (and therefore its effect) is either the creation of efficiency or some neutral result. It is proper to infer purpose from the objective possibility that a firm faces (unless we have clear evidence of a different purpose), and it is also proper to infer effect from purpose, even though we know that the effect will not always be what the firm intended. Businessmen make mistakes, and a particular efficiency-motivated contract or merger may, in fact, turn out miserably for the firm and hence be a poor use of society's resources. Antitrust cannot concern itself with this possibility, however, because prosecutors and courts simply cannot replace management by attempting to make business decisions through the litigation process. Antitrust must content itself with the identification of attempts to restrict output and let all other decisions, right or wrong, be made by the millions of private decision centers that make up the American economy.

---

[9]Arthur Conan Doyle, *The Sign of the Four,* Chap. VI.

There remains the difficult problem of the mixed case, the business practice that seems likely to produce both output restriction and efficiency. This is the case represented by Oliver Williamson's trade–off model, discussed in the preceding chapter. Horizontal mergers provide a primary example (indeed, almost the only example). If we disallow all horizontal mergers, no matter how small, we shall make a great sacrifice of productive efficiencies. If we allow all horizontal mergers, no matter how large, we shall make large sacrifices in allocative efficiencies. Somewhere on the spectrum between large and small mergers lies a range of mixed cases, and in these we do not know with certainty whether the efficiency or the trade restraint element predominates. How is the law to make a sensible decision in such cases?

The temptation is to reply: by making a showing of efficiencies an affirmative defense. But that is a temptation to be resisted, although its superficial plausibility lends the idea a certain attractiveness. After all, it might be said, facts are better than conjectures. They are, but only if you are sure that what you are dealing with are facts, and, unfortunately, the relevant ultimate facts for antitrust purposes cannot be perceived directly or quantified.

Making the existence and size of efficiencies a matter for proof, moreover, misleads the courts and the enforcement agencies into thinking that such direct proof is the only way efficiencies can be taken into account in antitrust litigation. Not surprisingly, they react by denying that efficiencies have any relevance to the law; this disastrous conclusion usually flows from a realization of what direct proof of efficiency would entail. Thus, it is customary to denounce proposals for performance tests as likely to plunge antitrust enforcement into "economic extravaganzas" or as being "prescriptions for the nonenforcement of the antitrust laws." Such invective misses the point.

If performance tests or efficiency defenses were the only way to reach intelligent decisions, then we ought either to stage economic extravaganzas or give up enforcing the laws. As Williamson says, "Filing (and winning) however many bad cases does not make for effective antitrust enforcement."[10] Simplicity of law enforcement is not worth having if the cost is law that does harm. We would not convict a man accused of theft without evidence on the argument that insistence upon unobtainable evidence is a prescription for the nonenforcement of the larceny laws.

The real objection to performance tests and efficiency defenses in antitrust law is that they are spurious. They cannot measure the factors relevant to consumer welfare, so that after the economic extravaganza was completed we should know no more than before it began. In saying this I am taking issue with some highly qualified authorities. Carl Kaysen and Donald Turner proposed that "an unreasonable degree of market power as such must be made illegal," and they suggested that all the relevant dimensions of performance be

---

[10]Williamson, "Allocative Efficiency and the Limits of Antitrust," 59 *Am. Econ. Rev.*, *Proceedings*, 105, 117 (1969).

studied.[11] Their idea, essentially, is that a court or agency determine, through a litigation process, whether there exists in a particular industry a persistent divergence between price and marginal cost; the approximate size of the divergence; whether breaking up, say, eight firms into sixteen would reduce of eliminate the divergence; and whether any significant efficiencies would be destroyed by the dissolution. The White House Task Force headed by Phil Neal came up with a similar proposal for litigating the desirability of restructuring concentrated industries.[12] Williamson thinks an efficiency defense is required if the trade–off relationship is to be recognized.[13]

These commentators are all entirely correct in perceiving the trade–off relationship and the crucial importance of efficiencies. There can be no rational antitrust policy that does not recognize and give weight to productive efficiency, and wide areas of present law are irrational precisely because they do not. The issue between these commentators and myself is simply the way in which efficiencies are to be given weight by the law.

A statement of what must be done in any direct measurement approach is sufficient to make its impossibility apparent. The court would have to make a reasonably accurate estimate of efficiency and dead–weight loss in an actual situation, and then make the same estimates of those two quantities in a hypothetical situation, in order to determine whether the real or the hypothetical situation is more favorable to consumers. Suppose that a merger is proposed and the government seeks to prevent its consummation. In order to explore the trade–off problem by direct study, trial would have to be had on the present contribution of the two firms to consumer welfare, their level of efficiency as separate firms, and the degree, if any, to which they were presently able to restrict output. As we shall see, that task is itself impossible. But trial would then have to proceed to the measurement of efficiency and restriction of output under an imaginary set of conditions: what would the net contribution to consumer welfare be if the two firms were merged into one? Judgment would be rendered according to a comparison of the two situations.

Passably accurate measurement of the actual situation is not even a theoretical possibility; much less is there any hope of arriving at a correct estimate of the hypothetical situation. Consider two of the factors that would have to be known: the demand curve over all possibly relevant ranges of output and the marginal cost curve over those same ranges. Only by knowing where marginal cost and demand intersect could one know whether there was a restriction of output and what its size was. Nobody knows these curves. Even the companies involved do not. The clarity of the graphs of firm behavior misleads many

---

[11]Kaysen and Turner, *Antitrust Policy* (Cambridge: Harvard University Press, 1959), pp. 111, 112.

[12]White House Task Force on Antitrust Policy, Report 1 (in Trade Reg. Rep., supp. to no. 415, May 26, 1969).

[13]Williamson, "Economies as an Antitrust Defense: The Welfare Trade-off," 58 *Am. Econ. Rev.* 18 (1968).

people. Companies do not compute these curves and then adjust output to equate marginal cost and marginal revenue. Rather, by a process of groping, by trial and error, they continually attempt, under constantly changing conditions, to make as much money as possible (or to lose as little as possible). The graph is a statement that in the process the firm will be driven toward the solution shown on the graph. Management may never think of demand curves or marginal cost curves. It may think in terms of a "fair return" and average costs, but rivalry and profit maximization will push it toward the solution shown by the graph.

There is a good reason why firms do not know these things, and it is the same reason why they cannot be know through an antitrust trial. The demand curve is not known because it changes continually and because the company is not constantly plotting it by running its prices up and down. The attempt to do so might make a minor contribution to science, but quite a research grant would be required, since the losses incurred in an attempt by a major company might make serious inroads on the resources of even the Ford Foundation.

But it is the quantification of the productive efficiency factor that renders the problem utterly insoluble. The point may be clarified by examining that class of efficiencies known as economies of scale, efficiencies related to the size of the firm. The variety of such efficiencies is suggested by E. A. G. Robinson's list of five forces that affect firm size:

> The forces which determine the best size of the business unit, assuming that the market is sufficient to absorb the whole production of at least one firm of optimum size, may be divided into five main categories: *technical forces*, making for a technical optimum size; *managerial forces*, making for an optimum managerial unit; *financial forces*, making for an optimum financial unit; the *influences of marketing*, making for an optimum sales unit; and the *forces of risk and fluctuation*, making for a unit possessing the greatest power of survival in the face of industrial vicissitudes. [Emphasis added.][14]

A noteworthy aspect of Robinson's list, for those who think of efficiency as an engineering concept and, therefore, of more importance to plant than firm size, is that only one of the influences mentioned, technical forces, is related at all closely to engineering or to the size of the plant (rather than the size of the firm).

The problem of technical efficiencies alone is likely to be beyond the capacities of the law. Imagine a large firm making several products and operating in distinct product and geographic markets. This would mean the study of not one but a number of technical marginal cost curves. For each of these, one would face the complex problem of separating fixed and variable costs and the insoluble problem of segregating and allocating joint costs. These things can

---

[14]Robinson, *The Structure of Competitive Industry* (Chicago: University of Chicago Press, 1958), p. 12.

be and are done by artificial accounting conventions, but that process, however useful it may be to a firm that wishes to compare its own performance during two different time periods, has little validity for the issues of real costs that antitrust policy must decide. Moreover, real marginal costs include a "normal" return to the various resources employed which includes opportunity costs, the latter being the return various resources could earn in the most profitable alternative use in the economy. We should be very skeptical, therefore, of any marginal cost curve that purported to reflect merely the technical efficiencies of a firm, particularly a large and complex firm.

Skepticism should turn to utter disbelief at the sight of cost curve purporting to reflect all the efficiencies of a firm. What could a court do when faced with a management claim that a merger would improve financial efficiency and a government contention that it would not, or with a claim that the merger would improve the new firm's chances of riding out unforeseen risks and fluctuations? And how could a court attach a number to such claimed efficiencies, for the firms separately and for the as yet hypothetical merged firm? Worse, a crucial component in any firm's efficiency is the skill of its management. How does one quantify judgement and imagination? We cannot begin to assign a quantitative value to a claimed future improvement (or decline) in the performance of firm A resulting from its acquisition by firm B, because that would require, among other impossibilities, precise statements about differences in the effects of unspecified future decisions concerning problems that cannot now even be identified. This unmeasurable factor may be the most important element of efficiency.

Williamson concedes that measurement of economies is difficult, but he thinks that admitting an economies defense would create an incentive to improve techniques. "To dismiss an economies defense on the prevailing state of the art is to employ an unacceptably narrow horizon."[15] I think it is the other way around: to admit an economies defense that proceeds by measurement would force us to an unacceptably narrow horizon. Economists, like other people, will measure what is susceptible of measurement and will tend to forget what is not, though what is forgotten may be far more important than what is measured. Williamson himself seems to have engaged in such a narrowing process. He speaks of an "economies defense" and seems to think of it as a cost–cutting defense. That in itself throws out those contributions to consumer welfare which arise from the conception and introduction of new products, new services, and variations of products and services.

The most important thing about the Ford Motor Co. in its early years was the genius of Henry Ford, just as the most important efficiency of General Motors Corp. in later years was the organizational genius of Alfred Sloan. The acquisition by one of those companies of a rival would have extended to a new group of resources a management that was enormously superior, even if there

---

[15]Williamson, supra n. 8, at 113.

were no cost cuts to be expected but only the doing of better things at higher costs.

The economies defense necessarily focuses on only half the problem, the cost–cutting side. And even within that half it will disallow efficiencies that are not easily proved. Thus Williamson: "if economies in both production and distribution expenses are claimed, and if the former are better specified than the latter, distribution economies would have to reach a higher threshold than would production economies to be admissible."[16]

Fortunately for both the time and cost of enforcement and the rationality of decisions, we can avoid attempts to measure dead–weight losses and efficiencies directly in order to compare a real situation with a hypothetical situation in terms of consumer welfare. We can avoid it because price theory tells us that many practices the law now views as dangerous do not contain any potential for restriction of output. In such cases there is no trade–off problem. The trade–off problem arises primarily in the context of horizontal mergers, and there we can take it into account by framing rules about allowable percentages that reflect the probable balance of efficiency and restriction of output.

Williamson criticizes this position (which I have taken previously):

> Lacking a tradeoff relation, Bork is forced to assert that "Economic analysis does away with the need to measure efficiencies directly. It is enough to know in what sorts or transactions efficiencies are likely to be present and in what sorts anticompetitive effects are likely to be present. The law can then develop objective criteria, such as market shares, to divide transactions [into those predominantly one type or another]." But this obviously leaves the mixed cases, which are the hard ones, unresolved.[17]

He says that without an economies defense "the mixed case which involves both scale economy and market power effects can only be handled arbitrarily—and this is satisfactory to no one."[18] But the nature of the problem shows that some degree of arbitrariness will have to be accepted as satisfactory by everyone because direct measurement of the conflicting factors cannot conceivably handle the trade–off dilemma. Indeed, it is precisely the introduction of an attempt to quantify economies that would make the law even more arbitrary than it need be, by eliminating the most important efficiencies from consideration.

This book will try to show that rules can be devised which reflect and resolve the tension between productive efficiency and allocative inefficiency accurately enough for the law to confer a net benefit. I hope it has already shown that performance tests and efficiency tests would multiply the costs of antitrust enforcement and defense without conferring any compensating advantage.

---

[16]Williamson, supra n. 11, at 24.

[17]*Id.* at 20.

[18]*Id.* at 24.

Suggested Qualifications

It is not surprising that Williamson, whose articles on the crucial but neglected subject of antitrust methodology are the best and most provocative of which I am aware, should also have suggested important qualifications to the trade–off model. Even though we must reject his suggestion of an economies defense, these qualifications require discussion because, to the degree they are significant, they also may affect an attempt to balance the tradeoff considerations through general legal rules.

Timing

The first proposed qualification is that of timing. Williamson argues that significant economies will ordinarily be realized eventually through internal expansion if not by merger. Growth of demand can facilitate this internal adjustment process; the necessity for part of the industry to be displaced in order that efficient size be achieved is relieved in a growing market. Thus, although a merger may have net positive effects immediately (cost savings exceed the dead–weight loss), when allowance is made for the possibility of internal expansion these effects can become negative eventually (the cost savings persist, but these could be realized anyway, and the dead–weight loss could be avoided by prohibiting the merger). . . . By contrast with a growing market, to force economies to be realized by internal expansion in a static market is generally without merit. The market power effects will occur here anyway, and the internal expansion route merely delays and may upset the market adjustment.[19]

This considerations seems entirely too speculative to deserve weight in framing rules. In the first place, the same economies may not be achieved by internal expansion. If merger was the preferred route, that preference may rest upon the lower cost of merger in achieving the new efficiencies. Blocking that route may very well impose higher costs, which must be subtracted from the efficiencies, and the costs may be high enough to prevent the achievement of the efficiencies altogether. Second, as Ward Bowman points out in this connection, the dead–weight loss may be reduced with the passage of time, both by the entry of new firms and because demand tends to become more elastic in the long run. This tends to counterbalance the prospect of achieving efficiency by growth. Finally, it is difficult to see that internal expansion is preferable in a growing market. It is true that internal expansion may have upsetting effects in a static market, but it should also be true that merger in a growing market would be unlikely to have lasting market power effects because of the greater likelihood of entry.

Incipiency

Ward Bowman and I once argued that applying the incipiency concept to halt a trend toward greater market concentration in its early stages is unfortu-

---

[19]*Id.* at 25.

nate because the existence of the trend constitutes evidence that greater concentration is desirable. The trend necessarily arises from emerging efficiencies.[20] Williamson comments:

> Their evaluation of the social desirability of a trend suggests a certain insensitivity to the relevant scale economy—market power tradeoff considerations, and they appear to read the significance of a trend somewhat too loosely. That a trend necessarily implies emerging efficiencies is incorrect: it may also indicate an emerging awareness that market power advantages might be realized through a series of combinations. Moreover, whereas they seem to suggest that to disallow a merger is to prevent the realization of scale economies altogether, ordinarily it is not a question of whether economies will be realized but when and with what market power effects. Thus, while Bork and Bowman may be correct in charging that scale economy justifications have not been given sufficient weight in the recent enforcement of the merger law, they are also guilty of a certain heavy–handedness in their own treatment of the incipiency question.[21]

To balance all this, Williamson drops a footnote to the second sentence in which he notes that I concede the possibility of an emerging awareness of market power advantages but that my "principal emphasis, which is probably correct, is that a trend signals emerging economies."[22] The upshot appears to be that I, along with Bowman, am insensitive and heavy–handed but probably correct. I will settle for that. I don't know about Bowman.

The incipiency concept appears to have no value whatever, and when the concept is applied to halt a trend (toward concentration, vertical integration, or what have you) in the early stages, it seems plain that the only effect is to halt (or perhaps only to delay and make more costly) the achievement of emerging efficiencies. It is altogether too much to believe that scores or hundreds of firms in a fragmented industry would at the same time begin growing by merger in the expectation that one day they would work the industry down to a highly concentrated state and achieve the power to restrict output. Each of them must rely upon all of the others to do the same thing and keep on doing it for a very extended period of time. More importantly, if we suppose there are not economies to be achieved by merger, we must, in order to accept the counterhypothesis, also suppose that there are no diseconomies, for if there were the process would be much too costly. Thus, we must imagine scores or hundreds of firms with perfectly flat marginal cost curves that permit expansion by merger to sizes perhaps twenty or more times their original sizes without diseconomy. And since we are asked to imagine that the beginning of the trend is not due to a change in cost conditions, we must wonder why, with

---

[20]Bork and Bowman, "The Crisis on Antitrust," *Fortune 68*, December 1963, pp.

[21]Williamson, supra n. 11, at 27.

[22]*Id.* at 27, n.6

marginal cost curves like that, the industry ever was fragmented in the first place.

It seems impossible to conclude that a merger trend signifies anything but emerging efficiencies unless the trend started from a condition so concentrated that one or two mergers would be sufficient to make output restriction a profitable course of action. That was not the case Bowman and I had under discussion, and the incipiency concept is not necessary to guard against that situation.

Weighting

"The economies that a merger produces are usually limited strictly to the combining firms. But the market power affects of a merger may sometimes result in a price increase across a wider class of firms." Where this occurs, Williamson suggests, the balancing of cost savings and dead-weight loss should be adjusted accordingly.[23] This seems clearly correct in any case in which the other firms can be expected to behave as conventional oligopoly theory predicts—that is, to cooperate in maintaining the new higher price rather than to erode it through rivalry. So clarified, this is a consideration to be taken into account in the framing of rules about allowable market shares. It will be argued later, however, that conventional oligopoly theory is not credible, and that argument, if it is accurate, greatly diminishes the consideration of "weighting."

Technological Progress and Managerial Discretion

Williamson suggests that technological progress may be related to market structure.

Presently, however, neither the arguments nor the evidence relating market structure to progressiveness is unmixed. Provisionally, it may only be judicious to withhold judgement on this dimension. But, as the evidence accumulates, sharper definition is ordinarily to be expected; and operational integration of progressiveness within the efficiency standard might, therefore, eventually be achieved.[24]

There can be no objection to the integration of effects upon progressiveness into the weight given efficiency when enough is know to predict the effects of structure upon progressiveness. My objection to progressiveness as a goal of antitrust,[25] an objection to which Williamson was responding, was to its consideration as a goal independent of consumer welfare. It is a component of consumer welfare. There is, moreover, a more fundamental difficulty with the notion of counting progressiveness as a goal of policy: it is not clear how much progressiveness is desirable. Progress requires the sacrifice of other resources, it costs something, and no one thinks it worth paying any price, no matter how

---

[23]*Id.* at 27.

[24]Williamson, supra n. 8, at 107.

[25]Bork, "The Goals of Antitrust Policy," 57 *Am. Econ.* Rev. 242, 251 (1967).

great, for faster progress. We are, therefore, necessarily ignorant of the "proper" rate of progress, and it may be wisest for that reason not to give the matter any weight in antitrust analysis.

Market power is also said to provide a firm "the opportunity to pursue a variety of other–than–profit objectives." This, if true and significant, would require that the efficiency component of a merger creating substantial market power be discounted because it would not be fully realized. Williamson characterizes this qualification, as well as that concerning technological progress, as "highly conjectural,"[26] and it too must await further evidence before being taken as a serious factor in the framing of legal rules.

The upshot of this consideration of the qualifications advanced as appropriate to the naive consumer welfare model is that weighting (the third suggested qualification) alone deserves to be worked into the trade–off relationship, but only in cases involving horizontal size. The argument of Chapter 8 suggests that this qualification is very minor and perhaps verges on nonexistence.

Tie Breakers

Cases may occur, primarily in the fields of horizontal mergers and horizontal ancillary restraints, in which changes seem roughly equal that the activity is beneficial or harmful. Instances of such uncertainty should be treated like cases of behavior that is neutral. The law should not intervene. One frequently hears the opposite contention: when in doubt "play safe," by banning the conduct in question. This is the sheerest folly. There is no way to "play safe." If the dead–weight loss and efficiency are not in fact equally balanced, then the conduct is either beneficial or detrimental. Assuming the odds are equal where we are unable to be sure, the would–be safe player is doing good in half the cases and inflicting harm in the other half.

A cluster of considerations require nonintervention in doubtful cases. First, antitrust enforcement is a very costly procedure, and it makes no economic sense to spend resources to do as much harm as good. There is then a net loss. Second, private restriction of output may be less harmful to consumers than mistaken rules of law that inhibit efficiency. Efficiency that may not be gained in one way may blocked because other ways are too expensive, but a market position that creates output restriction and higher prices will always be eroded if it is not based upon superior efficiency. Finally, when no affirmative case for intervention is shown, the general preference for freedom should bar legal coercion.

---

[26]Williamson, supra n. 11 at 29.

Barriers To Entry

Harold Demsetz

Although the notion of "barriers to entry" plays an important role in economic theory and antitrust litigation, the substantial problems inherent in it are not fully appreciated. Much existing discussion of barriers hardly pauses to recognize the difficulties, and even more careful treatments of the subject proceed as if the definition of barriers can be tied quite easily to some purely objective measure of the cost of doing business.[1] The burden of this paper is to demonstrate that this is not so.

The origin of the barriers concept is in the research custom of industrial organization economists during the post–World War II period. That custom was to seek monopoly explanations for data not obviously or directly implied by the perfect competition model. The perceived persistence of higher rates of return in some industries than in others was suggestive of barriers to entry, especially for industries exhibiting high levels of structural concentration. The equalization of profit rates through competition, however, is a proposition logically valid only with respect to investment on the *margin* of alternative economic activities. Only if all inputs are available in perfectly elastic supply does this imply equality between average profit rates. In addition, accounting profits are likely to be biased by the presence of uncapitalized assets, especially assets associated with advertising, research, and goodwill[2] (see Lester Telser; Leonard Weiss; my earlier article). But my purpose here is not to probe these measurement problems nor to compare the merits of these explanations, but to examine the usefulness of the concept of barriers. Accordingly, I will ignore the possibility that factors other than barriers may partly or wholly explain the phenomena that the barriers notion seeks to explain.

I. Prevailing Ambiguities

The discussion of barriers in economic literature hardly reflects concensus. Consider the definitions given by Joe Bain, George Stigler, and James Ferguson. Bain defines the conditions of entry as "the extent to which, in the long run, established firms can elevate their selling prices above the minimal average costs of production and distribution...without inducing

---

Reprinted from *American Economic Review* (1968) pp. 18–36 by permission of the American Economic Association.

[1] Recent contributions to the barriers literature by Franklin Fisher and C. C. von Weizsacker substantially improve the subject's treatment. Fisher's treatment is in some respects similar to the present paper's discussion, but our coverage and basic approach differ enough to warrant some duplication.

[2] If accountants could do in their ledgers what economists do with chalk and eraser, economic rent could be handled without risk in practical applications. Unfortunately, accountants are unable, conceptually and practically, to impute such rents, so the application of barriers in the courtroom will often confuse rent with profit, thus suggesting policy relevant barriers when there are none.

potential entrants to enter the industry" (p. 242). This suggests that the appropriate test is whether (long–run) price exceeds (long–run) average cost after entry has ceased. Ferguson defines barriers as "factors that make entry unprofitable while permitting established firms to set prices above *marginal* cost, and to persistently earn monopoly return" (p. 10). This adds to Bain's test of barriers a third condition, that price exceed marginal cost. Stigler defines barriers "as a cost of producing (at some of every rate of output) which must be borne by a firm which seeks to enter an industry but is not borne by firms already in the industry" (p. 67).

These differing definitions allow their authors to hold different opinions about specific sources of barriers. For Bain and Ferguson, economies of scale constitute a source of barriers, but not for Stigler so long as entrants have access to the same cost function. Advertising and capital requirements create barriers for Bain because they seem correlated with high profit rates, but, so long as these inputs are available on equal terms to all who wish to employ them, they create no barriers for Stigler; while for Ferguson, they create no barriers if they are not a source of scale economies.

The use of profit as the litmus test for barriers in Bain's and Ferguson's definitions, unlike Stigler's, uses a possible outcome of barriers, high profit rates, to substitute for the actual barriers. Barriers may or may not yield high profit. Even a securely protected monopolist may fail to cover his cost. Barriers that simply are sources of negatively sloped demand curves are easily overlooked by Bain's and Ferguson's definition.

These three definitions do agree on one matter. All focus attention on the different opportunities facing insiders and outsiders. This not only diverts attention from other types of barriers, but also hides the value judgments implicit in the barriers notion. As an example of the difficulty these definitions confront in identifying other types of barriers, consider those created by legal restrictions. A requirement that an official medallion must be owned by operators of taxis is a barrier to entry if the number of medallions available is less than the number of taxis that would operate without such a requirement or if the medallion is costly to obtain. Suppose it were true that such licenses, which may be resold subsequently, also must be purchased first from the city at *market–determined* prices. Insiders and outsiders face the same cost, the medallion price plus automotive costs, so Stigler's definition fails to identify the barrier, and, since the price of the medallion must dissipate profit, so do Bain's and Ferguson's. In these circumstances, the insider–outsider distinction fails to indicate the presence of a barrier to entering the taxi industry!

The reader will have recognized that what I have done is to use medallions as if they were scarce land, treating taxi owners as farmers who rent or buy "acres of" medallions from the city and/or other taxi owners. It might be supposed that lurking behind the scene are conditions with respect to medallion production that would allow one or more of the above definitions to identify the regulatory situation as one with barriers to entry. It would appear that there must be an abnormal return to the production of medallions and that, therefore, there are outsiders to the medallion industry who are barred by the city from profitably producing medallions. But this need not be the case. Let the city allow free entry into the medallion industry; let the city allow as many medallions to be manufactured as is called for by profit opportunities. As long as there is a significant cost to manufacturing (say, solid gold) medallions, fewer cabs would be in the industry than in the absence of licensure requirements. Indeed, medallions and licensure are not needed to keep some types of resources out of the taxi industry. Requirements to equip taxis with airbags, seatbelts, and costly bumpers will do. Even if the price of safety equipment equals it cost, and even if there were no bar to producing such equipment, would there not still be a barrier to putting taxis on the street?

Surely, the answer is "yes," but the policy implications of that answer depend very much on value judgments regarding the consequences of such barriers. A barrier to the use of resources for criminal activity will be judged by many to be desirable and socially productive, but not so many would take the same view toward a barrier to the importation of foreign goods. Even a barrier to the provision of low–cost, low–quality taxi services might seem desirable to those concerned about street congestion and dishonest drivers; licensing will reduce the number of taxis and also offer a premium for honest service that would otherwise be absent (the retention of a valuable license).

The insider–outsider framework assumes that consumer sovereignty will be served by allowing resources into the high profit industry. This hides the difficult problem of assessing the broader implications for consumer interest of the barrier. The barrier may reduce the severity of some externality or it may bring about improved levels of competition in activities other than that of direct concern. If the broader social constraints are accepted as serving consumer interest, then the fact that they block the free flow or resources in some directions is policy irrelevant.

Even the operation of an unregulated market system presupposes the general recognition of property rights, *but the problem of defining ownership is precisely that of creating properly scaled legal barriers to entry*. The essence of ownership is the general recognition that costs are to be borne if a person is to act in certain ways. These costs, like licensure, seat belts, etc., constitute hurdles that must be surmounted for an action, such as entry, to take place. An owner of resources may be barred legally from using (his) resources simply to occupy and operate the facilities of someone already in the industry. He must first meet the cost hurdle of securing the "owner's" permission. Similarly, he is barred by trademark protection from selling a product that he represents to be the product of his rival. But he may (or may not, depending on antitrust decisions) have the right to enter by selling a product priced below those of his rivals. The decision as to which actions are violative of someone's right implies a derivative decision about the protective measures (trademark enforcement, price reductions, etc.) socially sanctioned for defending against entry.

The denial of the right to burn down the factory of a rival implies a prior judgment about the utility derived from such an act, not only by the person protecting his market in this manner but also by those enjoying large bonfires or viewing factories as eyesores; their gains are deemed too small to offset the loss implies by a destroyed factory. Such a calculation may be so formidable that strict injunctions are avoided. Instead "ownership" is defined to allow voluntary consent to guide the use of resources. The factory owner's consent to the (controlled, safe) burning of his factory is required before its destruction (serving a legitimate purpose) can take place.

Positive transaction cost implies that these decisions about property rights influence the mix of output. The consensus that establishes his right to *bar* destruction, unless there is consent, reflects the implicit prior decision that the mix of output (or actions) encouraged is more desirable than the mix discouraged. Positive transaction cost implies that the encouraged mix will include less factory destruction that if factory owners were required to pay rivals not to destroy the factory.

When judging the social productivity of barriers, it may be useful to adopt the criterion of consumer sovereignty; but since the underlying property right system guides the operations of several industries, it is not possible to restrict the application of consumer sovereignty to the output of the specific industry. The broader question must be considered—how does a barrier which originates in and is justified by the right system affect consumer welfare generally? This question may be considered in the context of the traditional entry barriers.

II. Traditional Barriers as Choices Among Output Mixes

Traditional barriers are marshalled to explain industry profit rates that tend to be persistently high. Presumably, differences in cost between outsiders and insiders account for these high profit rates. These cost differences are described by Bain as deriving in some way from the use of advertising and/or capital, or from economies of scale. Industries using more advertising and capital, and those subject to scale economies, are seen as enjoying abnormal profits because of this protection from outsiders.

The right to promote one's product and the right to build appropriate factories, however, are legitimate exercises of the rights of ownership of resources, and scale economies remains a fact whether or not firms are allowed to produce relatively large rates of output. These uses of resources have not been treated as criminal by the evolving property right system. There is no obvious reason for believing that legally blocking or punishing the use of resources in these ways serves consumer interests. Prospective entrants must win buyers away from firms that have promoted and produced their products in ways that maximize profits in competition with other firms. Whether the mix of output that results is superior to one that would obtain in the absence of these rights cannot be inferred merely from the existence of either higher profit rates or lower costs for insiders. The fundamental consequences for the mix of goods require examination before the defeat of barriers can be judged.

Because of brand loyalty, new rivals, seeking to sell as much as existing firms, may need to advertise more than existing firms (or offer some other special compensating advantage). This may be required at the time of entry even though new and old firms produce the "same" product, and even though old firms may have had to advertise even more to promote a new product variety when they began to sell. Advertising expenditures, at least those incurred earlier by existing firms, may be called a source of "barriers" to entry. However, investments in advertising and promotion are worthwhile (for both old and new firms) only in the presence of significant information costs. Information costs are the more fundamental barrier to entry. These costs, not necessarily in identical amounts, constitute hurdles to all who would (and have) enter(ed) the industry. Complete knowledge about products and firms would make brand loyalty useless from both consumer and seller viewpoints. Where advertising and promotion are used extensively, and, therefore, where goodwill and brand loyalty are assets, there must also exist real costs of resolving uncertainties. In the presence of such costs, consumers will find it useful to rely on a firm's experience and reputation, or more correctly, on its *history* or on the fact that it has made sizeable investments specific to this industry.[3] New firms and recent entrants by virtue of their shorter histories or absence of specific investments (in particular, product lines) may not be able to impart to consumers, without some compensating effort, the same confidence as has already been secured by older firms through past investments in good performance. If new firms are to sell equal quantities at equal prices, they may need to incur higher costs of persuading and communicating than presently is required of older firms. In what sense, then, are advertising expenditures a barrier to entry? Entry by new firms might be even more difficult if such expenditures were disallowed because consumers would then be left to rely on *only* a company's history. It is the combination of information costs, the creation of a reputable history, and the commitment of industry–specific investment, not advertising per se, that constitutes the barrier (if that is how we choose to designate it).

Such histories and investment commitments must also play a role in the operation of capital markets. A large firm and a long history convey information about a firm's ability to weather unforseen risks and about its willingness to accept high risks. This information is not necessarily an overpowering determinant of risk of lending, since knowledge secured from other sources must also be taken into account, and these may indicate strongly an impending bankruptcy despite a brilliant history. But there is no reason to believe that such a history is irrelevant to the interest payment required by lenders. Larger,

---

[3]Consumer reliance on specific investments of sellers is discussed in Benjamin Klein and K. B. Leffler.

older firms generally will be able to borrow more cheaply than smaller, younger firms. It is not large capital "requirements," but the histories of successful firms, in a world in which information is costly to acquire, that constitute the source of such interest rate differentials.

Less obvious, but perhaps more important, the same factors are also the source of barriers that appear in the guise of scale economies. If each firm has available to it the same cost function for producing identical products or services, and if information is costless, then old and new firms can compete for the market on equal terms even if only a few (or one) wins(s) such a competition. Irrelevancy of a firm's historic record compels new and old firms to divide the market between them if their prices are equal, and, if not equals, compels delivery of the entire market to the firm with the lower price. Existing firms have an advantage only insofar as their existence commands loyalty. Existence commands loyalty only if it reflects lower real cost of transacting, industry-specific investments, or a reputable history, as, in general, it will. Long survival at least indicates that the firm has not been a fly-by-night operator. When the cost to consumers of overcoming uncertainty is taken into account—that is, when total system cost is gauged rather than some narrow definition of production cost—then long-lived firms can be seen to offer consumers risk reduction. Any price advantage enjoyed by such firms is limited to the value to consumers of the risk reduction provided by the demonstrated viability of older firms, whether or not there are scale economies. Scale economies make this risk reduction available at lower cost per unit as more consumers buy from one firm, so that entrants must compete for the entire market. With scale diseconomies, the benefits of risk reduction become available to additional buyers from a single firm only at rising marginal cost. Firms with less experience can gain a foothold when the price older firms would need to receive, if they are to increase their sales, rises sufficiently to offset the value to consumers of their longer experience.

A reputable history is an asset to the firm possessing it and to the buyer who relies on it because information is not free. A property right system that affords patent, copyright, and trademark protection, and that makes antitrust divestiture difficult, is one that encourages investment in "permanence" and discourages investment in fly-by-night operations. A property right system that weakens these legal protections, encourages investment in other means of information acquisition and transmission and in other methods of reducing risk. These choices are obscured by viewing advertising expenditures, capital requirements, and scale economies as if they were the basic sources of barriers rather than the cost of information. The Federal Trade Commission's antitrust action against leading producers of ready-to-eat breakfast cereals, being tried at the time of writing, certainly seeks to reduce the values of specific advertising capital and of the histories of these firms.

In a similar vein, the barrier to entry literature obscures the important issue raised by the phenomenon of firms facing negatively sloped demand curves. For both Bain and Ferguson, such negative slopes are identified as barriers to entry if price exceeds unit cost, but not otherwise. For Stigler, the limiting factor is more properly viewed as demand than as one of cost advantages, so (probably) from his viewpoint no barrier is involved. However, there must be a barrier to the production of some mix of output if the demand curves facing existing firms (and, possibly, potential entrants) are negatively sloped, and this must be true whatever the relationship between price and unit cost. The demand facing a producer is negatively sloped because there are "natural" or "legal" obstacles (such as trademark protection) to *perfect* imitation (meaning an imposter who duplicates product contents, name, and packaging). Trademark privileges may reduce the quantities sold of an *existing* product, but they may also increase the number of new products enjoyed by customers and even make some products profitable to produce that would be unprofitable in the absence of such legal protection. Elimination of such legal protection is likely to reduce prices and increase sales of products already produced, but it also reduces incentives to develop new ones. Whether these legal barriers are desirable cannot be judged without explicit or implicit comparison of the values of alternative mixes of outcomes. The judgmental valuation of the class of equilibria implied of product differentiation basically turns on such a comparison, not primarily on notions of excess capacity.

The degree to which it may be desirable to supplement natural barriers to imitation hinges on factual matters that vary from case to case. Considerable investment may be needed to develop a new product of one type, but little expenditure may be required to imitate it once someone else does the developing; here spillovers of knowledge beneficial to rivals are both significant and difficult to take into account through markets unaided by trademark, copyright, or patent; the case of legal barriers to imitation using the criterion for consumer sovereignty may be strong. Where such spillovers are slight, the case for such protection is weakened, again from the perspective of consumers.

These legal barriers define ownership and thereby facilitate the taking into account of the value of potential spillovers. The broader and more protective is the definition of ownership, the more likely it will be that nonspillovers will also be protected. A very broad patent right may give an inventor title to other inventions that benefit very little from knowledge of his. A much more limited patent tends to allow more spillover to be uncaptured by an inventor.

It bears repeating that the problem of defining ownership is precisely that of creating properly scaled legal barriers to entry. An appropriate trademark law equates the marginal value of a more finely tuned market for inventions to the marginal value of additional units of already invented goods. The equating of such marginal values may make it appear as if the product market is inefficient, because price may exceed the marginal cost of producing the good; but, of course, if greater imitation is tolerated, there is an element of the cost of increasing the output of already invented goods that is not explicitly recorded—the consequent cost of undermining the incentive to invent still other products. Because it is not recorded, the illusion is created that product price exceeds marginal cost. Whereas the existence of (appropriate) trademark protection is a barrier to greater production of known products, the absence of (appropriate) trademark protection is a barrier to invention of new products. *It cannot be said there is a barrier in one case and not (the potential of) a barrier in the other case.*

III. Predatory Pricing

Now, it would hardly seem serving of social purposes to establish legal rights requiring that the permission of one's rivals be obtained before a price reduction can be given to prospective buyers. The real costs of transacting and enforcing agreements that give such permission would be so great that most price reductions beneficial to buyers would be barred by legal rights of this sort. Yet, legislated or court–made prohibitions on price cutting establish precisely such legal rights under the guise of prohibiting "predatory pricing." This legal stance identifies some instances of price cutting as (undesirable) barriers to entry. The analysis of predatory pricing, however, is not less superficial than for other barriers to entry.

In principle, an objective of the legal framework that underlies the operation of markets is the specification of legal prohibitions of competitive methods judged socially unproductive. This prohibition should tend to channel rivalrous behavior into directions more likely to benefit consumers, such as product innovation, quality improvement, and price reductions. Since legal methods of competing are generally, or, at least, are in principle, those that transmit benefits to consumers, a practical policy problem of identification arises if a subset of these methods may be used sometimes in ways believed to be inimical to consumer interests. Allegedly prominent among these is predatory pricing, pricing designed to monopolize a market by punishing rivals until they cooperate by leaving the industry, reducing output, or merging on favorable terms with the predator. Presumably, the harm to consumers arises later in the form of higher prices undeterred by actions from rivals who have been disciplined into cooperation or into exiting the industry. The practical problem of an antipredatory pricing policy obviously is to distinguish beneficial from harmful price reductions. The ability of one firm to charge a lower price than another (for given quality), or to outlast another in a "price war," generally will be correlated with its efficiency, so that the prevention of price wars may merely prevent consumers from enjoying longlasting benefits of truly competitive pricing.

The problem of separating beneficial from harmful competitive acts is not so difficult when acts of violence are used to punish rivals; there is no necessary correlation between the efficiency with which a firm uses violence and the efficiency with which it produces goods desired by consumers. Sharp pricing practices require more precise policy tools than acts of violence if the consumer is to be benefitted. A barrier to competitors may arise from the superior efficiency of existing firms, in which case their low prices are precisely what competitive markets are expected to bring forth. Rivals of such firms will be discouraged from producing simply because they cannot produce at low enough cost. The policymaker cannot simply look to the harm done to the interests of entrants when determining whether low prices are to be encouraged or discouraged. Because of these difficulties, as with policy toward other barriers, a choice between alternative output mixes is involved. The attempt to reduce or to eliminate predatory pricing is also likely to reduce or eliminate competitive pricing beneficial to consumers.

It is thought that there is a clear way, at least in principle, to discriminate between these situations. A price that is below marginal cost is said to be predatory, whereas a price above or equal to marginal cost is not. Phillip Areeda and Donald Turner take this position, although they seek to employ shortrun average variable cost as a proxy for difficult to observe short–run marginal cost. The need for a proxy reveals the difficulty in measuring (*ex ante*!) marginal cost, but that is a matter I set aside here.[4] I also refrain from discussing in detail the issue raised by Richard Posner with regard to whether short- or long–run marginal cost is the relevant concept to use. (The relevant cost is the *ex ante* marginal cost of expanding output for whatever period and circumstances are expected to prevail during the pricing episode.) Both sides of the dispute fail to recognize more fundamental difficulties in the attempt to distinguish acceptable and unacceptable low prices. Profit–maximizing firms never seek to lower the relevant price below their relevant marginal cost, so such a test must fail.

Consider the situation when give–aways are used to attract potential customers. Drivers, when delivering milk to households, often give a free sample of milk to new residents. Price clearly *seems* below marginal cost. It does cost something to replace milk given away. Yet few would call this predatory pricing. Promotional pricing is the name accorded this unobjectionally low price. But the principle of price less than marginal cost would seem to have been violated, and if the principle fails to stand in such a case it may also fail to stand in more difficult cases.

As an example of a more difficult case consider a firm that advertises its product but sells at a price below cost for a month or two, or even longer, in the hope that buyers at the low price will so like the product that they will return to buy later at a higher price. In both this case and the dairy case, *price* is incorrectly measured by the economist or lawyer who relies on revenue per unit received at the time the below cost prices prevail. In both situations, the correct price is approximately the discounted value of the *future* higher price that is the objective of promotional selling. Neither the owner of the dairy nor

---

[4]The issue is not only of theoretical but also of practical import. The writings of Areeda and Turner, and of others, provide the rationale through which courts reach verdicts about pricing practices. Compare *Janich Bros. Inc. v. American Distilling Co.*

the advertiser would sell now at prices below marginal cost if he did not expect the future revenue stream to justify the promotion. Selling below cost now harms rivals, but in both cases the correctly perceived price exceeds (or equals) marginal cost.

It is important to recognize that predatory pricing involves exactly the same prospect—reducing price now, presumably below cost, with harm to rivals, in the hope of giving rise to a future stream of prices sufficient to make the "predatory promotion" worthwhile. *There is no obvious way to use the marginal cost criterion to distinguish the two cases.*

A second criterion for the presence of predatory behavior has emerged recently. Oliver Williamson argues that if entry prompts existing firms to expand output, then predation is involved, and, further, that public policy should prohibit such expansion in output by existing firms for a period up to twelve or eighteen months.

Again, the distinction between predatory and competitive prices is difficult to make. Suppose an existing firm begins from a monopoly situation, perhaps by virtue of being the first to produce a new product. An entrant adds to its output to the market and more entrants are in the offing. Let the monopolist of yesterday now view his situation as competitive, so that he takes the new lower price as given. At the lower price, *on the way* to the new long–run equilibrium price, the output of this erstwhile monopolist, now behaving competitively, will be where price equals his marginal cost. This generally will yield a larger output than he had produced before entry, or before price rivalry, because marginal cost in the neighborhood of the old monopoly price will be to the right of the previous output rate. Hence, purely competitive responses to entry can be expected to yield larger output rates from an existing firm until price has fallen enough to establish an equality with this firm's marginal cost to the left of its old monopoly rate of output. However, if scale economies prevail in the neighborhood of monopoly output, then even the final competitive equilibrium may call for an output from the erstwhile monopoly that exceeds its old monopoly rate of output. Only if the policymaker knew the price had reached the long–run competitive equilibrium, that it was not merely on its way down to that equilibrium, and, also, that scale economies were not present in the range of monopoly output, could he infer predatory behavior from the expansion of output by existing firms in response to entry. The fact of entry does imply a downward shift in demand, and this in and of itself will tend to reduce the output of an existing firm, but entry also makes the existing firm's demand more elastic, tending to increase output.[5] The net effect is unclear unless the existing firm's unit cost is deceasing in the region of its old output rate, for then entry must force it to increase output.

---

[5]For a more detailed criticism of Williamson's proposal and a general review of discussion about predatory pricing, see John McGee.

A third test for predation, this one legal rather than economic, centers on the *motivation* for the price cut. Did one firm cut price for the express purpose of harming its rivals? It is not clear to an economist why motivation matters at all. A price cut to obtain new customers imposes as much harm on rivals as a price cut whose objective is to harm them. The issue of motive arises in the legal mind not only because of the need for "evidence," but also because motive has played a role in the common law. However, it is not recognized that there are substantive differences between the predatory pricing problem and the "malice" situations in which intent seems relevant. The question of motive is clearly raised in the 1909 case of *Tuttle v. Buck*. The plaintiff, a barber in a Minnesota village, claimed that the defendant, a local banker, attempted to run him out of business by subsidizing a new barber shop, and that the defendant did this maliciously for personal gratification not because he intended to remain in the barbering business. Justice Elliot, after stating these allegations in his opinion, puts the problem as follows:

> For generations there has been a practical agreement upon the proposition that competition in trade and business is desirable, and this idea has found expression in the decisions of the courts as well as in statutes. But it has led to grievous and manifold wrongs to individuals, and many courts have manifested an earnest desire to protect individuals from the evils which result from unrestrained business competition. The problem has been to so adjust matters as to preserve the principle of competition and yet guard against its abuse to the unnecessary injury to the individual. So the principle that a man may use his own property according to his own needs and desires, while true in the abstract, is subject to many limitations in the concrete.... The purpose for which a man is using his own property may thus sometimes determine his rights. [p. 946]

It is desirable to consider the principle at issue in these allegations without regard to the facts or decision in this case. Suppose it true that the defendant disliked the plaintiff intensely, and that he was bent on destroying the plaintiff's economic opportunities in their home village. Should the pursuit of an otherwise unobjectionable act, say, the offer of free haircuts to all townspeople, be tolerated if this motive were known? Should the defendant be allowed to derive utility by harming plaintiff?

If the *only* effect from defendant's action was to harm the plaintiff (i.e., ignoring the price consequences for purchasers of haircuts), then there seems little difference between defendant's action in this case and the use of his financial resources to pay for the physical damage of plaintiff's barber shop. The Libertarian Anarchist might well claim there is a difference—that physically destroying defendant's place of business "invades' his property rights, while giving haircuts away does not. But this position tautologically evades the real issue, which is that of determining just what rights of use of property each party owns. Many judgers of this situation, I believe, would be disposed to deny the defendant the right to personally gratify himself if the sole effect and means of his doing so is to harm the plaintiff. Since no results productive to third parties emerges in such cases, whether "spite fences" or free haircuts are at issue, motive would seem to matter. The defendant's act would seem more tolerable if he provided free haircuts because of his joy in the act of barbering rather than in the act of harming a personal enemy.

The question here is purely one of how a person may spend his wealth in *consumption* activity. Is the defendant entitled to derive utility via the purchase of the harmful effects he imposes on plaintiff? The answer to this question frequently is no, but evidence is required as to whether this is the real source of utility. A person playing his radio outside while doing yardwork may really derive pleasure from annoying his neighbor and not from hearing the radio, but, if the volume of the radio is not turned too high, it will be difficult to identify this as the real source of enjoyment and so the law will tolerate his listening to music on the radio. The malicious harming of plaintiff is best viewed as a consumption activity, and for such an activity the relative wealth positions of plaintiff and defendants matter. The wealthier the defendant, the more such consumption he can finance.

The considerations change in important ways if we consider a more typical situation of alleged predatory pricing. First, like listening to music on the radio, the large numbers of buyers that are receiving a good at a lower price is a "gain" that must be counted as an offset to whatever "loss" rivals bear from lower prices. The larger the number of recipients of low prices, and the longer such prices are expected to prevail, the stronger is the case for legalizing the act of lowering prices, just as music played outside is easier to tolerate, even if played loudly, when it is servicing a large block party in which many derive benefit from the music.

Secondly, alleged predatory pricing is a business venture, not a consumption activity. The seeking of monopoly is motivated by the pursuit of profits; the magnitude of defendant's wealth relative to plaintiff's is neither here nor there in such a case because the capital markets stand ready to maintain the plaintiff in this price war if the prospect of profit is sufficient to cover the risk-determined cost of capital. The defendant pursuing his business interest also has no desire to lend his "own" capital to himself unless the prospect of profit is sufficient to cover the risk determined cost of capital. The two combatants are on equal footing if they represent the same risk to the capital markets. And if they do not represent equal risks, than one has cost advantages not possessed by the other. The motive to monopolize through predatory pricing is, therefore, difficult, if not impossible, to separate from real cost advantages of the kind that would lead to competitive (and "innocent") price reductions.

The use of motive by the courts is much safer in cases of personal malice than in cases of monopolization. In the former, no real cost advantages need be present for success and no benefits need be conveyed to third parties, but in the case of monopolization they must. Before the era of modern antitrust, it was precisely the personally malicious variety of activity, not price cutting, that fared badly before common-law courts. The motive that was important was the highly personal one that might provide evidence that this tall fence really was a spite fence; it was a motive that could identify consumption activity. That a firm seeks to expand its market is hardly a motive of this sort, even when a letter written by some middle management person alleges that price should be cut in order to teach some rival a "lesson." The lesson that is taught today often becomes the equilibrium price of tomorrow.

The objection to a low price that is allegedly predatory arises because of the expectation that price will be driven to monopoly levels once rivals are forced out of business, so that the benefit to consumers of immediately low prices may be offset by monopolistically high future prices. If we assume that this possibility is real in general, not merely reflective of the pursuit of the narrow interests of the harmed rivals through the good offices of the FTC, a question of legal tactics arises. Is it best to attack the practice which might after all be merely competitive or futile, or attack the monopoly should the practice succeed? To put the question as I have is to answer it, but one of the reasons for this answer may not be apparent. It is alleged that pricing practices are worth attacking because they nip monopoly in the bud; it has always seemed to me that the incipiency argument is weak, not only because competition might also be nipped in the bud, but because penalizing monopoly already successful also discourages the attempt to monopolize; any penalizing of monopoly nips monopoly in the bud by reducing the expected profits of monopolizing. Again, a choice of mix of outcomes must be made. One that is subject to all the usual uncertainties. We know that toleration of price cuts will deliver benefits to present consumers, but that future consumers may or may not be harmed by such toleration. Blocking price cuts certainly harms present consumers, but may benefit future consumers. A plausible policy is to take the bird in hand now because none may be in the bush tomorrow.

The distinction between limit-entry pricing and predatory pricing is only the difference in the level of price (relative to cost) that is assertedly necessary to bar entry. In the limit-entry model, because of scale economies, price need not be reduced below the cost of the existing firm(s) in order to make entry appear unprofitable to outsiders. It is not necessary here to explore the nuances of the model, nor to relate the entry barrier, supposedly based on scale economies, to its more logical source in firm history and existence. (See Section II, above.) All the objections raised to the attempt to tie predatory pricing to objective measures of cost apply even more strongly in this case, since existing firms need not experience even short-run loses in the limit entry model. It simply is impossible to distinguish such pricing from aggressive or promotional competitive pricing.

IV. Concluding Comment

The issue faced by the attempt to implement a policy toward barriers is that of defining which costs of undertaking activities are socially desirable and which are not. There presently is much too narrow a view about these costs, one that focuses on the cost of producing the physical output of an existing firm or industry. It tends to treat as unproductive the costs that must be incurred to create and to maintain a good reputation, to bear risks of innovation, and to build a scale of operations appropriate to the economical servicing of consumer demands, and it tends to neglect the incentives that will face future decision makers as a result of today's policy. Licensure, trademark, copyright, patent, entitlement to the fruits of past investment, including the investment in an honorable long history, and the right to reduce price may or may not be desirable, depending on how these broad implications are valued.

The valuation process must necessarily be one that is rich in intuition and faith, and poor in discernable measurements. A person possessing a deep faith in the strength and beneficient effects of competitive imitation will value the implied tradeoffs differently than a person possessing an equally deep faith in the process of "creative destruction." There exist neither cost–benefit analyses nor market–given prices by which to weight benefits and costs in most of these tradeoffs. If the concept of barriers to entry is to be policy useful, it must be able to distinguish these cases and attach value weights to them. The entire problem of desirable and undesirable "frictions" in economic systems has resisted analysis when it has not been simply ignored.

All policy preferences, of course, ultimately derive from a view of the world combined with one's preferences. The taste component remains a personal matter, but the view of the world can be convincing to others or not. Opposition to a tariff because of its impact on consumers is based on a convincing view of the world (to economists anyway!) because of our agreement as to the correctness of the underlying analysis. No such analysis exists for the notion of barriers. Our utterances in this regard may be accorded the skepticism appropriate to fairly unadorned opinion.

References

Areeda, Phillip, and Turner, Donald, "Predatory Pricing and Related Practices Under Section 2 of the Sherman Act," *Harvard Law Review*, February 1975, 88, 697–733.

Bain, Joe S., *Industrial Organization*, New York: Wiley & Sons, 1968.

Demsetz, Harold, "Accounting for Advertising As A Barrier to Entry," *Journal of Business*, July 1979, 52, 345–60.

Ferguson, James M., *Advertising and Competition: Theory, Measurement, Fact*, Cambridge: Ballinger, 1974.

Fisher, Franklin M., "Diagnosing Monopoly," *Quarterly Review of Economics and Business*, Summer 1979, 19, 7–33.

Klein, Benjamin, and Leffler, Keith, "The Role of Market Forces in Assuring Contractual Performance," *Journal of Political Economy*, August 1981, 89, 615–41.

McGee, John S., "Predatory Pricing Revisited," *Journal of Law and Economics*, October 1980, 23, 289–330.

Posner, Richard, *Antitrust Law: An Economic Perspective*, Chicago: University of Chicago, 1976.

Stigler, George J., *The Organization of Industry*, Homewood: Richard D. Irwin, 1968.

Telser, Lester, "Comment," *American Economic Review Proceedings*, May 1969, 59, 121–23.

von Weizsacker, C.C., "A Welfare Analysis of Barriers of Entry," *Bell Journal of Economics*, Autumn 1980, 11, 399–420.

Weiss, Leonard, "Advertising, Profits, and Corporate Taxes," *Review of Economics and Statistics*, November 1969, 51, 421–30.

Williamson, Oliver, "Predatory Pricing: A Strategic and Welfare Analysis," *Yale Law Journal*, December 1977, 87, 284–340.

Janich Bros. v. American Distilling Co, 570 F. 2d. 843, 1977.

Tuttle v. Buck, 107 Minn. 145, 119 N.W. 946.

CHAPTER 6 - Contestable Markets

Contestability and the Design of Regulatory and Antitrust Policy

Elizabeth E. Bailey

The theory of contestable markets, as advanced in a series of recent papers, encompasses a broad variety of market forms. (See William Baumol, Bailey, and Robert Willig; Baumol and Willig; and John Panzar and Willig.) However, its most dramatic results relate to natural monopoly. The theory pertains to markets which have substantial attributes of natural monopoly, but which are characterized by free and easy entry and exit. For such markets, the cost-minimizing market structure calls for a single seller, yet the theory asserts that these sellers are without monopoly power. In the case of contestable markets, potential entry or competition *for* the market disciplines behavior almost as effectively as would actual competition *within* the market. Thus, even if operated by a single firm, a market that can be readily contested performs in a competitive fashion.

In this paper, I advance the proposition that the theory of contestable markets can be extraordinarily helpful in the design of public policy. Particular markets can readily be observed to see whether the elements of contestability are present. Even more important, the tools of public policy do, by their nature, influence the degree of contestability. Just as traditional regulatory and antitrust policies often included elements that precluded contestability, so today there is a significant opportunity to redesign public policy so as to promote contestability. The new theory can facilitate the formulation of policy which permits toleration of factors that make for natural monopoly while at the same time lessening the need for public intervention.

I. The Elements of Contestability

The key element of contestability is that a market is vulnerable to competitive forces even when it is currently occupied by an oligopoly or a monopoly. That is, if any incumbent is inefficient or charges excessive prices or exploits consumers in any other way, successful entry must be possible and profitable. Thus, in contestable markets, entry and exit must be free and easy. There can

Reprinted from *American Economic Review* (1981) pp. 178–183 by permission of the American Economic Association.

be actual competition from either within the market or from a nearby substitute service, or there can exist potential entrants who face a cost structure that is no different than that of firms already in the industry. There must also be sufficient pricing flexibility so that potential entrants can undercut current suppliers. Economies of scale and/or large fixed costs are compatible with contestability. Even markets characterized by sunk costs may be contestable if these sunk costs are readily transferable or are borne by an entity other than the firm itself. The theory of contestability does not erase all problems associated with oligopoly or monopoly supply, for there is always the possibility that sustainable prices may not exist. This situation occurs, for example when a cost structure is such that the cost of supplying a subgroup of consumers is less per unit than the cost of supplying the entire group of consumers (see Gerald Faulhaber). But in all cases where sustainable prices can exist, the theory offers strong guidance for proper design of public policy.

Intuitively speaking, the theory of contestable markets builds on the tradition of Harold Demsetz, who first pointed out that it is sunk costs not economies of scale which constitute the barrier to entry that confers monopoly power. It is primarily the risk involved in expending large sums of money in order to acquire sunk–cost facilities that deters new entry when an otherwise profitable entry opportunity arises. Potential competition becomes an ever more effective force as the extent of large irretrievable entry costs declines. Similarly, incumbent firms, even those who have borne the burden of acquiring the sunk cost facility, are a problem for public policy only to the extent that they have permanent or exclusive access to that facility. Consequently, the single most important element in the design of public policy for monopoly should be the design of arrangements which render benign the exercise of power associated with operating sunk facilities.

One way to avoid the exercise of monopoly power is to have the sunk costs borne by a government or municipality, as they are in U.S. highway systems or airports, or by mandating that sunk costs be shared by a consortium, as is to some extent true of international broadcasting satellites, rather than to have the sunk costs incurred by the firm that is supplying the services. Virtually any method will do as long as there are contractual or other arrangements that are nondiscriminatory and permit easy transfer or lease or shared use of these cost commitments.

The theory tells us that when sunk costs are borne exclusively by a serving natural monopoly, as are railroad tracks in this country, and as are local telephone loops, then there may be a need for some form of government intervention to assure society that no excessive monopoly rents are earned from those facilities. By detaching sunk costs from the serving firm, much of the need for traditional economic regulation of the service industry disappears, even if the industry is still a natural monopoly. Instead, government intervention can often be limited to ensuring fairness of access to the sunk facility.

Fixed costs are not, according to the theory, a villain unless they also happen to be sunk. For example, although airplanes and barges might be individually costly, their mobility from market to market and their ability to be resold renders this cost unimportant as an entry barrier to a particular route and, consequently, as a source of monopoly power. Technological economies may be such that only one firm can actually serve in the market at any one time, but without exclusive rights to sunk facilities, the monopoly cannot expect to extract monopoly rents.

II. Design of Regulatory and Antitrust Policy

Unlike some policy prescriptions, the theory of contestable markets can readily be applied. The theory is clear about what types of policies enhance and what types interfere with the natural contestability of markets. In this section, I review traditional regulatory and antitrust policies which often served to preclude contestability, and describe how current policies are beginning to reverse this trend.

Consider, for example, the traditional licensing policies of the Civil Aeronautics Board (CAB) and the Interstate Commerce Commission (ICC). These policies restricted entry whether by new suppliers into the industry or by established suppliers into routes already served by others or not served by anyone. Entry was restricted both in dense markets which were structurally competitive and in thin markets where there might be expected to be only a single supplier. Authority was only conferred if it was likely to be used. There was no value placed on the benefit of having a pool of potential competitors who could respond to a potential profit opportunity by entering the market.

In contrast, the current policies of both the ICC and the CAB are to confer substantial new authority, whether actually used or not, thereby enhancing the degree of both actual and potential competition. The new policies are based on the theory that both trucking and aviation markets are, in the absence of regulatory intervention, naturally contestable. Capital is highly divisible in the trucking industry, and there is every reason to suppose that market mechanisms will work in allocating which exact commodities are carried by which particular trucking firm on which route. Even in nondense city-pair markets in aviation, where technological economies of scale with respect to aircraft size along with small traffic demand argue for a limited number of (turnaround) flights per day, potential competition should be able to act as a potent force. This is true because the major portion of airline capital costs, the aircraft, can readily be moved from one market to another. Thus, it is not surprising that John Panzar and I were able to cite evidence that, in late 1979 and early 1980 in the medium- and long-haul routes served by local service carriers, potential competition by trunk carriers was effectively policing the pricing behavior of the local carriers.

Regulation by the Federal Communications Commission (FCC) has also encouraged monopoly supply and prevented the emergence of contestable markets. There were rules that insisted upon monopoly supply of terminal equipment, even though the state of technology in that portion of the industry does not appear to favor, much less mandate the existence of a single supplier. Only in the last decade (after the Carterfone decision in 1968, the Equipment Registration Program in 1977–78, and a successful denial of AT&T's Primary Instrument Concept in 1979 by the Supreme Court), is economic control of equipment supply giving way to a policy which attempts to avoid network harm while permitting a variety of firms to supply the many terminal equipment devices that are now available for business and for household use.

Entry into the provision of transmission services was also precluded by government rule. At first, the rationale was to prevent destructive competition in an area that was considered to be a technological natural monopoly in which sunk costs played a major role. However, over time the sunk–cost aspects of cable technology have become mitigated by technical changes which led to the introduction of wireless transmission systems such as microwave services and more recently, of satellites. With these new techniques have come new policies which have attempted to encourage both actual and potential competition. The Above 890 Decision in 1959 gave a number of moderately large firms microwave transmission privileges. The Domestic Satellites decision encouraged firms other than AT&T to enter the domestic satellite business, and a later decision on Shared Use and Resale permitted customers of leased lines to resell their services. With the Execunet Decision in 1978, private carriers such as MCI and DATRAN were permitted to offer network services which compete in the broadest sense with the service offerings of the traditional telephone companies.

Traditional pricing policies of regulatory agencies have also interfered with the contestability of markets. One common practice has been to fix minimum or maximum rates. A typical result of this policy is that observable from stock brokerage regulation prior to 1975, where fixed rates meant that all customers paid for ancillary brokerage services, whether or not they used them. In the five years since the opening of these commission rates, a variety of price/service options have been introduced. These include discount brokers as well as arrangements whereby large buyers and sellers pay less per unit since the costs of serving them are lower.

Another practice common at the FCC and the CAB has been to set prices by formula, requiring equality of price for services over equal distance no matter whether the services involve sparsely traversed and hence costly rural routes, or routes which are heavily used and less costly. These formulas have many disadvantages. Perhaps the most obvious is the element of cross subsidy involved, with its concomitant requirement that competition be restricted on the lucrative routes. A second disadvantage of price formulas is that they tend to lag well behind technical changes. If, as in both aviation and communications technical change tends to reduce costs more for long- than for short-haul services, the formula tends to create a bias which under–values local services and overvalues long distance services. Yet a third disadvantage of the formulas is that they preclude price competition even where it involves innovative notions. For example, the CAB price formula of the early and mid–1970s precluded acceptance for interstate service of the high frequency/low fare proposals that are so successfully marketed by intrastate carriers, such as Southwest Airlines in Texas and Pacific Southwest Airlines in California.

In addition, antitrust policy has been used in ways that preclude the flexibility needed for contestability. One practice has been to grant antitrust immunity for rate conferences so that competing firms set rates jointly in a government approved cartel arrangement. At the ICC, these conferences not only serve to preclude price competition, but they have resulted in the pricing of trucking services at levels which have achieved rates of return for the major carriers of 30 to 40 percent or more and substantial rates of pay for teamster members. The recently enacted Motor Carrier Act of 1980 (Pub.L.96–296) has authorized a study commission to make a full and complete investigation upon the continued need or lack of need for continued antitrust immunity in this area.

Another practice has been to confer anti–trust immunity in situations where scarce capacity is allocated. This has been done, for example, by the CAB which has granted antitrust immunity to the incumbent airlines to meet and allocate among themselves the available landing slots at four major U.S. airports according to a rule of unanimity. The CAB and the FAA have recently commissioned a study by the Polimonic Research Laboratories of alternative, less anti–competitive methods for slot allocation. (See David Grether, R. Mark Isaac, and Charles Plott.)

Another step in altering antitrust policy to reflect contestability theory was taken by my colleagues and myself at the CAB when we refused to use traditional market share measures to preclude mergers. In the Texas International and National acquisition case, example, the Department of Justice recommended disapproval based in large part on market share data. They reasoned as follows: The Houston–New Orleans market shares for the twelve months ending June 30, 1978, were (in percent): National, 27, Delta 23, Texas International 24, Continental 17, and Eastern 7. The share of the two leading firms was therefore 51 percent and would be almost 75 percent after a combination of Texas International and National. This number was greater than comparable figures in mergers declared unlawful by the Supreme Court. The CAB countered by arguing that concentration ratios were not instructive in this case since with the passage of the Airline Deregulation Act of 1978 (Pub.L. 95–504), there was now relative ease of entry, even for small carriers, into such markets. In the Houston–New Orleans market in particular, there were eleven carriers with stations and functioning facilities already in place at both ends of this market. Therefore, the CAB reasoned that the markets were readily contested and did not find that a merger would be anticompetitive. Indeed, by the time the CAB order was written, a small regional carrier,

Southwest Airlines, had entered the market with a low fare turnaround service and was offering approximately 25 percent of the capacity of the market. (See CAB Order 79–12–163, 164, 165.)

III. Rules for Policy Design

The previous section has highlighted a number of the principles underlying reform policies. These principles include the removal of regulatory or antitrust barriers that prevent the access of competitors or that prevent competitive pricing. They include the examination of markets to ascertain whether potential competition is workable before actual share of market is taken to be a sign of monopoly power. The theory also suggests additional rules of thumb that can be used to guide policy design.

One such rule is that there should be coordination between pricing and entry policy. Freedom of entry into a market where incumbent suppliers are constrained to price according to a regulatory formula may result in "cream skimming." Freedom to price in a market where entry is precluded by regulatory fiat may well lead to gouging of consumers. Thus, to produce results that enhance the public welfare, freedom of entry should be accompanied by freedom of pricing and the reverse.

A second rule is a smallness doctrine, under which regulatory barriers to small entrants should be removed wherever possible. An example is the elimination by the FCC of all regulations for cable subscriber systems with fewer than 1,000 subscribers, or about 40 percent of cable systems. Another example was the decision of the CAB not to regulate route access or pricing for the commuter segment of the airline industry. Successful entry by small firms provides an excellent signal to a policymaker indicating that, under current economic conditions, there is room for enhanced competition. This competition often takes the form of the introduction of price/service innovations, such as Laker's Skytrain services from New York to London.

A third rule is that substantial pricing freedom can be granted if there is a competitive check offered by intermodal competition. It was sound policy when ICC recently permitted railroads total pricing freedom for transportation of fresh fruits and vegetables. The ICC reasoned that a competitive check existed since truck transportation of these commodities was already deregulated. The railroads responded strongly to their new freedom and increased their market share from 24 to 40 percent in only seven months. (See Darius Gaskins, Jr. and J. M. Voytko.) Thus, by segmentation of the industry, it may become possible to permit substantial pricing freedom in areas where carriers' ability to exploit market power is curtailed.

A fourth rule for the enhancement of contestability is that entry and exit should be made as easy as possible. Expedited procedures based on written pleadings rather than oral process can enhance this process. Another idea is to shift the burden of proof so that new entrants do not have the burden of showing that entry is in the public interest, but rather incumbents must argue that it is not. Both of these policy ideas have played important roles in the reform of aviation and transportation policy.

Other rules must be devised to handle sunk–cost problems. These may include encouraging technical changes that replace technologies involving large sunk costs with technologies that offer more opportunity for mobility or shared use. They may also include a careful look by policymakers of access rules to sunk facilities. For example, access problems can arise when airport authorities attempt to meet slot or noise constraints by banning new entry while allowing incumbent carriers to expand their operations at will. They can also arise under long–term lease arrangements which allocate airport space to particular carriers, and give these carriers the power to determine when, if, to whom, and at what price to sublease space to their competitors. The problem is illustrated by Laker Airways' search for gate and terminal space at Kennedy Airport in 1977 and 1978. Because the international terminal which is owned by the Port Authority was full, Laker contacted various airlines with no success, despite the fact that at least one terminal—National's—had unused space throughout the period. Laker was unable to get help from the Port Authority. It had to sell tickets at Queens Boulevard in Long Island and take passengers and their luggage to Kennedy by bus.

In the case of railroads, one of the most difficult problems blocking comprehensive rail deregulation is associated with the costs sunk in the rail lines to major coal using facilities, such as electric power plants. Once sites have been chosen for these plants, virtually no mobility is possible. The resulting problems should be dealt with using the principles laid out in contestability theory. Policymakers should look for solutions which permit and encourage competition from other sources, such as slurry pipelines. Or policymakers could supervise a transfer of the ownership of tracks to coal mines or to the public sector, which would then seek bids for shipping the coal. The theory provides a framework for the formulation of policies capable of coping with such problems.

In communications, the sunk costs of local telephone networks are, at present, fully borne by the Bell System. At issue now is the system of prices for access to these local networks. The design of "Exchange Network Facilities for Interstate Access" (ENFIA) tariffs with the principles of contestability in mind would call for the replacement of the current negotiated ENFIA tariffs with a system of prices that are the same for all vendors of network services so that the Bell System and others would all face the same costs of interconnection to the local network. With such equal opportunities afforded to all actual and potential competitors, with no barriers to entry, and with a policy of flexibility toward prices, the market might be expected to assure a socially efficient provision of network services.

IV. Summary

This paper has offered suggestions on how the theory of contestability can be used to organize the analysis of public policy. The theoretical concept of contestability has been shown to provide precisely the sort of guidance that has been needed for there to be an existing confluence between economic theory and the design of regulatory and antitrust policy.

References

E.E. Bailey and J.C. Panzar, "The Contestability of Airline Markets During the Transition to Deregulation," *Law Contemp. Probl.*, Dec. 1980.

W.J. Baumol,E.E. Bailey, and R.D. Willig, "Weak Invisible Hand Theorems on the Sustainability of Prices in a Multiproduct Monopoly," *Amer. Econ. Rev.*, June 1977, 67, 350–65.

W.J. Baumol and R.D. Willig, "Fixed Costs, Sunk Costs, Entry Barriers, Public Goods, and Sustainability of Monopoly," in eds., William J. Baumol et al., *Contestable Markets, Industry Structure, and the Theory of Value*, forthcoming 1981.

H. Demsetz, "Why Regulate Utilities." *J. Law Econ.*, Apr. 1968, 11, 55–65.

G.R. Faulhaber, "Cross Subsidization: Pricing in Public Enterprise," *Amer. Econ. Rev.*, Dec. 1975, 65, 966–77.

D.W. Gaskins, Jr. and J.M. Voytko, "Managing the Transition to Deregulation," *Law Contemp. Probl.*, Dec. 1980.

D.M. Grether, R.M. Isaac, and C.R. Plott, "The Allocation of Landing Rights by Unanimity among Competitors," *Amer. Econ. Rev. Proc.*, May 1981, 71, 166–71.

J.C. Panzar, "Equilibrium and Welfare in Unregulated Airline Markets," *Amer. Econ. Rev. Proc.*, May 1979, 69, 92–95.

_____ and R.D. Willig, "Free Entry and the Sustainability of Natural Monopoly," *Bell J. Econ.*, Spring 1977, 81, 1–22.

Contestable Markets: An Uprising in the Theory of Industry Structure

*William J. Baumol**

The address of the departing president is no place for modesty. Nevertheless, I must resist the temptation to describe the analysis I will report here as anything like a revolution. Perhaps terms such as "rebellion" or "uprising" are rather more apt. But, nevertheless, I shall seek to convince you that the work my colleagues, John Panzar and Robert Willig, and I have carried out and encapsulated in our new book enables us to look at industry structure and behavior in a way that is novel in a number of respects, that it provides a unifying analytical structure to the subject area, and that it offers useful insights for empirical work and for the formulation of policy.

Before getting into the substance of the analysis I admit that this presidential address is most unorthodox in at least one significant respect—that it is not the work of a single author. Here it is not even sufficient to refer to Panzar and Willig, the coauthors of both the substance and the exposition of the book in which the analysis is described in full. For others have made crucial contributions to the formulation of the theory—most notably Elizabeth Bailey, Dietrich Fischer, Herman Quirmbach, and Thijs ten Raa.

But there are many more than these. No uprising by a tiny band of rebels can hope to change an established order, and when the time for rebellion is ripe it seems to break out simultaneously and independently in a variety of disconnected centers each offering its own program for the future. Events here have been no different. I have recently received a proposal for a conference on new developments in the theory of industry structure formulated by my colleague, Joseph Stiglitz, which lists some forty participants, most of them widely known. Among those working on the subject are persons as well known as Caves, Dasgupta, Dixit, Friedlaender, Grossman, Hart, Levin, Ordover, Rosse, Salop, Schmalensee, Sonnenschein, Spence, Varian, von Weiszacker, and Zeckhauser, among *many* others.[1] It is, of course, tempting to me to take the view that our book is the true gospel of the rebellion and that the doctrines promulgated by others must be combatted as heresy. But that could at best be excused as a manifestation of the excessive zeal one comes to expect on such occasions. In truth, the immediate authors of the work I will report tonight may perhaps be able to justify a claim to have offered some systematization and order to the new doctrines—to have built upon them a more comprehen-

Reprinted from *American Economic Review* (1982) pp. 1–15 by permission of the American Economic Association.
*Presidential address delivered at the ninety-fourth meeting of the American Economic Association, December 29, 1981.

[1]Such a list must inevitably have embarrassing omissions—perhaps some of its author's closet friends. I can only say that it is intended just to be suggestive. The fact that it is so far from being complete also indicates how widespread an uprising I am discussing.

sive statement of the issues and the analysis, and to have made a number of particular contributions. But, in the last analysis, we must look enthusiastically upon our fellows rebels as comrades in arms, each of whom has made a crucial contribution to the common cause.

Turning now to the substance of the theory, let me begin by contrasting our results with those of the standard theory. In offering this contrast, let me emphasize that much of the analysis rests on work that appeared considerably earlier in a variety of forms. We, no less than other writers, owe a heavy debt to predecessors from Bertrand to Bain, from Cournot to Demsetz. Nevertheless, it must surely be acknowledged that the following characterization of the general tenor of the literature as it appeared until fairly recently is essentially accurate.

First, in the received analysis perfect competition serves as the one standard of welfare–maximizing structure and behavior. There is no similar form corresponding to industries in which efficiency calls for a very limited number of firms (though the earlier writings on workable competition did move in that direction in a manner less formal than ours).

Our analysis, in contrast, provides a generalization of the concept of the perfectly competitive market, one which we call a "perfectly contestable market." It is, generally, characterized by optimal behavior and yet applies to the full range of industry structures including even monopoly and oligopoly. In saying this, it must be made clear that perfectly contestable markets do not populate the world of reality any more than perfectly competitive markets do, though there are a number of industries which undoubtedly approximate contestability even if they are far from perfectly competitive. In our analysis, perfect contestability, then, serves not primarily as a description of reality, but as a benchmark for desirable industrial organization which is far more flexible and is applicable far more widely than the one that was available to us before.

Second, in the standard analysis (including that of many of our fellow rebels), the properties of oligopoly models are heavily dependent on the assumed expectations and reaction patterns characterizing the firms that are involved. When there is a change in the assumed nature of these expectations or reactions, the implied behavior of the oligopolistic industry may change drastically.

In our analysis, in the limiting case of perfect contestability, oligopolistic structure and behavior are freed entirely from their previous dependence on the conjectural variations of *incumbents* and, instead, these are generally determined uniquely and, in a manner that is tractable analytically, by the pressures of *potential* competition to which Bain directed our attention so tellingly.

Third, the standard analysis leaves us with the impression that there is a rough continuum, in terms of desirability of industry performance, ranging from unregulated pure monopoly as the pessimal arrangement to perfect competition as the ideal, with relative efficiency in resource allocation increasing monotonically as the number of firms expands.

I will show that, in contrast, in perfectly contestable markets behavior is sharply discontinuous in its welfare attributes. A contestable monopoly offers us some presumption, but no guarantee, of behavior consistent with a second best optimum, subject to the constraint that the firm be viable financially despite the presence of scale economies which render marginal cost pricing financially unfeasible. That is, a contestable monopoly has some reason to adopt the Ramsey optimal price–output vector, but it may have other choices open to it. (For the analysis of contestable monopoly, see my article with Elizabeth Bailey and Willig, Panzar and Willig's article, and my book with Panzar and Willig, chs. 7 and 8.)

But once each product obtains a second producer, that is, once we enter the domain of duopoly or oligopoly for each and every good, such choice disappears. The contestable oligopoly which achieves an equilibrium that immunizes it from the incrusions of entrants has only one pricing option—it must set its price exactly *equal* to marginal cost and do *all* of the things required for a first best optimum! In short, once we leave the world of pure or partial monopoly, any contestable market must behave ideally in every respect. Optimality is *not* approached gradually as the number of firms supplying a commodity grows. As has long been suggested in Chicago, two firms can be enough to guarantee optimality (see, for example, Eugene Fama and Arthur Laffer).

Thus, the analysis extends enormously the domain in which the invisible hand holds sway. In a perfectly contestable world, it seems to rule almost everywhere. Lest this seem to be too Panglossian a view of reality, let me offer two observations which make it clear that we emphatically do not believe that all need be for the best in this best of all possible worlds.

First, let me recall the observation that real markets are rarely, if ever, perfectly contestable. Contestability is merely a broader ideal, a benchmark of wider applicability than is perfect competition. To say that contestable oligopolies behave ideally and that contestable monopolies have some incentives for doing so is not to imply that this is even nearly true of all oligopolies or of unregulated monopolies in reality.

Second, while the theory extends the domain of the invisible hand in some directions, it unexpectedly restricts it in others. This brings me to the penultimate contrast I wish to offer here between the earlier views and those that emerge from our analysis.

The older theoretical analysis seems to have considered the invisible hand to be a rather weak intratemporal allocator of resources, as we have seen. The mere presence of unregulated monopoly or oligopoly was taken to be sufficient per se to imply that resources are likely to be misallocated *within* a given time period. *But where the market structure is such as to yield a satisfactory allocation of resources within the period*, it may have seemed that it can, at least in theory, do a good job of intertemporal resource allocation. In the absence of any externalities, persistent and asymmetric information gaps, and of interference with the workings of capital markets, the amounts that will be invested for the future may appear to be consistent with Pareto optimality and efficiency in the supply of outputs to current and future generations.

However, our analysis shows that where there are economies of scale in the production of durable capital, intertemporal contestable monopoly, which may perform relatively well in the single period, cannot be depended upon to perform ideally as time passes. In particular, we will see that the least costly producer is in the long run vulnerable to entry or replacement by rivals whose appearance is inefficient because it wastes valuable social resources.

There is one last contrast between the newer analyses and the older theory which I am most anxious to emphasize. In the older theory, the nature of the industry structure was *not* normally explained by the analysis. It was, in effect, taken to be given exogenously, with the fates determining, apparently capriciously, that one industry will be organized as an oligopoly, another as a monopoly and a third as a set of monopolistic competitors. Assuming that this destiny had somehow been revealed, the older analyses proceeded to investigate the consequences of the exogenously given industry structure for pricing, outputs, and other decisions.[2]

The new analyses are radically different in this respect. In our analysis, among others, an industry's structure is determined explicitly, endogenously, and simultaneously with the pricing, output, advertising, and other decisions of the firms of which it is constituted. This, perhaps, is one of the prime contributions of the new theoretical analyses.

I. Characteristics of Contestable Markets

Perhaps a misplaced instinct for melodrama has led me to say so much about contestable markets without even hinting what makes a market contestable. But I can postpone the definition no longer. A contestable market is one into which entry is absolutely free, *and exit is absolutely costless.* We use "freedom of entry" in Stigler's sense, not to mean that it is costless or easy, but that the entrant suffers no disadvantage in terms of production technique or perceived product quality relative to the incumbent, and that potential entrants find it appropriate to evaluate the profitability of entry in terms of the incumbent firms' pre-entry prices. In short, it is a requirement of contestability that there be no cost discrimination against entrants. Absolute freedom of exit, to us, is one way to guarantee freedom of entry. By this we mean that

---

[2]Of course, any analysis which considered the role of entry, whether it dealt with perfect competition or monopolistic competition, must implicitly have considered the determination of industry structure by the market. But in writings before the 1970's, such analyses usually did not consider how this process determined whether the industry would or would not turn out to be, for example, an oligopoly. The entry conditions were studied only to show how the assumed market structure could constitute an equilibrium state. Many recent writings have gone more explicitly into the determination of industry structure, though their approaches generally differ from ours.

any firm can leave without impediment, and in the process of departure can recoup any costs incurred in the entry process. If all capital is salable or reusable without loss other than that corresponding to normal user cost and depreciation, then any risk of entry is eliminated.

Thus, contestable markets may share at most one attribute with perfect competition. Their firms need not be small or numerous or independent in their decision making or produce homogeneous products. In short, a perfectly competitive market is necessarily perfectly contestable, but not *vice versa*.

The crucial feature of a contestable market is its vulnerability to hit–and–run entry. Even a very transient profit opportunity need not be neglected by a potential entrant, for he can go in, and, before prices change, collect his gains and then depart without cost, should the climate grow hostile.

Shortage of time forces me to deal rather briefly with two of the most important properties of contestable markets—their welfare attributes and the way in which they determine industry structure. I deal with these briefly because an intuitive view of the logic of these parts of the analysis is not difficult to provide. Then I can devote a bit more time to some details of the oligopoly and the intertemporal models.

A. Perfect Contestability and Welfare

The welfare properties of contestable markets follow almost directly from their definition and their vulnerability to hit–and–run incursions. Let me list some of these properties and discuss them succinctly.

First, a contestable market never offers more than a normal rate of profit —its economic profits must be zero or negative, even if it is oligopolistic or monopolistic. The reason is simple. Any positive profit means that a transient entrant can set up business, replicate a profit-making incumbent's output at the same cost as his, undercut the incumbent's prices slightly and still earn a profit. That is, continuity and the opportunity for costless entry and exist guarantee that an entrant who is content to accept a slightly lower economic profit can do so by selecting prices a bit lower than the incumbent's.

In sum, in a perfectly contestable market any economic profit earned by an incumbent automatically constitutes an earnings opportunity for an entrant who will hit and, if necessary, run (counting his temporary but supernormal profits on the way to the bank). Consequently, in contestable markets, zero profits must characterize any equilibrium, even under monopoly and oligopoly.

The second welfare characteristic of a contestable market follows from the same argument as the first. This second attribute of any contestable market is the absence of any sort of inefficiency in production in industry equilibrium. This is true alike of inefficiency of allocation of inputs, X–inefficiency, inefficient operation of the firm, or inefficient organization of the industry. For any unnecessary cost, like any abnormal profit, constitutes an invitation to entry. Of course, in the short run, as is true under perfect competition, both profits and waste may be present. But in the long run, these simply cannot withstand the threat brandished by potential entrants who have nothing to lose by grabbing at any opportunity for profit, however transient it may be.

A third welfare attribute of any long–run equilibrium in a contestable market is that no product can be sold at a price, p that is less than its marginal cost. For if some firm sells y units of output at such a price and makes a profit in the process, then it is possible for an entrant to offer to sell a slightly smaller quantity, $y - \epsilon$ at a price a shade lower than the incumbent's, and still make a profit. That is, if the price p is less than MC, then the sale of $y - \epsilon$ units at price p must yield a total profit $\pi + \Delta\pi$ which is greater than the profit, π, that can be earned by selling only y units of output at that price. Therefore, there must exist a price just slightly lower than p which enables the entrant to undercut the incumbent and yet to earn at least as much as the incumbent, by eliminating the unprofitable marginal unit.

This last attribute of contestable equilibria—the fact that price must always at least equal marginal cost—is important for the economics of anti-trust and regulation. For it means that in a perfectly contestable market, no cross subsidy is possible, that is, no predatory pricing can be used as a weapon of unfair competition. But we will see it also has implications which are more profound theoretically and which are more germane to our purposes. For it constitutes half of the argument which shows that when there are two or more suppliers of any product, its price must, in equilibrium, be exactly equal to marginal cost, and so resource allocation must satisfy all the requirements of first best optimality.

Indeed, the argument here is similar to the one which has just been described. But there is a complication which is what introduces the two–firm requirement into this proposition. $p < MC$ constitutes an opportunity for profit to an entrant who drops the unprofitable marginal unit of output, as we have just seen. It would seem, symmetrically, that $p > MC$ also automatically constitutes an opportunity for profitable entry. Instead of selling the y–unit output of a profitable incumbent, the entrant can now offer to sell the slightly larger output, $y + \epsilon$ using the profits generated by the marginal unit at a price greater than marginal cost to permit a reduction in price below the incumbent's. But on this side of the incumbent's output, there is a catch in the argument. Suppose the incumbent is a monopolist. Then output and price are constrained by the elasticity of demand. An attempt by an entrant to sell $y + \epsilon$ rather than y may conceivably cause a sharp reduction in price which eliminates the apparent profits of entry. In the extreme case where demand is perfectly inelastic, there will be no positive price at which the market will absorb the quantity $y + \epsilon$. This means that the profit opportunity represented by $p > MC$ can crumble into dust as soon as anyone seeks to take advantage of it.

But all this changes when the market contains two or more sellers. Now $p > MC$ does always constitute a real opportunity for profitable entry. The entrant who wishes to sell a bit more than some one of the profitable incumbents, call him incumbent A, need not press against the industry's total demand curve for the product. Rather, he can undercut A, steal away all of his customers, at least temporarily, and, in addition, steal away ϵ units of demand from any other incumbent, B. Thus, if A and B together sell $y_a + y_b > y_a$, then an entrant can lure away $y_a + \epsilon > y_a$ customers, for ϵ sufficiently small, and earn on this the incremental profit $\epsilon(p - MC) > 0$. This means that the entrant who sells $y_a + \epsilon$ can afford to undercut the prevailing prices somewhat and still make more profit than an incumbent who sells y_a at price p.

In sum, where a product is sold by two or more firms, any $p > MC$ constitutes an irresistible entry opportunity for hit–and–run entry in a perfectly contestable market, for it promises the entrant supernormal profits even if they accrue for a very short period of time.

Consequently, when a perfectly contestable market contains two or more sellers, neither $p < MC$ nor $p > MC$ is compatible with equilibrium. Thus we have our third and perhaps most crucial welfare attribute of such perfectly contestable markets—their prices, in equilibrium, must be equal to marginal costs, as is required for Pareto optimality of the "first best" variety. This, along with the conclusion that such markets permit no economic profits and no inefficiency in long–run equilibrium, constitutes their critical properties from the viewpoint of economic welfare. Certainly, since they do enjoy those three properties, the optimality of perfectly contestable equilibria (with the reservations already expressed about the case of pure monopoly) fully justifies our conclusion that perfect contestability constitutes a proper generalization of the concept of perfect competition so far as welfare implications are concerned.

B. On the Determination of Industry Structure

I shall be briefer and even less rigorous in describing how industry structure is determined endogenously by contestability analysis. Though this area encompasses one of its most crucial accomplishments, there is no way I can do justice to the details of the analysis in an oral presentation and within my allotted span of time. However, an intuitive view of the matter is not difficult.

The key to the analysis lies in the second welfare property of contestable equilibria—their incompatibility with inefficiency of any sort. In particular, they are incompatible with inefficiency in the *organization* of an industry. That is, suppose we consider whether a particular output quantity of an industry will be produced by two firms or by a thousand. Suppose it turns out that the two-firm arrangement can produce the given output at a cost 20 percent lower than it can be done by the 1,000 firms. Then one implication of our analysis is that the industry cannot be in long–run equilibrium if it encompasses 1,000 producers. Thus we already have some hint about the equilibrium industry structure of a contestable market.

We can go further with this example. Suppose that, with the given output vector for the industry, it turns out that *no* number of firms other than two can produce at as low a total cost as is possible under a two–firm arrangement. That is, suppose two firms can produce the output vector at a total cost lower than it can be done by one firm or three firms or sixty or six thousand. Then we say that for the given output vector the industry is a *natural duopoly*.

This now tells us how the industry's structure can be determined. We proceed, conceptually, in two steps. First we determine what structure happens to be most efficient for the production of a given output vector by a given industry. Next, we investigate when market pressures will lead the industry toward such an efficient structure in equilibrium.

Now, the first step, though it has many intriguing analytic attributes, is essentially a pure matter of computation. Given the cost function for a typical firm, it is ultimately a matter of calculation to determine how many firms will produce a given output most efficiently. For example, if economies of scale hold throughout the relevant range and there are sufficient complementarities in the production of the different commodities supplied by the firm, then it is an old and well–known conclusion that single firm production will be most economical—that we are dealing with a natural monopoly.

Similarly, in the single product case suppose the average cost curve is U shaped and attains its minimum point at an output of 10,000 units per year. Then it is obvious that if the industry happens to sell 50,000 units per year, this output can be produced most cheaply if it is composed of exactly five firms, each producing 10,000 units at its point of minimum average cost.

Things become far more complex and more interesting when the firm and the industry produce a multiplicity of commodities, as they always do in reality. But the logic is always the same. When the industry output vector is small compared to the output vectors the firm can produce at relatively low cost, then the efficient industry structure will be characterized by very few firms. The opposite will be true when the industry's output vector is relatively far from the origin. In the multiproduct case, since average cost cannot be defined, two complications beset the characterization of the output vectors which the firm can produce relatively efficiently. First, since here average cost cannot be defined, we cannot simply look for the point of minimum average costs. But we overcome this problem by dealing with output bundles having fixed proportions among commodity quantities—by moving along a ray in output space. Along any such ray the behavior of average cost is definable, and the point of minimum ray average cost (RAC) is our criterion of relatively efficient scale for the firm. Thus, in Figure 1 we have a ray average cost curve for the production of boots and shoes when they are produced in the proportion given by ray OR. We see that for such bundles y^m is the point of minimum RAC. A second problem affecting the determination of the output vectors the firm can produce efficiently is the choice of output proportions—the location of the ray along which the firm will operate. This depends on the degree of complementarity in production of the goods, and it also lends itself to formal analysis.

We note also that the most efficient number of firms will vary with the location of the industry's output vector. The industry may be a natural monopoly with one output vector, a natural duopoly with another, and efficiency may require seventy–three firms when some third output vector is provided by the industry.

This, then, completes the first of the two basic steps in the endogenous determination of industry structure. Here we have examined what industry structure is least costly for each given output vector of a given industry, and have found how the result depends on the magnitudes of the elements of that output vector and the shape of the cost function of the typical firm. So far the discussion may perhaps be considered normative rather than behavioral. It tells us what structure is most efficient under the circumstances, not which industry structure will emerge under the pressures of the market mechanism.

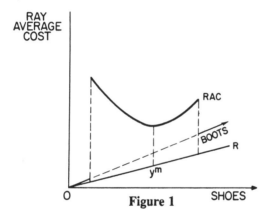

Figure 1

The transition toward the second, behavioral, stage of the analysis is provided by the observation that the optimal structure of an industry depends on its output vector, while that output vector in turn depends on the prices charged by its firms. But, since pricing depends on industry structure, we are brought full circle to the conclusion that pricing behavior and industry structure must, ultimately, be determined simultaneously and endogenously.

We are in no position to go much further than this for a market whose properties are unspecified. But, for a perfectly contestable market, we can go much further. Indeed, the properties of perfect contestability cut through every difficulty and tell us the equilibrium prices, outputs, and industry structure, all at once.

Where more than one firm supplies a product, we have already characterized these prices precisely. For we have concluded that each equilibrium price will equal the associated marginal cost. Then, given the industry's cost and demand relationships, this yields the industry's output quantities simultaneously with its prices, in the usual manner. Here there is absolutely nothing new in the analysis.

But what is new is the format of the analysis of the determination of industry structure. As I have already pointed out, structure is determined by the efficiency requirement of equilibrium in any contestable market. Since no such equilibrium is compatible with failure to minimize industry costs, it follows that the market forces under perfect contestability will bring us results consistent with those of our normative analysis. Whatever industry structures minimize total costs for the equilibrium output vector must turn out to be the only structures consistent with industry equilibrium in the long run.

Thus, for contestable markets, but for contestable markets *only*, the second stage of the analysis of industry structure turns out to be a sham. Whatever industry structure was shown by the first, normative, portion of the analysis to be least costly must also emerge as the industry structure selected by market behavior. No additional calculations are required by the behavioral analysis. It will all have been done in the normative cost–minimization analysis and the behavioral analysis is pure bonus.

Thus, as I promised, I have indicated how contestability theory departs from the older theory which implicitly took industry structure to be determined exogenously in a manner totally unspecified and, instead, along with other recent writings, embraces the determination of industry structure as an integral part of the theory to be dealt with simultaneously with the determination of prices and outputs.

At this point I can only conjecture about the determination of industry structure once we leave the limiting case of perfect contestability. But my guess is that there are no sharp discontinuities here, and that while the industry structures which emerge in reality are not always those which minimize costs, they will constitute reasonable approximations to the efficient structures. If this is not so it is difficult to account for the similarities in the patterns of industry structure that one observes in different countries. Why else do we not see agriculture organized as an oligopoly in any free market economy, or automobiles produced by 10,000 firms? Market pressures must surely make any very inefficient market structure vulnerable to entry, to displacement of incumbents by foreign competition, or to undermining in other ways. If that is so, the market structure that is called for by contestability theory may not prove to be too bad an approximation to what we encounter in reality.

II. On Oligopoly Equilibrium

I should like now to examine oligopoly equilibrium somewhat more extensively. We have seen that, except where a multiproduct oligopoly firm happens to sell some of its products in markets in which it has no competitors, an important partial monopoly case which I will ignore in what follows, all prices must equal the corresponding marginal costs in long–run equilibrium. But in an oligopoly market, this is a troublesome concept. Unless the industry output vector happens to fall at a point where the cost function is characterized by locally constant returns to scale, we know that zero profits are incompatible with marginal cost pricing. Particularly if there are scale economies at that point, so that marginal cost pricing precludes financial viability, we can hardly expect such a solution to constitute an equilibrium. Besides, we have seen that long-run equilibrium requires profit to be precisely zero. We would thus appear to have run into a major snag by concluding that perfect contestability always leads to marginal cost pricing under oligopoly.

This is particularly so if the (ray) average curve is U shaped, with its minimum occurring at a single point, y^m. For in this case that minimum point is the only output of the firm consistent with constant returns to scale and with zero profits under marginal cost pricing. Thus, dealing with the single product case to make the point, it would appear, say, that if the AC-minimizing output is 1,000, in a contestable market, equilibrium is possible if quantity demanded from the industry happens to be exactly 2,000 units (so two firms can produce 1,000 units each) or exactly 3,000 units or exactly 4,000 units, etc. But suppose the demand curve happens to intersect the industry AC curve, say, at 4,030 units. That is, then, the only industry output satisfying the equilibrium requirement that price equals zero profit. But then, at least one of the four or five firms in the industry must produce either more or less than 1,000 units of output, and so the slope of its AC curve will not be zero at that point, precluding either MC pricing or zero profits and, consequently, violating one or the other of the requirements of equilibrium in a perfectly contestable market.

It would appear that equilibrium will be impossible in this perfectly contestable market unless by a great piece of luck the industry demand curve happens to intersect its AC curve at 2,000 or 3,000 units or some other integer multiple of 1,000 units of output.

There are a variety of ways in which one can grapple with this difficulty. In his dissertation at New York University, Thijs ten Raa has explored the issue with some care and has shown that the presence of entry costs of sufficient magnitude, that is, irreversible costs which must be borne by an entrant but not by an incumbent, can eliminate the existence problem. The minimum size of the entry cost required to permit an equilibrium will depend on the size of the deviation from zero profits under marginal cost pricing and ten Raa has given us rules for its determination. He has shown also that the existence problem, as measured by the required minimum size of entry cost, decreases rapidly as the equilibrium number of firms of the industry increases, typically attaining negligible proportions as that number reaches, say, ten enterprises. For, as is well known, when the firm's average cost curve is U shaped the industry's average cost curve will approach a horizontal line as the size of industry output increases. This is shown in Figure 2 which is a standard diagram giving the firm's and the industry's AC curves when the former is U shaped. As a result, the deviations between average cost and marginal cost will decline as industry output increases and so the minimum size of the entry cost required to preserve equilibrium declines correspondingly.

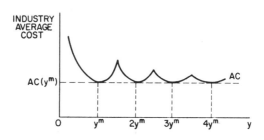

Figure 2

However, here I want to describe another approach offered in our book to the problem of existence which I have just described—the difficulty of satisfying simultaneously the zero–profit requirement and the requirement of marginal cost pricing. This second avenue relies on the apparently unanimous conclusion of empirical investigators of the cost function of the firm, that AC curves are not, in fact, characterized by a unique minimum point as they would be if they had a smooth U shape. Rather, these investigators tell us, the AC curve of reality has a flat bottom—an interval along which it is horizontal. That is, average costs do tend to fall at first with size of output, then they reach a minimum and continue at that level for some range of outputs, after which they may begin to rise once more. An AC curve of this variety is shown in Figure 3. Obviously, such a flat segment of the AC curves *does* help matters because there is now a *range* of outputs over which MC pricing yields zero profits. Moreover, the longer the flat-bottomed segment the better matters are for existence of equilibrium. Indeed, it is easy to show that if the left–hand end of the flat segment occurs at output y^m and the right–hand end occurs at ky^m,

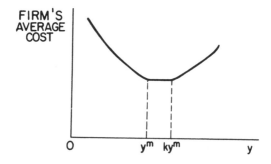

Figure 3

then if k is greater than or equal to 2 the existence problem disappears altogether, because the industry's AC curves will be horizontal for any output greater than y_m. That is, in any contestable market in which two or more firms operate the industry AC curve will be horizontal and MC pricing will always yield zero profits. To confirm that this is so, note that if, for example, the flat segment for the firm extends from $y = 1,000$ to $y = 2,000$, then any industry output of, say, $9,000 + \Delta y$ where $0 \leq \Delta y \leq 9,000$ can be produced by nine firms, each of them turning out more than 1,000 but less than 2,000 units. Hence, each of them will operate along the horizontal portion of its AC curve, as equilibrium requires.

Thus, if the horizontal interval (y^m, ky_m) happens to satisfy $k \geq 2$, there is no longer any problem for existence of equilibrium in a contestable market with two or more firms. But fate may not always be so kind. What if that horizontal interval is quite short, that is, k is quite close to unity? Such a case is shown in our diagram where for illustration I have taken $k = 4/3$.

I should like to take advantage of your patience by dealing here not with the simplest case—that of the single product industry—but with the multiproduct problem. I do this partly to offer you some feeling of the way in which the multiproduct analysis, which is one of the hallmarks of our study, works out in practice.

Because, as we have seen, there is no way one can measure average cost for all output combinations in the multiproduct case, I will deal exclusively with the total cost function. Figure 4 shows such a total cost function for the single firm, which is taken to manufacture two products, boots and shoes.

Let us pause briefly to examine its shape. Along any ray such as OR, which keeps output proportions constant, we have an ordinary total cost curve, OST.

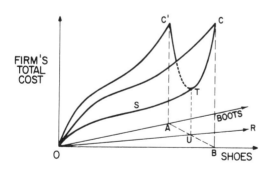

Figure 4

With one exception, which I will note soon, I have drawn it to have the usual sort of shape, with marginal costs falling near the origin and rising at points much further from the origin. On the other hand, the trans ray cut above AB yields a cross section $C'TC$ which is more or less U shaped. This means that it is relatively cheaper to produce boots and shoes together (point U) than to produce them in isolation (point *A* or point *B*). That is, this convex trans ray shape is enough to offer us the complementarity which leads firms and industries to turn out a multiplicity of products rather than specializing in the production of a single good.

Now what, in such a case, corresponds to the flat bottom of an *AC* curve in a single product case? The answer is that the cost function in the neighborhood of the corresponding output must be linearly homogeneous. In Figure 5 such a region, $\alpha\beta\gamma\delta$, is depicted. It is linearly homogeneous because it is generated by a set of rays such as *L, M,* and *N.* For simplicity in the discussion that follows, I have given this region a very regular shape–it is, approximately, a rectangle which has been moved into three–dimensional space and given a U–shaped cross section.

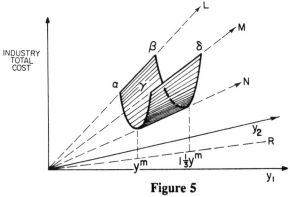

Figure 5

Now Figure 6 combines the two preceding diagrams and we see that they have been drawn to mesh together, so that the linearly homogeneous region constitutes a portion of the firm's total cost surface. We see then that the firm's total cost does have a region in which constant returns to scale occur, and which corresponds to the flat-bottomed segment of the AC curve.

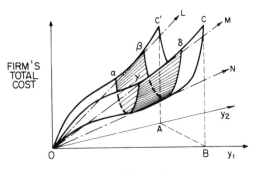

Figure 6

Moreover, as before, I have deliberately kept this segment quite narrow. Indeed, I have repeated the previous proportions, letting the segment extend from a distance y^m from the origin to the distance $11/3y^m$ along any ray on the floor of the diagram.

Let us now see what happens in these circumstances when we turn to the total cost surface for the *industry*. This is depicted in Figure 7 which shows a relationship that may at first seem surprising. In Figure 7 I depict only the linearly homogeneous portions of the industry's cost surface. There we see that while for the firm linear homogeneity prevailed only in the interval from y^m to $11/3y^m$, in the case of industry output linear homogeneity also holds in that same interval but, in addition, it holds for the interval $2y^m$ to $22/3y^m$ and in the region extending from $3y^m$ to infinity. That is, everywhere beyond $3y^m$ the industry's total cost function is linearly homogeneous. In this case, then, we have three regions of local linear homogeneity in the industry's cost function, $\alpha\beta\theta\omega$, which is identical with that of the individual firm, the larger region abcd, and the infinite region *aleph beth....*

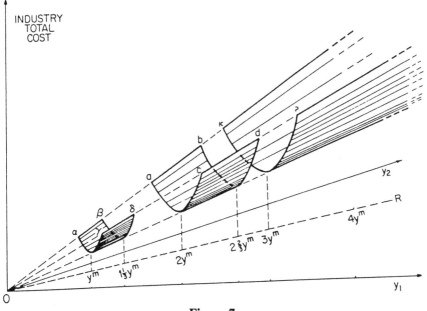

Figure 7

Before showing why this is so we must pause to note the implications of the exercise. For it means that even a relatively small region of flatness in the *AC* curve of the individual firm, that is, of linear homogeneity in its total cost function, eliminates the bulk of the existence problem for oligopoly equilibrium in a contestable market. The problem does not arise for outputs nearer to the origin than y_m because such outputs are supplied most efficiently by a monopoly which is not required to price at marginal cost in a contestable market equilibrium. The problem also does not arise for any industry output greater than $3y^m$ in this case, because everywhere beyond that marginal cost pricing yields zero profits. There are two relatively narrow regions in which no equilibrium is, indeed, possible, but here we may conjecture that the vicissitudes of disequilibrium will cause shifts in the demand relationships as changing prices and changing consumption patterns affect tastes, and so the industry will ultimately happen upon an equilibrium position and remain there until exogenous disturbances move it away. Thus we end up with an oligopoly equilibrium whose prices, profits, and other attributes are determined without benefit of the conjectural variation, reaction functions, and the other paraphernalia of standard oligopoly analysis.

To complete this discussion of oligopoly equilibrium in a contestable market, it only remains for me to explain why the regions of linear homogeneity in the industry's cost function are as depicted in Figure 7. The answer is straightforward. Let $C(y)$ be the firm's total cost function for which we have assumed for expository simplicity that in the interval from y^m to $1\ 1/3y^m$ along each and every ray, total cost grows exactly proportionately with output. Then two firms can produce $2y^m$ at the same unit cost, and three firms can produce $3y^m$ at that same unit cost for the given output bundle, etc. But by exactly the same argument, the two firms together, each producing no more than $1\ 1/3y^m$, can turn out anything up to $2\ 2/3y^m$ without affecting unit costs, and three firms can produce as much as $3\ 3/3y^m$, that is, as much as $4y^m$. In sum, the intervals of linear homogeneity for the industry are the following:

Interval 1: from y^m to $1\ 1/3y^m$
Interval 2: from $2y^m$ to $2\ 2/3y^m$
Interval 3: from $3y^m$ to $4y^m$
Interval 4: from $4y^m$ to $5\ 1/3y^m$
Interval 5: from $5y^m$ to $6\ 2/3y^m$
....

That is, each interval begins at an integer multiple of y^m and extends $1/3\ y^m$ further than its predecessor. Thus, beyond $3y^m$ successive intervals begin to touch or overlap and that is why linear homogeneity extends everywhere beyond $3y^m$ as I claimed.[3]

There is one complication in the multiproduct case which I have deliberately slid over, feeling the discussion was already complicated enough. The preceding argument assumes implicitly that the firms producing the industry output all employ the same output proportions as those in the industry output vector. For otherwise, it is not legitimate to move outward along a single ray as the number of firms is increased. But suppose increased industry output were

---

[3]The reader can readily generalize this result. If the flat–bottomed segment for the firm extends from y^m to $y^m(1+1/w)$, where w is an integer, then there will be w regions of linear homogeneity in the industry cost function and it will be linearly homogeneous for any output $y \geq wy^m$.

to permit savings through increased specialization. Might there not be constant returns with fixed output proportions and yet economies of scale for the industry overall? This problem is avoided by our complementarity assumption used to account for the industry's multiproduct operation—our U-shaped trans-ray cross section. This, in effect, rules out such savings from specialization in the regions where linear homogeneity also rules out savings from increased scale.

This, then, completes my discussion of oligopoly equilibrium in perfectly contestable markets, which we have seen, yields a determinate set of prices and outputs that is not dependent upon assumptions about the nature of incumbent firm's expectations relating to entrants' behavior and offers us an concrete and favorable conclusion on the welfare implications of contestable oligopoly.

III. Intertemporal Vulnerability to Inefficient Entry

Having so far directed attention to areas in which the invisible hand manifests unexpected strength, I should like to end my story by dealing with an issue in relation to which it is weaker than some of us might have expected. As I indicated before, this is the issue of intertemporal production involving durable capital goods.

The analysis is far more general than the following story suggests, but even the case I describe is sufficiently general to make the point. We deal with an industry in which a product is offered by a single firm that provides it period after period. The equilibrium quantity of the commodity that is demanded grows steadily with the passage of time in a manner that is foreseen without uncertainty. Because of economies of scale in the production of capacity the firm deliberately builds some excess capacity to take care of anticipated growth in sales volume. But there is some point, let us say, $z = 45$ years in the future, such that it would be uneconomic to take further growth in sales volume into account in the initial choice of capacity. This is so because the opportunity (interest) cost of the capacity that remains idle for 45 or more years exceeds the savings made possible by the economies of scale of construction. Thus, after 45 years it will pay the firm to undertake a second construction project to build the added capacity needed to produce the goods demanded of it.

Suppose that in every particular period our producer is a natural monopolist, that is, he produces the industry's supply of its one commodity at a cost lower than it can be done by any two or more enterprises. Then considering that same product in different periods to be formally equivalent to different goods we may take our supplier to be an intertemporal natural monopolist in a multiproduct industry. That is, no combination of two or more firms can produce the industry's intertemporal output vector as cheaply as he. I will prove now under a set of remarkably unrestrictive assumptions that despite its cost advantages, there exists no intertemporal price vector consistent with equilibrium for this firm. That is, whatever his price vector, his market will at some time be vulnerable to partial or complete takeover by an entrant who has neither superior skills nor technological superiority and whose entrance increases the quantities of resources used up in production. In other words, here the invisible hand proves incapable of protecting the most efficient producing arrangement and leaves the incumbent producer vulnerable to displacement by an aggressive entrant. I leave to your imaginations what, if anything, this says about the successive displacements on the world market of the Dutch by the English, the English by the Germans and the Americans, and the Americans, perhaps, by the Japanese.

The proof of our proposition on the intertemporal vulnerability of incumbents to entry that is premature from the viewpoint of cost minimization does require just a little bit of algebra. To keep our analysis simple, I will divide time into two periods, each lasting $z = 45$ years so that capacity in the first period is, optimally, just sufficient to satisfy all demand, but in the second, it requires the construction of added capacity to meet demand growth because, by assumption, anticipatory construction to meet growth more than z years in the future simply is too costly. Also for simplicity, I will assume that there are no costs other than cost of construction. Of course, neither this nor the use of only two periods really affects the argument in any way. My only three substantive assumptions are that demand is growing with time, that there are economies of scale, that is, declining average costs in construction, and that there exists some length of time, z, so great that it does not pay in the initial construction to build capacity sufficient for the growth in quantity demanded that will occur beyond that date.

The argument, like the notation, is now straightforward. Let y_t be output in period t, p_t be price in period t, and $K(y)$ be the cost of construction of capacity sufficient to produce (a maximum of) y units per period. Here, both p_t and $K(y)$ are expressed in discounted present value.[4]

Then, by assumption, our firm will construct at the beginning of the first period capacity just sufficient to produce output y_1 at cost $K(y_1)$ and at the beginning of the second period it will produce the rest of the capacity it needs, $y_2 - y_1 > 0$, at the cost $K(y_2 - y_1)$.

The first requirement for the prices in question to be consistent with equilibrium is that they permit the incumbent to cover his costs, that is, that

(1) $\qquad p_1 y_1 + p_2 y_2 \geq K(y_1) + K(y_2 - y_1).$

Second, for these prices to constitute an equilibrium they must protect the incumbent against any and all possible incursions by entrants. That is, suppose an entrant were to consider the possibility of constructing capacity y_1 and not expanding in the future, and, by undercutting the incumbent, selling the same output, y_1, in each period. Entry on these terms will in fact be profitable unless

---

[4]That is, if p^*_1, p^*_2, represent the undiscounted prices, $p_1 = p^*_1$, $p_2 = p^*_2/(1 + r)$, where r is the rate of interest, etc.

the prices are such that the sale of y_1 in each period does not bring in revenues sufficient to cover the cost, $K(y_1)$, of the entrant's once-and-for-all construction. That is, entry will be profitable unless

(2) $\qquad p_1 y_1 + p_2 y_1 \leq K(y_1).$

Thus, the prices in question cannot constitute an equilibrium unless (2) as well as (1) are satisfied.

Now, subtracting (2) from (1) we obtain immediately

$$p_2(y_2 - y_1) \geq K(y_2 - y_1)$$

or

(3) $\qquad p_2 \geq K(y_2 - y_1)/(y_2 - y_1),$

but, by the assumption that average construction cost is declining, since $y_1 > 0$,

(4) $\qquad K(y_2 - y_1)/(y_2 - y_1) > K(y_2)/y_2.$

Substituting this into (3) we have at once

$$p_2 > K(y_2)/y_2$$

or

(5) $\qquad p_2 y_2 > K(y_2).$

Inequality (5) is our result. For it proves that any prices which satisfy equilibrium requirements (1) and (2) must permit a second–period entrant using the same techniques to build capacity y_2 from the ground up, at cost $K(y_2)$, to price slightly below anything the incumbent can charge and yet recover his costs; and that in doing so, the entrant can earn a profit.

Thus, our intertemporal natural monopolist cannot quote, *at time zero*, any prices capable of preventing the take over of some or all of his market. Moreover, this is so despite the waste, in the form of replication of the incumbent's plant, that this entails. That, then, is the end of the formal argument, the proof that here the invisible hand manifests weakness that is, perhaps, unexpected.

You will all undoubtedly recognize that the story as told here in its barest outlines omits all sorts of nuances, such as entrants' fear of responsive pricing, the role of bankruptcy, depreciation of capital, and the like. This is not the place to go into these matters for it is neither possible nor appropriate here for me to go beyond illustration of the logic of the new analysis.

IV. Concluding Comments

Before closing let me add a word on policy implications, whose details must also be left to another place. In spirit, the policy conclusions are consistent with many of those economists have long been espousing. At least in the intratemporal analysis, the heroes are the (unidentified) potential entrants who exercise discipline over the incumbent, and who do so most effectively when entry is free. In the limit when entry and exit are completely free, efficient incumbent monopolists and oligopolists may in fact be able to prevent entry. But they can do so only by behaving virtuously, that is, by offering to consumers the benefits which competition would otherwise bring. For every deviation from good behavior instantly makes them vulnerable to hit-and-run entry.

This immediately offers what may be a new insight on antitrust policy. It tells us that a history of absence of entry in an industry and a high concentration index may be signs of virtue, not of vice. This will be true when entry costs in our sense are negligible. And, then, efforts to change market structure must be regarded as mischievous and antisocial in their effects.

A second and more obvious conclusion is the questionable desirability of artificial impediments to entry, such as regulators were long inclined to impose. The new analysis merely reinforces the view that any proposed regulatory barrier to entry must start off with a heavy presumption against its adoption. Perhaps a bit newer is the emphasis on the importance of freedom of exit which is as crucial a requirement of contestability as is freedom of entry. Thus we must reject as perverse the propensity of regulators to resist the closing down of unprofitable lines of activity. This has even gone so far as a Congressional proposal (apparently supported by Ralph Nader) to require any plant with yearly sales exceeding $250,000 to provide fifty-two weeks of severance pay and to pay three years of taxes, before it will be permitted to close, and that only after giving two years notice!

There is much more to the policy implications of the new theory, but I will stop here, also leaving its results relating to empirical research for discussion elsewhere.

Let me only say in closing that I hope I have adequately justified my characterization of the new theory as a rebellion or an uprising. I believe it offers a host of new analytical methods, new tasks for empirical research, and new results. It permits reexamination of the domain of the invisible hand, yields contributions to the theory of oligopoly, provides a standard for policy that is far broader and more widely applicable than that of perfect competition, and leads to a theory that analyzes the determination of industry structure endogenously and simultaneously with the analysis of the other variables more traditionally treated in the theory of the firm and the industry. It aspires to provide no less than a unifying theory as a foundation for the analysis of industrial organization. I will perhaps be excused for feeling that this was an ambitious undertaking.

References

Bain, Joe S., *Barriers to New Competition*, Cambridge: Harvard University Press, 1956.

Baumol, William J., Bailey, Elizabeth E., and Willig, Robert D., "Weak Invisible Hand Theorems on the Sustainability of Multiproduct Natural Monopoly," *American Economic Review*, June 1977, 67, 350–65.

_____, Panzar, John C., and Willig, Robert D., *Contestable Markets and the Theory of Industry Structure*, San Diego: Harcourt Brace Jovanovich, 1982.

Bertrand, Jules, *Review of Theorie Mathematique de la Richesse and Recherches sur les Principes Mathematiques de la theorie des Richesses, Journal des Savants*, 1883, 499–508.

Cournot, A.A., *Researches into the Mathematical Principles of the Theory of Wealth*, New York: A.M. Kelley, 1938; 1960.

Demsetz, Harold, "Why Regulate Utilities?," *Journal of Law and Economics*, April 1968, 11, 55–65.

Fama, Eugene F. and Laffer, Arthur B., "The Number of Firms and Competition," *American Economic Review*, September 1972, 62, 670–74.

Panzar, John C. and Willig, Robert D., "Free Entry and the Sustainability of Natural Monopoly," *Bell Journal of Economics*, Spring 1977 8, 1–22.

ten Raa, Thijs, "A Theory of Value and Industry Structure," unpublished doctoral dissertation, New York University, 1980.

CHAPTER 7 - Modern Rivalry

Competition Theory and the Market Economy

Dominick T. Armentano

It might be appropriate to begin a theoretical discussion of the foundations of antitrust law with the familiar historical observation that business competition was declining in the post–Civil War period. Joseph W. McGuire, in his classic *Business and Society*, provides a typical expression of the conventional wisdom regarding the state of competition in the marketplace.

> There have always existed many forces which tend to reduce competition. In the thirty years following the Civil War, these forces began to predominate in the United States.... Competition, so effective as a regulating force on business operations in the decades prior to the war, was steadily decreasing as a few firms began to dominate our important industries and as these and other concerns turned more and more to collusion.[1]

Now this seems entirely straightforward. Competition was an effective process prior to the Civil War, but in the post–war period it steadily declined. Major industries came to be dominated by large combinations that either monopolized the market or conspired to restrain trade and competition. The impression here and elsewhere is that these combinations were effective and that the Sherman Act was a logical response to a deteriorating economic situation. In short, the free market was amended to save it.

And yet there is something curious about this perspective, particularly in the McGuire text. For only a paragraph earlier it had informed the reader that:

> From 1865 to 1897, declining prices year after year made it difficult for businessmen to plan for the future. In many areas new railroad links had resulted in a nationalization of the market east of the Mississippi, and even small concerns in small towns were forced to compete with other, often larger firms located at a distance. At the same time there were remarkable advances in technology and productivity. In short it was a wonderful era for the consumer and a frightful age for the producers especially as competition became more and more severe.[2]

Reprinted by permission of the publisher from *Antitrust and Monopoly: Anatomy of a Policy Failure*, by D.T. Armentano. Copyright ©1990, The Independent Institute, 134 Ninety-Eighth Avenue, Oakland, California 94603.
[1]Joseph W. McGuire, *Business and Society* (New York: McGraw–Hill Book Co., 1963), pp. 39–40.
[2]*Ibid.*, pp. 38–39.

Something appears amiss here. It is not immediately obvious how competition could be "steadily decreasing" on the one hand while it was becoming "more and more severe" on the other. In addition, if competition was declining as large firms came to dominate certain industries, how could the period have been a "wonderful era for the consumer"? If the growth of large-scale enterprise reduced competition in the market, why did overproduction occur, and why were there "remarkable advances in technology and productivity"? Further, how are we to reconcile increasing monopoly and collusion with the general price deflation that occurred in this period, and with McGuire's conclusion that this era was a "frightful" age for the producer? And finally, if the second perspective quoted above is in fact the correct one, what becomes of the standard explanation for regulatory antitrust?

It should be apparent that a theory of competition—and monopoly—is required before we can proceed further. We must have a theory of competition before we can judge whether it is increasing or decreasing. And we must have a theory of "resource allocation" before we can assert, or understand the assertion that monopoly power can arise in a free market and can misallocate economic resources and reduce consumer and social welfare. As the quotations from McGuire have illustrated, the facts in any historical situation can provide an ambiguous picture of what is occurring. What is required is a theory that can integrate the relevant facts and make business history intelligible.

Neoclassical Competition Theory

Competition can be defined as "the effort of two or more parties acting independently to secure the business of a third party by offering the most favorable terms."[3] This definition is entirely consistent with the everyday usage of the term. In business, for instance, competition is seen as a continuous process of rivalry between sellers for the patronage of potential customers. The emphasis is upon strategies involving price, product differentiation, advertising, service, research and development, technological change, and a whole host of activities that are designed to secure sales and ultimately profits for the business organization. Competition is not simply a mechanical optimization within known constraints, but is seen as an exploratory process whereby opportunities for profit are discovered and exploited over time under uncertain circumstances. Resources are allocated efficiently if rival producers (entrepreneurs) are in the process of discovering and responding correctly to the uncertainties of changing market conditions.

Economists, by and large, have held sharply differing views of competition and resource allocation, and it is their views which have tended to legitimize antitrust regulation. This is not to say that the views of the economists have been correct and that antitrust policy is appropriate in a market economy. Indeed, it will be argued below that such views are fundamentally misguided. Yet it is vitally important to understand the orthodox theories of competition

---

[3]By permission. From Webster's New Collegiate Dictionary 1981 by G. & C. Merriam Co., Publishers of the Merriam–Webster Dictionaries.

and monopoly, and to understand how to criticize them, since they still serve as the intellectual foundation of antitrust policy. Indeed, it is difficult to comprehend the classic antitrust cases to be discussed in this volume, and the decisions reached in those cases, without a clear understanding of conventional competition and monopoly theory.

Perfect Competition and Resource Allocation

For more than 100 years, economists have been building economic models describing an ideal or optimal competitive situation, that is, a situation that would produce the greatest benefit to consumers and to society at the lowest possible economic cost. If this optimal condition could be achieved, scarce resources would be employed in their highest valued use, and their efficient employment would imply that no alternative allocation could make anyone better off without making someone else worse off. This situation is referred to as a *Pareto optimal* condition and it can occur in a perfectly competitive equilibrium.[4]

In its simplest expression, pure and atomistic competition is said to exist in any market if all suppliers of commodities in the market are small relative to total market supply; the commodity produced and sold by the various suppliers is homogeneous in the minds of the consumers; and resources are mobile and no artificial restrictions exist with respect to entry, demand, supply, or price. In addition, a condition of perfect competition is said to exist if all relevant market information is correct and fully known to market participants.[5]

To understand why many economists hold this conception of competition as optimal, it is necessary to review briefly the mechanics of the competitive model. The model begins by assuming that a substantial number of small firms already exist in some relevant market, and that they are already producing homogeneous products, that is, products that are identical in the mind of the consumer. If the firms are small, such that their individual outputs cannot noticeably affect the total market output of the product under discussion, then all sales by these sellers are made at some given market price that is determined by market demand and market supply (see Figure 1).

In a purely competitive market, atomistic firms are said to have no control over their own prices. No firm could sell its output at a price higher than the market price since the same homogeneous product is available from all other suppliers at the (lower) market price. And no firm would charge a price lower than the market price, since all of its output can be sold at the market rate.

---

[4]On the development of this model of competition between 1880 and 1933, see Donald Dewey, *The Theory of Imperfect Competition: A Radical Reconstruction* (New York: Columbia University Press, 1969), pp. 5–10.

[5]For a review of the assumptions and operations of the perfectly competitive model, see any modern microeconomics text, or specifically, Richard H. Leftwich, *The Price System and Resource Allocation*, 7th ed. (Hinsdale, Ill.: Dryden Press, 1979).

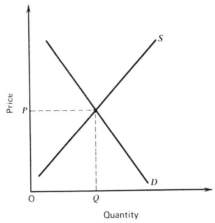

Figure 1 Supply and demand determine market price and output.

Hence, the market price becomes a horizontal demand schedule facing each and every firm in the market, and indicates, at any relevant price, how many units of the commodity consumers would be willing and able to purchase.

Firms under short–run competitive conditions are assumed to be powerless to adjust the price of their commodity or of any other relevant product variable (e.g., quality). Consequently, sellers are induced to maximize their profits by adjusting their outputs such that their marginal costs of production and sale just equal the market price of the commodity. At such output levels, the extra costs (marginal cost) of producing and selling the commodity would just equal the extra revenue (marginal revenue) received from the sale of the commodity. And if average costs including "normal" profits are below average revenues at such outputs, total net income (economic profit) would then be maximized for some representative firm (see Figure 2).

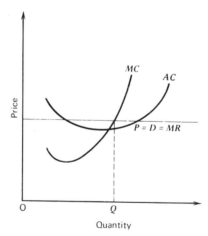

Figure 2 A firm's marginal costs are equated with market price (marginal revenue) to determine firm output.

Economic profits would only be temporary under pure competition. Eventually, it would pay entrepreneurs to mobilize additional resources and supply additional homogeneous products (entry is easy) in an effort to earn the economic profits available in this industry. But the entrepreneurial adjustments in output will soon lower the market price of the commodity and narrow economic profits of any representative supplier. In fact, pushed to its logical conclusion, it is possible to argue that outputs will be increased until market prices fall and eliminate all economic profits (normal profits included as a "cost" still being earned). With appropriately drawn average–cost functions, price will settle at the very minimum point of the average cost function where there is a triple identity between price, marginal cost, and minimum average cost (see Figure 3). And since economic profits and losses are entirely absent, and demand and supply are assumed to be known and stable, and equilibrium condition is now established in this industry. Resource allocation is as efficient as possible and social welfare, given the distribution of income, is said to be maximized.

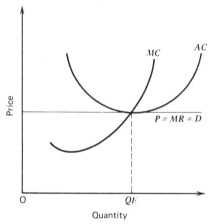

Figure 3 Equilibrium for the individual firm in pure competition.

Perfect Competition and Regulatory Policy

It should be apparent that there may be important policy implications associated with this equilibrium condition and with this theory of atomistic competition. For instance, if this is a correct theory of competition, and if this is the sort of competition that actually exists in the marketplace, antitrust policy would be unnecessary. Since a perfectly competitive market would automatically generate socially beneficial conduct and performance on the part of the suppliers, little if any additional social benefit could be accomplished by antitrust intervention.

On the other hand, if economic markets are not perfectly competitive, then there can be no corresponding guarantee that resources would be allocated efficiently. Indeed, from a perfectly competitive perspective, economic resources would be misallocated and some waste and inefficiency would exist under imperfectly competitive conditions.[6] Markets that contain large firms, locational advantages, price discrimination, differentiated products, tie-in sales, promotional advertising, collusion, and interdependent rivalry are not perfectly competitive markets, and firms in such markets are said to possess some *monopoly power*. Consistent with this perspective, such markets might require government antitrust regulation to make them more competitive and more socially efficient.[7]

This is not to say that regulatory enthusiasts believe that the actual business world can (or even should) be transformed by law, into pure or perfect competition. That would be the ultimate "straw man" position and it is not being maintained here or elsewhere in this volume. It is to say, however, that the atomistic model described above is still the standard welfare benchmark, the guidepost, the optimal referent that most proponents of regulation employ when they argue that concentrated industries can misallocate resources, or that waste and inefficiency can occur under imperfectly competitive market conditions.[8] It is the implicit acceptance of perfect competition as some sort of optimal standard of economic performance that allows a condemnation of activities such as large mergers, or product differentiation and advertising. Consumers that prefer product variety are said to be willing to sacrifice "efficiency" in order to obtain it.[9]

Reference to the perfectly competitive model also allows proponents of business regulation to talk of "more competition" as an industrial situation that structurally approaches atomistic competition; alternatively, resource misallocation is any allocation that does not coincide with the pattern of resource use under perfect competition. From a neoclassical perspective, competition declines, and some economic waste occurs, as we move away from perfect competition, and competition increases, and markets become more

[6]F.M. Scherer, *Industrial Market Structure and Economic Performance*, 2nd ed. (Chicago: Rand McNally College Publishing Company, 1980), p. 18. For a contrasting view, see Harold Demsetz, "The Nature of Equilibrium in Monopolistic Competition," *Journal of Political Economy*, Vol. 67 (February 1959), pp. 21–30, and "The Welfare and Empirical Implications of Monopolistic Competition," *Economic Journal*, Vol. 74 (September 1967), p. 623.

[7]This is a widely held view among academic economists. See Robert L. Bishop, "Monopolistic Competition and Welfare Economics," in Robert E. Keunne, ed., *Monopolistic Competition Theory: Studies in Impact* (New York: John Wiley & Sons, 1967), pp. 251–63; Edwin Mansfield, *Microeconomics* (New York: W.W. Norton and Company, 1975), pp. 282, 315; Willard Mueller, *A Primer on Monopoly and Competition* (New York: Random House, 1970), p. 8; Richard E. Low, "Introduction," in R.E. Low, ed., *The Economics of Antitrust: Competition and Monopoly* (Englewood Cliffs,N.J.: Prentice-Hall, Inc., 1968), pp. 1–42. See also Lee Preston and Benjamin King, "Proving Competition," *The Antitrust Bulletin*, Vol. 24, No. 4 (Winter 1979), p. 787.

[8]See the discussion by Roger Sherman in *Antitrust Bulletin* (January 1976), p. 947. See also Milton H. Spencer, *Contemporary Microeconomics* (New York: Worth Publishers, Inc., 1975), pp. 240–243 and Peter Asch, "Industrial Concentration, Efficiency and Antitrust Reform," *The Antitrust Bulletin*, Vol. 22, No. 1 (Spring 1977), pp. 129–143, esp. p. 130.

[9]Douglas F. Greer, *Industrial Organization and Public Policy* (New York: Macmillan Publishing Co., 1980), p. 44.

efficient, as we move towards perfect competition. The explicit relationship between this perspective and government antitrust regulation should now be clear. As a leading microtheorist puts it:

> ...in the theory of a market economy pure competition tends to lead toward the set of conditions defining maximum economic welfare or well-being, given the distribution of income. The actual performance of the economy can then be appraised against its potential "best" performance. Imperfectly competitive or monopolitic forces are important in preventing the attainment of the "best" allocation and use of economic resources. Thus, the purely competitive model frequently is used as the basis for public regulation of imperfectly competitive situations. Presumably it underlies the philosophy and enforcement of the Sherman Antitrust Act of 1890...[10]

Imperfect Competition and Resource Misallocation

It is important to understand why business organizations are judged to be misallocating resources under monopoly or imperfect competition. The explanation begins with the observation that under imperfectly competitive conditions, firms have some control over the prices of their products. This control may stem from the fact that the commodities being produced by suppliers are differentiated, or that market knowledge is not perfect, or that firms are colluding to restrict production. Differentiation of product, imperfect knowledge, and collusion are the primary ingredients of imperfectly competitive situations.

For instance, if products are differentiated, individual sellers discover that the demand curve for their own product is downward sloping and not horizontal, and that they will not lose all of their customers with a price slightly higher than a competitor's. Such sellers are said to have price control or monopoly power relative to competitive sellers of homogeneous products. And it is this price and product control, and the subsequent business rivalry, that so typify monopolistically competitive or imperfectly competitive market situations.

Similarly, if firms collude to restrict production, prices can be higher than under perfectly competitive conditions. Consumers may buy less and pay more, and are said to be injured by the restriction of production. Moreover, there is said to be a social welfare–loss due to the misallocation of resources associated with the collusive output restriction.

Firms under monopolistic or imperfect competition still attempt to maximize their profit by selling an output where marginal revenue equals marginal cost. But if products are not perfect substitutes, the demand function each firm faces is downward sloping, and the price that each firm charges will tend to be greater than both marginal revenue and marginal cost (see Figure 4).

---

[10]Leftwich, *op. cit.*, p. 32 [Copyright 1979 by Dryden Press, Inc., Reprinted by permission of Dryden Press, Inc.].

Thus, when profits are maximized, the prices that consumers pay will exceed the extra costs associated with bringing those products to the consumers. Even if economic profits are zero, prices will still exceed marginal costs, production will not occur at minimum average costs, and resources are said to be misallocated due to monopoly power.

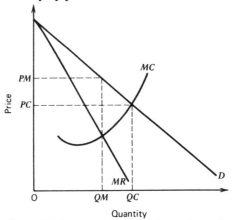

Figure 4 A firm with "monopoly power" produces less (QM) and charges more (PM) than a "competitive" firm.

Most economists would hold that this particular economic situation compares unfavorably with price, output, and cost under perfect competition. Under atomistically competitive conditions, price is always identical to marginal cost, and within a competitive equilibrium, market price is always driven to the minimum point of the average–cost function such that production tends to occur at its most efficient point. Thus neoclassical analysis appears able to demonstrate scientifically what has always been assumed concerning monopoly, namely, that the prices tend to be higher, the outputs less, and the equilibrium costs greater than under comparably competitive conditions.[11]

The Cost–Benefit Welfare Model

Since a classic journal article by Arnold Harberger in 1954, it has been convenient to portray the economic difference between monopoly and competition, and the consequent welfare loss and resource misallocation, as a so–called welfare-loss triangle[12] (see Figure 5). In this basic diagram, OX is the competitive price and is equal to long–run average and marginal cost. OPM is the monopoly price and is higher than the competitive price for reasons explained previously. It should be clear that if governmental antitrust regulation could prevent or reduce this monopoly power, it could, consistent

---

[11]Antoine Cournot made this determination as early as 1838. See Joseph A. Schumpeter, History of *Economic Analysis* (New York: Oxford University Press, 1954), pp. 972–977. And despite some qualifications this is still the determination today. See Roger A. McCain, *Markets, Decisions, and Organizations* (Englewood Cliffs, N.J.: Prentice Hall, Inc., 1981), pp. 257–259.

[12]"Monopoly and Resource Allocation," *American Economic Review, Papers and Proceedings*, Vol. 44 (May 1954), p. 77.

with this perspective, improve economic performance and allocative efficiency by lowering prices and increasing output. Presumably it is this fundamental economic principle that underlies any rational antitrust policy in this country.[13]

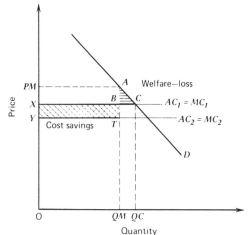

Figure 5 The cost–benefit model.

The basic economic model outlined above can be broadened to highlight the economic effects, and regulatory implications, of business collusion, merger, deconcentration, and increased business efficiency. If, for example, monopoly power established through collusion or horizontal merger threatens to reduce output and increase prices, resources would be misallocated and social welfare would be reduced (as explained above). The triangle area ABC in Figure 5 is said to represent the deadweight welfare–loss associated with a restriction of output from QC to QM. Or, alternatively if antitrust policy could prevent or end such output restrictions, it could increase social welfare by improving the allocation of scarce economic resources. This analysis would also apply, similarly, to proposals aimed at the governmental decentralization of highly concentrated industries. Presumably, a reduction in economic concentration would lessen monopoly power and lead to increased outputs at lower prices.

Whether society would gain on balance from such governmental regulation would depend upon whether costs were affected adversely by such policies.[14] With respect to so–called naked price-fixing and market division

[13]William Long, Richard Schramm, and Robert Tollison, "The Economic Determinants of Antitrust Activity," *Journal of Law and Economics*, Vol. 16, No. 2 (October, 1973), pp. 351–364. See also Philip Areeda, *Antitrust Analysis: Problems, Text, Cases*, 2nd ed. (Little, Brown & Company, 1974), pp.12–23, and esp. p. 195.

[14]Oliver Williamson, "Economics as an Antitrust Defense: The Welfare Tradeoffs," *American Economic Review*, Vol. 68, No. 18 (March 1968), and a correction in *American Economic Review*, Vol. 69 (December 1969), pp. 954–959). For an excellent discussion of the cost–benefit trade off model, see Wesley J. Liebeler, "Market Power and Competitive Superiority in Concentrated Industries," *UCLA Law Review*, Vol. 25 (1979), pp. 1232–1297.

agreements, the standard economic literature is practically unanimous: to prevent or end such agreements by law would not raise business costs and thus, would clearly serve the public interest in terms of increased social efficiency.[15] Indeed, costs might even be reduced since it has been maintained by some commentators that firms expend resources to attain monopoly power, and then expend monopoly profits in socially wasteful non-price competition. Thus, the social costs of monopoly are alleged to be greater than just the dead-weight welfare-loss triangle.[16]

The matter becomes still more complicated with antimerger and business deconcentration policies. As can be observed from Figure 5, even the slightest gains in actual economic efficiency associated with a merger or increased business concentration (the decrease in costs from AC_1 to AC_2), could easily overwhelm the strict allocative welfare losses associated with pure monopoly power (output restriction). In general, if area XYBT exceeds area ABC, regulatory action to prevent the merger or reduce the industrial concentration is said to harm society's welfare, and could not be justified even from a utilitarian perspective. If output restriction is difficult or impossible, and if there are more than negligible economies and efficiencies associated with large-scale business organization, antimonopoly policy—even on its own terms—would not tend to improve social welfare.

A Criticism of Neoclassical Competition Theory

The orthodox theories of competition and monopoly just reviewed have hardly gone unchallenged by economists over the last thirty years. Baumol, for instance, has admitted that if monopoly were to exist in every industry in the economy, it would be difficult to conclude that resources were misallocated.[17] Lipsey and Lancaster have acknowledged that it is uncertain whether a public policy that leads to a reduction in some but not all monopoly would necessarily result in a more efficient allocation of resources.[18] Further, it has long been admitted that the entire long-run cost function might be lower under monopoly than under competition. And finally, the traditional analysis and its welfare implications does not take account of market externalities, factor indivisibilities and noneconomic elements of social welfare.

Horizontal Demand and Resource Misallocation

Although these critical observations are interesting, the orthodox approach to competition and monopoly theory is open to more serious and fundamental difficulties. The first difficulty concerns the internal logic of the

---

[15]This position has recently been stated most emphatically in Robert Bork, *The Antitrust Paradox* (New York: Basic Books, 1978).

[16]Richard A. Posner, *Antitrust Law: An Economic Perspective* (Chicago: University of Chicago Press, 1976), pp. 10–15.

[17]William Baumol, *Economic Theory and Operations Analysis* (Englewood Cliffs, N.J.: Prentice-Hall, 1961), p. 257.

[18]R.G. Lipsey and K. Lancaster, "The General Theory of Second Best," Review of Economic Studies, Vol. 24 (1956–57), p. 11.

competitive model itself, and specifically the logic of the horizontal demand function that is the hallmark of competition and its welfare implications. Atomistic competition assumes that the demand curve that faces each firm is horizontal and that the coefficient of elasticity is infinite. But is such a circumstance logically possible?

There are several objections that can be raised to the notion of a perfectly horizontal demand function. The first is that market price is determined by total market demand and total market supply. At the equilibrium price consumers are purchasing (or are willing to purchase) some *precise* amount of market product—and no more. It would seem logical, therefore, to conclude that any increase in supply—if it is to be sold—must have some perceptible effect on market supply and market price. The effect may be "small" but there must be some effect in order to sell the additional output.

It will not suffice to assert that an atomistic firm is so tiny that its output has no "appreciable" effect on the market. What is an appreciable effect? If the additional output is to be sold there must be an appreciable effect as far as consumers are concerned. The economic world, unlike the pure mathematical model in which price can be parametric, does not contain the "infinitely small steps" of the calculus or limit. Output adjustments, even small ones, are nonetheless discrete changes, and must have some noticable effect on prices. Although individual demand functions may appear to be *nearly* horizontal, and may indeed be extremely elastic under certain circumstances, a perfectly elastic demand function confronting each seller would not appear to be logically possible.[19]

Prices in openly competitive markets may tend to remain stable even though there are "small" increases in supply. But this observation does not demonstrate that individual demand functions are perfectly horizontal or that sellers have no influence on market price. It simply demonstrates that market demand has shifted (slightly) to purchase the (slightly) larger supply that is in the market. If the demand curve is held constant, however, the slightly larger output must be sold at a slightly lower market price.

An additional objection to the horizontal demand curve is that in strict mathematical terms, the curve is not a "function." In the mathematics methodology, a functional relationship between two variables always implies that for every value of the *independent* variable there exists one, and only one, value for the *dependent* variable. In economic models, although the familiar axes have been reversed, "price" is clearly the independent variable and "quantity demanded" is the dependent variable. Yet a perfectly elastic demand curve implies that there are an infinite number of values for the dependent variable ("quantity demanded") associated with any one independent variable

---

[19]This is admitted in some of the older and more careful microeconomic texts. See Albert Levenson and Babette Solon, *Outline of Price Theory* (New York: Holt, Rinehart and Winston, Inc., 1964), p.111.

("price"). Clearly, then, the perfectly elastic line in competition (assuming for the moment that it could exist) is not a demand *function.*

We must conclude, therefore, that the notion of a perfectly elastic demand function is not legitimate and must be rejected even on its own terms, aside and apart from any criticism of the realism or optimality of the atomistic model.

This criticism has important welfare and policy implications. If actual demand curves cannot even in theory be perfectly horizontal, the entire orthodox theory of resource misallocation under imperfect competition simply collapses. The fact remains that if all demand curves are downward sloping, price diverges from marginal revenue under all selling conditions. All sellers now must restrict their output to a point where marginal cost is just equal to marginal revenue and not price. It should be obvious, however, that such behavior can no longer be uniquely associated with market power, but is, instead, the natural conduct and performance of all business organizations.

Orthodox theory is able to conclude that resources are misallocated under such circumstances only by comparing these selling situations with the perfectly competitive equilibrium. Since price is greater than marginal cost and since output is restricted, the result is termed socially inefficient. But if such an equilibrium situation with a horizontal demand function is logically impossible, then this particular notion of resource misallocation is incorrect. "Misallocation" is relative to what possible standard? "Restricted" output is relative to what possible standard of output? "Inefficient" is relative to what possible standard of efficiency? Without perfect competition as a standard, monopoly power and monopolistic competition are indistinguishable from any selling situations where firms face a downward sloping demand curve, and where they attempt to maximize their profits by equating marginal revenue with marginal costs.

Indeed, why continue to refer to such situations as "monopolistic"? All firms in a free market tend to produce an output where marginal revenue and marginal cost are equal. This allocation of resources is the allocation that one would expect under free-market competition with legally open entry; monopoly power has nothing to do with this at all. Such openly competitive markets would tend towards an equilibrium condition where marginal revenue and marginal costs were equal, and where firms were earning returns comparable to returns earned elsewhere in the market (see Figure 6).

This general theory of entry, pricing, and output determination can easily be broadened to incorporate the competitive process in which several large firms sell the bulk of the market output. The primary behavioral characteristic of oligopoly and, indeed, of all business competition, is that there is extreme interdependence (rivalry) between the sellers in the marketplace. Business organizations realize that their competitors will respond and react to their actions. The demand function facing each seller, therefore, would incorporate the most likely reactions of rivals to price and no-price changes. The equilibrium solution towards which such markets theoretically tend, would be precisely the same as depicted in Figure 6.

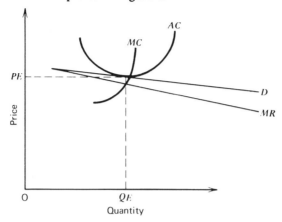

Figure 6 Equilibrium for a firm in an openly competitive market.

Competition as a Dynamic Discovery Process

There are still more fundamental difficulties with the perfect competition perspective. Certainly one of the most important is that perfect competition theory is not really concerned with the process of competition. Perfect competition theory is fundamentally static, and not a theory of market process.[20] Standard competition theory assumes conditions to exist that automatically result in an equilibrium. But such assumptions avoid the tough questions concerning the nature of the competitive process and can easily lead to inappropriate policy conclusions.

Neoclassical competition theory begins with given conditions—with information that is already known, and correctly known, to all market participants. The economic activity that occurs under such conditions is purely routine, that is, maximization of profit, with no room for discovery, error, or learning. Correctly understood, the perfectly competitive model does not actually move toward equilibrium but is, itself, an equilibrium condition.

Since perfect competition theory starts with equilibrium assumptions, it must assume away the significant aspects of a genuinely competitive process. For instance, the question of how businessmen come to understand what

---

[20]The discussion that follows draws heavily on the following works: Murray N. Rothbard, *Man, Economy and State*, Vol. 2 (Princeton: D. VanNostrand & Co., 1962); Israel M. Kirzner, *Competition and Entrepreneurship* (Chicago: University of Chicago Press, 1973); Friedrich Hayek, "The Meaning of Competition," *Individualism and Economic Order* (Chicago: Henry Regnery Company, 1972), pp. 92–106; Paul McNulty, "Economic Theory and the Meaning of Competition," *Quarterly Journal of Economics*, Vol 82 (1968), reprinted in Yale Brozen, *The Competitive Economy: Selected Readings* (General Learning, 1975), pp. 64–75. Also, see a recent treatment by Arthur A. Thompson, Jr., "Competition as a Strategic Process," *The Antitrust Bulletin*, Vol. 25, No. 4 (Winter 1980), pp. 777–803.

consumer demand is becomes, in the standard analysis, the assumption that such information is already known, and correctly known, to all businessmen. How businessmen discover which factor combinations are the most efficient becomes, in the orthodox model, the assumption that such combinations are already known and have already been adopted by suppliers. How businessmen determine which products to produce with what degree of differentiation, becomes the assumption that all the products are already homogeneous. In short, the model assumes the existence of information that a competitive process aims to discover.

Moreover, the competitive equilibrium condition is optimal in an entirely trivial sense. Perfect competition is optimal if all relevant information is given, and then only if that information never changes. The optimality of the perfectly competitive solution depends upon a static world of unchanging data and preferences. But is should be apparent that the passage of time in any real market situation must change knowledge and preferences and, thus, must weaken seriously the relevance of the neoclassical model. A perfectly competitive equilibrium in a changing world could not be efficient, since a changing world would allow for new products, new factor combinations, and new insights into what consumers prefer and at what prices. A changing world would allow for rivalry, for error and error corrections, and for continuous entrepreneurial activity. But such a perpetual disequilibrium process is incompatible with the assumptions of the perfectly competitive model and with its static perspective.

Entrepreneurial Competition. Business competition is always a dynamic process, not a given static state of affairs, in which suppliers continually strive to offer improved alternatives to market participants. Unlike the perfectly competitive world, competition is a process of discovering opportunities for profit, and then adjusting market conditions so that these opportunities tend to be exploited. If there is any movement toward equilibrium, this process of discovery and market adjustment is that movement, and this is why it occurs. Competition is the equilibrating process, not the equilibrium condition, in which businessmen attempt, in the absence of perfect knowledge and homogeneous products, to more closely coordinate their supply plans with the anticipated plans of other market participants.

As an illustration of the process, imagine that we are concerned with the buying and selling of ballpoint pens. If we assume at the start that market knowledge is perfect, then we have assumed away the entire competitive process. If, instead, we assume that the knowledge concerning consumer preferences, technology, factor prices, advertising, location, and dozens of other variables is only understood vaguely, then the competitive process is the social vehicle through which a closer economic coordination is achieved. During the process some firms may differentiate their products; others may not. Some firms may stress durability and choose to sell their pens in retail stores; others may stress only price and choose to mail order. Some pens may be produced by large business organizations that formerly offered only fountain pens to consumers. Other pens may be sold by new organizations equipped with radically different manufacturing technologies. Since market knowledge is imperfect, some firms may choose to spend substantial amounts of resources on advertising and on alerting and persuading potential consumers to purchase; others may decide on minimal amounts of advertising, or even, perhaps, on none at all. The point to be emphasized here is that all of these entrepreneurial activities are competitive, and it is only through this discovery process that firms are able to determine how to allocate resources efficiently. These entrepreneurial activities do not spoil competition or efficiency, as they would in the atomistic model, but are the very essence of market competition.

Neoclassical Competition and Social Welfare. The real perversity inherent in the traditional competitive perspective is that it can treat as resource–misallocating the very business practices that are, in fact, essential to any competitive process. Business organizations compete by differentiating products, innovating new products, discounting list prices, locating in areas convenient to consumers, advertising prices and services, and purchasing resources cheaper than rivals. Yet because these activities are not discovered in the competitive maximization process or in the equilibrium condition, they have often been classified as monopolistic and inefficient. What some have labeled monopolistic may simply be a competitive market process in a necessary state of disequilibrium.

This mislabeling is most pernicious in the case of product differentiation. Since the atomistic model starts with the given assumption of homogeneous product, it is forced by its own logic to treat product differentiation as inefficient. But why begin an analysis of competition by assuming that products are already homogeneous? If, instead, a competitive model is begun with revealed consumer preferences, homogeneous products become one, but only one, possible competitive outcome. Other competitive outcomes include various degrees of product differentiation that are supported by the voluntary demonstrated preferences of consumers. Once it is acknowledged that differentiated goods have subjective value that buyers are willing to pay for, perfect competition with homogeneous products can no longer be considered universally optimal or efficient.

It is a serious analytical error to mistake a competitive market process for resource–misallocating monopoly. It is also a serious error to continue to associate the simple price–and–profit behavior of atomistic firms (in equilibrium), with competitive business conduct and performance. For example, it is now arbitrary to associate zero economic profits with efficient resource allocation or alternatively, to associate the total absence of a pricing policy with competitive behavior; price takers are now no more competitive than price makers. Indeed, radically different price–and–profit strategies are compatible and desirable if competition is defined in dynamic terms. Nor ought anyone to expect any actual industrial situation to settle down into some impossible, long–run equilibrium (if we could only wait long enough); long–run equilibria are not of this world. In short, every aspect of the perfectly competitive model must be rejected for policy purposes. Far from being useful or predictive, as has often been maintained, the atomistic model leads to incorrect expectations concerning socially desirable structure, conduct, and performance. To attempt to apply the model as a standard in antitrust for determining competition or monopoly power would be nothing short of disastrous.

The Welfare Models Revisited

The welfare model analysis reviewed earlier in this chapter can now be confronted directly. It will be recalled that resource misallocation in that model occurred relative to some objectively determined "competitive" price and output. But if perfect competition is both illogical and non–optimal, the standard of optimality and efficiency for measuring welfare–loss evaporates. If all firms in open markets face downward sloping demand functions, then price diverges from marginal cost in all economic markets, and outputs are always restricted. Further, even if this "restriction" was meaningful, why do the higher prices and profits *not* attract entry, increase production and lower prices? In the absence of a governmental restriction on production, why is the welfare triangle not competed away?

But even more fundamentally, the standard welfare models assume that both costs and benefits are measurably objective phenomena, knowable to outside observers. From a strictly theoretical perspective, however, the notion of objective and aggregate costs and benefits for society as a whole is seriously misleading. Not only are costs imprecise and difficult to measure in an accounting sense, but a strictly theoretical understanding of costs and benefits is that they are ultimately and fundamentally personal and subjective.[21] The costs of an action are the subjective values attached to the foregone opportunities by the decision maker at the moment of the decision. Such subjective values can never be known to any outside observer and thus, cannot be objectively aggregated for society as a whole.

If social costs and social benefits cannot be known or aggregated, the alleged usefulness of the neoclassical welfare models in support of a rational antitrust policy is now open to the most serious question. In short, how is it to be demonstrated that, say, "restrictive" agreements between business organizations are socially inefficient when the gains and losses associated with such arrangements are incapable in principle of discovery, measurement, or comparison? How are we now to know that cartel prices injure consumers or "society"? How are we now to compare social utility before and after some

---

[21]James M. Buchanan, *Cost and Choice* (Markham Publishing 1969). Also see an excellent discussion by Thomas Sowell, *Knowledge and Decisions* (New York: Basic Books, Inc., 1980), pp. 50–52, and Bork, *op. cit.*, pp. 110–113.

cartelization or monopolization? How are we now to conclude that certain forms of non-price competition are socially wasteful? It would appear that even the best and most reasonable neoclassical analysis is mired in a serious *methodological* difficulty.

An Alternative Theory of Efficiency

A very different perspective on economic efficiency and resource alloca-tion can be developed directly from a strict subjectivist approach to cost and utility. This approach would hold that individual human action is purposeful and aims at accomplishing selected ends by adopting patterns of resource use (plans) consistent with those ends. If the means employed in the pursuit of selected ends are consistent with those ends, then the means or plans are said to be efficiently employed.

The efficient accomplishment of ends in a social context requires that particular planned activity dovetail or coordinate with the planned activity of other market participants. Yet given the complex division of labor and the difficulty of obtaining accurate information, such a dovetailing is not auto-matic; indeed, mutually inconsistent plans must be anticipated. If market participants had perfect information, all plans would be fully coordinated and markets would be efficient, by definition. But to assume perfect information is to assume away the problem of explaining social efficiency. The question of social efficiency is not how resources would be allocated if everyone had perfect information. The issue, instead, is an understanding of the process by which more accurate information is produced, transmitted, and utilized such that a more consistent pattern of social plan coordination can be achieved.

An unhampered market economy automatically generates price informa-tion that can be utilized by decision makers in an effort to coordinate divergent plans. Decision makers are able to monitor behavior with strong incentives to pursue patterns of resource use that are more fully coordinated with the plans of others. Since information is not perfect and is constantly changing, this process of plan adjustment can never achieve any final equilibrium. What must be emphasized, however, is that the competitive market process creates powerful incentives to discover and utilize information and to correct plans that fall short of objectives. In short, an unhampered market provides the context within which individuals can engage in efficient action. It is both a necessary and a sufficient condition for an efficient market process.[22]

Seen in this light, voluntary market agreements—even agreements that intend to "restrict" production in some neoclassical sense—can be efficient, since they aim to more fully coordinate the plans of the respective parties. Such arrangements are judged appropriate *ex ante* to bring about some desired end or goal. To prohibit or restrict (by law) such agreements, from this perspec-

---

[22]Israel Kirzner, *Market Theory and the Price System* (Princeton: D. Van Nostrand, Inc., 1963), pp. 34–45. See also Roy E. Cordato, "Austrian Theory of Efficiency and the Role of Government," *Journal of Libertarian Studies,* Vol. 4, No. 4 (Fall 1980), pp. 393–403.

tive, would result in an unambiguous reduction in efficiency and social coordination.

There are some distinct advantages associated with this theory of efficiency. The first is that the entire professional tirade against highly advertised differentiated products simply collapses as an irrelevant discussion of ends; social efficiency relates only to means. Second, nothing said or implied in this discussion of efficiency requires the aggregation of individual costs and benefits; individual decision makers perform all of their own cost/benefit calculations, and social welfare can be enhanced by free trade since individuals can coordinate their plans more fully and engage in any arrangements that they judge to be efficient. Finally, all government restrictions or prohibitions of trade and contractual agreement are now revealed to be socially inefficient in a scientific sense that is independent of the natural rights argument for open markets sketched briefly in Chapter 1.

Economists and Competition Theory

Some of the preceding criticism of the atomistically competitive paradigm and its regulatory implications has been noted in the orthodox literature, although it has yet to dislodge that perspective from its foremost position in matters of public policy. Some economists have argued eloquently that perfect competition is a misleading notion, and that simple welfare comparisons between the real world and the model are fraught with danger. The criticism first became important in the 1930s when Joan Robinson and Edward Chamberlin developed their respective theories of imperfect and monopolistic competition. Joan Robinson, for instance, stated that:

> In order to make a valid theoretical comparison between competitive output and monopoly output in a particular industry it is necessary to make very severe assumptions. First, we must have a definite idea of what we mean by the commodity that we are considering. Secondly, if we wish to discuss what will happen to output and prices if a certain commodity, heretofore produced by competing firms, is monopolized, we must assume that neither the demand curve for the commodity nor the costs of production of any given output are altered by the change. These assumptions are unlikely to be fulfilled in any actual situation.[23]

In addition, there were whole classes of industrial activity (she specifically mentioned railways and the distribution of gas and electricity) where, because of vast cost differentials, any general comparisons were meaningless.[24]

Professor Chamberlin was even more explicit in his criticism of neoclassical competition theory. He put the matter bluntly:

> The explicit recognition that product is differentiated brings into the open the problem of variety and makes it clear that *pure competition may no*

---

[23]Joan Robinson, *The Economics of Imperfect Competition*, 2nd ed. (New York: St. Martin's Press, 1961), pp. 143–144.

[24]*Ibid.*, p. 166.

longer be regarded as in any sense an ideal for purposes of welfare economics....
Differences in tastes, desires, incomes, and locations of buyers, and differences in the uses which they wish to make of commodities all indicated the
need for a variety and the necessity of substituting for the concept of a
'competitive ideal' an ideal involving both monopoly and competition.
How much and what kinds of monopoly and with what measure of social
control become the questions.[25]

In addition, economists such as J.M. Clark, J.K. Galbraith, and Sumner H.
Slichter all rejected pefect competition as a welfare ideal as far as public policy
is concerned.[26] Finally, two intellectual giants, Joseph Schumpeter and F.A.
Hayek, while holding quite different views of the competitive process, were
unanimous in their condemnation of the purely competitive model as a benchmark for policy analysis.

The Schumpeter Criticism. Schumpeter constantly chided his fellow economists for thinking of competition, and hence, of capitalism, in static termi-
nology. Instead, competition was always a continuous process of "creative
destruction" that came from the "new commodity, the new technology, the
new source of supply, the new type of organization—which commands a decisive cost or quality advantage and which strikes not at the margins of the
profits and the outputs of the existing firms, but at their foundations and their
very lives."[27] This sort of innovative competition was incompatible with
perfect competition, and incompatible with the sort of ideal business organization envisioned under competitive conditions. Instead, the large capital–inten-
sive firm was the "the most powerful engine" of dynamic competition.
Schumpeter concluded that

> perfect competition is not only impossible but inferior, and has no title to
> being set up as a model of ideal efficiency. It is hence a mistake to base the
> theory of government regulation of industry on the principle that big busi-
> ness should be made to work as the respective industry would work in
> perfect competition.[28]

The Hayck Criticism. Austrian economist F.A.Hayck delivered a severe attack
on the neoclassical theory of competition in a talk at Princeton University in

---

[25]Edward H. Chamberlin, *The Theory of Monopolistic Competition* (Cambridge, Mass.:
Harvard University Press, 1948), p. 214.

[26]J.M. Clark, "Toward a Concept of Workable Competition," *American Economic Review,*
Vol. 30 (June 1940, pp. 241–56, and *Competition as a Dynamic Process* (Washington: Brookings
Institution, 1961). See Summer H. Slichter, "In Defense of Bigness in Business," and John
Kenneth Galbraith, "The Economics of Technical Development," in Edwin Mansfield, ed.,
Monopoly Power and Economic Performance: The Problem of Industrial Concentration, 3rd ed.
(New York: W.W. Norton and Company, 1974),pp. 13–18 and pp. 36–44.

[27]Joseph Schumpeter, *Capitalism, Socialism and Democracy* (New York: Harper and Row,
1962), p. 84.

[28]*Ibid.*, p. 106.

1946.[29] Hayek argued that most economists assumed away the competitive process, or simply took it for granted, when they postulated that firms already knew the tastes of consumers, the least–cost combination of resources, and all other relevant market information. If these bits of information were already known, Hayek reasoned, then the markets must already be in equilibrium. As Hayek put it so cogently, the "modern theory of competitive equilibrium *assumes* the situation to exist which a true explanation ought to account for as the effect of the competitive process."[30]

For Hayek, and for all modern neo–Austrians, competition is the discovery process itself, and not the final and static equilibrium condition. Equilibrium theory, which assumed away the entrepreneurial process, was simply no help in an understanding of market competition.

Summary

Perfect competition theory is both illogical and irrelevant. Moreover, it simply assumes conditions to exist which necessarily result in an equilibrium. Business competition, on the other hand, is always a process in which entrepreneurs, with imperfect information, attempt to make adjustments in market conditions such that a closer coordination between supply and demand plans is achieved. Importantly, these adjustments are not limited to price and output, as in the standard model, but may encompass any aspect of exchange that consumers believe to be relevant. Finally, even collusive agreements can be efficient if one adopts a coordinating theory of efficiency and market process.

These theoretical arguments concerning competition have important practical implications. Antitrust policy in the United States has often been associated with that vision of competition inherent in the perfectly competitive equilibrium. Consequently, many of the elements of the entrepreneurial adjustment process, such as product differentiation, price cutting, and advertising have been consistently misidentified by business critics as inefficient, and as resource–misallocating activities. In addition, horizontal price agreements have almost always been seen as inherently inefficient and antisocial.[31] Yet if this standard theory of competition and resource allocation is incorrect or irrelevant, then the legitimacy of all antitrust policy must be open to the most serious question.

---

[29]Hayek's talk is reprinted as "The Meaning of Competition," in his *Individualism and Economic Order* (Chicago: Henry Regnery Company, 1972), pp. 92–106.

[30]*Ibid.*, p. 94.

[31]An interesting exception to this general position is taken by Donald Dewey, "Information, Entry, and Welfare: The Case for Collusion," *American Economic Review*, Vol. 69, No. 4 (September 1979), pp. 588–593.

Market Structure and Industrial Organization

One might think that this criticism of the standard competitive perspective would have settled the policy issues decisively. It would seem that no serious student of antitrust could hold perfect competition as an optimal benchmark, or attempt to employ the perfectly competitive structure as an ideal one for real-world competition. And yet this position, far from being abandoned, is the essence of the still popular "structural" approach to competition, and forms the core of industrial organization theory. This is not to say that all economists—even those who support antitrust—support the structuralist approach, or that there are not vigorous disagreements over the significance of certain structural factors. It is to say, however, that much of the academic and nonacademic support for antitrust regulation is based primarily on structural considerations.[32]

The tie-in between a structuralist approach to competition and a perfectly competitive perspective ought to be made explicit. The market-structure approach to competition assumes that structure "determines the behavior of firms in the industry, and that behavior determines the quality of the industry's performance."[33] But this is precisely the perspective of the perfectly competitive benchmark school. Perfect competition theory assumes the same sort of one-way determinism between structure, conduct, and performance. And as will be shown, what is in fact proper behavior and performance for the structuralists is identical to what is proper behavior and performance from a perfectly competitive perspective.[34]

An attack on the perfectly competitive perspective, therefore, is an attack on the entire structuralist methodology. If perfect competition is illogical and irrelevant, then market structures, or market structure changes, reveal nothing *a priori* concerning competition or welfare. And without reference to some acceptable welfare ideal, structuralist discussions of concentration, barriers to entry, high-profit rates, product differentiation, wasteful advertising, and mergers are indeterminate discussions at best, and totally misleading discussions at worst. It will be useful to review, critically, some of the more common tools of analysis in industrial organization theory to further substantiate this position.

---

[32]See, for example, Stanley E. Boyle, *Industrial Organization: An Empirical Approach* (New York: Holt, Rinehart and Winston, 1972). See also, Joe S. Bain, *Industrial Organization*, 2nd ed. (New York: John Wiley & Sons, 1968); F.M. Scherer, *Industrial Market Structure and Economic Performance*, 2nd ed. (Chicago: Rand McNally & Company, 1980).

[33]Richard Caves, *American Industry: Structure, Conduct Performance*, 2nd ed. (Englewood Cliffs, N.J.: Prentice-Hall, 1967), p. 17.

[34]Boyle, *op. cit.*, p. 8.

Lerner Index

The so-called Lerner Index is one of the oldest devices for measuring monopoly power and estimating social welfare loss.[35] Assume that some commodity is produced and sold under imperfectly competitive conditions. For reasons already explained, the price of the product and the marginal costs associated with producing it will not be the same: the price will always exceed the marginal costs. The Lerner coefficient of monopoly is determined by dividing the price of the product into the difference between the price of the product and its marginal costs. The index number will be greater if there is a wider divergence of price from marginal costs. If perfect competition exists, on the other hand, the index number is zero.

But what is all of this supposed to mean? If perfect competition is a welfare ideal—and Lerner accepted it as such—it is apparent that the index number is intended to be a handy, short-cut method for measuring monopoly power and the subsequent resource misallocation associated with such power. With little encouragement, many economists have proceeded to determine the degree of monopoly power and the subsequent welfare losses due to monopoly in the economy as a whole, under the Lerner-like assumption that a simple divergence of price from marginal cost is indicative of wasteful economic performance.[36]

It should be apparent that if costs and benefits are subjective, and if perfect competition is not a welfare ideal, then all of this so-called measurement of monopoly and welfare-loss is illegitimate. Once it is recognized that heterogeneous firms, products, and tastes are desirable facts of economic life, and that equilibria with perfect information and product homogeneity cannot actually exist in a dynamic market, a divergence of selling price from marginal cost cannot prove inefficiency or resource misallocation in any meaningful sense. Prices diverge from marginal costs in all market situations since demand curves are never perfectly elastic. The alleged comparison of the real world with the perfectly competitive wonderland is simply not legitimate.

Profit-Concentration Studies

The same sort of methodological error is made in the ever-popular profit-concentration study, where economists seek to discover the relationship between profit rates (rates of return on investment or equity) in various

---

[35]A.P. Lerner, "The Concept of Monopoly and the Measurement of Monopoly Power," *Review of Economics and Statistics*, Vol. 1 (June 1934), pp. 157–175. For a review of the other "monopoly indexes," see Eugene M. Singer, *Antitrust, Economics and Legal Analysis* (Columbus, Ohio: Grid Publishing, Inc., 1981), pp. 181–186.

[36]Arnold Harberger, "Monopoly and Resource Allocation," *American Economic Review,* Vol. 44 (May 1954), pp. 77–87; David Schwartzman, "The Burden of Monopoly," *Journal of Political Economy,* Vol. 68 (December 1960), pp. 627–630; Dave R. Kamershen, "An Estimation of the 'Welfare Losses' from Monopoly in the American Economy," *Western Economic Journal,* Vol. 4 (Summer 1966), pp. 221–36; Keith Cowling and Dennis Mueller, "The Social Costs of Monopoly," *Economic Journal,* Vol. 88 (December 1978), pp. 727–748.

industries, and the degree of concentration in those industries.[37] The idea for such a relationship is derived directly from neoclassical competition theory where, under perfect competition, economic profits are eliminated and accounting profits among industries are brought into equality, neglecting risk, in equilibrium.

A handy way to determine which industries might require antitrust attention, therefore, would be to correlate industrial concentration with rates of return. If industries really behave competitively, it is argued, such correlations should be weak or nonexistent. If correlations are high and persist over time, however, serious resource misallocation may be occurring, and the U.S. Justice Department might do well to correct such market failure.[38]

But as with the welfare–loss studies already criticized, all this measurement of monopoly and misallocation is meaningless. If zero economic profits or equalized accounting returns are not a competitive or a welfare ideal in a dynamic and changing world, profit differences need not demonstrate monopoly power or resource misallocation and consumer injury. The fundamental error here is to assume that long–run equilibria actually exist, or that the movement toward equilibrium is smooth and continuous after some initial exogenous shock to the system. Long–run equilibria cannot actually exist, and changes in tastes, costs, risk, information, and uncertainty are not short–run phenomena whose effects on profitability somehow disappear in the static long–run. Change and entrepreneurial adjustment to change are continuous in the market process and are as much in evidence in the long view as in the short. There is, to be sure, an ever present process of equilibration and coordination occurring, but it would be sheer fantasy to assume or expect such a process ever to be completed. Thus profit rate differentials, should they exist between industries, would be explainable within the contest of a fully competitive market process that has not achieved, and could never achieve, any final long–run equilibrium.

Even if the differentials in profit rates were to statistically correlate with particular market structures, the results need not be interpreted negatively, that is, that monopoly power in concentrated markets produce the high rates of return and the social inefficiency. As Harold Demsetz has suggested, it may

---

[37]There have been dozens of such studies and we cannot review them here. For a good review and criticism of the more important profit/industrial organization studies, see John M. Vernon, *Market Structure and Industrial Performance: Review of the Statistical Findings* (Boston: Allyn & Bacon, 1972). The first and perhaps most influential concentration/profit study was Joe S. Bain, "Relation of Profit Rates to Industry Concentration," *Quarterly Journal of Economics* (August 1951). For an important criticism of the Bain study, see Yale Brozen, "Concentration and Profits: Does Concentration Matter?," *The Antitrust Bulletin*, Vol. 19, 1974. For an important methodological criticism of all such studies, see Almarin Phillips, "A Critique of Empirical Studies of Relations Between Market Structure and Profitability," *Journal of Industrial Economics*, Vol. 24 (June 1976), pp. 241–249.

[38]H.M. Mann, "Seller Concentration, Barriers to Entry, and Rates of Return in Thirty Industries: 1950–1960," *Review of Economics and Statistics*, vol. 48 (August 1966), pp. 296–307, esp. p. 300.

make more sense to reason that efficient business organizations expand their market share faster than less efficient rivals and that, therefore, efficiency and profits tend to produce specific levels of concentration (rather than vice-versa).[39] Far from concluding that resources are misallocated, one should conclude that such resource allocations are entirely consistent with social efficiency and consumer preferences.

Cross–Elasticity and Competition

Cross–elasticity tests have been another popular method of attempting to measure competition and monopoly in markets. The cross–elasticity coefficient records the responsiveness of buyers of one commodity to a change in the price of some other commodity. Assume that pencils are made and sold by a group of small manufacturers in some market area. A change in the price of pencils made by manufacturer X might well affect the sales of pencils by manufacturer Y. For example, higher X prices, other things being equal, might mean higher Y sales; lower X prices might mean lower Y sales. If changes in the price of one commodity affect sales of another commodity in the manner just described (termed high cross–elasticity), then one might infer that the products are relatively good substitutes for each other, that is, that the goods are competitive with each other in the market. On the other hand, if a change in the price of X has little or no effect on the sales of Y (termed low cross–elasticity) then one might infer that the goods are not close substitutes, and do not really compete with each other in the market. Indeed, the relevant market itself might be defined in terms of cross–elasticity coefficients.

There are serious methodological difficulties in attempting to measure competition in this manner, or to infer anything meaningful concerning an efficient allocation of resources. The most serious difficulty is that any cross-elasticity test over time would inevitably confuse a change in sales due to a price change, and a change in sales due to any and all other factors. Since other things are never constant in an actual situation, there is never any guarantee that one is, in fact, testing cross–elasticity at all. Economic principles such as elasticity are unlikely to be verified by empirical experiments that are, of necessity, a mosaic of complex and nonrepeatable historical events.

Further, all close substitutes in markets differ on the basis of appearance, reliability, quality, service, technical assistance, ease of shipment, warranty, and many other factors that buyers may consider important. If final selling price were the only relevant variable then, in principle, cross–elasticity might indicate which products compete in the market at some point in time. But if price were not the only relevant selling factor, and if everything else were not constant, then such measurements might only indicate the relative insignifi-

---

[39]Harold Demsetz, "Industry Structure, Market Rivalry and Public Policy," *Journal of Law and Economics*, Vol. 16 (April 1973), pp. 1–70, and "Economics as a Guide to Antitrust Regulation," *Journal of Law and Economics*, Vol. 19 (August 1976), pp. 371, 384. For an independent confirmation of the Demsetz hypothesis, see John R. Carter, "Collusion, Efficiency, and Antitrust," *Journal of Law and Economics,* Vol. 21, No. 2 (October 1978), pp. 434–444.

cance of price differentials as a competitive factor in the market. Cross–elasticity tests implicitly assume that competition is one–dimensional; they neglect non–price–competitive factors employed by firms in rivalrous market situations.[40]

Finally, even if cross–elasticity could measure competition, it would have nothing unambiguous to say concerning social welfare. If consumers decide a product is special and don't abandon it because of a price reduction in a supposed substitute, so what? Does low cross–elasticity imply injury to buyers or society when it is presumably the very same buyers that decide to ignore the price change? Once it is recognized that disequilibrium and differentiation are inherent in all competitive situations, cross–elasticity tests cannot reveal anything meaningful concerning resource allocation and welfare.

Barriers to Entry

The subject matter of so–called barriers to entry occupies a crucial position in the structuralist orthodoxy. For it is these supposed barriers, erected by leading firms in an industry, that limit competition and misallocate resources away from their highest valued use. The three most important barriers for the critics are: product differentiation, scale economics, and advertising.

Product Differentiation. Product differentiation allegedly limits competition and injures consumers since it makes competitive market entry more costly. Relative to the ease of entry into homogeneous product markets, firms must expend extra resources to differentiate their products. To use a favorite example of the critics, the fact that the major automobile companies change styles each year increases the entry costs of competing in this industry.[41] Would–be–entrants must be willing and able to undergo similar style–change procedures (e.g., retooling) or they cannot compete in the industry. Hence the high costs of differentiation (a "phony" product differentiation for most critics) block entry into the business an tend to perpetuate the market positions of the leading companies. Even worse, once competition is limited, the auto companies routinely pass along the higher costs in the form of higher prices which contribute to a further reduction in consumer and social welfare.

It can be argued that the critics have gotten the matter completely and precisely backwards. It is only because consumers find resources satisfactorily allocated that potential competitors find entry difficult or impossible. Product differentiation, especially a differentiation that increases prices, can act as a barrier to entry *only if* consumers prefer that differentiation, and are willing to pay the presumably higher prices associated with, say, new annual auto style

---

[40]Edward H. Chamberlin, *Towards a More General Theory of Value* (New York: Oxford University Press, 1977), pp. 78–83. See also Ken D. Boyer, "Degrees of Differentiation and Industry Boundaries," in Terry Calvani and John Siegfried, eds, *Economic Analysis of Antitrust of Antitrust Law* (Boston: Little, Brown, 1979), pp. 88–106.

[41]Mark J. Green, *The Closed Enterprise System* (New York: Bantam Books, 1972), p. 396. See also Franklin Fisher, Zvi Griliches, and Carl Kaysen, "The Costs of Automobile Model changes Since 1949," *Journal of Political Economy*, Vol. 70 (October 1962), pp. 433–451.

changes. If consumers do not prefer such changes and instead reward the firms that change styles less often, or not at all, then product differentiation could hardly act as a barrier to entry. Indeed, in the case just suggested, differentiation would be an open invitation to entry and to a more rivalrous competition.

To condemn commercially successful product differentiation as a misallocation of resources, therefore, is to condemn the very allocations that consumers apparently prefer and support. It is the faulty vision of an allegedly optimal allocation under purely competitive conditions that product differentiation upsets, and not any allocation that can be associated with free buyer choice in open markets.[42]

Scale Economies. The barriers–to–entry argument become particularly irrational when applied to cost savings associated with large–scale production. The fact that certain firms realize lower average costs because of larger volumes may, indeed, make it difficult for smaller, higher–cost firms to enter or compete in the market.[43] Thus we are supposed to regret the reduced competition and the consequent resource misallocation, since relatively inefficient firms cannot compete successfully with relatively more efficient firms! But consumers do not regret the economies nor the consequent reduction in competition; why should critics? Consumers could increase competition any time they choose by indicating their willingness to pay higher prices to cover the higher costs of the smaller less efficient firms. That consumers do not usually do this indicates that resources are correctly allocated as far as they are concerned. Again, it is the vision of the purely competitive wonderland that is threatened by large, efficient firms, and not efficiency from a free–market perspective.

Advertising. The same sort of errors in analysis are evident in much of the orthodox criticism of advertising. Certainly it can be admitted readily that advertising might be wasteful in the perfectly competitive equilibrium. But advertising is wasteful there only because that model already assumes perfect information.[44] To simply *assume* perfect information, however, is not to explain how information comes to exist, or how information comes to be noticed by market participants. In the competitive world, noticed information cannot be assumed; it must be accounted for within a theory of market process.

Product advertising is a legitimate way of accounting for noticed information, and information transfer, within a theory of market process. Indeed, it is

[42]Some structuralists attempt to meet this criticism by simply asserting that consumers, in the absence of perfect knowledge, really don't know what they are doing! See Boyle, *op. cit.,* p. 73.

[43]Caves, *op. cit.,* pp. 24–25.

[44]Yale Brozen, "Entry Barriers: Advertising and Product Differentiation," in Goldschmids, Mann & Weston, eds., *Industrial Concentration: The New Learning* (Boston: Little, Brown and Company, 1974), pp. 115–37. Also see Dean A. Worcester, Jr., *Welfare Gains from Advertising: The Problem of Regulation* (Washington, D.C.; American Enterprise Institute, 1978).

difficult to imagine how any products could be sold without some advertising, since they could not even be know without it.

A popular criticism of advertising holds that it attempts to persuade rather than to inform. But once it is recognized that advertising occurs in disequilibrium, where selling is not automatic, it is difficult to appreciate the relevance of this criticism. All advertising, even the so–called informational advertising, is intended to sell products. Why advertisements that are loaded with "pure" information ought to be preferred to advertisements that are highly emotional and persuasive is not immediately obvious from this perspective.[45]

It is also difficult to appreciate the traditional distinction that some economists have made between production costs and selling costs. All expenditures, including advertising, are selling costs in the sense that they are made only in order to sell products to consumers. Products only sell themselves in the perfectly competitive equilibrium. Since products are intended to be sold, advertising expenditures are as legitimate as any other resource expenditure for the firm, and are a crucially important activity in a competitive market. To separate out such expenditures for special treatment and special criticism thus appears arbitrary and indefensible.[46]

It is also indefensible to assert that advertising is socially efficient only if it shifts market demand and allows scale economies to be realized. It is still common in some elementary textbooks to see a comparison of the costs and prices of a product before advertising with the costs and prices of the same product after advertising.[47] But such comparisons cannot be legitimate, since the alleged products being compared are *not* the same product. The price and cost of apples after advertising cannot be meaningfully compared to the price and cost of apples before advertising; in the mind of the consumers, they are now different products. Whether higher expenditures are socially efficient or legitimate is to be determined ultimately by competition and not by outside observers.

Advertising may, of course, lower the average total costs of a product and act as a barrier–to–entry to competition. This could occur if media advertising expanded the market for a product or if it substituted for more expensive and less effective marketing techniques. But as with the achievement of any economy in the use of resources, such circumstances are never to be regretted, and certainly not from any consumer perspective. If consumers want more competition between products they are always free to increase their patronage of the higher–cost, higher–priced sellers; indeed, consumers in legally open markets should have all the competitors they are willing to pay for.

On the other hand, if advertising tends to raise costs and prices, then it could hardly act as a barrier to entry or to competition. To raise costs and prices in markets where there are no legal restrictions on entry is to encourage entry

---

[45]Kirzner, *Competition and Entrepreneurship, op. cit.* pp. 159–163.

[46]*Ibid.,* pp. 146–151.

[47]See, for instance, Milton Spencer, *Contemporary Economics,* 2nd ed. (New York: Worth Publishers, Inc., 1974), p. 433.

and competition. Therefore inefficient advertising would always act as an invitation to entry and to competition, and requires no remedial antitrust activity.

Concentration

Concentration has been the most popular and important tool of analysis in industrial organization. *Market concentration* (concentration ratio) refers to the percentage of assets or sales held by the largest firms in a particular industry or market. *Average market concentration* measures the degree of concentration in all markets sampled, by averaging the market concentration data for those markets. *Aggregate concentration* refers to the percentage of assets (sales) held by the largest manufacturing firms in the economy, without reference to specific industries or markets. All three concentration indicators have been used by structuralists to imply that certain degrees of market control, or changes in these percentages over time, infer something significant concerning monopoly power, competition, and social welfare. The implication is that a high level of concentration, or increasing concentration in an industry, or in the economy, is bad for competition and is socially inefficient.[48]

Once the arbitrary optimality of the atomistic model is admitted, however, concentration or changes in concentration reveal little concerning business competition or consumer welfare. An industry or industrial sector with a high level of concentration, or one with increasing concentration, is quite compatible with competition defined in dynamic terms. If competition is a process of rivalry between firms in open markets, then that process could increase in intensity and could be more efficient because of increasing concentration. Concentration could increase as smaller firms grow larger due to increased efficiency, relative to other firms. Concentration could also increase as firms innovate new products that are popular with consumers, relative to other firms. Companies could merge to enjoy economics of scale in production, distribution, research and development, or capital financing, and the resultant economies could also result in growth and concentration, relative to other firms. In all of these cases, concentration could increase, but it is not at all clear that business competition would necessarily decline, or that social welfare would automatically be lowered (even if we could measure welfare) and resources wasted. Concentration may upset the perfectly competitive wonderland, but it is not clear that it upsets the efficiency of the competitive process.

This perspective is even more apparent when consumers themselves concentrate an industry or market by concentrating their expenditures on the products of one firm or group of firms, to the consistent neglect of others. Are we to equate this concentration with monopoly power, with a misallocation of resources, and with a reduction in consumer satisfaction? Here as elsewhere,

---

[48]For example, the influential *Studies by the Cabinet Committee on Price Stability* (Washington, D.C.: U.S. Government Printing Office, 1969) boldly asserted that "market concentration is directly related to the intensity of competition in an industry" (p. 54). For an excellent criticism of the notion that high concentration endangers competition or consumer welfare, see John S. McGee, *In Defense of Industrial Concentration* (New York: Praeger Publishers, 1971).

structuralists have gotten the matter backwards. Starting with given levels of concentration they proceed, using neoclassical price theory, to pessimistic conclusions about conduct and market performance. Yet if they started with revealed consumer preferences in an open market, they would see that concentrated market structures may only reflect buyer choice and entrepreneurial efficiency: that is, that structure is determined by performance and not vice versa. If concentration reflects tastes, technology, and increased coordination, then it clearly would be absurd to condemn such situations as wasteful or inefficient.

But even on its own structural terms, the concept of market concentration is subject to much criticism.[49] What are "high" levels of concentration, how much of an increase in concentration is dangerous, and are the benchmarks the same for all markets? If concentration in a market stays the same over time, and yet the leading firms change position and shares of the market or are replaced by new firms, what conclusions are to be drawn from the structural information? How are the markets under discussion to be defined in the first place: are imports and used goods to be included in the concentration data, and are foreign and nonindustrial assets to be excluded from the calculations? How are these questions to be answered objectively and unambiguously?

As an example of the ambiguity, an influential government study of concentration was released in 1969, titled *Studies by the Staff of the Cabinet Committee on Price Stability*. The study employed data for 213 industries, even though the Census of Manufacturers classifies over 400 different industries in manufacturing. Nearly half of all industries in the economy were excluded from the study, since their product in 1963 had become too differentiated from their product in 1947, making it infeasible to draw any valid comparisons. The trends in concentration, therefore, were developed for the older, more conservative industries, whose product lines had not changed markedly. Further, the study employed unweighted averages of concentration ratios for the different markets, did not exclude foreign assets and nonindustrial assets held by the domestic manufacturing firms included in the study, and made no allowances for imports or second-hand goods in the concentration ratios.[50] And even though it concluded that "average market concentration of manufacturing industries has shown no marked tendency to increase or decrease between 1947 and 1966,"[51] no unambiguous conclusions concerning competition or consumer welfare could ever be drawn from such a methodological nightmare.

Even if market concentration were a completely reliable measure of competition, there is surprising little empirical evidence that there has been any

---

[49]Sanford Rose, "Bigness is a Numbers Game," *Fortune,* Vol. 80 (November 1969), pp. 113, 115, 226, 228, 230, 232, 234, 237–38.

[50]*Ibid.,* pp. 230–32.

[51]*Studies by the Cabinet Committee on Price Stability,* p. 58.

marked tendency for average market concentration to increase sharply over time (with a resultant decline in competition in the economy). Studies of industrial concentration in the period 1901–47, and some through 1976, reveal a modest upward trend, at best. The early work of Adelman,[52] Nutter,[53] and Nelson[54] all tend to support the idea that general levels of industrial concentration reached at the turn of the present century have remained relatively stable since.

If average market concentration is a methodological nightmare, aggregate or overall concentration is still more ambiguous in terms of competition and consumer welfare.[55] Market concentration is at least concerned with competition between business organizations in the same market; aggregate concentration, on the other hand, is not derived from microeconomic market data, but is determined by computing the percentage of the total manufacturing industry's sales or assets held by the largest corporations in manufacturing. But what a given level of concentration, or rising or falling aggregate concentration would mean in terms of prices, costs, innovation, competition or resource allocation in any given industry is unknowable. In short, aggregate concentration even on its own terms cannot measure competition or social inefficiency.

Conclusions

It has been argued here that atomistic theory and the structuralist approach to competition are inherently flawed notions that cannot serve as the foundation for any rational antitrust policy. What these theories identify as manifestations of monopoly power are simply economic advantages and efficiencies that specific business organizations have earned—absolute and scale economies, for instance—or they are consumer preferences for one brand of product over another. Moreover, what these theories describe as a misallocation of resources is only inefficient when compared with the irrelevant perfectly competitive equilibrium. Clearly, this theory of monopoly power must be rejected for antitrust purposes.

Monopoly and the Market Process

To reject the standard theory of monopoly power and resource misallocation is not to reject all such theories. If competition is a process in which entre-

[52]Morris A. Adelman, "The Measurement of Industrial Concentration," in Mansfield, *op. cit.*, pp. 83–88.

[53]G. Warren Nutter, *The Extent of Enterprise Monopoly in the United States, 1899–1939* (Chicago: University of Chicago Press, 1951).

[54]R.L. Nelson, *Concentration in the Manufacturing Industries of the United States* (New Haven: Yale University Press, 1963).

[55]Morris A. Adelman, "Monopoly and Concentration: Comparisons in Time and Space" in Richard E. Low, ed., *The Economics of Antitrust: Competition and Monopoly* (Englewood Cliffs, N.J.: Prentice–Hall, 1968), p. 52. See also Willard F. Mueller and Larry G. Hamm, "Trends in Industrial Concentration, 1947 to 1970," *Review of Economics and Statistics,* Vol. 56 (November 1974), pp. 511–513.

preneurs are free to offer more "attractive opportunities to other market participants,"[56] then the power to arbitrarily restrict such offers and market adjustments can be defined as monopoly power. And since the adjustment process is inherent in the very working of the free market itself, the power to restrict entry and market adjustment must arise from outside the market.

Government can impede the competitive process with certain legal restrictions as barriers to exchange and entry. Such legal restrictions harm consumers (and excluded suppliers) by restricting or preventing mutually advantageous exchanges and plan coordinations from occurring.[57] Consequently consumers can be injured and resources can be misallocated since production and resource use is not fully determined by the voluntary preferences of market participants. Government franchises, certificates of public convenience, license, tariffs, price–support programs, patents, and any other governmental interference with voluntary trade and production are all instances of monopoly, and all can prevent plan coordination and generate monopoly power for the firms protected from open competition.[58] With this perspective, government, and not the free market, would be the actual source of resource–misallocating monopoly.

One of the implications to be drawn from this perspective is that monopoly power could not exist without direct governmental support. Yet it has been widely believed that competitive markets could deteriorate into monopoly without antitrust protection. Certain business organizations could presumably attempt to eliminate rivals through predatory practices and eventually monopolize the market. Moreover, once in control of a market, such firms could exploit their power by restricting output and raising prices to consumers.

But there have always been serious problems with this argument. Even if such a scenario were likely (it is unlikely, since predatory practices to eliminate rivals are expensive in open markets),[59] the process of attempting to eliminate rivals is inherently competitive. Large firms bent on eliminating competitors would presumably seek to reduce final prices, increase their own efficiency and productivity, and offer additional services to potential buyers, all in order to secure business from rivals. But such competitive activity is delightful from a consumer perspective, and ought not to be discouraged in any way.

---

[56]Kirzner, *op. cit.,* p. 20.

[57]Legal barriers are to be distinguished sharply from the nonlegal barriers discussed earlier in this chapter. As we have already argued, nonlegal barriers are created or perpetuated by free consumer choice and cannot be said, therefore, to harm consumer welfare.

[58]Yale Brozen, "Is Government the Source of Monopoly?" *Intercollegiate Review* (Winter 1968–69), reprinted in Tibor R. Machan, ed., *The Libertarian Alternative: Essays in Social and Political Philosophy* (Chicago: Nelson–Hall Company, 1974), pp. 147–169.

[59]Wayne A. Leeman, "The Limitations of Local Price Cutting as a Barrier to Entry," *Journal of Political Economy* (August 1956), pp. 329–332. In addition, see John S. McGee, "Predatory Price Cutting: The Standard Oil (N.J.) Case," *Journal of Law and Economics,* Vol. 1 (October 1958), pp. 137–169, and the discussion of McGee's analysis in Chapter 3. Also see Roland H. Koller II, "The Myths of Predatory Pricing," *Antitrust Law and Economics Review,* Vol. 4 (Summer 1971), pp. 105–123.

In addition firms are driven ultimately from open markets by consumer choice. It is buyers that decide to end supplier rivalry (temporarily, perhaps) by abandoning some producers in favor of what they perceive to be more desirable alternatives. They could ignore the lower prices and better services and stay with the existing market structure. Instead, they reduce the number of firms in the market by concentrating the bulk of their purchases on outputs that promise to maximize their subjective utility. Are consumers to be prevented from exercising free choice in order to protect these very same consumers from the consequent monopoly? Resources are not misallocated when they are allocated in accordance with revealed consumer preferences in open markets.

Finally a free-market monopolist does not "control the market" (a misleading phrase of the industrial-organization theorists) and cannot misallocate resources, as traditional theory assumes. The market, far from being "monopolized" or controlled, is still perfectly open to competition; that is, open to any entrepreneur who correctly sees a way to more efficiently service consumers than the existing firm. The existing firm is correctly seen as monopolizing existing preferences, and not the market for the product or service.[60] Should such preferences change, the open market monopoly can dissolve into a more familiar supply pattern.

Actually, extended discussions of monopoly in a completely free-market context strain credibility since such situations, though not regrettable—as already argued—would be extremely rare in fact. To establish monopoly in a free market would require perfect entrepreneurial foresight, both in the short run and the long run, with respect to consumer demand, technology, location, material supplies and prices, and thousands of other uncertain variables, it would also require an unambiguous definition of the relevant market. Few, if any, firms in business history, before or since antitrust, have ever approached such unerring perfection, let alone realized it for extended periods of time. The so-called quiet life that is reputed to be enjoyed by the free-market monopolist is, as we shall discover below, part of the folklore of antitrust history.

Business interests, however, have employed the state in an attempt to achieve legal monopoly positions of influence and power within the capitalistic system. Indeed it may have been their inability to achieve free-market monopoly that prompted such interests to seek government regulatory control over entry and restricted competition in many industries. In the chapters that follow, we will attempt to document both the fact that free-market monopoly is an illusion, and the fact that pernicious monopoly power can be associated with government regulation of the economy.

---

[60]Free market monopoly is consistent with consumer choice as long as markets are legally open to entry. To "monopolize" existing buyer preferences is not harmful and should not be illegal.

General and Partial Equilibrium Theory in Bork's Antitrust Analysis

Richard H. Fink

In applying economic theory to evaluate antitrust laws, Judge Robert Bork explicitly favors a partial equilibrium over a general equilibrium approach. He believes the general model assumes away too many real–world aspects to be usefully employed as a criterion by which to judge real–world laws.

However, Bork's partial equilibrium replacement, the Oliver Williamson trade–off model, implicitly contains many of the same assumptions as general equilibrium theory. Equilibrium prices in all industries, an absence of external effects, and well–defined demand curves are assumptions of both general equilibrium theory and the Williamson trade–off model. If one theory is judged inadequate because of these assumptions, so should the other.

Bork's analysis is more consistent with market process theory than with his own partial equilibrium approach. Market process theory assumes neither the absence of externalities, nor the presence of well–defined demand and equilibrium prices in all industries.

I. Introduction

Although Robert Bork's work in antitrust is part of the Chicago tradition of law and economics, it is also much more. In its most developed form, *The Antitrust Paradox* (Bork 1978), Bork's contribution is a unique blend of legislative history, judicial scholarship, economic theory, and antitrust policy. These subjects are not merely juxtaposed, but are brilliantly integrated. We can, in fact, state the central themes of Judge Bork's analysis using these four categories:

Legislative History: The intent of Congress in passing the Sherman Act (and most subsequent legislation) was to promote consumer welfare (Bork 1978, 20).

Judicial Scholarship: The courts have misunderstood congressional intent and tried to use antitrust laws to promote goals (such as the preservation of small businesses) that are incompatible with consumer welfare. This has produced a "policy at war with itself," the subtitle of Bork's 1978 book.

Economic Theory: Only economic theory can provide us with a knowledge of those business practices that are likely to help, or likely to harm, consumer welfare (Bork 1978, 90).

Antitrust Policy: Of the many practices that the law now restricts, restrictions on only three are justified on consumer–welfare grounds. The three are horizontal agreements, horizontal mergers creating concentrated markets,

Reprinted from *Contemporary Policy Issues*, pp. 12–20 by permission of the Western Economic Association.

and predatory behavior. Other practices (vertical and conglomerate mergers, and resale price maintenance, for example) that are now prohibited should be permitted (Bork 1978, 406).

This paper will focus primarily on the last two categories—economic theory and antitrust policy. Because Bork's ideas are interconnected, our analysis also will have implications for his historical interpretation of antitrust law. But we will not draw out those implications here.

Our main thesis can be briefly stated. We do not believe that equilibrium theories provide a consistent framework for much of Bork's analysis. Judge Bork rejects perfectly competitive, general equilibrium theory as a guide to antitrust policy, and adopts the partial equilibrium (Oliver Williamson trade-off) model instead. We will argue that the Williamson trade-off model is a "tight prior" partial equilibrium model (see Reder 1982), and that Bork should reject it for the same reasons he spurned the general competitive model. We will argue further that a "loose prior" equilibrium model, or a process theory of the market, is more congenial to Bork's pioneering work in antitrust analysis.

II. Bork's Criticism of General Equilibrium Theory

Antitrust law has traditionally been supported by "general competitive analysis," that is, by general equilibrium theory, which uses perfect competition as its model. For example, using general equilibrium theory, economists have claimed to show that a large number of small firms maximizes consumer welfare. Therefore, it would follow that many smaller firms are better for consumers than one larger firm. On this basis, economists have argued that smaller is better, and that antitrust should not let firms get too big relative to others in the industry.

Bork has vigorously criticized this argument. To illustrate his objections to general competitive theory—objections which we believe are compelling—we quote him at length:

"Competition" may be read as that state of the market "in which the individual buyer or seller does not influence the price by his purchase or sales. Alternately stated, the elasticity of supply facing any buyer is infinite, and the elasticity of demand facing any seller is infinite." Stigler, whose words these are, lists four conditions under which a competitive market will normally arise: perfect knowledge; large numbers; product homogeneity; and divisibility of output. This is an enormously useful model for economic theory, but it is utterly useless as a goal of law. The model deliberately leaves out considerations of technology (in the broadest sense) that prevent real markets from approximating the model. For the law to move either national markets (in such products as steel, automobiles, computers) or local markets (in motion picture exhibitions, newspapers, department stores, education) as close as possible the model of perfect competition (perfect knowledge could not be either required or supplied by the law) would entail an unbelievable loss in national wealth for no particular purpose. The economic model of perfect competition was never intended as a policy prescription, and it is a basic, though extremely common, error to suppose that markets do not work efficiently if they depart from the model. As we shall see, antitrust must use the model and its implications as a guide to reasoning about actual markets, but the pure model must never be mistaken for that "competition" we wish to preserve (Bork 1978, 59–60).

At bottom, it is Bork's realistic turn of mind that rejects the perfectly competitive model as a welfare ideal. In order for consumer welfare to be maximized by perfectly competitive criteria, we have to assume that there are no external effects (i.e., that no one takes any action without considering all the effects that the action will have on others). We also have to assume that there is perfect knowledge of pertinent information (i.e., that producers know their demand curves, know the most efficient methods of production, and know the present and future prices of all the resources they use and labor they hire). And we also must assume that small firms can use resources as efficiently as large ones. The first two assumptions are obviously absurd, and the third will often be false. Yet, all three are *necessary* to prove that perfect competition maximizes welfare. Little wonder then that Bork rejects this ideal, and casts about for a more realistic one.

III. Bork's Partial Equilibrium Alternative

In place of the conventional structure, performance, and conduct criteria derived from the perfectly competitive model, Bork proposes using Williamson trade–off assessments to evaluate whether market structures of business practices benefit or harm consumers (see appendix). The Williamson model recognizes that small firms may not be the most efficient way to conduct business. If larger firms are more efficient, then we must weigh what we gain in efficiency against what we lose by having the market dominated by larger firms.

The Williamson trade–off model is the basis on which Bork derives his antitrust policies. All those practices that increase consumer welfare more than they harm it should be declared legal. All those practices that harm consumer welfare more than they help it should be declared illegal.

There is no doubt that the Williamson trade–off model, at least as it is used by Bork, improves judgments about the desirability or undesirability of various business practices. But this method is not without serious faults. In fact, in the next section we will see that this method of evaluating practices which fall under antitrust law is open to many of the same objections that apply to general equilibrium theory.

IV. Is The Williamson Trade–Off Model
a Sensible Guide to Antitrust Policy?

We can illustrate this model and its application to antitrust by considering a manufacturer that wants to introduce a new product into the market using independent retail stores. (Cuisinart Inc. is a recent and successful example.) The manufacturer will want retailers to provide information about the product to prospective customers. However, a retail store that does not provide information has lower costs than a store that does, and can therefore sell at a lower price. This adversely affects the store that provides the information because customers will get the information at the high-priced store, then purchase at the low-priced store. This adverse effect can be eliminated if the manufacturer imposes uniform retail prices for his product.

It appears that this example fits neatly into the Williamson trade-off mold. This is an example of a monopolistic practice (resale price maintenance) being more efficient than a large number of independent retailers at eliminating adverse external effects. However, permitting the manufacturer to set price also means that the consumer might pay a higher price than he would if there were many independent retailers. Consequently, a valid normative assessment would seem to require comparing the welfare loss resulting from the monopoly with the efficiency gains generated by eliminating external effects. But when we inquire into this comparison, we find that it, like the perfectly competitive model of general equilibrium theory, requires a number of questionable assumptions.

First, in order to conclude that the cost curve measures the value of using resources elsewhere, we have to assume that there are no external effects anywhere else in the economy. If there are external effects elsewhere, then price will not equal marginal cost in other industries, and the cost curve in the industry under consideration does not measure opportunity costs. The very condition that gives rise to resale price maintenance in our example must be assumed away in all other industries in the economy.

We can put this point another way. Because of external effects, resale price maintenance may be an effective way to introduce a new product. But in order to apply the Williamson trade-off, we must assume that there are no external effects elsewhere in the economy. Not only is this a peculiar assumption, it is very close to the assumption made in general competitive analysis (Arrow and Hahn 1971, 132-136). A second assumption we have to make to apply the Williamson trade-off is that all markets are in equilibrium. For markets not in equilibrium, price does not equal marginal cost, and the cost curve in any one industry does not accurately measure the value of using resources in other industries. But if we assume all markets are in equilibrium, then we are back to general competitive analysis.

Perhaps we should make more explicit what underlies the assumption that a market is in equilibrium. We take equilibrium to mean a state in which there is no endogenous tendency to unanticipated change (Hahn 1973, 2). The cause of change on the firms' side of the market is unfulfilled production or sales plans. Thus, in order for equilibrium to exist, the plans of everyone in the market must be compatible with one another. All firms in an industry must expect the same prices to prevail for all of their inputs. The suppliers of each of these inputs must be planning to sell just those amounts that firms are planning to purchase. The production targets, payrolls, and revenues of each firm must all turn out exactly as the firm anticipated.

Many economists who use partial equilibrium analysis are quite willing to make the assumption that all markets are in (or very close to) equilibrium. Reder (1982, 11) calls this "tight prior equilibrium theory" and identifies this theory with the modern Chicago school. Our point is not simply that the assumption is highly unrealistic, but that, if we are willing to make it, we are engaging in general competitive analysis. Of course, in general equilibrium, perfect competition is the welfare ideal. Thus, if we wish to employ the Williamson trade–off model, we are back to that ideal which Bork originally rejected because it was too unrealistic.

A third assumption we have to make to apply the Williamson trade–off diagram is that the demand curve for a product already exists. We have chosen the example of resale price maintenance because this practice is often an important part of creating the demand curve. Had Cuisinart retailers not provided information about their new product, their demand may not have been sufficient to manufacture the product. But once the firm has created the demand curve through advertising, product demonstration, and resale price maintenance, can we rightly say that the firm is exploiting consumers, or using resources inefficiently, by charging a price above marginal cost? If not, then we cannot call the triangle underneath the demand curve a welfare loss.

We see here a conflict between resale price maintenance and the trade–off diagram. Resale price maintenance is used to introduce new products. Its usefulness depends on its ability to "create" a demand curve. However, the imperfect information that gives resale price maintenance its usefulness goes against the assumptions of the Williamson model. Unless the demand curve exists, and is known by the firms, the welfare conclusions of the diagram do not follow.

If the above considerations are valid, then the basis for Bork's proposal that we employ the Williamson trade–off model to assess resale price maintenance is questionable. The conditions required to apply trade–off assessment are the very ones whose existence obviates the economic functions of resale price maintenance. This stricture against the Williamson trade–off assessment applies to all business practices that exist primarily because of imperfect information.

V. Bork's Analysis and Market Process Theory

Bork's economics is much more compatible with a market process approach than with either general or partial equilibrium theory. We can make this point briefly by considering Bork's ideas on resale price maintenance.

Bork criticizes economists who work strictly within equilibrium theory for assumptions that are "divorced from reality," and chides economists for using a model of businessmen who, in any world outside the hypothetical, "would have to be accompanied by a guardian." Bork thinks it important to postulate normal intelligence, which we can do only if we postulate the normal amount of knowledge (Bork 1968, 959–960).

Bork thinks that resale price maintenance will rarely lead to inefficiency because manufacturers would know of its inefficiency and, therefore, not use it (Bork 1968, 952). Of course, businessmen will make mistakes, but if resale price maintenance is legal, "any manufacturer is free to try another policy anytime he thinks it worthwhile... That seems infinitely preferable to a rule argued in terms of discovery of information which prohibits the discovery of information" (Bork 1967, 740).

Bork believes that one of the main reasons firms implement resale price maintenance is to provide consumers with information about products. This, he argues, is something that benefits rather than exploits consumers (Bork 1968, 956).

Finally, Bork argues that one of the main reasons for property rights is that individual persons know best how to use their resources. He believes that "[r]esale price maintenance is best viewed as an instance of this general principle" (Bork 1968, 956).

Incomplete knowledge, uncertainty, judgment, experiment, success and failure, spreading of information, reliance on individual knowledge for decisions—these are all characteristic of economic theory in the tradition of Knight, Hayek, Shackle, Simon, and others. It is these elements of Bork's analysis that fit in well with market process analysis, but not with equilibrium theory. And although we have demonstrated these elements of Bork's analysis only through his discussion of resale price maintenance, they run throughout his work.

If market process theory is so compatible with Bork's analysis, why has he chosen to formulate his work within the partial equilibrium theory? We can only speculate here. Probably this is due partly to the predominance of equilibrium analysis in the economics profession and partly to the influence of his training at Chicago. But it also is attributable to an unwarranted stress that economists, including market process economists, place on the virtue of competition.

Properly conceived, a market system is seen as a process in which consumers and producers interact under a system of property rights. Much of this interaction is competitive (i.e., rivalry between two or more persons to gain access to scarce resources). This rivalry has many beneficial aspects, of course; it is a driving force behind innovation and the efficient use of resources by entrepreneurs. But rivalry is not always beneficial everywhere, and should not be promoted to excess. To do so would destroy the market's cooperative activity, which is fully as important to the efficient use of resources as is competition.

Bork is acutely aware of the efficiency that results from cooperation and thus rejects the characterization of competition and rivalry as a goal that antitrust should foster. He writes:

Our society is founded upon the elimination of rivalry, since that is necessary to every integration or coordination of productive economic efforts
and to the specialization of effort. No firm, no partnership, no corporation, no economic unit containing more than a single person could exist
without the elimination of some kinds of rivalry between persons. Taken
seriously, Justice Clark's policy would be what Justice Holmes believed to
be the policy of Justice Harlan in *Northern Securities,* a prescription for the
complete atomization of society. That policy is unthinkable, of course,
since it would call not only for general abject poverty but for the death by
starvation of millions of people. We may assume the antitrust laws were
not designed to place the United States in worse economic condition than
Bangladesh. So long, therefore, as we continue to speak of antitrust's
mission as the preservation of competition, we must be on guard against
the easy and analytically disastrous identification of competition with
rivalry. . . (Bork 1978, 59).

Of course, we can equate competition and rivalry without, at the same
time, advocating that rivalry should be promoted without limit. Equating
competition and rivalry is *not* disastrous analytically, as long as we recognize
the beneficial effects of cooperation, and as long as we do not try to make
rivalry the sole end of law and public policy.

Recognizing that the law should promote both competitive and cooperative behavior consistent with property rights carries implications for Bork's
historical interpretation of the Sherman Act, implications that we have
neither the inclination nor the space to enter into. All we wish to stress here is
that if we look at the market as a process of competition and cooperation,
market rivalry need not be rejected as a tool of economic analysis.

VI. Summary and Conclusions

Bork's work in antitrust analysis represents a landmark because of its brilliant integration of legislative history, judicial scholarship, economic theory,
and public policy. Yet, despite its obvious virtues, Bork's analysis contains a
serious flaw. Although he rightly rejects the perfectly competitive model as a
welfare ideal, his alternative—the Williamson trade-off model—possesses
many of the same faults. The Williamson analysis, like perfect competition,
requires the absence of external effects, the presence of perfect knowledge,
and the existence of equilibrium in all markets in order to legitimately draw
welfare conclusions. Bork should reject the Williamson model for the same
reasons that he rejected the perfectly competitive, general equilibrium model.

Bork's analysis fits in better with market process theory, which stresses
incomplete knowledge, uncertainty, and change. Resale price maintenance
and many other business practices can be understood only within this theoretical framework. Part of the reason Bork rejected process theory is because
of the undue stress that is placed on competition. Properly understood,
competition is only part of a process which also includes cooperation. By placing the beneficial results of the market almost entirely on the process of

competition, economists (and perhaps legislators) have ignored the enormous benefits that result from cooperation. Bork's perceptive recognition of the importance of cooperation led him to reject the process notion of competition. However, as long as we remember that the exclusive focus on unlimited competition is inappropriate, and that cooperation is as important to consumer welfare as rivalry, market process theory can serve well as a theoretical framework for Bork's impressive contributions to antitrust analysis.

Appendix

The trade-off Bork (1978, 107) presents is illustrated in figure 1 below. Cost curve AC, is the average cost of producing a unit of output when there are many small firms in the market, and point Q_1 represents industry output, Cost curve AC_2 is the lower cost to the monopolist of producing a unit of output, and point Q_2 represents industry output. The shaded triangle represents lost exchanges in moving from perfect competition to monopoly, and is the "welfare loss" to consumers. The shaded rectangle represents the lower cost of production in moving from perfect competition to monopoly, and is the "welfare gain" to consumers. In Bork's view, antitrust law must recognize this trade-off if it is to fulfill its appointed mission of promoting consumer welfare.

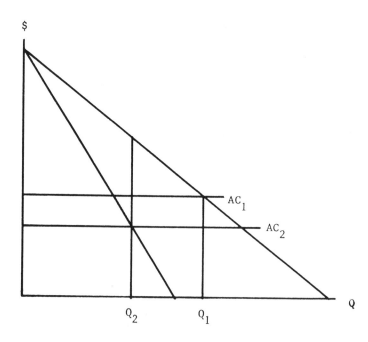

FIGURE 1

References

Arrow, Kenneth J., and F.H. Hahn, *General Competitive Analysis*, Holden–Day Inc., San Francisco 1971.

Bork, R.H., *The Antitrust Paradox*, Basic Books Inc., New York 1978.

_____, "Resale Price Maintenance and Consumer Welfare," *Yale Law Journal*, April 1968, 77, 950–964.

Fink, R.H., "Partial Equilibrium and the Analysis of Resale Price Maintenance," in the Center for the Study of Market Processes, Working Paper Series, George Mason University, 1983.

Fink, R.H., and T. Cowen, "Equilibrium, Information and Public Goods," (unpublished).

Hahn, F.H., "Reflections of the Invisible Hand," *Lloyds Bank Review*, April 1982, *144*, 1–21.

_____, *On the Notion of Equilibrium in Economics*, Cambridge University Press, Cambridge 1973.

Hayek, F.A., "Economics and Knowledge," in *Individualism and Economic Order*, University of Chicago Press, Chicago 1948.

Reder, M., "Chicago Economics: Permanence and Change," *Journal of Economic Literature*, March 1982, *20*, 1–38.

Richardson, G.B., "Equilibrium, Expectations, and Information," *The Economic Journal*, June 1959, *69*, 223–237.

Simon, H.A., "Rationality as Process and as Product of Thought," *American Economic Review*, May 1978, *68*, 1–16.

The Analysis of Competition and Monopoly

Franklin M. Fisher,
John J. McGowan & Joan E. Greenwood

The economic analysis of competition, especially perfect competition (numerous small sellers of a single homogeneous product), is a familiar one. Unfortunately, such familiarity can lead to misuse in the analysis of antitrust cases. A relatively superficial understanding of the competitive model—and, by contrast, its monopoly opposite—can lead to a number of errors when considering real situations. Such errors include the belief that a large market share must be due to monopoly and the consequent belief that the definition of the "market" is crucial; the view that anything that makes it expensive or time-consuming to enter constitutes a "barrier to entry"; the interpretation that all or most profits are due to monopoly; and the view that the "invisible hand" works anonymously so that price cutting by incumbent firms, particularly large ones, is likely to be predatory.

To a large extent, all these errors stem from a common source, a focus on the long-run equilibrium of the competitive model to the neglect of the process that brings that equilibrium about. Because disequilibrium is transient (and perhaps because of the beauty of the analysis of equilibrium), there is sometimes a tendency to view disequilibrium as necessarily very short-lived. This in turn gives rise to a tendency to analyze real markets as though they were always in long-run equilibrium and, indeed, sometimes to forget the precise nature of the definitions (profits, costs, entry barriers) that make the beautiful equilibrium propositions true.

Such a focus on long-run equilibrium can be a major error in the analysis of a real industry. This is particularly so in an industry like the computer industry in which the driving force has been technological change and which has again and again experienced a totally unexpected explosion of demand as new users of and new uses for computers came into being.[1] In such an industry, the competitive process—including the special role of innovation—is what matters. That process cannot be understood and monopoly power cannot be evaluated by assuming, in effect, that all innovations have long since been made, that all demand has been anticipated, and that the industry has settled down to a comfortable steady state.

Competition and Monopoly in Different Types of Markets

Most real markets fall in between pure competition and pure monopoly. Thus, virtually all firms possess some "market power" in that they are not constrained at every moment of time to follow a single set of decisions on

---

Reprinted from *Folded, Spindled and Mutilated* by permission of The MIT Press, 1983, pp. 19–41.
[1]Historical Narrative, pp. 923–943 and 1067–1068; Akers, Tr. 96932.

outputs, prices, product quality, investments, and so forth. A firm has monopoly power when it is sufficiently insulated from competitive pressures to be able to raise its prices or withhold the introduction of new technology, either in product innovations or in process (cost–reducing) innovations, without concern about the actions of its competitors and with relative impunity because its customers lack reasonable alternatives to which to turn. Monopoly power is the ability to *raise* prices above competitive levels or to market inferior products while excluding competition. This is the economist's version of the law's definition of monopoly as the "power to control prices or exclude competitors."[2] The ability to gain business through lower, remunerative prices or through better products is not monopoly power but the manifestation of "superior skill, foresight, and industry."[3]

Homogeneous Products and Many Firms

It is relatively easy to analyze competition in a market in which there are many small, equally efficient sellers of a single homogeneous product for which there are (by assumption) no close substitutes. In particular, such a case presents no problem of market definition. There are few, if any, markets such as this in the real world, however; hence the usefulness of such an analysis is as a theoretical polar case with which to start.

In such a market, price differences among sellers cannot persist forever. A supplier who offers the homogeneous product at a higher price than do other suppliers will lose business as soon as his customers detect the differences and shift to cheaper sources of supply. How long that takes will depend in part on how informed customers are about price offerings. The more information customers have about the prices that the various suppliers are charging, the faster they will shift their purchases from high–priced to low–priced suppliers and the faster price differences will be eliminated.

Moreover, in such a market when customers have good information about prices, prices will tend toward costs. When the general price level in the market is well above costs, some firms will reason correctly that they can attract business from their competitors and earn increased profits by shading the price somewhat while leaving it enough above cost to earn a profit. The firms losing customers will be forced to follow suit and lower their prices too or see their customers and profits dwindle away. The lower prices will therefore inevitably spread to all sellers. This process will tend to drive prices to a level that just covers costs, which are here defined to include "normal profits"—the return necessary to keep the firms in this business (as opposed to some other) with neither investment nor disinvestment taking place.[4]

---

[2]See *U.S.* v. *de Nemours and Company,* 351 U.S. 377 (1956) at 391.

[3]*U.S.* v. *Aluminum Company of America,* et al., 148 F. 2d 416 (1945) at 430.

[4]There are other differences between accounting definitions of costs and profits and those used in economic analysis. These important matters are discussed in chapter 7.

Thus, in such a classically competitive market, prices tend toward equality among suppliers, and the common value of price tends toward costs. Moreover, the same competitive process will force all the firms in the market to adopt the most efficient means of production available so that all firms will produce at the lowest possible cost. As soon as any firm realizes that it can adopt a more efficient mode of production (a process innovation), it will do so, and if a firm continues to sell at the preexisting price (equal to the costs of the inefficient firms), it will earn higher than "normal profits" as a reward. Indeed, such a firm will make even greater profits by lowering its price below the costs of its inefficient competitors and bidding away their business. As the efficient firm does this, the remaining firms will either have to follow suit by adopting the most efficient means of production or lose business. Costs will be driven down as far as possible, and prices will come to reflect these minimum costs.

Note that this says nothing about how fast such adjustments will occur. If the innovative firm can adopt the new method of production and expand its production very substantially and rapidly, then the process will occur rather quickly, especially if other firms can promptly copy the innovation. In real life, however, such changes take time, and firms face practical constraints on their ability to expand. Thus, the innovative firm may earn "economic profits" (above normal profits) for some period, and prices will gradually, not immediately, reach the new cost level.

Familiar as this model is, there are several lessons to be drawn from it about competitive markets that will be helpful in considering more complicated cases. These include the question of who benefits from competition; the role of profits and losses; competition and "predatory pricing"; and indicia of competition: constraints on behavior.

Who Benefits from Competition? The ultimate beneficiary of the competitive process is the customer. Suppliers are driven to adopt efficient means of production by the reward of positive economic profits if they are among the first to do so and the threat of losses if they lag behind other firms in this regard. Prices are driven down as competitors vie with each other to keep their own customers, take customers away from others, and win the business of new customers. Customers are able to obtain efficiently produced goods at prices that are continually pushed downward toward the level of the costs necessary to amass the resources required for production and distribution.

Those firms quickest to perceive that more efficient methods of production are possible, and therefore earning extra profits before the less efficient firms copy them, are also beneficiaries, but only in the short run. The efficient firms are unable to continue earning high profits, since their new methods are adopted by others, prices are lowered, and the extra profits are competed away. Only if further efficiencies become possible, can a new cycle of temporary extra profits arise. As we shall see in considering technological change and innovative competition, continual improvements and continued new technical opportunities can lead to repeated "temporary" and hence long–lasting profits.

There are also victims of the competitive process. Those firms slow to adopt the most efficient methods suffer losses as customers turn from them to more efficient firms charging lower prices. If they are slow enough in responding, such inefficient firms will go out of business. Losses and the failure of some firms are inevitable results of competition, particularly when new technical opportunities exist.

The Role of Profits and Losses The foregoing description of the competitive process underlines the important role that profits and losses play in it. Profits and losses are, respectively, the carrot and the stick of the marketplace. The hope of higher profits draws firms into the use of more efficient productive methods. The inevitability of losses, if they do not adopt such methods once discovered, prods sluggards to follow suit or drives them out if they remain sluggish. Profits are both the reward and the incentive for efficiency in serving customer needs. Losses are the penalty for not doing so.

Profits and losses also provide the incentives and punishments that lead a competitive economy to produce goods that customers desire. Thus, when customer needs change, with customers desiring more of good A and less of good B—so that, at given prices, the demand for good A rises and the demand for good B falls—the price of good A will increase, creating an opportunity for economic profit for firms offering good A. That profit opportunity will lead existing suppliers of good A to expand their production and, possibly, lead new firms into the production of good A. Firms quick to expand or enter will earn profits. As the supply of good A expands, its price will fall (although generally not back to the original level) until the profit opportunities disappear.

Similarly, the decline in demand for good B will produce a lower price. If price originally just covered cost, it will now not do so, losses will be incurred, and firms will find it to their advantage to cut back on their production of good B. Some firms, the least efficient ones, may find that they have to leave the production of good B altogether. Firms that are sluggish in responding to such signals will suffer the greatest losses. The reduction in supply of good B will cause its price to increase (although generally not back to the original level) until it is once again just profitable to produce. The net result of all this will be a transfer of resources from the production of good B to the production of good A, matching the changed needs of customers. These roles played by profits and losses remain essentially the same in more complex market situations.

Competition and "Predatory Pricing" In the simple case we have been discussing, competitive price formation is the mechanism that forces firms to adopt efficient means of production and forces prices down to costs. Customers seek lower prices, and more efficient firms increase their profits by lowering prices and bidding away business from less efficient ones. Firms set prices above their own costs but below those of less efficient firms. Pricing below costs of inefficient rivals is the natural and desirable result of the competitive process and is not "predatory pricing" even though inefficient firms are driven from the market. Were firms unable (for legal reasons, for example) to cut prices below other firms' costs (while still making a profit themselves), competition could not force inefficient firms to adopt more efficient modes of production, and prices might never fall below the level of the *least* efficient firm's cost. Efficiency would be somewhat rewarded (since the efficient firms would make higher profits), but inefficiency would not be discouraged. Most important, the inefficient firms would survive at the expense of customers who would be paying excessive prices to keep them in business. Price cutting by some firms and losses by others are not only natural but essential to the workings of competition. The competitive process favors the customer and not the competitor.

Indicia of Competition: Constraints on Behavior The most important lesson of the simple competitive model is the way in which each firm's behavior is constrained and compelled by external market forces. Firms in a competitive market cannot choose to use inefficient methods of production and hope to survive. If they attempt to follow that course, the competitive pressure of lower–cost, lower–priced rival offerings will threaten their survival. They also cannot choose to charge unduly high prices, for if they do, they will lose business and ultimately fail. The requirements of efficient production and consumer demand determine the price of the product and the quantity sold, even though they do not determine the identity of the firms that survive in the market.

To be sure, it generally will take time for customers to switch from a high-price firm to a low–price firm, and it will take time for new means of production to be adopted. Thus, even firms in a competitive market can avoid the external compulsion of the marketplace to be efficient and to set prices that just cover costs (including a return to capital)—but only for a time. In all real markets, firms have power to avoid competitive constraints on prices and costs to some degree. The hallmark of monopoly is the power to avoid such constraints to a great degree and for an extended period of time. The inability to avoid such constraints to any great degree or for more than a short period of time is the hallmark of competition.

There are two basic features of competitive markets that provide constraints on the firms participating in them. First is the existence of alternative sources of supply. Second is the presence of customers who are knowledgeable about the prices charged by alternative suppliers.

When there are alternative sources of supply, customers are not forced to deal with any specific firm; rather, they can choose from a variety of suppliers bidding for their business and seeking to meet their needs. In the model sketched earlier, we assumed that there are numerous firms in the market none of them having a large share of it. All are actively bidding for the customer's business. Competition could be equally effective and could work in the same way if there were only a few firms in the market and one or more of them had large shares, provided either that entry into the market were easy or that smaller firms could readily expand.

If entry is easy, an attempt by the incumbent firms to exploit their positions by charging higher prices would prompt the entry of more firms, lured by the profits to be made by bidding away the business of the incumbents. New firms would charge lower prices than those charged by the incumbent firms, since the profits earned by selling at lower prices would be enough to induce their entry. Incumbent firms would lose business if they did not lower their prices, exactly as if they had been faced with all of those competitors initially. Thus, when entry is easy, competition is effective and monopoly power is absent. Moreover, this is true whether or not entry does in fact occur. If incumbent firms are forced to lower their prices to avoid losing business to new entrants or to potential new entrants, competition is effective. Lower prices are the result it produces.

Furthermore, even without easy entry by new firms, competition will be equally effective if existing firms can readily expand. Thus, even if entry is difficult, the question of whether a particular firm has monopoly power does not directly depend on its current share of the market but on what would happen to its share if it attempted to charge high prices. This, in turn, depends on the ability of existing competitors to expand, which has the same effect as entry.

To illustrate this point, consider two cases in which entry is difficult. Suppose there is a single firm with a very high share, say over 70 percent of current sales, and a collection of competitors that both individually and in the aggregate have a small share. In one case, the small competitors are, for some reason, unable to expand their output. The large firm in that position is referred to in economic theory as a "dominant firm." It can set prices, calculating the demand it will face at any given price as the total industry demand minus the necessarily limited supply that its competitors will be able to offer at that price. It faces a demand curve consisting of the industry demand curve less the limited supply curves of the other firms. When that supply is limited and small relative to the total market, the large firm has a great deal of market power and may have monopoly power. When a full monopolist (one who faces a situation in which its competitors can, by definition, only supply zero because they never exist) can raise prices without losing any share, the large firm in this case can raise prices without losing very much share.

The dominant firm model, however, is very misleading when competitors can expand their supply. If competitors can easily increase their supply, then a sustained attempt by the firm with a large share to depart from competitive behavior by raising prices or offering inferior products will lead to an expansion by competitors, who will bid away its business. Its share will drop rapidly as a result of such an attempt. The same result occurs when new entrants appear and bid away the business of the large firm. When either new or existing competitors can readily expand, the firm is not "dominant" and does not have monopoly power even though it has a much larger share than those of its rivals. In such a situation, the firm in question can only keep that share by keeping prices low, by being more efficient than the others in the market, and by passing the benefits of that efficiency along to consumers in the form of lower prices. Thus, it is never the case that monopoly power can be inferred from a high market share. Only in the presence of blockaded conditions of entry and the inability of competitors to expand their outputs will a large market share provide evidence of monopoly power.

There is some apparent tension here between this formulation in terms of economic analysis and judicial interpretation of Section 2 of the Sherman Act. As discussed in chapter 1, such interpretations have long recognized that "superior skill, foresight, and industry" is a defense to a monopolization charge.[5] A defendant who is deemed to have attained and kept monopoly power solely by such means is not to be found in violation of the antitrust laws. The formulation given here has the same practical effect but expresses the matter differently. A defendant who maintains a large share solely through superior skill, foresight, and industry has no monopoly power at all. In this view, the necessity for the superior skill, foresight, and industry defense comes from falsely equating large share with monopoly power.

The second basic feature of the simple model that constrains sellers' behavior is the information possessed by customers. Where customers know about the range of price offerings in the market, high–price firms are forced to lower their prices. This point is obvious in the context of the simple market with a single homogeneous product, but it has an important corollary for more complex situations involving technological change and innovation: when customers are sophisticated and informed about both the prices and the product offerings of suppliers, suppliers will be forced to meet the real needs of customers in terms of the value of the products that they offer or suffer losses and eventually go out of business.

In short, then, it is the presence of alternative sources of supply (either actual or potential but readily available) together with sophisticated and informed customers that creates the essential constraints that characterize competition. In the absence of high barriers to entry and competitive expansion, when customers have alternatives and are informed about them, monopoly power cannot exist.

Many Firms with Differentiated Products

The second kind of market setting to be examined is somewhat more complex than the first. Each firm in this type of market offers a product that differs from the products offered by other firms. The differences among products may

---

[5]See, for example, *U.S.* v. *Aluminum Company of America, et al.,* 148 F. 2d 416 (1945) at 430 and *U.S.* v. *United Shoe Machinery Corporation,* 100 F. Supp. 295 (1953) at 297.

be physical differences or they may be differences perceived by customers but perhaps not readily apparent to uninformed outside observers. The markets for furniture or clothing illustrate the former case; preference for brands of beer or cigarettes exemplify the latter.

Product and Quality Competition The significant distinction between the present market and one for a homogeneous product lies in the area of product competition. In a market for a homogeneous product, firms are distinguished in the eyes of the customer only by the prices they charge. Customers, given good information, automatically find it advantageous to buy from the firm with the lowest price. In a market with differentiated products, firms are distinguished not only by the prices they set but by the products they offer. A large number of additional dimensions are thus added to the user's evaluation and choice and thus to the firm's competitive efforts. Importantly, customers will not necessarily buy from the firm that offers its products at the lowest price. Those products must also meet the customers' needs reasonably well, and their deficiencies relative to other product offerings may more than offset any price advantage.

Indeed, when products are differentiated, simple price comparisons are meaningless, since the prices charged by different firms relate to different products. Customers who pay an apparently higher price and receive a product better suited to their needs may in a real sense be paying less than those who pay a lower price for a product less suited to their needs. If it is possible to construct a measure of product quality as perceived by customers, then nominal prices can be converted to prices per unit of quality, and comparisons among such quality adjusted prices will be meaningful. Such adjustments, however, are always difficult and often impossible for an outside observer to make. The customers themselves are the best judges of how much they get for their money, at least provided that they are informed and sophisticated in their understanding of the alternatives that different suppliers offer to them. And, the customer's judgments are demonstrated by their actions in the market.

If the choice among product varieties is important and involves expending large amounts of money, customers will undoubtedly find that it pays to become sophisticated if they are not so already. When, in particular, customers are businesses themselves, they will tend not to make procurement decisions without appropriate information, for they run the risk of unnecessarily increasing their own costs. Indeed, if the customers themselves operate in competitive environments, they will be compelled to make rational, economic choices. If they are large, they may find it profitable to acquire the necessary expertise within their own organizations. However, even small customers can often achieve sophistication in their important purchasing decisions, for when there are numerous small customers, it will be profitable for consultants to offer the necessary expertise.[6]

When products differ in complex ways, price comparisons will be similarly complex because there is unlikely to be a readily constructed unidimensional measure of quality. Discussions of "price/performance" in the computer business, for example, represent attempts to correct price for rather rough measures of technical attributes of computer equipment. In general, such attempts cannot adequately account for all such attributes. Moreover, such discussions do not and cannot take into account equipment reliability, responsiveness of the supplier's service organization, the supplier's reputation for supplying reliable equipment suitable to customer needs, or the functions offered by the supplier's software. Yet these are important parts of product quality, however difficult they are to measure. Different customers will generally differ in the weight they give each such attribute, just as different customers will generally differ in the weights they give the various more tangible attributes.

This discussion provides the major points for an understanding of how competition works in a market with differentiated products. Customers are presented with an array of products with attributes more or less suitable for them; associated with each product of the array is a price. Customers who are sophisticated and informed enough to understand the alternatives facing them, or who hire sophisticated consultants to advise them, choose that product from the array that gives them the best value, taking into account their particular needs, the characteristics of the product, and its price. Firms that do well in serving customers' desires per dollar of price will do well in sales. Firms offering unnecessarily expensive items or, similarly, products less suited to customer needs at the same prices as their rivals will lose business.

Competition in a market with differentiated products will take the form of product innovation as well as price and cost reduction. As discussed later, a successful product innovation by a firm in an industry characterized by competition and product differentiation will stimulate imitation of the innovation by others. Firms that are initially less successful will be forced either to lower their prices or to change their products so that they meet customer demands as well as their more successful rivals do.

As in the homogeneous product case, prices in theory ultimately will reflect costs. A firm pricing its products above cost will eventually find business bid away by imitators offering essentially the same product at lower prices. Firms unusually successful in meeting customers' needs will initially make extra profits, but those profits will be eroded over time unless the firms continue to offer successive products that customers find exceptionally desir-

---

[6]Large sophisticated customers are common in the computer business (Union Carbide is an example well brought out at the trial). Consultants are also common (Mancke Testimony, pp. 921–929; Historical Narrative, pp. 1412–1426).

able. Those profits (as in the homogeneous case) are the rewards that spur the firm to meet customers' needs well in the first place. Unfortunately for the successful firm they are also the lure that draws imitators to produce similar or even more attractive products and compete away the business. The speed of successful imitation or new product introduction will determine the duration of high profits. Only if the first firm continues to meet customer needs consistently better than its rivals can it continue to make extra profits over the long run.

As in the homogeneous product case, costs will tend to be driven down to the lowest level allowed by the state of the technology at any moment of time. Inefficient firms will find that they cannot afford to continue to be inefficient; their more efficient rivals will produce the same product at lower cost or a better one at the same cost, offer equivalent quality for lower prices or higher quality for the same price, and thus bid away their business. In addition with differentiated products, there may often be different production techniques or technologies in use by different firms, and it may not be immediately clear which technology is in fact the most efficient one for a particular quantity and quality of product. Therefore, differences in economic profits, resulting from differences in cost levels and prices, may persist longer than would theoretically be expected in the case of the homogeneous product. It may take quite some time for one firm's choice of technology and production processes to be proven inferior in the competitive struggle, and it may be difficult for that firm to shift direction and catch up when it becomes apparent that it is going the wrong way.

As in the homogeneous product case, there will be both winners and losers in the competitive race. The winners will be those firms that are technically efficient, that have the lowest costs and are thus able to offer given products at a low price, that are most adept at meeting customer needs, that offer products preferred by at least some customers over the alternative products available, or that combine these attributes. The losers will be firms that use technically inefficient means of production or that are unable to offer products well-suited to customers' desires, and for either or both reasons cannot supply satisfactory products at acceptable prices while covering their costs.

But here, as in all competitive markets, the ultimate winners are the customers. They are offered a variety of products from which they choose those best suited to their needs and desires, given their budgets, and they spend only those amounts of money technically necessary to get those products. The rewards that the efficient and well-performing firms earn are not earned at customers' expense but are the result of serving their customers better than do alternative suppliers.

Again, it is noteworthy that good performance (low prices, efficiency in production, and a variety of products well-suited to customers' desires) is not a matter of choice for the firms offering it if imitation is rapid. Rather, the competitive constraints of the market enforce good performance. Only well-performing firms survive. Their less competent rivals are penalized by the market process to the benefit of their customers. As before, the presence of responsive alternative suppliers and informed customers cognizant of alternatives compels the results, at least in the absence of substantial barriers to entry and expansion. Given these two ingredients, competition must emerge (absent collusion and regulatory impediments).

The Role of Market Definition In this analysis, we have deliberately begged the question of how the "market" is defined, a question that all too often becomes central in antitrust cases. In the simple case of a single homogeneous product, that question is settled by assumption and does not arise, but it is hard to avoid in more complex cases. When there is a range of differentiated products, each substituting for the others to some extent, but not perfectly, should one group these products in a single market, consider each of them as constituting a single market, or group clusters of them in one market and other clusters in other markets? Moreover, how should one draw the boundary between the spectrum of products to be considered and other products in the economy?

To understand how a market or group of markets should be delineated, one must keep in mind the purpose to which market definition is to be put. For antitrust purposes, the goal of market definition is to facilitate the analysis of the way in which competition works or, alternatively, the assessment of whether a particular firm possesses monopoly power with respect to a particular group of its products and services.

Market definition is a convenient and useful tool for these purposes, but it is not an end in itself. Further, it must not be a tool that determines the outcome of the analysis. The underlying facts of the market situation are what they are no matter how the products bought and sold have been categorized into "markets" for the purpose of analysis. The way competition works in a particular market cannot and does not depend on how an observer organizes or classifies the products traded in it. Thus, in examining whether a particular firm possesses monopoly power, the behavior of the firm either is or is not constrained by market forces to a greater or lesser degree. The presence of absence of such constraints does not depend on how one looks at them. The basic facts cannot be changed by choosing to describe the products of a particular firm (which in the differentiated product case are to some extent unlike those of any other firm) as constituting a separate market by themselves or choosing to include them in a market with similar products of other sellers.

Thus, consider the analysis just given of competition with differentiated products. Suppose that the market is defined somewhat more narrowly, leaving out the products and firms placing the least constraints on the alleged monopolist. Competition among the firms within the more narrowly defined market would operate in exactly the same way as described earlier in terms of a broader market definition. Customers would choose those product best suited to their desires in terms of both the quality and the price of the products. However, the effects of the substitute products now placed outside the market and of entry into the market as defined must also be considered when the somewhat narrower definition of the market is used. Customers may find that they can better satisfy their needs for the same price (or satisfy them as well at lower prices) by dealing with firms and buying products now excluded from the more narrowly defined market. Further, if the firms inside the market are the ones who are receiving the rewards of adeptly satisfying customer needs (that is, economic profits), then the kind of imitation of success discussed earlier will appear as entry into the narrowly defined market by firms previously outside it.

If the question is whether a particular firm is so insulated from the compulsions of competition as to warrant the attribution of monopoly power to it, it does not matter which market definition is used, so long as it is used consistently. In the first case, with all the relevant firms included in the market, however, mistakes of omission are less likely to occur than in the second case of the narrowly defined market, since it will be immediately apparent in the former case that there are many alternative suppliers constraining the behavior of the firm or firms in the market. If the slightly narrower market definition is used, a large market share of the firm or firms in question might appear itself to warrant an inference about monopoly power. Such a conclusion, however, drawn without considering the facts of entry and potential entry would be plainly wrong. To assess market power, the constraints on the alleged monopolist's behavior from substitute products outside the market and from entry and potential entry into it must be taken into account as well as those arising from the offering of firms inside the more narrowly defined market.

The fact that the precise locations of the boundary does not matter does not make market definition a matter of no consequence, however. It is one thing to consider placing firms or products near the boundary outside rather than inside the market, bearing in mind the way in which they compete; it is quite another to do this with much of the market, arbitrarily deciding on a narrow definition that excludes much of the real competition constraining the behavior of the included firms. To do so while attempting to bear in mind the way in which the excluded firms and products compete is to defeat the purpose of market definition by adopting a course designed to confuse rather than to aid analysis. Similarly, it is true that defining a market so broadly as to include many things that do not much constrain the power of the alleged monopolist is to misuse market definition.

As this suggests, what matters are the constraints themselves, not the way in which they are classified. A market with heterogeneous products will include some that constrain the alleged monopolist less than do others. Analysis and understanding of these different effects is what is important, and this can be done without deciding on a definition of the market.

Despite this, market definition tends to play a major role in antitrust cases and certainly in Section 2 cases. This is largely due to the mistaken belief that a large market share (generally according to the guidelines laid down by Judge Hand in *Alcoa*[7]) can prove monopoly and that a large share can be proven by definitional arguments about the "market." While we believe such emphasis to be totally misplaced, the importance of the issue in practice requires an extended discussion (both in general and in terms of the IBM case), and we give that discussion in the next chapter.

Technological Change and Innovative Competition

Technological change has not been present as a major factor in the market models considered so far. Yet the most apparent and distinctive characteristic of the computer business is dramatic technological change.

The groundwork for an analysis of the case of "innovative competition" has already been laid in the consideration of markets with a number of competitors and differentiated products. What happens when the prospects of the continual introduction of new, improved or innovative products or new, improved production techniques are added to the model?

Under competition, firms that cannot meet customer needs as well as their rivals will lose business. When innovation is possible, the threat that others will produce better or cheaper products puts pressure on firms to find new and better ways of meeting customer needs. Under that pressure, firms will continually introduce new products that serve customers' needs better than existing products. The first firm successfully to market a superior new product[8] is rewarded for the risks it took in developing that new product by acquiring the ability to attract customers preferring the improved product or the ability to charge a premium price reflecting the improvement. Thus, in the period immediately after it introduces a new product, an innovating firm earns higher profits than firms in the market that do not make such an innovation. Those profits are both the incentive for innovation and the reward for success in producing it. They are also an incentive for other firms to equal or better the innovation.

This is only the first step of the competitive process, however. Other firms are induced to imitate or improve on the innovation to defend their existing business and to attempt to reap similar high profits. Gradually, as other firms learn how to make the same or similar products, the innovative firm's capacity to attract additional customers or charge higher prices for its special products is diminished. The period in which business is competed away from firms with existing products by an innovator who has created a new one is followed by a period in which the profits of the innovator are competed away by the price

---

[7]*U.S.* v. *Aluminum Company of America,* et al., 148 F. 2d 416 (1945) at 424.

[8]It is the bringing of an invention to commercial practicability—the successful marketing of a superior product—and not the invention itself that characterizes an innovating firm in the only sense relevant for economic analysis.

competition of imitators. Ultimately, the innovative firm will be on a par with everyone else, unless it is able to respond to the competitive pressure by making further innovations. Of course, a given innovation is followed not only by direct imitators and price competition but by further innovation by others and by the original innovator. These, in turn, tend to make the first innovation obsolete. Under technological change, both price competition and product competition are present. The latter, in terms of both imitative development and leapfrogging innovations, plays a particularly significant role in the competitive process.

As in all competitive markets, the presence of alternatives to which customers can turn and their knowledge of those alternatives provide both the incentive and the threat causing firms to seek to discover better ways of meeting customers' demands more effectively and more cheaply. In a market with technological change, absolute prices may rise. However, that rise is illusory. While the innovative firm may well be able to charge a higher price for its new products than other firms charge for their old ones, it can do so only because the new product offers more value for the money. On a properly measured basis (taking product characteristics into account), the innovator has actually cut prices. That is why it attracts customers. Further, even such a "higher" price will fall as imitation or further innovation occurs and forces prices down. The cycle is then repeated—in innovative competition, time and the time sequence of events are of critical importance.

The Benefits of Innovation

In the process of innovative competition, as always in competitive markets in general, customers are the ultimate beneficiaries. They receive a succession of better products and lower prices. There are, however, other beneficiaries in the short run; and there are also losers.

The innovative firms, the risk takers, benefit from the competitive process. They run the risk that the potential innovation will not be technically feasible, that it will not be accepted by customers, and that other simultaneous or closely following innovations will make it obsolete as it is born. If such risk taking is successful, innovative firms will reap rewards. By succeeding in serving customer needs better, they achieve a profit. But in the face of continuing technological competition and price competition from imitators, their ability to earn high profits from any single innovation is transitory, although such "transitory" effects may last for several years. Innovating firms can continue to earn profits only if they continue to innovate. It is true, however, that a firm having forged ahead in the race may be in a better position than others to remain ahead, provided it keeps running.

The profits earned by the innovative firm in these circumstances are in no helpful sense "monopoly profits." One important difference between these profits and monopoly profits is that the firms must keep on serving customer needs better in order to continue to earn high profits. If they slow down, become less innovative, or incorrectly predict the movement of customer preferences or technology, their profits will not last. The monopolist, by contrast, can continue to earn high profits simply by virtue of its monopoly position. It does so by restricting output and by not offering product improvements while retaining customers who have nowhere else to turn.

Other firms may also earn profits in markets where technological change is occurring. Successful imitators who are quick to see what makes a particular innovation successful and who quickly follow the lead of the innovator may also make profits. However, imitators of new products are likely to earn smaller profits than do successful innovators because their products will be on the market for a shorter period of time before they are made obsolete by further innovations. In addition, the first imitator is likely to be followed soon by others so that the profits in that type of product will soon be competed away. Thus, successive imitators are likely to earn diminishing profits in comparison with those of the first imitator.

In a market with rapid technological change, some firms also suffer losses. Those who invest in new products that turn out not to be particularly well suited to customer needs will lose money. Those who are slow to perceive that new ways of doing things have arisen and that the old ways are no longer favored by customers will also lose. The process of innovative competition is like a race in which it is necessary to run and run well to endure and to prosper, but the race is more like a marathon than a sprint.

Other Forms of Innovation

Beyond product innovation—the development and marketing of a new product—other kinds of innovation exist that may be less visible but of equal importance. The first of these has already appeared in part: innovation in the techniques of production, sometimes called "process innovation." Such innovation involves an invention that makes production techniques more efficient. This may be a technological innovation or a reorganization of the way in which production is structured or both. Firms successful at process innovation will make profits because they will reduce their costs. Such profits, which are the rewards of efficiency, will last until other firms become equally or more efficient by imitating the innovation or surpassing it.

How long that will be depends on the kind of innovation involved. Unlike a product innovation, which is produced and can be seen and possibly copied by competitors, a process innovation may remain relatively invisible to the outside world. Thus, as opposed to product innovation, the competitive process here is more likely to proceed by other firms innovating and discovering alternative ways of reducing costs than by imitating a particular process. This will be particularly so where the firm making the innovation does so using only its own personnel and resources and has no particular incentive to publicize it.

When the innovation is patentable, however, the innovating firm may be induced to reveal it. If patents are relatively freely available, then so will be the innovation (perhaps with a share of revenues going to the innovator). Further, process innovations may be prompted by inventions from wholly outside the market, where they are available to all firms. In such cases, process innovations are likely to be imitated fairly quickly. In an intermediate case, the innovating firm, if it has to design or use special manufacturing equipment, may cooperate with outside vendors in its design or procurement. In time, the equipment so designed may become available to other firms competing with the innovator.[9] In any event, as with product innovation, process innovation will result in an advantage for the innovating firm, leading to profits.

Other forms of innovation may not be technological at all. One form of process innovation can involve reorganizing the way production is structured. Another form of innovation is the creation of a management system that keeps the decisionmakers in touch with the marketplace and links that awareness with the design and manufacturing activities. In competitive markets with differentiated products and product innovation, firms that best serve customers' needs and desires are the ones that survive and prosper. This, in turn, requires knowing what customer needs and desires are, and firms that create effective methods for discerning them will be able to take better advantage of innovative opportunities. Moreover, firms with good market information systems are more likely to perceive when better products are being offered by others, imitate them, and enter successful areas quickly. Customers benefit when firms have the information to respond quickly to changes in their needs and market situations. A firm that develops better ways of gaining and using such information and organizes itself in a manner that helps to ensure that the products it develops and manufactures are responsive to customers' needs and desires will be rewarded in the competitive process.

Another important related form of innovation is the perception of new uses for existing products, or new versions of them, and the expansion of business through the education of potential customers. This form of innovation may be especially important when combined with new product development to make product lines more suitable for use by those new customers.

Finally, to succeed in a market with shifting customer demands and rapid technological change, a firm must be able to make informed, intelligent decisions quickly. In addition, the firm cannot be paralyzed by disputes; they must be resolved quickly and effectively. Thus, the internal organization of management is of considerable importance to the results of the firm over time. Superior management can bring profits; ineffective management can bring losses.

---

[9] The Gardner–Denver wire wrapping machines, for example, originally designed by IBM in cooperation with the manufacturer, became generally available throughout the computer industry.

The Importance of Time

An obvious but important lesson from this analysis of the process of competition in a market with rapid technological change is that in assessing whether a firm in such a market has monopoly power, one must be sure to examine the market over a sufficiently long period of time to be able to observe the process of innovative competition at work. A snapshot taken at a single moment in time can be entirely misleading. It might, for example, show one firm (the innovator) well ahead of its rivals and with a substantial share of even a reasonably well–defined market. But since the snapshot could not reveal either the competitive process whereby the firm attained its position or the competitive response of rival firms, it could not form a reliable basis for making inferences about the presence or absence of monopoly power.

Similarly, a short period analysis might be misleading in other ways. If one observes the process of innovative competition in the period after a successful innovation has been made and when imitators begin to enter, one will see the innovator with a large share and high profits. As other follow that lead, prices, as we have seen, will be bid down as part of the competitive process. The "invisible hand" is not literally invisible, however. Such price adjustment comes about through the actions of imitators (who may not have had the same research and development costs as the original imitator) offering similar products at a price lower than that originally set by the innovator. As those products prove reliable, customers will turn away from the innovator to take advantage of such prices. Then the original innovator *must* lower prices or lose share. That is the essence of competition. If the innovator were able to retain its share without lowering its prices or improving its product, one might infer that it had monopoly power. If, looking at the process during this period, one sees the original innovator lowering prices in an attempt to ward off competitors, it would be a complete mistake to regard such lowering of prices as the action of a monopolist determined to drive out competition. Rather, that lowering is the result that competition inevitably brings about and that benefits the consumer.

Consideration of the entire process is important in the analysis of all kinds of competitive markets, not merely those characterized by innovative competition. In the real world, in which things take time, competitive markets will often not be at equilibrium with prices equal to marginal costs equal to average costs and no economic profits being made. When demand or cost conditions change and, especially, when new opportunities appear, competitive markets will be thrown into disequilibrium, and the process of adjustment will begin. That adjustment may not be complete before the next change occurs. Under innovative competition, this is particularly important. Only in a world in which new opportunities do not arise and old ones disappear as competitors take advantage of them can one be sure that the competitive process will even approach equilibrium.[10] When new opportunities continually arise, one will see under competition a continuing process of change that carries with it continual opportunities for profit and growth. One cannot hope to understand the competitive nature of such a process by examining it in the terms of static competitive equilibrium. Such an examination will tend to lead to the false conclusion that the market is not competitive when in fact competition is operating fiercely.

A snapshot taken at a moment in time might show one firm ahead. It would give only a very incomplete picture, however, for it would fail to show that what is going on is a continuing race. What matters is not the snapshot but the movie. Even though a firm initially ahead may well be in a better position to stay ahead than firms that are initially behind, what matters is whether it can do so only by continuing to compete and whether the race is fair.

Structure, Conduct, and Performance: Indicia of Competition or Monopoly

Our discussion of the several market models presents a description of the competitive process and competitive activity as distinguished from the presence of monopoly power. Often an examination of the actual activity of firms in the market and the results of their interaction can reveal whether the market is effectively competitive. Economists, however, have traditionally undertaken the analysis of the competitiveness of a market by an examination of indicia of competition and monopoly categorized under the headings of market structure, market conduct, and market performance.

Market structure consists of the environment within which a given firm does business. It comprises such things as the number and strength of competitors, the technological opportunities, and the underlying conditions of entry. Other relevant factors are the pattern and rate of growth of the market, the sophistication and nature of the customers, and the availability of product and price information to the participants in the market. In the language used earlier, analysis of market structure is an examination of the more or less fixed constraints within which a firm does business, viewed in the perspective of several years rather than a month or a year.

In some situations, analysis of market structure alone answers the questions of interest. In markets with several suppliers, with customers sophisticated about the alternatives presented, and in which either no one supplier has a particularly large market share or entry and expansion are easy, the market structure constraints compel competition. Little more need be discussed. In other situations, however, the relationship between market structure and the outcome (performance) or behavior (conduct) in that market is not so clear. In particular, a situation in which there are several supplying firms but one has a

---

[10]This is true on several levels. For a formal treatment as regards the stability of equilibrium, see Franklin M. Fisher, "Stability, Disequilibrium Awareness and the Perception of New Opportunities," *Econometrica,* vol. 49, no. 2 (March 1981), and especially *Disequilibrium Foundations of Equilibrium Economics* (Cambridge, U.K.: Cambridge University Press, 1983).

much larger market share than any others and the conditions of entry and expansion are not favorable may be either competitive or monopolistic. For example, assuming that the large share is not simply a product of an inappropriately narrow market definition, that share may reflect a firm that has been successful innovative competition in a particularly risky and rapidly changing market. Alternatively, it may mean that customers are limited in their capacity to find alternatives to the offerings of the firm with the large share, even if that firm does not offer good value. In such situations, further analysis is necessary.

Consideration of the case in which a large market share is the product of success in innovative competition reveals the fact that there are circumstances in which some aspects of market structure, at least, cannot be treated as exogenous—taken as given for the analysis of competition. Particularly when technological change is important, certain aspects of market structure will be endogenous—themselves produced by the workings of the competitive (or noncompetitive) process. In innovative competition, one cannot understand the significance of a large market share without understanding how that share came to be and how it is maintained. Similarly, in such circumstances, the number and identity of firms in the market are not immutably given but are determined by the competitive process itself. One must understand that process as a dynamic whole rather than as a static situation.

Market conduct consists of the ways in which firms interact with each other and the ways in which individual firms decide to do business. Conduct encompasses the actual competitive activity: pricing practices, terms and conditions, marketing policies, product offerings, and the like, whether such activity reflects vigorous rivalry, predatory behavior, or an inability or unwillingness to compete aggressively. An examination of market conduct can help to decide whether the market position of the alleged monopoly is due to conduct constituting an exercise of monopoly power that frees it from competitive constraints or from the threat of such constraints, or is due to successful risk taking, superior products or services, excellent business management, or a particular skill in meeting customer demands.

Market performance consists of the results of the working of the market in terms of the major economic variables of prices, costs, product quality, variety of customer alternatives, responsiveness of the suppliers to the demands of the customers, and the interrelations among these variables. An examination of market performance may determine whether the workings of the given market structure and market conduct result in the kind of outcome that competition is designed to produce; efficient production, technological improvement (with the implementation of technological advances in the products and services offered to customers), ample and expanding customer alternatives, responsiveness to customer demands, and prices tending to fall toward costs. If the outcome differs significantly from that which a competitive market is expected to produce, then the market is not competitive. If the performance is what is expected from a competitive market, then one should suspect that the market is competitive. As a matter of theory, it is possible that, even though the market is not competitive, firms with freedom of action and monopoly power may choose to act in such a way as to duplicate the workings of the competitive market, but this theoretical possibility is not likely to be realized in observable market situations. A judgment that observed performance is compatible with competition supports, as a practical matter, a judgment that the market is in fact competitive. This judgment will be inevitable if the analysis of the market shows behavior on the part of all firms that can only be interpreted as being responses to market constraints. When one can observe that the competitive process is at work and that vigorous rivalry among independent firms is creating strong pressure to push market performance toward the desired results, monopoly power cannot exist.

CHAPTER 8 - Public Choice

Use of Antitrust to Subvert Competition

William J. Baumol   *Janusz A. Ordover*

> The day after Congress passed the changes in the clean air legislation which substantially tightened emissions standards the Japanese automakers called an emergency meeting of their engineers. On the same day the carmakers in Detroit called an emergency meeting of their lawyers. [JOKE CIRCULATING AT THE TIME]

There is a specter that haunts our antitrust institutions. Its threat is that, far from serving as the bulwark of competition, these institutions will become the most powerful instrument in the hands of those who wish to subvert it. More than that, it threatens to draw great quantities of resources into the struggle to prevent effective competition, thereby more than offsetting the contribution to economic efficiency promised by antitrust activities. This is a specter that may well dwarf any other source of concern about the antitrust processes. We ignore it at our peril and would do well to take steps to exorcise it.

The problem is not an easy one. In a sense it is inherent in the very nature of the antitrust process. There is no doubt, for example, that mergers can sometimes inhibit or undermine competition and that predatory pricing can sometimes serve as an instrument of monopolization. But then, because of that, a merger that promises to introduce efficiencies that make it necessary for other firms in the industry to try harder is vulnerable to challenge by those rivals, who will claim that it is anticompetitive. Similarly, a firm that by virtue of superior efficiency or economies of scale or scope is able to offer prices low enough to make its competitors uncomfortable is all too likely to find itself accused of predation. Such attempts to use the law as an instrument for the subversion of competition do not confine themselves to private lawsuits. All too often the enterprise seeking to erect a protective umbrella about itself will be tempted to try to subvert the antitrust authorities, Congress, and even the president's office as partners in its purpose. One suspects that the costs in terms of the efficiency of the firm and the economy that is subject to this sort of attack are high. One knows that the costs in terms of the time of management,

Reprinted from the *Journal of Law & Economics*, (1985) pp. 247–65 by permission of the University of Chicago Press.

lawyers, economists, and others absorbed in the litigation process itself are enormous. And it is almost all economic waste.

I. Protectionism as Rent Seeking

Few observers will deny that some firms succumb to the temptation to seek governmental protection from the unpleasantness of effective competition. The blatant attempts by some steel and auto firms to have foreign imports restricted, the transparent purpose underlying a number of private antitrust suits, among other examples, can leave little doubt that the phenomenon is a reality. Yet, at least in some discussions, the volume of such protectionist activity is viewed as fortuitous, explainable largely in terms of cultural characteristics, political climate, and other influences beyond the purview of economic analysis. For example, American litigiousness is sometimes contrasted with Japanese distaste for direct confrontation as an explanation of the differences in the volume of private suits in the two countries.

Economic theory nonetheless has a good deal to say about the matter. The theory of rent seeking contributed by James Buchanan and extended to a variety of legal issues by Richard Posner tells us just how much protectionist effort one can expect in any particular set of circumstances. To summarize the argument very briefly, rent is defined by economists as any earnings by the supplier of an activity that exceed the minimum amount necessary to elicit the services of that supplier. Any supercompetitive (monopoly) profits of a firm are a rent. The theory of rent seeking tells us that where entrepreneurs are free to spend money in an attempt to gain control of such a source of rent, that is, when entry into a rent–seeking activity is completely free, when rent seeking is perfectly competitive or at least perfectly contestable, the resources devoted to the attempt will reach just the amount necessary to consume the entire rent. Rent seekers suing one another to gain control of a source of monopoly profit will spend so much on lawyers, consultants, and so on, that they will dissipate the entire expected monopoly profit in the process. That is just a corollary of the theorem that under perfect competition (excess) profits must be zero. In the circumstances posited, the struggle for the monopoly profits is a perfectly competitive process (or, at least, one that is perfectly contestable).

The result may seem to constitute a mere transfer of wealth from the monopolist to lawyers and economists, but it is much worse than that. In the process the latter are led to devote considerable (and valuable) time in a way that yields no socially valuable product. In other words, here rent seeking transforms into pure waste a quantity of resources equal in value to the rent that is sought.

The search for protection, which is the subject of this paper, is rent seeking (or rent preserving), as we now show. But it is not necessarily competitive, and so the analysis requires some modification. Envision the following scenario. Firm A offers generous salaries to its management, and firm B, with a leaner compensation package, undercuts A's prices, thereby eliminating the rents constituted by the overcompetitive salaries. A can hope to force B to cease and desist and perhaps even to collect treble damages from B by suing it for predatry pricing. What quantity of resources will A devote to this purpose?

First we note that even if other firms in the industry are hurt by A's pricing behavior, there is no competitive pressure driving A to use up its entire expected gain in its rent–preserving outlays. To see what will occur, let us first assume that A is the only firm affected by B's prices and then consider the case where several enterprises have their rents threatened.

Where A alone is involved, and assuming that its chances of achieving its protectionist goal increase monotonically with the quantity of resources it devotes to the purpose, then, as usual, profit maximization requires it to spend on its litigation effort up to the point where an additional dollar in outlay increases the expected rent yield by no more than $1.00. This may well leave firm A with a considerable expected gain from the undertaking. But it is also likely to involve a very substantial total outlay, that is, a very large amount of waste.

Where several other firms C, D, and E will benefit along with A if B is forced to end its "unfair competition," each of them will find it profitable to spend some money to increase the probability of victory. The joint profitmaximizing outlay will be greater, in general, than when only A's rents are at stake, since the marginal expected yield to the group as a whole must be at least as great as the marginal yield to A alone. However, in the absence of effective collusion, the behavior of the group may well not be (joint) profit maximizing, and it may involve outlays by the group lower than those that maximize their joint profits. This is so because an externality (free–rider) issue is involved. Any increment in probability of success against B achieved by an increase in A's expenditure will also benefit firms C, D, and E. As a result, when the marginal net benefit of such outlays to firm A reaches zero, its marginal benefit to the group of firms will still be positive. It follows that the total rent–seeking expenditure of the group can be expected to be less than that which maximizes their combined expected rent return.[1] The group's outlay will almost certainly be at least as large as the largest of the outlays of any of the four rent–seeking firms would have been had it been the only competitor of B. To see this, it would have paid, say, firm C to spend X dollars in litigation if A and D were not spending anything for the purpose. If C finds that A and D together are spending on $X - \Delta$ for the purpose, then surely it will pay C to obtain the same probability of success as it would have in isolation since now it only costs him $\Delta < X$ dollars to do so. The Slutsky theorem for the firm not subject to a budget

---

[1] We cannot be certain of this since it depends on the concavity–convexity properties of the pertinent relationships. The presence of externalities themselves is likely to cause problems on that score. On this see William J. Baumol & David F. Bradford, Detrimental Externalities and Non–Convexity of the Production Set, 40 Economica 160 (n.s. 1972); or William J. Baumol & Wallace E. Oates, The Theory of Environmental Policy (1975), at ch. 8.

constraint tells us that this must be so because what is involved is a reduction in the price of increased probability of success in the rent–seeking undertaking.

We conclude from all this that while protectionist activity is a form of rent seeking, its expected benefits to the rent seeker are not likely to be dissipated completely in wasteful litigation expenditure. But the theory suggests nevertheless that the expenditures may typically be very substantial and that the social costs stemming from such direct waste may well prove very high.[2]

This is by no means the only type of social costs of protectionism. There are at least two other sorts of cost: monopolistic resource misallocation, and disincentives for internal operating efficiency for the individual firms, which may prove far more serious. The nature of the first of these is obvious to anyone familiar with welfare economics. After all, the immediate purpose of the protectionist activity is to subvert the forces of competition, and if the effort succeeds, it will lead to pricing and other decisions that are different, perhaps very different, from those that would emerge under competition. It follows that resources can be expected to be misallocated, as is always true under unregulated monopoly in a market that is not contestable.

The second social cost takes the form of inefficiency in the protected firm. First, if a company is insulated from competition, the pressures that would otherwise force it to operate with maximal efficiency are simply removed.[3] It is freer than it otherwise would be to engage in nepotism and sloppy supervision, to display excessive caution in risky decisions, and to avoid innovations that require management to exert itself. In short, protectionist activity frees the firm to engage in the degree of inefficiency that suits the proclivities and abilities of its management.

The third social cost of protectionism is its effect on the immediate objectives, and hence the organization, of the firm. If such rent seeking is the easier way to increase its profits or to achieve other managerial objectives, the firm's energies will be directed toward preparation for its litigative ventures, which will receive priority over efforts to increase productivity or to improve the

---

[2]The astonishing outlays by major firms on the antitrust litigations in which they have been involved confirms that these expenditures can indeed be substantial. For example, Alan A. Fisher & Robert H. Lande, Efficiency Considerations in Merger Enforcement, 71 Calif. L. Rev. 1580, 1673 (1983) estimate that Du Pont, Seagram, and Mobil spent about $13.5 million in private legal fees to acquire Conoco. In addition, they estimate at 1673 n.308 that an average merger antitrust case costs anywhere between $700,000 and $1.4 million. To this one must add costs incurred by the DOJ, or the FCC, and the courts.

[3]Some sense of magnitude of the expenditures that insulation from competition can elicit is suggested by the surprising size of the cut in wage and salary outlays in aviation that followed airline deregulation.

product line. Engineers will become relatively less numerous in the ranks of top management, and lawyers will assume a correspondingly larger share.[4]

In sum, the social costs of rent-seeking protectionism can be very high (though we have no estimate of their magnitude). Indeed, if it is true that productivity growth in the United States is suffering from a serious longer-term malaise, it is not implausible that the incentives for firms to undertake the sort of rent seeking we are discussing has played a role that is not negligible.

We repeat that the antitrust and regulatory institutions have shown themselves to be sources of substantial incentives and opportunities for such rent-seeking activity. Whenever a competitor becomes too successful or too efficient, whenever his competition threatens to become sufficiently effective to disturb the quiet and easy life his rival is leading, the latter will be tempted to sue on the grounds that the competition is "unfair." Every successful enterprise comes to expect almost as a routine phenomenon that it will sooner or later find itself the defendant in a multiplicity of cases. It is an enchanted topsy-turvy world in which vigorous competition is made to seem anticompetitive and in which "fair competition" comes to mean no competition at all.

The runners-up, the firms that despair of succeeding through superior efficiency or more attractive products, use different instruments in seeking protection from rivals. The antitrust laws are not always useful as means to handicap competition from abroad, but they are apparently a prime instrument for the creation of impediments to effective competition by American rivals. The reason the antitrust laws can be used in this way is clear. The borderline between measures that are legitimate competitive moves and those that are destructive instruments of monopolization is often difficult to define even in principle (witness, for example, the intricacies of the concept of predatory innovation). Moreover, whatever the criteria adopted, in practice they rarely lend themselves to clear-cut evidence and unambiguous conclusions.

---

[4]A simple model making use of the Slutsky theorem readily confirms that if the antitrust laws increase the expected returns to litigation, they will also increase the firm's outlays on lawyers and other inputs that contribute to the probability of success in such litigation. A very elementary model for the purpose maximizes the profit function.

$$\Pi^*(Z,x) = \Pi(Z) + vr - x \tag{1}$$

subject to

$$r = f(x), f'(x) > 0, \tag{2}$$

where Z = the vector of the firm's inputs and outputs, x = its litigation-related expenditure, r = its probability of victory in litigation, v = its expected increase in profit as a result of victory, $f(x)$ = probability of litigative success as a function of the firm's expenditure on litigation, and $\Pi(Z)$ = the firm's profit from its normal production activities in the absence of litigation.

We may regard r, the probability of success, as an additional output of the firm and v as the per unit return to an increase in the value of r. Then, if the sufficient conditions for the Slutsky theorem are satisfied, we know that we must have $\delta r/\delta v > 0$. That is, if the availability of the antitrust rules increases the payoff to litigative rent-seeking activity, the profit-maximizing firm will act to increase the probability of success in this arena. But by (2), in order to do so it must increase x, so that we have our result, $\delta x/\delta v > 0$.

The runner–up firm then finds itself with the opportunity to claim that almost any successful program by a rival is "anticompetitive" and and that it constitutes monopolization. Antitrust, whose objective is the preservation of competition, by its very nature lends itself to use as a means to undermine effective competition. This is not merely ironic. It is very dangerous for the workings of our economy.

II. Antitrust Provisions That Encourage Protectionism

We cannot hope to provide an exhaustive list of the antitrust institutions that lend themselves to the purposes of the protectionist. We simply offer several illustrations. We discuss the treble–damages provisions, vagueness of criteria of predation and other types of unfairness of competition, and excessive severity of tests of anticompetitiveness.

Treble Damages[5]

The availability of trebled damages payments to the plaintiff has several arguments in its favor. First, there is evidence that in antitrust suits private plaintiffs have a relatively low probability of winning their cases.[6] If private antitrust suits are considered desirable in at least some cases, the plaintiffs must be offered an expected return at least equal to the heavy litigation costs they are likely to incur. While treble damages do not generally increase the probability of victory (and may well decrease it by forcing the defendant to expend larger resources to protect his interests), they almost certainly increase the expected award to a plaintiff. Second, in some cases (such as successful price fixing), in addition to the culprit's ill–gotten gains, his victims suffer a deadweight loss in the form of distorted relative purchase quantities which the courts do not recognize in their damage calculations. A multiplied damage payment then serves as very rough compensation for such deadweight losses, though any resemblance between the two magnitudes is certain to be purely coincidental. Third, no doubt some violators of the antitrust laws escape unscathed and sometimes are not even brought to trial, let alone convicted and punished. Optimal deterrence requires such firms to face ex ante a probable punishment that does fit the crime. This means that the higher the probability that any particular violator of the law will get away with it, the higher must be the fine exacted from those who are brought to justice.

All of these arguments are legitimate so far as they go, but they neglect the other side of the matter. From the point of view of society, escalated damages awards also increase the probable payoff to protectionist activity. The runner–up who hopes to impose legal obstacles on the vigorous competitive efforts of his all–too–successful rival is offered the prospect of also acquiring a

[5]See Kenneth G. Elizinga and William Breit, Private Antitrust Enforcement: The New Learning, in this issue, and Frank H. Easterbrook, Detrebling Antitrust Damages, in this issue, for an extensive discussion of the social costs and benefits of the trebling of damages.

[6]See Richard A. Posner, A Statistical Study of Antitrust Enforcement, 13 J. Law & Econ. 365 (1970); National Economic Research Associates, Statistical Analysis of Private Antitrust Enforcement, Final Report (1979).

substantial amount of funding in the process. It has even been charged that runners–up have been known to start such suits in the hope of acquiring the funding that the capital market denied them.

Trebled damages also increase the amounts it pays both defendant and plaintiff to expend in combating the case, for such damages increase the pool of rents to be disputed. And, as usual, the waste of economic resources elicited can be expected to be proportional to the size of the available rents. It is noteworthy that, as in the case of rivalrous advertising, such enhanced outlays on a legal battle will tend to cancel one another, at least in part. They will benefit neither the plaintiff nor the defendant, while raising the cost to society.

All in all, the case against trebled damages is far from clear–cut. Yet the fact that they provide a direct incentive for protectionist activity suggests that the issue requires reconsideration. We will return to this subject later, when we discuss policy appropriate for the phenomenon of protectionist misuse of antitrust institutions.

Vagueness of Antitrust Criteria

Knowledgeable students of antitrust issues often are impressed with the difficulty of determining and defining in a manner that is universally applicable the borderline between acceptable and unacceptable behavior. Scherer's attack on the famous Areeda–Turner article is a classic illustration, carefully cataloguing a variety of circumstances under which almost any reasonable but explicitly defined standard of predatory pricing can be expected to condone activities that are anticompetitive or to condemn activities that are innocent or even benign.[7] No categorical rule can fully encompass intentions, antecedent and subsequent circumstances and developments, interdependence with actions other than those under immediate consideration, and the host of other pertinent considerations. Such a point of view would seem to lead toward heavy reliance on the good judgment of the courts, toward a universal reign of some form of rule of reason. It leaves matters subject to vague and general guidelines derived from the obscure admonitions of the pertinent law and the available precedents, and beyond that it gives the courts the duty of deciding matters case by case, on the basis of individual judgment and in light of attendent circumstances.

Here is not the place to examine all the likely consequences of such a procedure or to consider the implications of wide range in capability and economic sophistication that one encounters among judges. Rather, our concern here is that obscurity and ambiguity are convenient tools for those enterprises on the prowl for opportunities to hobble competition. As we know, it is not always necessary to win cases in order to blunt a rival's competitive weapons. Harassment by lawsuit or even the threat of harassment can be a marvelous stimulus to timidity on the part of competitors. The potential

---

[7]F.M. Scherer, Comment on Areeda and Turner, 89 Harv. L. Rev. 869 (1976). Phillip Areeda and Donald F. Turner, Predatory Pricing and Related Practices under Section 2 of the Sherman Act, 88 Harv. L. Rev. 697 (1975).

defendant who cannot judge in advance with any reasonable degree of certainty whether its behavior will afterward be deemed illegal is particularly vulnerable to guerrilla warfare and intimidation into the sort of gentlemanly competitive behavior that is the antithesis of true competition.

Thus, to continue with our example, whatever one may think of the Areeda–Turner test (and we do consider it to constitute a major infusion of logic into the arena), it seems to us certainly to have made a critical and beneficial contribution simply by reducing vagueness in the criterion of predation in pricing. This makes protectionist misuse of the antitrust laws much less easy.

Severity of the Tests of Anticompetitiveness

A third phenomenon that facilitates protectionist efforts is reliance on rules increasing the range of private activities subject to condemnation as "anticompetitive." Here, too, the Areeda–Turner contribution provides an excellent illustration. The long debate between advocates of fully distributed cost tests of anticompetitiveness in pricing and advocates of incremental or marginal costs for this purpose has a straightforward interpretation in terms of our discussion. Though we are not disinterested observers of this debate, we are reasonably confident that it is not bias alone that leads us to interpret advocacy of the fully distributed cost approach as a systematic protectionist onslaught. We believe the evidence strongly supports the thesis that it is a standard put forward almost exclusively by firms that were unlikely to compete successfully on the merits of their performance alone. They advocate their costing approach as a device to limit the price–cutting opportunities of rivals rendered more efficient by economies of scale or scope, by superior management, or by other legitimate sources of superiority. This is surely attested to by the frequency of cases in which full distribution has been used to argue that some prices are unacceptably low, when the pricing behavior that should most be feared by guardians of the public interest in the presence of market power is overcharging, not underpricing.

Thus, rules that make vigorous competition dangerous clearly foster protectionism. That point is obvious enough. What is perhaps only a bit less obvious is that protectionists are not prone to wait passively for such overrestrictive rules to fall into their laps. Rather, a central element in their strategy is persistent expenditure of money and effort to change the rules in ways that favor their cause, and resistance to any attempt to reduce impediments to effective competition. When an agency such as the FTC proposes to hold hearings on the advisability of revision of one of its rules that may be suspected of discouraging competition, those who stand to bear the brunt of any enhanced competitive pressures can be expected to resist energetically.

In sum, it seems plausible that rules defining unacceptable competitive practices that lean toward potential plaintiffs are a major source of encouragement to protectionist efforts. The presence of such rules is not happenstance. They are often attributable to the deliberate efforts of those who stand to gain by using the antitrust mechanism to emasculate competition.

The preceding paragraphs are intended to suggest that the search for protection from competition by runner-up firms, and the use of antitrust institutions for the purpose, is encouraged by a number of attributes of those institutions themselves. We do not mean to apportion blame or even to claim that any one group can be said to be at fault. Our purpose is to look for strategic points that lend themselves to modification and that are therefore appropriate foci for ameliorative policy—a subject to which we will return presently.

It must, however, be pointed out that even if antitrust rules were modified to make them less susceptible to rent–seeking activities described here, such activities might not disappear or even decline materially. More likely, firms might merely divert their rent–seeking resources to other political and legal arenas.

III. Case Examples of Strategic Uses of Antitrust

The purpose of this section is to illustrate by means of a few actual cases the protectionist uses of antitrust and associated forms of government intervention such as regulation. Our examples involve mergers and joint ventures, as well as monopolization cases.

A. The GM–Toyota Joint Venture

The GM–Toyota joint venture illustrates clearly the strategic role of antitrust litigation. Here, it is Chrysler and Ford, the horizontal competitors of the joint venturers, that have pressed the Federal Trade Commission to reject the joint venture on the ground that it will restrain competition in the automobile market in general and in the subcompact segment of the market in particular. Recently the FTC approved the joint venture. Undeterred, Chrysler has been pressing a private antitrust action in an attempt to accomplish what it failed to do at the FTC.

This sort of opposition is predictable, and in a manner that is rather ironic it can signal clearly the likely effects of the joint venture. If the enterprise were in fact likely to acquire monopoly power and charge excessive prices, other U.S. auto firms undoubtedly would benefit from the resulting protective umbrella, which would enable them to raise their prices as well. If this is the probable outcome, then those rivals can be expected to view the joint venture with equanimity and silent acquiescence. But if the joint venture really is likely to introduce economies or improve product quality, it is sure to make life harder for the domestic rivals of the participants who will then have to run correspondingly faster in order to stand still.[8] Paradoxically, then and only then, when the joint venture is really beneficial, can those rivals be relied on to

---

[8]Admittedly, it is possible that the joint venture will make GM a more formidable competitor not because of any gains in economic efficiency but merely because it will make it easier for GM to satisfy the asinine Company Average Fuel Efficiency (CAFE) regulations.

denounce the undertaking as "anticompetitive."[9] That is exactly the response of Chrysler and Ford, who have presented themselves here as defenders of consumers' interests even though before other forums they have not hesitated to argue for blatantly protectionist measures such as higher trade barriers. Once again, consistency has given way to expediency.

B. MCI v. AT & T: The Economics of Price Inflexibility[10]

MCI was perhaps the first firm to challenge AT&T's monopoly in the long–distance telecommunications market. Beginning in 1963, MCI embarked on an extensive investment program in microwave transmission facilities. Because of its (and the FCC's) policy of "universal service" or "nationwide averaging," AT&T's relative rates along different routes did not correspond closely to relative costs, with service along sparsely used routes comparatively underpriced. This was a clear invitation for "cream skimming" entry. Under-standably, MCI at least initially attempted to specialize in serving the high-density routes in which AT&T earned more substantial profit margins.

MCI's moves to enter these routes predictably led to an attempt by AT&T to adjust it relative rates to correspond more closely to costs. MCI alleged that these responses were anticompetitive. Litigation ensued.[11] Of course, MCI's initial entry primarily into AT&T's more profitable routes is unobjectionable. The benefits of competition depend on the willingness of entrants to seek out profitable opportunities. What is far more questionable is MCI's attempt to use antitrust litigation as a means to restrain AT&T's ability to respond to competitive incursions. It was charged that by adjusting its prices on different routes to correspond more closely to costs, even on routes where competition had not yet appeared, AT&T was launching "preemptive strikes." One can imagine what would have been said if instead AT&T had reduced prices *only* on the routes where MCI had opened for business.

MCI insisted during the trial and in its appellate brief that a "full–cost" approach should be used to calculate AT&T's costs and to perform the tests of predatoriness.[12] Indeed, according to MCI, citing Dr. William Melody's testi-mony, many "economists advocate the use of fully distributed costs as the

---

[9]Steven Salop suggested to one of us that a merger of joint venture may be a part of a strategy employed by the merging partners, or co–venturers, to elevate the rivals' costs and thereby harm competition. We doubt that "predatory" mergers or joint ventures are a frequent occurrence. In such a rare instance, the rival would have to assume the standard of proof of a potential anticom-petitive effect that is appropriate for monopolization cases, rather than that which is appropriate for a merger case.

[10]We are not disinterested disussant of this case. Both of us have carried out work for AT&T. One of us not only served as a witness for AT&T in the MCI case but also recommended the type of price response to MCI's entry that AT&T later adopted.

[11]MCI Communications Corp. v. AT&T, 369 F. Supp. 1004 (E. D. Pa. 1973) vacated and remanded, 496 F.2d 214 (3d Cir. 1974); MCI Communications Corp. v. AT&T, 462 F. Supp. 1072 (N. D. Ill. 1978), rev'd, 708 F.2d 1081 (7th Cir. 1983).

[12]Brief of Appellees, MCI Communications Corp. and MCI Telecommunications Corp. (March 5, 1981), at 112.

proper test for below-cost predatory pricing in the telecommunications industry."[13]

There is no need to dwell here on the inefficiencies that result from the use of fully allocated costs as constraints on the price responses of regulated and unregulated firms. It suffices to note that insistence that such costs are the appropriate price floors invites socially inefficient entry that is elicited not by genuine cost advantages and productive efficiencies but by false profitability signals. There is no doubt that potential and actual entrants (such as MCI) have a strong incentive to rigidify the price responses open to an incumbent who is confronted with newly emerging competition. It seems clear that the staunchest advocates of full-cost pricing have been firms anxious to hobble their disquietingly effective rivals.

C. Strategic Uses of Antitrust in Takeover Cases

The targets of tender offers frequently initiate antitrust suits against their unwanted suitors. The critical issues are whether the targets should be allowed to institute injunction proceedings or whether instead the enforcement of merger statutes should be left to the government and to customers who are likely to be injured if the merger brings competition to an end, elevates prices, and causes resource misallocation. The issue is not straightforward. While the incentive for management to bring an antitrust case need not coincide with the interests of the consumers,[14] it is nevertheless true that the management of the target is probably better informed than any other group about the likely consequences of the acquisition for future competition.

There is no question that a target's management, bent on derailing the tender offer, has a potent weapon in the antitrust laws. The two most recent instances in which highly lucrative offers were defeated with the aid of the antitrust laws were *Grumman Corp. v. LTV Corp.*[15] and *Marathon Oil Co. v. Mobil Corp.*[16] The latter case illustrates the problem clearly. Marathon's management possessed extensive, firsthand information about the scope of its geographic operations and about the marketing of gasoline to independents, which was at issue in the antitrust proceedings. On the other hand, Marathon's management hardly shared the interests of the automobile owners in cheap and plentiful gasoline.[17] Indeed, if the target's management were truly guided by shareholders' interests, it ought to sell the company to the bidder likely to

---

[13]*Id.* at 113–14. The court of appeals disagreed and decided against MCI on most points.

[14]This point is made in Frank H. Easterbrook & Daniel R. Fischel, Antitrust Suits by Targets of Tender Offers, 80 Michigan L. Rev. 1155 (1982).

[15]665 F.2d 10 (2d Cir. 1981).

[16]669 F.2d 378 (6th Cir. 1982).

[17]In fact, if the management had wanted to trigger an auction for Marathon by impeding Mobil's actions, it might have been implying that it was expecting another oil company as the next suitor.

obtain the highest profit from the transaction.[18] But when such enhanced profits result from the elevation of market power in the postmerger market, the interests of the consumers and of the target's stockholders clash directly.

IV. Alternative Enforcement Procedures: Japan and the EEC

In this section we briefly compare antitrust procedures in the United States with those of our major trading partners: Japan and the EEC. We do not claim any expertise on the antitrust laws of other countries. However, expertise is not required in light of our limited objective—to explore how other countries have held in check the use of antitrust litigation as a strategic weapon in the hands of competitors. (Of course, none of the discussion is meant to imply that the antitrust policies in other countries constitute ideal models for the United States that should recommend themselves to American scholars and policymakers.)

A. Japan[19]

Japan has dealt with the problem of strategic use or abuse of the antitrust laws by largely consolidating enforcement in its Fair Trade Commission (JFTC). In Japan a person injured by acts in violation of the antimonopoly laws has a right to sue for damages under Section 709 of the Civil Code. And any person injured by conduct found illegal by the JFTC has a right, under Section 25 of the Antimonopoly Act, to recover damages.[20] Yet as of 1983 only five damage suits had been filed under Section 25. The reasons for the reluctance of private Japanese plaintiffs to seek damages in court are not easy to determine. We think that the national distaste for litigation cannot explain it fully. In particular, the fact that damages are not readily awarded in Japan and that plaintiffs can sue under Section 25 only if the JFTC has found the conduct complained of to be illegal surely discourages private actions for damages.[21]

---

[18]That is, if the target's managers can somehow share in these incremental profits.

[19]Information in this section is culled from notes by Matsushita; see M. Matsushita, Informal Notes for the conference on Japan's Antimonopoly Legislation and Doing Business with Japan, Japan Society (January 5, 1978).

[20]Hiroshi Iyori & Akinori Uesugi, The Antimonopoly Laws of Japan 127 (2d ed. 1983). We are grateful to Edward Glynn of the FTC for correcting our earlier discussion of private enforcement in Japan.

[21]Economists are usually loath to seek explanations in alleged differences in "national character" to explain the Japanese record. Arguments based on national character are difficult to test and are, in any event, treacherous, as the following illustrative story suggests: "An Australian expert, invited by the Japanese government, had this to say in his Report, as excerpted in the *Japan Times* of August 18th 1915: 'Japan commercially, I regret to say, does not bear the best reputation for executing business. Inferior goods, irregularly and indifferent shipments have caused no end of worry... My impression as to your cheap labour was soon disillusioned when I saw your people at work. No doubt they are lowly paid, but the return is equally so; to see your men at work made me feel that you are a very satisfied easy–going race who reckon time is no object. When I spoke to some managers they informed me that it was impossible to change the habits of national heritage... First class managers...are required to wake things up and get out of the go–as–you–please style that seems universal at present.'" Cited in J.N. Bhagwati, Development Economics: What Have We Learnt (mimeographed, Columbia Univ. 1984), at 27.

Japan's FTC is basically an administrative agency with some quasi–judicial powers. Its judicial powers are exercised only rarely. According to the Japanese antitrust expert M. Matsushita of Sophia University, only four antitrust criminal cases have occurred in the past thirty years of antitrust enforcement. The main channel through which the JFTC shapes competition is informal. The JFTC may issue "warnings" that are usually respected. In addition, the JFTC provides "guidance" that helps the companies to avoid conflict with the antitrust laws, especially in international contracts.

When the JFTC brings a formal action, it usually ends with the company (or companies) accepting the JFTC's recommendation decision. Available estimates indicate that some 90 percent of these recommendations are accepted. Those that are not accepted usually are resolved during trial through consent decisions that embody the proposals of the respondent.

Private complaints are filed with the JFTC. The JFTC must then investigate but need not take an enforcement action. However, according to the Japanese experts, frequently investigation alone suffices to induce the investigated firm (or firms) to stop the activity that has been challenged. Thus, here there does remain some scope for strategic use of the JFTC investigatory powers.

Yet the incentives for the allegedly harmed petitioners to use this process are limited. They receive no financial recompense for any harm they have suffered. Their only benefit derives from the JFTC's ability to require cessation of the allegedly anticompetitive activity. The incentive to use the JFTC for protection from competition is thereby weakened, especially if the cost of filing the complaint is high.

It is noteworthy that in a few cases complaining parties have attempted to sue the JFTC for the failure to act on their complaints. However, appellate authorities have ruled that only respondents can appeal a JFTC decision and have thereby severely restricted the complainants' standing to sue.

In sum, in Japan antitrust enforcement is placed almost exclusively in the hands of its JFTC, which relies heavily on informal mechanisms such as warnings and reviews. The strategic use of the antitrust mechanism is circumscribed because the parties who claim they were harmed must first convince the JFTC to act and cannot appeal from the JFTC decisions.

One may well feel that this arrangement goes too far and that its protection of anticompetitive activities is excessive. However, it does certainly help to check the litigiousness of business firms and their use of antitrust as a means to restrain effective competition.

B. The EEC Member States

It would add unduly to the length of this paper, and strain the information at our disposal, to analyze the vulnerability to strategic abuse of the national laws on competition where they exist in the EEC countries. It is safe to say, however, that the incentives for abuse probably are significantly weaker in the

EEC member states than they are in the United States, at least for the following reasons. First, in the EEC member states the plaintiff who wins a case is not entitled to treble damages. Second, in the EEC member states contingent free arrangements with lawyers do not exist in antitrust cases. Third, discovery procedures are less developed in Europe than they are in the United States, which may make it more difficult for a plaintiff to obtain the "incriminating" evidence with which to fuel rent–seeking anticompetitive activities.[22] Fourth, in the EEC member states the right to trial by jury in money damages cases is not available. Fifth, in Britain especially an unsuccessful plaintiff must bear the defendant's costs.[23] And, finally, in Europe some aspects of the competition law, for example merger statutes, fall only within the purview of governmental bodies. This greatly reduces the opportunity for strategic use of these laws.

Having said all this, we must emphasize one important continuing development in the EEC member states that bears directly on the issues raised in this paper. It has by now become fairly well established through judicial authority that "actions for injunctions and for compensation may be brought in national courts by plaintiffs claiming to suffer loss as a result of infringements of Articles 85–86 and 90 EEC Treaty.... This confirms that Articles 85–86 are laws for the protection of individual interests and *not* merely laws for the protection of the public interest or the community."[24] Thus, for example, rivals now can avail themselves of EEC statutes on competition if they can claim to have been affected in their intracommunity business activities by allegedly anticompetitive actions of dominant firm.

This extension of the enforcement of the EEC competition statutes in general, and of Article 86 in particular, opens an opportunity for strategic use of the statutes. The leading United Kingdom case that has established that plaintiffs can, in fact, sue shows that the EEC competition statutes can be used to retard rather than promote allocative efficiency.[25] In that case, the plaintiff was purchasing most of its "bulk butter" from the Milk Marketing Board (which apparently had a dominant position in the relevant market) for resale to a single purchaser in the Netherlands. At some point the defendant changed its marketing strategy and decided to sell its bulk butter to four distributors in England and Wales. The plaintiff was instructed to purchase its butter requirements from the designated distributors. Allegedly, this would

---

[22]However, as Edward Glynn has noted, extensive "discovery" available under American law can at times also be used to "bludgeon" a financially weak plaintiff into dropping his case.

[23]We note, however, that the effects of fee shifting on litigation incentives are not as clear as one might expect. See Steven Shavell, Suit, Settlement and Trial: A Theoretical Analysis under Alternative Methods for the Allocation of Legal costs, 11 J. Legal Stud. 55 (1982); and Janusz A. Ordover & Ariel Rubinstein, A Sequential Concession Game with Asymmetric Information (mimeographed, C.V. Starr Center for Applied Economics, New York Univ., July 1984).

[24]John Temple Lang, Enforcement in National Courts of Community Competition Rules on Enterprises, Notes for Lecture, Brussels (March 1983).

[25]Garden Cottage Foods, Ltd. v. Milk Marketing Board (1983) 2 ALL ER 770.

have rendered its resale activities unprofitable. The plaintiff sued and asked for injunctive relief. The relief was not granted. Nevertheless, the case set a precedent for future suits.

The preceding sequence will be familiar to the American students of antitrust. Vertical relations between a manufacturer and his dealers have been a subject of frequent litigation, often of doubtful merit. It appears that now, by involving Article 86, dealers in the EEC may have acquired an important weapon with which to attack the distribution arrangements of their suppliers.[26] This has occurred at a time when, in the United States, various commentators have suggested that per se legality be granted to such arrangements. Time will tell whether competitors in the EEC will use the statute against one another.

V. What is to be Done?

There are no easy and costless remedies for the abuse of antitrust by those who use it for protection from competition. The difficulty is inherent in the problem, for anything that is done to make it harder for plaintiffs to use our antitrust institutions anticompetitively automatically also makes it easier for others to get away with acts of monopolization. This trade-off is apparently unavoidable, because anything that makes conviction of the defendant more likely necessarily makes suits more attractive to plaintiffs in pursuit of protection from effective competition. The Japanese, as we have seen, have largely solved the problem of protectionism, but only by virtual prohibition of initiatives by the victims of monopolistic behavior. In dealing with the shortcomings of our antitrust institutions that are the subject of this paper, we must be careful not to undermine the antitrust laws themselves.

The most obvious remedial change is a restriction of the sort of circumstances to which treble damages apply. One should consider both the use of a multiple smaller than three, at least in those types of cases, such as predatory pricing, in which rent-seeking protectionist activity seems to abound, and in some types of cases one might even consider restriction of the amount of the award to the magnitude of the damage actually shown to have been sustained.

Such proposals are not new, but we do have a new wrinkle to suggest. The choice of multiplicand in damages payments faces at least two conflicting goals. Given the possibly low probability of discovery of an antitrust violation and of conviction on the charge, optimal deterrence clearly calls for a multiplicand greater than unity, and on that score trebling of damages may perhaps not be too bad an approximation to the optimum. On the other hand, if this

---

[26]In the United Kingdom, such practices are also examined in the Restrictive Practices Court in which there is "a great deal of wasted time particularly with economists swearing against each other—canceling each other out!" As was observed extrajudicially by Advocate-General Warner of the Court of Justice of the European Communities, in Enterprise Law of the 80's 235 (F.M. Rowe, F.G. Jacobs, & M.R. Joelson eds. 1980).

encourages rent seeking we may want, on this score, a much smaller damages award.

Environmental economics has shown how an analogous problem can be dealt with. There, deterrence policy can use the polluter pays principle as an effective instrument. But if that payment is used to compensate the polluter's victims on the basis of the amount of damage they suffer, a moral hazard problem arises—for it undermines the incentive for potential victims to seek pollution-avoiding locations or to take other measures to protect themselves from damages. Indeed, it can be proved that *any* such compensation to utility–maximizing victims will reduce their pollution–deterrent resource outlays below the socially optimal level. The solution implicitly advocated by economists for pollution policy is simple. The polluter should indeed pay, but the payments should be collected by government, at least in part, and should not go to the victims. In that way the payment scheme is provided with two parameter values—the price the polluter is charged, and the amount that victims are compensated. These parameter values can then be chosen so as to elicit both the optimal reduction of polluter emissions and the optimal selfdefensive effort by the victim.

In private antitrust suits a similar solution is at least worth considering. That is, the defendant who is found guilty might continue to pay three times (or some other multiple of) the estimated damages. But the plaintiff can be made eligible to a smaller multiple (and perhaps even a multiple less than unity) of that damages figure. The difference would then go into the public treasury as a tax on violators of the antitrust laws. Once again, this provides two distinct parameters (the defendant's multiple and the plaintiff's multiple) to the designers of public policy who can select their values separately so as to provide the proper incentive for deterrence of violations while at the same time offering an appropriate disincentive for rent–seeking protectionism.

One may want to take a further step in this direction. Mere accusation and trial subjects the defendant firm to enormous expenses and even greater ex ante risks of an expensive adverse decision, even if it transpires ex post on the basis of convincing evidence that it is completely innocent. The possibility of required compensation to the defendant for these damages caused by the plaintiff might well discourage frivolous and mischievous suits, including those undertaken in the hope that an out–of–court settlement will prevent the latter from having to reveal the weakness of his case. Thus, the third remedy we propose for consideration is liability of the plaintiff for costs incurred by the defendant in the event of acquittal.

A fourth line of defense against protectionism is the adoption of clearer criteria of unacceptable behavior, such as the predation tests proposed by

Areeda and Turner or those we have suggested.[27] For reasons already discussed, vagueness in the standards of unacceptable behavior plays into the hands of those who would use the antitrust laws as anticompetitive weapons.

Fifth, one may well consider it desirable, for similar reasons, to inhibit, if not necessarily prohibit, the ability of the management of a company that is a takeover target to bring an antitrust suit against the unwanted acquirer.[28]

Here is should be emphasized that we do not want to immunize mergers or acquisitions from the antitrust laws. Rather, we suggest the possibility that (only) those most likely to misuse the process for protectionist purposes be limited in their ability to bring private suits against the transaction on antitrust grounds. Others, including the pertinent government agencies, should clearly remain free to do so.

All of these suggestions are offered very tentatively and with great hesitation. They are mostly untried, and our lack of competence in the law surely raises questions about their workability, their consistency with other legal rules, and perhaps even (in some cases) their constitutionality.

We end by repeating an earlier caveat. It is not by accident that every one of our very tentative proposals incurs some social cost in that it reduces to some degree the available deterrents to monopolistic behavior. This is unavoidable, because any measure that offers some promise of dealing effectively with the problem discussed in this paper must necessarily involve some reduction in the incentive to bring litigation and hence must weaken to a degree the position of the potential plaintiff. It seems clear to us that *some* move in this direction is urgent if antitrust and regulation are to be prevented from becoming major impediments to competitiveness, efficiency, and productivity growth in the U.S. economy. The question is not whether some such moves are justified. The issue, rather, is how substantial those moves should be—how great a modification constitutes a social optimum in the tradeoff between the two competing perils to true competition—excessive weakening of the deterrents to monopolization and excessive facilitation of attempts to subvert effective competition through protectionist misuse of our antitrust institutions.

---

[27]William J. Baumol, Quasi Permanence of Price Reduction, 89 Yale L.J. 1 (1979); Janusz A. Ordover & Robert D. Willig, An Economic Definition of Predation: Pricing and Product Innovation, 91 Yale L.J. 8 (1981).

[28]In a recent case, the U.S. District Court for the Central District of California ruled that the target of a tender offer lacks standing to seek a preliminary injunction to halt the acquisition as a violation of the Clayton Act. Carter Hawley Hale Stores. Inc. v. The Limited, Inc., 587 F. Supp. 246 (C.D. Cal. 1984).

PUBLIC CHOICE AND ANTITRUST

Robert D. Tollison

I. Introduction

The field of antitrust and industrial economics is one of the last bastions of the economics profession to be untouched by the public choice revolution. Economic analysis in this area proceeds in roughly the following way. First, the efficiency of market arrangements and organizations is analyzed. Second, those markets found wanting on the efficiency scorecard are assigned to government, through an antitrust case, to correct. The first step in this process is unobjectionable and represents one of the richest applied parts of modern economics. The second part is weak because it rests on a public interest theory of government. A market failure (monopoly) is found in the private sector, and government (an unexamined alternative) is invoked to correct it. Judges and antitrust bureaucrats are assumed to operate in the public interest, which in this case means the promotion of economic efficiency in the economy.

This is not a very useful way to approach antitrust (or any other) economic analysis. As a positive theory, it is wrong. As many critics have shown, the historical record of antitrust decisions will not support the public interest theory. If we are to understand the course of antitrust better, the behavior of the relevant actors must be made endogenous to our explanation of antitrust outcomes. As a normative basis for criticizing antitrust, the public interest approach is not very helpful. When all is said and done and government is not following one's conception of the public interest in antitrust, we are reduced to such tried and true nonsense as "better people make better government." Change the decision makers and the policy will change. This sounds good but it never seems to work. Government cranks along by an internal logic of its own, which in this case we do not know because we have not tried to find out what it is. If we want to have a powerful critique of antitrust, the first thing that must be done is to achieve a positive understanding of how antitrust decision makers behave. Launched from such a platform, antitrust criticism and reform can be more effective.

My interest in this paper is to review the state of the (small) art with respect to developing a positive public choice theory of antitrust and to illustrate the potential of this approach. In Section II, I offer the reader a brief introduction to public choice. In Section III, I briefly outline the prevailing public interest approach to antitrust commentary. In Section IV, I survey some of the useful steps that have evolved in the literature away from the public-interest perspective. In Section V, I present some of the literature directly on the positive economics of antitrust and detail a couple of examples of the approach. Finally, in Section VI, I offer some concluding remarks.

Reprinted by permission of the *Cato Journal*, (Winter 1985), pp. 905–916, published by the Cato Institute.

One caveat is in order at the outset. I have not tried to be copious in my search of the literature. As a result, I have undoubtedly missed work that bears on the issues of this paper. My apologies are offered in advance for any glaring omissions.

II. Public Choice

"Public choice" refers to a revolution in the way government is analyzed. Before public choice, government was treated as exogenous to the economy, a benign corrector of the market economy when it faltered. After public choice, the role of government in the economy became something to be explained, not assumed. As a result of the public choice revolution, economists now place government failure alongside market failure as a useful category of analysis.[1]

What is public choice? I advance my own particular answer to the question. Public choice is an expansion of the explanatory domain of economic theory. Traditional economic analysis uses the apparatus of economic theory to explain the behavior of individuals in private settings. Public choice represents the use of standard economic tools (demand and supply) to explain behavior in nonmarket environments, such as government.

This expansion of economic theory is based on a simple idea. Individuals are the same people whether they are behaving in a market or nonmarket context. The person who votes also buys groceries; the workers in government bureaucracies do not have radically different temperaments from workers in corporations; and so on. There is no Dr. Jekyll and Mr. Hyde dichotomy in economic behavior whereby we behave one way in the private sector and another way in the public sector. As a practical working hypothesis, individuals seek to promote their self–interest in any given situation. Public choice represents the application of this axiom to behavior in nonmarket settings. This approach has been employed by public choice analysts to explain the behavior of voters, bureaucrats, politicians, interest groups, and other political actors and organizations.

Obviously, this is not an argument that rational behavior in private and public settings leads to the same types of outcomes. The result of self–interest in government manifests itself in a different way than elsewhere because the constraints on individual behavior are different. The managers of a private corporation and a government bureau behave differently, not because they are different people but because the rules that govern their behavior are different. This is a simple but important point.

Finally, note that public choice closes the behavioral system of economic analysis (Buchanan 1972). It incorporates the behavior of government actors into economic theory, and it pushes us beyond the Pigovian fantasy that the market is guided by private interest and the government is guided by public

---

[1]See Mueller (1979) and Buchanan and Tollison (1984) for useful surveys of public choice research.

interest. It is this step that is sorely needed in the field of antitrust and industrial organization.

III. The Antitruster's View of Government

There is a nearly unanimous tendency in antitrust commentary toward a public interest theory of government. In short, there is an implicit and unexamined view in the literature that antitrust decision makers are benign seekers of the public interest. If they knew better, they would do better. This case can be made without much effort by drawing selective references from the literature.

The primary U.S. antitrust statutes—the Sherman Antitrust Act (1890), the Clayton Antitrust Act (1914), and the Federal Trade Commission Act (1914)—are largely seen as being without economic motivation. Rather they are seen as efforts by the Congress to protect the public interest (Bork 1966, p. 7). Moreover, the role of the antitrust bureaucrats put in place by this legislation is seen as that of maintaining a competitive economy (Bain 1968, p. 515). Scherer (1980, p. 491) summarizes when he observes that antitrust is "one of the more important weapons wielded by government in its effort to harmonize the profit–seeking behavior of private enterprises with the public interest." In a similar vein Posner (1976, p. 4) suggests that the importance of economic efficiency as a social norm "establishes a prima facie case for having an antitrust policy." Neale and Govder (1980, p. 441) put the matter as well as anyone when they observe that "it is tempting (and common) to regard the antitrust policy simply as a kind of economic engineering project."

I could go on in this vein, quoting famous students of antitrust of various ideological and methodological stripes, but the point is the same. Antitrust policy, whether discussed in terms of the origin of antitrust laws, the behavior of the antitrust bureaucracies, the behavior of judges, and so on, is predominantly discussed in public interest terms. The market fouls up; government corrects.

Of course, the public interest approach may be right, although the trenchancy of the antitrust critics with respect to selected policies and decisions seems to suggest that it is not. Moreover, the solutions that the public interest approach offers do not seem to work. The public interest approach says that more information or better people will lead to better antitrust. There is obviously some truth to such an argument, but it does not seem to be very important in the actual conduct of government affairs.

An alternative way to approach the problem is by the route of positive public choice. What can be said about the *actual* or *predicted* course of antitrust policy, as opposed to the *desired* course? By learning first about how antitrust decisions are actually made and how antitrust decision makers behave, we are surely in a better position to reform antitrust institutions— if that is what we want to do.

IV. Steps in the Right Direction

The idea that I espouse, the application of positive economics to antitrust issues, is not new. Efforts in this direction have just not been systematic, and they have been scattered around in the literature for some time. This section briefly reviews some of these early steps toward positive analysis.

Empiricism

One way to find out what antitrust authorities do is to look. In this spirit there have been several statistical studies of antitrust enforcement. The primary example is a paper by Posner (1970). Other studies include those by Stigler (1966), Gallo and Bush (1983), Clabault and Block (1981), Shughart and Tollison (forthcoming), Elzinga (1969), Asch and Seneca (1976), Hay and Kelley (1974), and Palmer (1972).

What can this approach teach us? Primarily, it can yield clues about the interworkings of the enforcement agencies. Shughart and Tollison (forthcoming), for example, study the incidence of recidivism in Federal Trade Commission (FTC) enforcement activities since 1914. They find that the rate of repeat offenses is very high, constituting about one–quarter of historical agency enforcement actions. Why is this rate so high? Is it because it is bureaucratically easier to keep track of and to prosecute the same firms over time (cost–minimizing bureaucrats), or is it because offenders find it worthwhile to violate the antitrust laws repeatedly over time? While these questions cannot be resolved on purely empirical grounds, the data point to an interesting process in FTC enforcement to be explained. This is one way in which the empirical study of antitrust can be useful.

As Posner (1970, p. 419) concludes, "antitrust enforcement is inefficient and the first step toward improvement must be a greater interest in the dry subject of statistics."

Organizational Behavior

Another way to find out what antitrust authorities do is to ask them. This is essentially what Weaver (1977) and Katzman (1980) have done in providing organizational studies of the Antitrust Division of the U.S. Department of Justice and the FTC respectively. Both of these authors base their analyses on extensive interviews with agency staff. The primary value of such studies is that they point the way to a bureaucratic model of agency behavior, Katzman, for example, finds that the desire to gain trial experience biases FTC lawyers toward shorter and less complicated initiatives as opposed to the FTC economists who are for the most part long–term employees with an interest in more time–consuming structural assaults on industry. The moral is that personnel turnover patterns may provide an important clue about agency behavior.[2]

---

[2]Also see Clarkson and Muris (1981) for an organizational–type study of the FTC.

Cost–Benefit Analysis

There has been an attempt to apply cost–benefit analysis to antitrust case-bringing activity. The basic paper here is by Long, Schramm, and Tollison (1973), with follow–up studies by Asch (1975) and Siegfried (1975). The thrust of applying the cost–benefit approach to antitrust is interesting. On the benefit side, industries are ranked according to their estimated degree of deadweight costs attributable to monopoly power. The cost side is represented by the costs of legal action by the government. Cases are then targeted according to a rule of marginal benefit equal marginal cost until the enforcement budget is exhausted.

There are many pitfalls in such an idealized approach to antitrust. At the theoretical level, it is not clear, for example, how deterrent effects should be treated in the case–allocation decision. At a practical level, reliable empirical estimates of monopoly deadweight costs are hard to obtain, and legal action against firms and industries based on such evidence is probably not sustainable (antitrust as economic surgery seems out of fashion). For such reasons no one has ever pushed very hard on applying the cost–benefit calculus to antitrust problems. Long, Schramm, and Tollison (1973), however, find that the actual cases brought by the Justice Department do *not* correspond to what a welfare-loss model would imply. In other words, *ceteris paribus*, cases are not brought where welfare losses are higher. This is fairly strong evidence that the goal of antitrust enforcement is not linked closely to the economist's conception of social welfare.[3]

V. Antitrust as a Problem in Positive Economics

The literature that takes the positive public choice approach to antitrust is small in quantity and admits of no easy organizing principle. In this section, accordingly, I first offer a brief survey of this literature and then produce two applications of the approach to illustrate more clearly its potentiality.

Explaining Antitrust

The papers using the positive approach fall mainly into two broad categories. In the first category are papers that apply the so–called interest group theory of government to antitrust. In the second category are papers that seek to identify the winners and losers from particular antitrust actions.

The interest group theory of government, in its modern form, is normally credited to Stigler (1971). This theory suggests the forces by which some groups win at the expense of others in the political process. Efforts to model antitrust in this spirit include Stigler's (1984) attempt to explain the origin of the Sherman Antitrust Act, Baxter's (1980) insightful paper on the political

---

[3]In recent years the standard Harberger treatment of monopoly welfare loss has been modified by the concept of rent seeking. Briefly, rent seeking means that trapezoids and not triangles are the relevant geometrical unit of calculation for measuring welfare loss. For more details see Tollison (1982).

economy of antitrust, the work of Faith, Leavens, and Tollison (1982) and of Weingast and Moran (1983) on the influence of congressional committees on FTC activities, a paper by Amacher et al. (forthcoming) on the counter-cyclical and cartelizing nature of historical antitrust enforcement activity, and a paper by Higgins and McChesney (1983) explaining the FTC ad substantiation program in interest–group terms.

This small body of literature is distinguished by the development of a testable model of an antitrust process and a test of the model on available data. The main conclusion of this work seems to be that government works in this area much the same way as it works in others; namely, that antitrust is at least partly a veil over a wealth–transfer process fueled by certain relevant interest groups. Moreover, where the conventional wisdom points to policy failure to explain deviations in antitrust, this work suggests that the deviations are readily understandable as self–interested behavior under the relevant constraints. Thus, for example, the Robinson–Patman Act is not a mistake of antitrust policy but a rationally designed law to buffer certain firms against losses when aggregate demand falls.

The second category of positive literature looks directly at the wealth losses and gains from antitrust actions. These papers differ from those in the first category in that the unit of analysis is the firm and the concern is not with modeling the political process that guides antitrust. In a way this work can be seen as searching for important clues (who wins? who loses?) about the identity of the relevant interest groups that undergird antitrust activities. Important papers in this tradition are a study by Ellert (1976) of mergers and antimerger law enforcement, an examination by Burns (1977) of the famous oil and tobacco dissolutions in 1911, and a study by Ross (1984) of the origin of the Robinson–Patman Act suggesting that the wealth effects of the law and its enforcement transferred wealth from large chain stores to small firms and brokers. These papers are all heavily empirical, and, in particular, they employ capital market data to test hypotheses. This movement away from the reliance on accounting data is a heartening development in industrial organization research.

At base, then, the positive approach to antitrust analysis is represented by a small body of literature. Although I have undoubtedly missed some papers and other efforts, my aim is not to be comprehensive in reviewing the literature, but to show something about what has been done and, more important, what can be done.[4]

---

[4]I should also mention a particular effort to study the FTC that grew out of my experience as director of the FTC's Bureau of Economics from 1981 to 1983. A group of my FTC colleagues and I undertook systematic studies of several aspects of FTC activities that will appear in Mackay, Miller, and Yandle (forthcoming).

Dual Enforcement

Antitrust laws in the United States are enforced by the Antitrust Division of the Department of Justice and by the FTC. The critical literature on this dual enforcement system has been exclusively normative. Some observers have criticized the quality of FTC cases, and some have criticized the FTC internal procedure whereby commissioners sometimes sit as both prosecutors and judges for the same cases. Normally the brunt of dual-enforcement criticism is aimed at the FTC, with many calls being made for its abolition.

There is a prior problem, however, which is that of how well the dual-enforcement system works in practice. That is, what are the positive economics of dual enforcement? Higgins, Shughart, and Tollison (forthcoming) recently have tackled this problem. Their approach is simple. Dual enforcement can be modeled as an example of two bureaus competing with one another. Thus, Higgins, Shughart, and Tollison posit a model—the H–S–T model—of two budget-maximizing bureaus that behave according to Cournot output conjectures. The results of this analytical exercise are straightforward. Independent agency dual enforcement leads to more output (cases) per budget dollar than either single agency or collusive dual-agency enforcement. Begging the question for the moment of what is being produced, competition in government operates as it does anywhere else—it acts to increase output.

History provides a natural experiment for the H–S–T model. From 1890 to 1914 the Antitrust Division was the sole antitrust agency (single-agency enforcement). From 1914 to 1948 the FTC competed vigorously with the Antitrust Division (independent dual-agency enforcement). From 1948 to this day the two agencies have colluded under a liaison agreement with respect to who will bring what case or contest which merger (collusive dual-agency enforcement). Moreover, budget and output data are available for the two agencies for the years 1931 to the present. The model's implications about cases per budget dollar can therefore be tested.

Using the period 1932 to 1948 as the period of competition between the two agencies and the period 1948 to 1981 as the period of collusion, the H–S–T model has been used to compare mean annual case output, real budgets, and real output per budget dollar for the two agencies over the two periods. The authors have found that in the two periods, total cases remained roughly the same, but average cases per budget dollar fell substantially (by about half) in both organizations. This implies that more inputs were used per case in the period of collusion, or that, put another way, collusion led to increased rents to bureaucratic input suppliers (lawyers, economists).

Positive economics thus teaches us a familiar lesson in this application. For a given enforcement budget, independent dual enforcement will yield more cases per dollar spent. On such grounds one may mount a serious scientific case for dual enforcement without collusion; that is, for scrapping the so-called liaison agreement. There remains, however, a major question: Are these agencies producing "goods" or "bads"? If the latter (as the first part of this paper more or less argued), single or collusive dualagency enforcement would be preferred on the grounds of restricting the output of a "bad." If the former, then competition between the two bureaus is the best policy. Either way, however, a positive understanding of the implications of dual enforcement provides a basis for knowing what to recommend.

Antitrust and Jobs

Time after time, regulatory programs have failed a cost-benefit test, and the econometric assault on regulation has spawned a significant regulatory reform movement in this country and abroad. For some reason, though, antitrust activities have largely escaped this type of careful, applied analysis.

In a recent paper Shughart and Tollison (1984) seek to take a first step toward remedying this situation. They propose to look at the impact of antitrust on the economy, and as a start, they look at the impact of antitrust on the level of unemployment. The purpose of this work is to try to achieve a preliminary understanding of how antitrust is related to basic economic welfare. Jobs seemed a good place to start in this regard.

The methodology used by Shughart and Tollison is quite simple. They searched the literature for a standard model of the unemployment rate in the United States and then augmented this model with a measure of antitrust activity—cases per real budget dollar brought per year by the Antitrust Division under the Sherman and Clayton Acts (a complete set of data is available for the 1947–81 period). Estimating this relationship by using ordinary least squares analysis reveals that over this period a 1 percent increase in Justice Department cases leads to a 0.17 percent increase in the economy's unemployment rate, *ceteris paribus*. Moreover, accounting for the fact that the aggregate economy and antitrust are jointly determined leaves this basic result intact.

The results yield to a natural interpretation. What Shughart and Tollison have found is an antitrust Phillips curve. When the model is run on definitions of expected (predicted) and unexpected (unpredicted) antitrust cases, it has been found that unexpected antitrust drives the result. This is analogous to unexpected money in the traditional Phillips relation. Furthermore, the numerical results are consistent in this specification of the problem. Using conservative estimates, the Shughart-Tollison study suggests that over the 1947–81 period, a 1 percent increase in annual enforcement activity added about 7,000 individuals to the mean stock of unemployed persons in the economy.

Now to the important question: How can this be? If antitrust causes unemployment in one sector, will not these workers and resources find employment in an untargeted sector? The answer is yes where antitrust activities are predicted. If antitrust actions are accurately forecast, the indicated resource adjustments will take place. It is the unexpected component of antitrust that causes unemployment.

Consider the following hypothetical situation. Suddenly the merger rules are changed for large tire firms. New mergers are challenged under stricter rules and old mergers are dissolved. Firms react by reducing the optimal scale of tire production, laying off workers as planned production falls. Unemployment rises during the adjustment period. Other industries face similar antitrust uncertainty, and they expand less as a consequence. Economywide, the unemployment rate goes up and stays up owing to the uncertainty over being targeted for an antitrust complaint. This simple Phillips curve theory explains the Shughart–Tollison results.

Some other points worth noting about these results are (1) they do some damage to the esteem with which the Sherman and Clayton Acts are held by most observers; (2) the Phillips curve explanation is quite consistent with the new learning critique of antitrust decisions, which suggests that antitrust normally attacks efficient firms or commercial practices; (3) the idea that antitrust is about equity suffers in this analysis; and (4) we are at some distance here from the public interest theory.

VI. Conclusion

The thesis of this paper is that we need to know how and why antitrust decision makers behave before we can make intelligent criticisms of antitrust policies; science must precede prescription if prescription is to be meaningful. My focus has been on enforcement officials. Judges also are important antitrust decision makers, but they have been largely exempt from the discussion. How do judges behave and why? The flat answer is that we simply do not know. We know that their antitrust decisions often evoke reams of criticism, but we have made almost no progress in developing a theory of judicial decision making in antitrust or any other area of the law.[5]

So there is work, much work, to be done to achieve a fusion of public choice with antitrust law and economics. I predict that this work will emerge, and that it will provide a rich empirical basis for deciding whether antitrust is a boon or bane for the economy. Moreover, this work will help to cast the role of antitrust in more reasonable terms. Our choice in this area of government policy, as in all others, is between imperfect markets and imperfect government. In the public interest approach, government always gets a green light in antitrust. In the public choice approach, government will often face red and yellow lights, and a little bit more laissez faire will be allowed to prevail in the world.

---

[5]See, however, the work of Landes and Posner (1975) on the independent judiciary.

References

Amacher, R.C.; Higgins, R.S.; Shughart, W.F., II; and Tollison, R.D. "The Behavior of Regulatory Activity Over the Business Cycle." *Economic Inquiry* (forthcoming).

Asch, P. "The Determinants and Effects of Antitrust Policy," *Journal of Law and Economics* 17 (October 1975): 578-81.

Asch, P., and Seneca, J.J. "Is Collusion Profitable?" *Review of Economics and Statistics* 58 (February 1976): 1-10.

Bain, J. *Industrial Organization*, 2d ed. New York: John Wiley & Sons, Inc., 1968.

Baxter, W. "The Political Economy of Antitrust." In *The Political Economy of Antitrust: Principal Paper by William Baxter*, pp. 3-49. Edited by Robert D. Tollison. Lexington, Mass.: D.C. Heath & Co., 1980.

Bork, R.H. *The Antitrust Paradox.* New York: Basic Books, 1978.

Buchanan, J.M. "Toward Analysis of Closed Behavior Systems." In *Theory of Public Choice*, pp. 11-23. Edited by J.M. Buchanan and R.D. Tollison. Ann Arbor: University of Michigan Press, 1972.

Buchanan, J.M., and Tollison, R.D., eds. *The Theory of Public Choice—II*. Ann Arbor: University of Michigan Press, 1984.

Burns, M.R. "The Competitive Effects of Trust-Busting: a Portfolio Analysis." *Journal of Political Economy* 85 (August 1977): 717-39.

Clabault, M.M., and Block, M. *Sherman Act Indictments, 1955-1980.* 2 vols. New York: Federal Legal Publications, 1981.

Clarkson, K.W., and Muris, T.J., eds. *The Federal Trade Commission Since 1970: Economic Regulation and Bureaucratic Behavior*. Cambridge: Cambridge University Press, 1981.

Ellert, J. "Mergers, Antitrust Law Enforcement and Stockholder Returns." *Journal of Finance* 31 (1976): 715-32.

Elzinga, K. "The Antimerger Law: Pyrrhic Victories." *Journal of Law and Economics* 12 (April 1969): 43-78.

Faith, R.; Leavens, D.; and Tollison, R.D. "Antitrust Pork Barrel." *Journal of Law and Economics* 25 (October 1982): 329-42.

Gallo, J.C., and Bush, S. "The Anatomy of Antitrust Enforcement for the Period 1963-1981.: Manuscript. May 1983.

Hay, G.A., and Kelley, D. "An Empirical Survey of Price-Fixing Conspiracies," *Journal of Law and Economics* 17 (April 1974): 13-38.

Higgins, R., and McChesney, F. "Truth and Consequences: The Federal Trade Commission's Ad Substantiation Program." Manuscript, 1983.

Higgins, R.S.; Shughart, W.F., II; and Tollison, R.D. "Dual Enforcement of the Antitrust Laws." In *The Federal Trade Commission*. Edited by R. Mackay, J.C. Miller, and B. Yandle, Stanford, Calif.: Hoover Institution Press, forthcoming.

Katzman. R.A. *Regulatory Bureaucracy: The Federal Trade Commission and Antitrust Policy.* Cambridge, Mass.: MIT Press, 1980.

Landes, W.M., and Posner, R.A. "The Independent Judiciary in an Interest-Group Perspective." *Journal of Law and Economics* 18 (December 1975): 875–901.

Long, W.F.; Schramm, R.; and Tollison, R.D. "The Determinants of Antitrust Activity." *Journal of Law and Economics* 16 (October 1973): 351–64.

Mackay, R.; Miller, J.C.; and Yandle, B., ed. *The Federal Trade Commission.* Stanford, Calif.: Hoover Institution Press, forthcoming.

Mueller, D.C. *Public Choice,* Cambridge: Cambridge University Press, 1979.

Neale, Alan D., and Goyder, D.G. *Antitrust Laws of the U.S.A.* 3d ed. Cambridge: Cambridge University Press, 1980.

Palmer, J. "Some Economic Conditions Conducive to Collusion." *Journal of Economic Issues* 6 (June 1972): 29–38.

Posner, R.A. "A Statistical study of Antitrust Law Enforcement." *Journal of Law and Economics* 13 (October 1970): 365–419.

Posner, R.A. *Antitrust Law, An Economic Perspective.* Chicago: University of Chicago Press, 1976.

Ross, T.W. "Winners and Losers Under the Robinson–Patman Act." *Journal of Law and Economics* 27 (October 1984): 243–72.

Scherer, F.M. *Industrial Market Structure and Economic Performance.* 2d ed. Chicago: Rand McNally, 1980.

Shughart, W.F., II, and Tollison, R.D. "The Employment Consequences of Antitrust." Manuscript. 1984.

Shughart, W.F., II, and Tollison, R.D. "Antitrust Recidivism in Federal Trade Commission Data: 1914–1982." In *The Federal Trade Commission.* Edited by R. Mackay, J.C. Miller, and B. Yandle, Stanford, Calif.: Hoover Institution Press, forthcoming.

Siegfried, J.J. "The Determinants of Antitrust Activity." *Journal of Law and Economics* 17 (October 1975): 559–73.

Stigler, G.J. "The Economic Effects of the Antitrust Laws." *Journal of Law and Economics* 9 (October 1966): 225–58.

Stigler, G.J. "The Theory of Economic Regulation." *Bell Journal of Economics* 2 (Spring 1971): 7–21.

Stigler, G.J. "The Origin of the Sherman Act." *Journal of Legal Studies* 14 (January 1985): 1–12.

Tollison, R.D. "Rent Seeking: A Survey." *Kyklos* 35 (1982): 575–602.

Weaver, S. *Decision to Prosecute: Organization and Public Policy in the Antitrust Division.* Cambridge, Mass.: MIT Press, 1977.

Weingast, B.R., and Moran, M.J. "Bureaucratic Discretion or Congressional Control: Regulatory Policymaking by the Federal Trade Commission." *Journal of Political Economy* 91 (October 1983): 765–800.

CHAPTER 9 - Antitrust Enforcement

What Is Publicity?

Henry Carter Adams

It is commonly acknowledged that publicity is an essential agency for the control of trusts. Evidence of this appears on every hand. In the Conference on Trusts, held in Chicago in 1899, a conference which embraced all interests from all parts of the country and all schools of economic thought, there was scarcely a paper which did not give direct or implied assent to the proposition that trusts are under moral obligation, and should be placed under legal obligation, to expose their financial and operating accounts. The Industrial Commission, to whose investigation we are indebted for what little is known of trusts in this country, submitted three independent and, in some respects, conflicting sets of recommendations, but all of them acknowledged the significance of publicity. Most important treatises on this phase of the monopoly problem, such as those of *von Halle, Ely, Jenks*, and *Clarke*, while presenting different analyses of the situation, are united in their demand for publicity. The utterances of President Roosevelt upon this point are strong and emphatic; and even Mr. Dill, the avowed advocate of industrial combination, uses the phrase when discussing remedial measures.

So universal a consensus of opinion commonly indicates that the question involved is well advanced towards a satisfactory adjustment; but such a conclusion would be far from correct if applied to the present relation of publicity and trusts. Unfortunately, the word is capable of many meanings, and must be defined before it can serve as the rallying point of a constructive policy. Such being the case, an endeavor to analyze the principle of publicity, and to point out what should be the form of the law designed to secure its realization, seems pertinent and timely.

Any fruitful analysis of publicity requires that it be considered from at least three points of view. One must learn, first, its general significance, or the state of the public mind which publicity is designed to create; second, its particular significance, or the interests which publicity is designed to serve; and, third, its administrative significance, or the claim which publicity submits for successful realization.

Reprinted from the *North American Review* (1903) pp. 895–904 by the permissions department, *North American Review*, University of Northern Iowa.

The General Significance of Publicity

The fundamental purpose of publicity is to establish in the community a condition of confidence. Secrecy in the administration of a power which in any way touches the interests of the community, gives birth to the suspicion that the power is unwisely or tyrannously administered. Not only does this state of mind impair the most successful use of the power in question, but, if the interests which believe themselves jeopardized are sufficiently important, it becomes a prolific source of political agitation and social unrest. The task of publicity is to allay this suspicion, and the statutory definition of publicity, in any particular case, must be as broad as the ground of suspicion which makes appeal to it necessary.

It may be said that this view of publicity is correct so far as the power in question is a public or political power, but that it does not apply in the case of private or commercial power. I am quite willing to admit this theoretic limitation, because it raises the question whether or not highly centralized commercial power can longer be regarded as a private power. There was a time when even political power was claimed as a private possession, and when the sovereign urged his right to administer that power without accountability to the people. We need not dwell upon the struggle that followed. The result is well known. The counter claim prevailed, and the public character of political power was irrevocably established for all peoples who acknowledge the principles of constitutional government. Accountability of public officers—that is to say, publicity in political affairs—followed as a matter of course. Commerce, trade, and industry, on the other hand, continued to be regarded as matters of private concern. For more than two centuries, English jurisprudence and English political philosophy have given formal consent to the distinction between political or public power, on the one hand, and commercial or private power, on the other; and, until comparatively recent years, no serious criticism has been heard based upon the practical workings of this distinction.

It would be a mistake, however, to read from this fact the conclusion that English jurisprudence has ever given sanction to the doctrine that the rights of private property are superior to the necessities of public welfare. The courts upheld the claim of secrecy in business affairs because they assumed the efficacy of competition; and it must be admitted that, while industries were small, markets were local, and the relations between producer and consumer continued to be personal relations, this assumption of the courts was reasonable. Wherever healthful competition holds sway, there is no ground for suspecting a tyrannous use of commercial power and, consequently, no demand for publicity. But industrial conditions have changed. Industries are becoming colossal. The local market is a thing of the past. The personal relation between producer and consumer, which for generations exercised a powerful moral restraint upon business conduct, no longer exists. The automatic restraints being weakened, artificial restraints have, in consequence, become a necessity. Neither the assumption of publicity for industries superior to the satisfactory control of competition, nor the assumption of secrecy for industries subject to such control, may be said to possess inherent vitality; they are merely working hypotheses for the administration of justice and for the organization of the State. Secrecy against a competitor is, doubtless, a right carried by the institution of private property; secrecy against the State is a privilege which the State sees fit to grant, but which can be recalled if necessary to allay the suspicion that the privilege conferred endangers the public welfare. Interpreted in this way, publicity seems to have ample legal justification, for it rests upon a fundamental principle of English jurisprudence.

I might refer, in further support of this distinction, to the fact that the socialization of the industrial process has, in large measure, destroyed the private character of business enterprises, and that, in so far as this is the case, the power which it generates is a public power, which, like all public powers, should be administered under conditions of strict accountability. It does not, however, seem appropriate to encumber this article with a line of reasoning which would render necessary the use of unfamiliar words. The conclusion would be the same as that already reached, relative to the right of government to such information as may be necessary to enable the people to live in the enjoyment of equity and justice. The important fact is, reverting again to the definition of the phrase, that publicity should be defined by its functions, and that one of its functions is to dispel the suspicion that industrial power is used in a tyrannous manner, or to make it possible to specify the ground of complaint should investigation prove the suspicion well founded. Such is the general significance of publicity, and such the aim which a law that provides for publicity should hold in view.

The Particular Significance of Publicity

The second suggestion for defining publicity holds in mind the particular interests jeopardized, or believed to be jeopardized, by the growth of colossal enterprises operating in a world's market. It will suffice for our present purpose to mention only the more important of these interests. These are: the interest of the investor; the interest of the independent or potential producer; and the interest of the consumer.

It would be a mistake to say that the public has no interest in easy and safe investments. Under the institution of private property in its present undeveloped stage, there is no other means of making provision for declining years. Moreover, it is of the utmost importance to continuous prosperity that consumption be steady and uniform from year to year. The economic necessity of high wages regularly paid is coming to be generally recognized; but the argument upon which this necessity rests applies with equal force to high dividends and regular interest, provided stocks and bonds are widely diffused among the people. The permanent interest of the investor coincides in every particular with what is known as the permanent interest of society.

It would also be a mistake to say that the investor can take care of himself. This is just what he can not do, unless he possessed of sufficient property to protect his capital by becoming a promoter. It is a statement of stupendous significance, as indicating the insecurity of small investments, that the amounts paid by life insurance companies are, on the average, lost to the beneficiaries within seven years of the death of the insured. The small investor is exposed to the danger of the speculative prospectus, which not infrequently is so highly colored as to be utterly untrustworthy; he is exposed also to the danger of being forced to sell, or induced to sell, through false rumors or incomplete statements relative to the industry in which he has placed his capital. Whatever the precise remedy for this unfortunate state of affairs may prove to be, it is evident that appeal in some form must be made to the principle of publicity, whose function it is to let in the light and let out the facts. Any comprehensive definition of publicity must hold in mind the continuance of the existence, and the encouragement of the growth, of the small investor. To kill the small investor is to make socialism inevitable.

The second of the particular interests named is that of the independent and potential producer. The chief argument in support of trusts rests upon the assumption that colossal corporations are essential to a low cost of production and on this account are the forerunners of low prices. It seems to me that this argument is sadly overworked; but, out of deference to the large number of conservative economists who judge it proper to march with the procession of present tendencies, it is temporarily conceded, in order to bring their view of the situation within our definition of publicity. Says Professor Clarke: "The key to the solution of the grave problems that are thus presented lies in the fact, that the independent producer is the natural protector of all the other threatened interests." Social and political considerations, also, urge the preservation of the independent man in industrial affairs. So far as his disappearance is due to the decrease of cost through the aggregations of large capital, no help, perhaps, can be offered. Possibly, none is to be desired. But so far as this is due to the fact that the small producer is exposed to "predatory competition," the government is in duty bound to grant its protection. This phrase "predatory competition" is taken from Professor Clarke's book, "The Control of Trusts." As defined by him, it embraces three classes of improper acts; namely, "favors exacted from railroads," "the local cutting of prices" (by which is meant the placing of goods on local markets at a sacrifice, in order to destroy local competition), and "the type of boycotting termed 'factor's agreement.' " Predatory competition thus defined is not competition at all; it is, again to quote Professor Clarke, "refined robbery;" and a citizen has the same right to protection from this refined robber as from the footpad or the pirate.

Can publicity reinstate normal competition? Possibly not, in and of itself; but, when government shall undertake the task of restoring to the public the liberty of individual enterprise which the institution of private property assumes to be the inalienable right of every business man (and which, taken away, means inevitably the destruction of the historic institution of private property), it will be found necessary to assign to publicity a broader and more comprehensive interpretation than seems at present to be contemplated by many of its most pronounced advocates. Publicity is whatever is necessary to perform the work of publicity, and one of its tasks is to assist in keeping open the door of opportunity for the independent producer.

The third interest to be considered is that of the consumer. From the time of Moses to the present, industrial philosophy has interpreted the fair price to mean the cost price. Wherever competition guarantees this fair price, government is excused from the task of supervision; but wherever exclusive possession of the source of raw material, monopoly of the process of manufacture, or factious control of the market, enables a corporation to charge either more or less than the fair price for the service which it renders, it is encumbent upon the government to substitute the bookkeeping price for the monopoly price, which, in the absence of effective competition, is sure to be exacted. The determination of the bookkeeping price by which the purchaser is guaranteed justice against a monopolistic producer, is, or may become in extreme cases, one of the functions of publicity, and any definition of publicity which ignores this fact is an incomplete definition.

The Administrative Significance of Publicity

Theorists are too apt, in their study of particular questions, to overlook administrative considerations. It seems sufficient to them to conclude that a certain thing should be done, without inquiring what is implied in the doing of it. Statute makers, also, are prone to the same error. Their besetting sin seems to be the enactment of laws which impose tasks, but which do not, in clear and unmistakable language, grant adequate power for the performance of the tasks imposed. This fact goes far toward explaining what is called the incompetency of governmental administrative bureaus. It seems appropriate, therefore, in discussing the character and scope of publicity, to go beyond a simple statement of the ends desired, and to inquire respecting the powers to be conferred, if the desired ends are to be attained. Three suggestions are offered as bearing on this phase of the subject.

First. A law designed to secure publicity, such as is necessary to enable government to dominate the industrial situation, must provide for the final determination of the industries which are to be subject to its jurisdiction. This implies, of course, an authoritative classification of industries. The general principle according to which such a classification should be made is manifest. Our industrial constitution—that is to say, that scheme of industrial rights and duties imposed by English jurisprudence—assumes not only the persistence of competition, but that the competition which persists will be normal in character and healthful in its working. The present necessity for an appeal to government is found in the fact that certain industries, or industries operated under certain peculiar forms of organization, lie beyond the influence of the healthful regulation of competition. It is this class of industries to which the rule of publicity applies, a fact which the law providing for publicity should definitely express.

Unfortunately, however, although the principle is simple, its application in our complex industrial order would be attended with difficulty. It is not easy to enumerate the tests of normal competition, nor is the idea of monopoly a simple idea. There are many degrees in monopolization; there are many conditions which give vitality to monopolistic organization. Some industries are by nature monopolistic, others are monopolistic through ownership of the source of supply, and still others become monopolistic through their dependence upon or agreement with what may be termed the fundamental industries—as, for example, railways. The situation is not, then, a simple one. It can not be understood without an investigation more far-reaching and exhaustive than would be possible for any legislative committee. While, perhaps, one cannot go so far as to say that the determination of what industries are to be brought within the jurisdiction of a law providing for publicity is in its nature an administrative act, it is certain that better results are likely to follow if the law contents itself with a statement of the end to be attained, with a delineation of the principles to be followed, and with the creation of such executive machinery as may be necessary for its effective administration. It is clear to me, although the Federal Court in its treatment of the Inter-State Commerce Commission seems to hold a different opinion, that the realization of the principles of publicity and control means, among other things, a further development of judicial or semi-judicial functions on the part of the executive branch of the government. It is either this or a further development of administrative functions on the part of the judiciary; and, when the real meaning of such a tendency is appreciated by the people, I am confident they will choose the former alternative.

Second. The law should confer upon the bureau or commission intrusted with its administration, power to prescribe a legal form of accounts for all concerns which come under its jurisdiction. To one who has had experience with government investigations into corporate accounts, no argument is needed in support of such a suggestion. It is easy for an accountant, so disposed, to give a false coloring to a transaction by an unusual distribution of charges. A current expense may be carried as an investment in such a manner as to increase unduly net earnings, and thus deceive the investor as to the value of the property. An improvement, on the other hand, may be charged as a current expense, which results in an erroneous statement of cost, thus misleading both court and legislature, should either be called upon to consider the question of a just or reasonable price for service rendered. Statutory bookkeeping is the only remedy for the many mischiefs incident to uncertain accounting.

A system of prescribed accounting finds further support when one considers that, even with the best intention on the part of accounting officers, a compilation of the reports which they render will not accurately portray the industrial situation, unless the reporting corporations keep their books according to uniform rule. The basis of accounting is classification, and sound classification consists in collecting items of the same sort under the same title. If, now, there is no uniformity in the use made of the titles of accounts by the several accounting officers, it is evident that a combination of their reports will result in bringing together incongruous items, thus rendering impossible the determination of a true average or the disclosure of a safe generalization. This consideration in favor of statutory accounting is especially pertinent to those who rely upon that indefinite though powerful force called "public opinion" for the control of corporate powers.

The man interested in corporate securities as an investor, has a special reason for the advocacy of statutory accounting. His judgment relative to an investment rests quite as much upon a comparison of the current report with previous reports as upon an analysis of the current report itself. If, then, the corporate financier is at liberty to distribute the items of income and expenditure in an arbitrary manner, the usefulness of the report to the investor is very largely destroyed. It will be said that most corporations do, at the present time, maintain uniformity in their current reports. This may, perhaps, be true; but, in the same way that a small amount of false coin gives rise to the suspicion that all coins may be false, so the listing of securities of corporations whose accounts can not be trusted may be the occasion of widespread distrust with regard to all securities. The government ought to guarantee, not only the integrity of the reports which corporations make, but that the charges in the books from which the reports are made shall be uniform from month to month and from year to year.

The government, on its part, has a peculiar interest in the demand for statutory bookkeeping from all corporations subject to its supervisory jurisdiction. If each of these corporations—and their number, it may be assumed, will be very large—retains the privilege of formulating its own classification of charges, the task of gaining mastery over their accounts lies beyond the ability of any single office. If, however, the mastery of a single system of accounting implies the mastery of all, as would be the case if all industries of the same class follow the same accounting rules, this task would be greatly simplified. Each item would then mean the same thing for every reporting corporation, and it would not be necessary to enter upon a detailed analysis of each in order to arrive at its true meaning. Moreover, it would be impossible to locate reasonable suspicion relative to improper administration by the comparison of individual reports with what may be termed the typical report, were each corporation at liberty to follow its own whim in the classification of its charges. Such considerations as these, and there are others of the same sort, make it evident that the only hope for the successful exercise of supervisory control over the administration of private corporations, through the agency of an administrative bureau, lies in granting that bureau the right to prescribe the manner in which corporation accounts shall be kept.

Third. The law designed to realize publicity must, in some manner, make the accounting officer of the corporations in question personally responsible for the report which he submits. The most direct method of arriving at this result would be to follow the suggestion of a man who, at the time of his death, was the treasurer of one of the largest railway interests in the country. "In my opinion," he said in the course of a conversation upon this point, "you will never get what you are after until railway accountants are made public officials." This, perhaps, is an extreme suggestion. It may have been made in levity, though many a sane word has been spoken in jest. It is certainly true that the accounting officers of the class of industries for which publicity is demanded, should be forced to recognize a broader allegiance than to the corporations which give them employment. As a practical proposition, it may at least be urged, in the name of the principle of publicity, that a government bureau created for the purpose should have the right of visitation and examination, and that any deviation which may be discovered from the method of accounting prescribed by law, should be regarded as a misdemeanor chargeable to the accounting officer. Unless one is willing to go this length in providing for governmental supervision over corporate administration, one had better abandon the advocacy of publicity.

It is, of course, understood that the foregoing is merely an attempt to formulate a practical definition of publicity. The analysis does not touch the deeper question of governmental supervision and control over monopolistic corporations. It is evident, however, that, whatever the character of that supervision or control, adequate provision must be made for getting at the facts. This is essential, whether we rely upon public opinion to exercise a conservative influence in the management of corporations, or upon the legislature to prescribe reasonable conditions for corporate activity, or upon a semi–judicial administrative bureau to supervise monopolistic combinations. Indeed, from whatever point of view the trust problem is considered, publicity stands as the first step in its solution; and there is reason to believe that the further the government is willing to go in its statutory definition of publicity the greater likelihood is there that it may be excused from the necessity of exercising direct administrative control.

Fines: The Efficient Solution

William Breit and Kenneth G. Elzinga

The Coasian Framework

Chapter 5 argued that monopoly damages are reciprocal in nature. The real issue is where to place the liability for the untoward economic repercussions of anticompetitive practices. Placing the liability squarely on the antitrust violator by requiring him to pay compensation to his "victims" does not permit an efficient solution since it changes the incentives of those potentially compensated, thus generating unintended and adverse side effects. These side effects would persist even if the reparations process were costless, which it assuredly is not.

The Coasian analysis would suggest that consideration should be given to placing the liability on the consumer and then comparing the results under such a system with the results of the strict liability approach of present treble damage law. It is clear, however, that shifting the liability to the consumer with no liability placed on the monopolist would not be efficient. Furthermore, it would be equivalent to having no antitrust laws. The consumer would then bear the entire burden of damages arising from monopolistic practices. Since the consumer's surplus lost would be larger than the monopolist's profits, there is still a potential for "gains from trade." But the large numbers problem and the free rider argument dash the hope that strictly private transactions would eliminate the monopolistic market structure. It is unlikely that even the most assiduous and prudent conduct on the part of shoppers by itself would deter, for if there were always effective substitutes in the market there would be no monopoly problem. There are thus sharp limits to the benefits to be had from a completely laissez–faire approach. To achieve optimality in the Coasian sense (that is, to maximize the value of total output), *some* liability must be placed on the monopolist. Since negotiation is impractical and perfect substitutes do not exist, consideration must be given to finding a solution through governmental action. In this case, it appears that the optimal solution is precisely the kind that Coase once suggested might prove correct in the case of other social costs. The optimal solution calls for neither compensation for damages suffered nor for allowing monopoly to persist unabated. Coase himself, in discussing another type of liability issue, suggested that in some

---

Reprinted by permission of William Breit and Kenneth G. Elzinga.

instances the liability for damages must be *shared* in order to reach an optimal solution.[1]

But what could such a prescription mean in the context of antitrust policy? The answer is to place the liability for monopolistic behavior on *both* buyers and sellers. Under the ideal solution, the monopolistic sellers would be fined enough to cause them to cease and desist from all monopolistic behavior, but they would be exempt from paying compensation to anyone who purchased from them. Buyers as well as sellers would then share the "liability." With no potential compensation, perverse incentives and misinformation effects would be eliminated and the perplexities and costs of the reparations process would vanish.

To die-hard advocates of private enforcement, such a prescription might appear unwarranted. They might argue that increasing the amount of damages that plaintiffs could receive would at some point completely deter monopolistic behavior.[2] This increase could be accomplished by increasing the multiple of damages that is paid to successful plaintiffs to one that would lead to complete deterrence, by easing the process of successfully consummating private suits, or by a combination of the two.

Although it might at first appear that appropriately increasing the amount of damages, in deterring all monopoly, would surely eliminate the moral hazards of private actions, further examination renders this conclusion dubious. Increasing private payments to the point where monopoly is deterred would eventually eliminate the perverse incentives effect, because if no one could be damaged by monopolists there would be no damages to be avoided. In addition, an individual could not modify his behavior to increase his damage, since without monopolies there would be no monopolistic damages to be increased.

However, the amelioration of one adverse effect of a private action can be obtained in this way only by exacerbating the other. For the higher the amount of damages that could be collected, and the greater the ease with which such suits could be consummated, the greater will be the misinformation effect. As has been shown, nuisance suits are more likely to occur when a defendant cannot easily show that the claimant's charges are groundless and when the

---

[1]R. H. Coase, "The Problem of Social Cost," *Journal of Law & Economics* 3 (October 1960): 1, reprinted in William Breit and Harold M. Hochman, *Readings in Microeconomics* 2d ed. rev. (New York: Holt, Rinehart, and Winston, 1971), p. 515. Buchanan and Stubblebine have also suggested that a bilateral approach to liability might sometimes be necessary to achieve full Pareto equilibrium. See James M. Buchanan and William Craig Stubblebine, "Externality," *Economica* 29 (n.s.) (November 1962): 371. Guido Calabresi in *The Costs of Accidents: A Legal and Economic Analysis* points out that an efficient approach to automobile liability law would stress the reciprocal nature of accidents involving both cars and pedestrians noting that "the cheapest way of avoiding costs, is often a reduction of *both* activities, walking and driving" [New Haven: Yale University Press, 1970], p. 154.

[2]Gary S. Becker is a leading exemplar of this point of view. See his "Crime and Punishment: An Economic Approach," *Journal of Political Economy* 76 (March–April 1968): 169. Reprinted in Breit and Hochman, *Reading in Microeconomics,* pp. 339–369, esp. 360.

defendant predicts that he has a good chance of being found guilty. If a defendant is risk averse, and his expected payment to allegedly injured claimants is relatively large, the greater will be his desire to settle without litigation. We would predict that any attempt to deter monopolistic activity through increasing payments to plaintiffs or easing the way to their bringing and winning suits would increase the amount of misinformation that the system generates regarding the extent of monopolistic activity. Even total deterrence, then, under a system of private actions, would not be efficient deterrence because of the resources misallocated to nuisance and *in terrorem* suits. Indeed the closer the approach to total deterrence, the greater would be the extent of this misallocation.

To obviate these problems under a private actions approach, it would be necessary to consider a complicated multipronged attack on the problem. First, only unavoidable damages could merit compensation. This change would require an alteration in the present attitude of the courts toward this problem. Otherwise, the magnified perverse incentives effect would persist under a regime of compensation. But even if this effect were eliminated, the perverse incentives effect would remain unless compensation were not paid to those actually damaged. This might be accomplished through a system of entrepreneurial law firms that, in return for rewards, detected antitrust law violations. Second, even assuming that the perverse incentives effect were completely eliminated, the misinformation effect would persist. It would be greatly reduced, of course, if the law were changed so as to assign all legal fees to unsuccessful plaintiffs. If this action did not eliminate the misinformation effect, it would be necessary to impose heavy penalties upon those bringing unsuccessful suits.[3] The superiority of this approach is not persuasive, however. For one thing, such a system of penalties might dampen the enthusiasm not only of those with groundless claims but those with viable grievances as well. And even if it is assumed that the perverse incentives effect and the misinformation effect could be eliminated by these actions, there remain two seemingly incorrigible problems of a full–fledged reliance on private antitrust enforcement: (1) substantive reform of the antitrust laws would have to be undertaken so that only procompetitive actions would be brought; (2) in the event that such a system led to overenforcement of the antitrust laws, one would have to calculate an optimal tax on private enforcement in order to lower the equilibrium probability of conviction to the desired level.[4]

As a first approximation to an optimal solution, a monetary fine should be levied that would be sufficient to deter most risk averse managers and that would enable society to achieve at least the present degree of deterrence at far

---

[3]We are indebted to Gary Becker for an illuminating discussion of these points with us.

[4]On the general subject of private law enforcement, see Gary S. Becker and George J. Stigler, "Law Enforcement, Malfeasance, and Compensation of Enforcer," *Journal of Legal Studies* 3 (January 1974): 1.

less cost and a greater degree of deterrence at the same cost. Given this mandatory fine, the Antitrust Division and Federal Trade Commission could then increase or decrease the amount of monopolistic activity by altering the amount of resources used in detecting and convicting antitrust violators. In other words, the antitrust authorities could adjust policy through marginal increments in the amount of investigatory and litigative activity permitted. Under public enforcement of the antitrust laws, the optimal combination of probabilities and punishments would more readily be approximated. Under a private actions approach, on the other hand, it is unlikely that such an outcome could be obtained. The amount of resources devoted to the apprehension and conviction of violators could only be changed through the use of the blunt instruments of congressional legislation or court decisions, which could ease or hinder the bringing of private actions. With public enforcement, however, a change in total antitrust activity could be accomplished by simply changing the congressional appropriations for these agencies and the discretionary use to which the antitrust authorities put these resources. This policy (permissible only through public actions) would thus entail faster and more predictable antitrust enforcement.

One likely criticism of a proposal to rely upon a high monetary exaction combined with governmental control over the mechanisms that initiate enforcement is the argument that the antitrust authorities would be subject to temptations to accept bribes in lieu of bringing charges against a violator. Since the gain to the violators is potentially greater than that to the antitrust authorities from preventing or punishing those who would infringe the law, the quality of enforcement might be lessened. The higher the fine, the greater would be the temptation of malfeasance, and the greater would be the costs of monitoring the antitrust authorities. However, as Becker and Stigler have demonstrated, a compensation structure that would eliminate malfeasance can be developed.[5] The higher the salary paid to enforcers, the greater is the cost to them of violations of trust. An alternative would be to increase the penalties for dishonesty. In other words, the cost of dismissal to a public law enforcer could be made greater than the gain he received from dishonesty.

What Do Entrepreneurs Want?

Can economic reasoning shed any light on the question of the efficiency of fines—the remaining antitrust penalty? In other words, what kind of fine would be appropriate and how high should it be? In order to analyze this problem it will be necessary to examine the motivations of the entrepreneurs whose behavior these fines are presumably designed to affect. Stated in its starkest form, assuming that the entrepreneur is attempting to maximize his expected utility, then antitrust violations will occur if the expected utility from

---

[5]Ibid.

anticompetitive behavior exceeds the expected utility from competing. But the economists' term "expected utility" is a portmanteau that requires unpacking.

The entrepreneur's "expected utility" simply refers to the average or mean level of his satisfactions from his business activities. They are "expected" because he operates under conditions of uncertainty and he cannot know in advance whether he will actually realize any particular amount of profits. Only a set of probabilities is known. There are essentially three items that must be taken into account in order to predict accurately the behavior of, say, a potential cartelist. First, the entrepreneur is interested in the additional profits he will realize from joining the cartel. But he actually interested in the present value of those profits. This value tells him how much his firm is worth. He then discounts these profits by the probability of his being detected and convicted, and by the risk of high fines he must pay, an exercise that gives him his expected value. The second item is thus the probability of detection and conviction as well as the size of the fine. This risk is part of his costs and reduces the present value of his monopoly profits and therefore the capitalized value of his enterprise. Insofar as it is a deterrent, antitrust policy works by making the present value of monopoly profits less by increasing the risk facing the potential and actual cartelist. But how much this policy will actually deter the firm from illegal behavior depends on the entrepreneur's attitude toward risk. The more averse he is to risk, the more he will be deterred by any given reduction in the present value of his monopoly profits resulting from increased risk. The more of a risk lover he happens to be, the less will he be deterred by any reduction in the present value of his monopoly profits resulting from increased risk. So the third important item in appraising any antitrust policy is the attitude of the businessman toward risk. His attitude toward risk determines the utility or satisfaction that he expects to get from his monopoly profits. And, as already noted, his expected utility from monopoly profits must be greater than his expected utility from his competitive returns before he would be willing to collude. With these functional relationships in mind, under what conditions will the entrepreneur enter a cartel or engage in monopolistic behavior?

The present value of a firm is the discounted stream of expected profits. Any increase in the financial penalties or in the probability of detection and conviction would increase the risk facing this firm. This increase would cause a rise in the firm's average costs because shareholders would insist on a higher return because the riskiness of the enterprise has increased.[6] They will sell shares, reducing the market value of the stock and increasing its yield. The increased yield indicates a higher cost of capital to the firm. Consequently the rising probability of antitrust conviction or the risk of paying higher financial penalties increases average costs and reduces the present value of the profit

---

[6]See William Fellner, "Average-Cost Pricing and the Theory of Uncertainty," *Journal of Political Economy* 56 (June 1948): 249.

accruing to the firm. If the goal of antitrust activity was totally to deter this cartel, then the best policy would be to increase the risk, making the firm's average costs rise so high that the expected utility of monopoly profits would be zero. At that point there would be no incentive to collude since the expected utility of profits under competitive conditions would be the same as those under collusive conditions.

By now it should be clear that Congress can affect monopoly behavior by acting on two variables: the probability of detection and conviction and fines. For example, if society wishes to increase competition, one variable to modify would be the amount of resources devoted to the detection and conviction of anticompetitive behavior; another would be the size of the financial penalty.

There is widespread agreement that, everything else being equal, an increase in the probability of detection and conviction will decrease the number of offenses an individual will commit. Whether this decrease will be negligible or substantial, however, is open to question. There has long been a presumption among sociologists, government officials, and even businessmen that the decrease will be substantial, because, it is alleged, the severity of a sentence is less important than the likelihood that it will be imposed. In 1949, for example, Ellis Arnall, former governor of Georgia and president of the Society of Independent Motion Picture Producers, testified before a congressional committee to study monopoly power. He suggested that "in most criminal laws the deterrent from crime is the certainty of the punishment." But in the case of the antitrust laws, "the certainty of punishment is not a deterrent because the punishment does not amount to anything."[7] In 1961, Lee Loevinger, the chief of the Antitrust Division, repeated the conventional view:

> It is the general experience of law enforcement officials that severity of punishment is not nearly as effective a deterrent to law violation as certainty of apprehension and punishment. Increasing the severity of punishment does not aid in the detection and apprehension of violators. It is the enforcement machinery and the tools of detection and apprehension that are the indispensable weapons of law enforcement.[8]

In like fashion, when urging stronger antitrust laws, Henry Ford II stated his view that increasing the penalties would not be as effective a deterrent as greater enforcement efforts. The "threat of fairly certain detection, [and] conviction for violation would be enough to deter all but the most incorrigible offenders."[9] If these statements are correct, then a plausible argument can be made in favor of enlarging the budgets of the Antitrust Division and the

---

[7]Testimony of Ellis Arnall in U.S., Congress, House, Committee on the Judiciary, *Hearings on the Study of Monopoly Power,* 81st Cong., 1st Sess., 1949, p. 278.

[8]U.S., Congress, Senate, Committee on the Judiciary, *Hearings, Legislation to Strengthen Penalties Under the Antitrust Laws,* 87th Cong., 1st Sess., 1961, p. 17.

[9]Letter from Henry Ford II to Estes Kefauver, cited in *ibid.,* p. 107.

Federal Trade Commission. And precisely such measures have been endorsed, recently by the Nader antitrust study group.[10] Willard Mueller, a former director of the Federal Trade Commission's Bureau of Economics, has written that "antitrust policy has never been given a fair test" because of its lean funding.[11]

As a second alternative, society could act upon the variable of fines by increasing their magnitude. Chapter 3 noted a number of proposals to do just that.[12] However, the appropriate choice or "mix" between the level of the fine and probability of detection and conviction depends upon the precise extent to which manipulating them will deter monopolistic behavior. And this deterrence is a direct function of the attitude of the businessmen toward risk. Consequently it is now necessary to examine the meaning of risk preference as it relates to managerial behavior.

Risk Preference and Antitrust Policy

An illustration comparing a given large loss with a given smaller loss will prove instructive in clarifying the meaning of risk preference. Assume that the large loss is ten times the smaller loss. The expected value of these two losses is said to be equal if the probability of the occurrence of the small loss is ten times as great as that of the large loss. However, although the expected values are the same, individuals may have different expected disutilities from these losses depending upon their attitudes toward risk. The risk averse person will prefer the large probability of the small loss to the small probability of the large loss. The risk preferrer, on the other hand, will prefer the small probability of the large loss to the larger probability of the smaller loss. More technically, for the risk averse person the disutility of the larger loss is more than ten times as great as the disutility of the smaller loss. For the risk preferrer, the larger loss disutility is less than ten times that of the smaller loss.

Let us apply this risk attitude analysis to our antitrust policy problem of choosing between a primarily fine–oriented an a primarily detection–oriented deterrence system. Assume that the enforcement agencies are considering two alternative proposals. The first calls for both the imposition of a higher fine on convicted antitrust violators and a reduction in the amount of resources going into detection and conviction. The second calls for reducing the financial penalties but also for increasing the resources devoted to enforcement, thereby causing an increase in the probability of detection and conviction. Let us assume further that the high financial penalty is ten times the lower penalty, but that because of the difference in the quantity of

---

[10]Mark J. Green, et al., *The Closed Enterprise System* (New York: Grossman Publishers, 1972), pp. 129–130. Arguing that the present budget of the Antitrust Division is "absurdly too small," the study group recommended an increase from the present budget of $12 million to "at least $100 million," p. 130.

[11]Willard F. Mueller, *A Primer On Monopoly and Competition* (New York: Random House, 1970), p. 117.

[12]See pp. 55–62 supra.

resources devoted to enforcement, the probability of being required to pay the lower penalty is ten times as great as the probability of being required to pay the high penalty. Based on these assumptions, the expected value of monopoly profits under either proposal is the same. The businessman's expected utility from antitrust violations, however, will vary depending upon his attitude toward risk. The risk manager's attitudes will lead him to practice more collusion under the policy involving the larger probability of paying the smaller financial penalty. The risk preferrer, on the other hand, will practice more collusion under the policy involving the smaller probability of the large penalty.

The indifference maps of figure 4 provide graphic illustration of the attitudes of both a risk preferrer and a risk averter. On the horizontal axes of panels A and B is measured the probability of detection and conviction of antitrust violations. On the vertical axes is measured fines paid when the firm is apprehended and convicted of restraints of trade.[13] Unlike relative magnitudes in the usual construction of such diagrams, the magnitudes measured on each axis become smaller as they move away from the origin. The indifference curves depicted will be called "iso–expected utility" curves. They show for a given businessman combinations of antitrust polices associated with a particular expected utility from monopoly profits. A movement along any curve indicates the amount by which a decrease in the use of one policy instrument must be compensated by an increase in employment of the other instrument in order for a given businessman to maintain a given degree of utility from monopolistic activity. As the businessman moves out to higher iso–expected utility curves–that is, as he moves further away from the origin—the greater satisfaction that he can achieve from monopoly profits will encourage him to engage in more anticompetitive behavior.

A preliminary issue that figure 4 can help illuminate is the inefficiency of incarceration as an antitrust weapon. In chapter 3 this penalty was seen to have little deterrent effect because of the paucity of its use, an understandable situation given the reluctance of judges and juries to believe either that antitrust violators merit jail or that the chief corporate culprits have been identified. But the analysis in this chapter allows one to go beyond such a purely pragmatic consideration. For if the horizontal axis of figure 4 is understood as depicting incarceration in terms of the length of the sentence (rather than probability of detection and conviction), the indifference curves would then represent a plausible trade-off between financial penalties and time to be served in jail. In other words, the geometry brings out clearly that there is some marginal rate of substitution between financial penalties and *any* other

---

[13]The magnitude of fines is independent of the probability of conviction and detection. Congress could increase the fines and not vote any additional resources to the enforcement agencies. Furthermore, increased fines provide no significant inducement to private parties either to prosecute or to inform the government of antitrust violations.

penalty, including jails, which means that the jail penalty, like any other penalty, can always be collapsed into its monetary equivalent. Thus the inefficiency of the jail penalty can be easily seen. For any given period of time spent

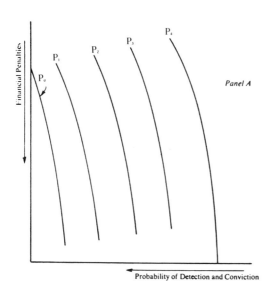

Panel A

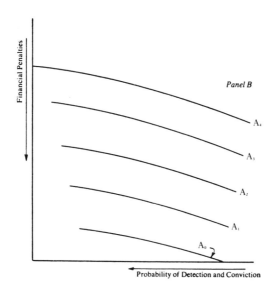

Panel B

Figure 4

in jail, there is some fine capable of securing the same deterrent effect. However, since the size of a fine can be changed without the expenditure of additional resources, while increased use of incarceration always involves greater costs to society, incarceration is an inferior penalty. Whenever any penalty can give the same amount of deterrence at less cost, or additional deterrence for the same cost, that option is economically superior.

More important, this geometrical construct can be used to see the implications of managerial risk attitudes in the design of antitrust policy. Panel A depicts the case in which the manager is a risk preferrer. His indifference curves indicate that a relatively small reduction in the probability of apprehension and conviction must be compensated by a relatively large increase in financial penalties in order for him to maintain any given degree of expected utility from his monopolistic behavior. Precisely the opposite attitude is depicted in panel B, which illustrates the case of a risk averse manager. In this case, a relatively large reduction in the probability of detection and conviction needs to be compensated by only a relatively small increase in penalties in order to maintain any given expected utility.

The implications of attitudes toward risk for antitrust policy can be illustrated by superimposing the expected utility indifference curves of the risk preferrer (the curves depicted as P) on those of the risk averter (the curves depicted as A), as is done in figure 5. Assume that in terms of current expenditures of resources, antitrust policy places society at point Q, where the A3 indifference curve of the risk averter cuts curve P3 of the risk preferrer. The line KL passes through point Q and is drawn as an iso-expected value curve. By definition, any movement along KL leaves constant the expected value of the monopolist's profits, with any change in the financial penalty exactly compensated in terms of expected value by an opposite change in the probability of detection and conviction. The iso-expected value curve, a rectangular hyperbola, also represents the iso-expected utility curve of a risk-neutral businessman, a businessman who has no preference, say, between a 10 percent probability of a $10 loss and a 100 percent probability of a $1 loss. KL can thus be thought of as the line that divides risk preference from risk aversion.[14] The slopes of iso-expected utility curves at each point of intersection with KL are

---

[14]That criminals are risk neutral (i.e., that line KL accurately depicts their psychology) is implicitly assumed by Gordon Tullock. In discussing the question of whether the severity of the penalty or the certainty of punishment is more important in deterring criminal behavior, Tullock stated his opinion that "this is not a very important question. Suppose a potential criminal has a choice between two punishment systems: One gives each person who commits burglary a one-in-100 chance of serving one year in prison; in the other there is a one-in-1,000 chance of serving 10 years. It is not obvious to me that burglars would be very differently affected by these two punishment systems, although in one case there is a heavy sentence with a low probability of conviction, and in the other a lighter sentence with a higher probability of conviction." See Gordon Tullock, "Does Punishment Deter Crime?" *The Public Interest* 36 (Summer 1974): 103, 107. Our indifference curve analysis makes clear, however, that the probability that a potential burglar would commit more crime under one or the other of these two systems depends on his attitude toward risk.

greater or less than the slope of KL, depending upon whether they represent risk preferrers or risk averters.

If one were to start at point Q on KL and were to allow both P and A to design any antitrust policy they wished, with the only constraint being that the expected value of their monopoly profits would have to remain constant, one would expect each businessman to travel up or down the iso–expected value curve KL until he reached his highest iso–expected utility indifference curve. In figure 5, the risk averter reaches his highest indifference curve at point T, while the risk preferrer reaches his highest expected utility at point S. Point T represents relatively low monetary losses with a high likelihood of detection, while point S represents relatively high losses with a low probability of detection.

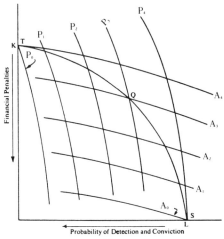

Figure 5

Of course, in reality both risk averse and risk loving managers must adjust their behavior to the same antitrust policy. The law cannot allow each of them to choose the combination he prefers under the constraint of a specific expected value of monopoly profits. With an initial policy placing them both at point Q, a new policy that would place them both at point S would move the risk preferrer to a higher indifference curve than he was on at point Q, but it would move the risk averter to a lower curve than *he* was on at point Q. By moving to point S, therefore, the expected utility of the risk lover would rise relative to that of the risk averter. The risk preferrer would engage in or "demand" more anticompetitive collusion, boycotts, mergers, and the like. He will receive more satisfaction from his monopoly profits when the probability of detection is low and the financial penalties high. On the other hand, the risk averter at point S will choose business practices and policies that involve less monopolistic activity because such activity offers him less expected utility.

With any given antitrust enforcement policy, then, the degree of monopoly in the economy depends on whether managerial classes consist mainly of risk preferrers or risk averters. Changes in the risk attitudes of the managing classes may demand corresponding changes in antitrust policies. It is therefore highly pertinent to examine the development of the risk attitudes of American business management since the enactment of the Sherman Act.[15]

The Psychology of Managers and Its Implications for Antitrust Policy

There is considerable evidence that today's business management is distinctly more cautious than its late nineteenth-century counterpart; furthermore, this tendency toward greater risk aversion appears to be centered in the nation's oligopolies, those firms most subject to antitrust scrutiny. Joseph Schumpeter and Robert Aaron Gordon were among the earliest observers of this attitudinal change.[16] Schumpeter's sweeping description of capitalism, in its very success, smothering and making obsolete the entrepreneurial spirit dovetails with Gordon's careful investigation of large enterprise management. Gordon argued that the desire for security is "very probably...stronger among the leading executives of large and mature concerns than it was among an earlier generation of 'big' businessmen."[17]

Since Schumpeter and Gordon made their observations, other economists have also argued convincingly that American business prudence has sharply increased in recent decades. Both Robin Marris and John Kenneth Galbraith contend that control of large enterprises has passed from the individualistic entrepreneur to the organization-minded, group-oriented manager who is highly concerned with minimizing risk and uncertainty.[18] In the Galbraith-Marris corporate world, concern for individual and corporate security acts as an overriding constraint on desires for growth and profits:

> Today, when one young executive describes another as a "good businessman," more often than not he does not mean...a man with a good nose for profits, but rather a man who keeps his records in order, his staff contented, his contacts active and his pipelines filled...not rash, but not

---

[15]In enacting the Sherman Act, Congress in all likelihood did not explicitly or implicitly consider the risk attitudes of American businessmen. The earlier discussion of legislative history indicated that such matters were at best peripheral to the consideration of the legislation. Nevertheless, the ultimate effectiveness of the antitrust laws is in fact intimately related to management's attitudes toward risk.

[16]Robert A. Gordon, *Business Leadership in the Large Corporation* (Washington: The Brookings Institution, 1945), pp. 271–351; Joseph A. Schumpeter, *Capitalism, Socialism, and Democracy,* 3d ed. (New York: Harper, 1950), pp. 121–163.

[17]Robert A. Gordon, *Business Leadership,* p. 283. See also pp. 310–311.

[18]John Kenneth Galbraith, *The New Industrial State,* 2d ed. rev. (Boston: Houghton-Mifflin, 1971), pp. 11–178; Robin Marris, *The Economic Theory of "Managerial" Capitalism* (New York: Free Press of Glencoe, 1964), pp. 1–109, 204–288.

suffering from indecision; a good committee man who knows both when to open his mouth and when to keep it shut.[19]

The use of complex decision theory and organization theory has led other economists similarly to conclude that contemporary management wishes to avoid risk and uncertainty.[20] These analysts portray a hired management interested not solely in maximizing profits but rather in pursuing a variety of goals; they describe a management geared to "homeostatic" business conduct rather than impetuous, swashbuckling strategies. According to many economists, the risk attitudes of contemporary management are well summarized by Sir J. R. Hicks's observation mentioned earlier: "The best of all...profits is a quiet life."[21]

Observers in other disciplines have also noticed the changed risk attitude of contemporary management. William Whyte has argued that the displacement of the Protestant Ethic by the Social Ethic has led to the professionalization of management, strict pressures to conform, and constraints on individual expression.[22] Political scientist Antony Jay has compared the large corporation with the large state, arguing that both generate strong pressures to maintain the status quo. Jay believes that any risky moves that are made by today's management are aberrations, atypical phenomena that have little connection with the risk attitudes of management in general.[23]

Observers find, then, that modern enterprise lacks the Carnegies, Fricks, and Firestones of an earlier era. Such entrepreneurs have been displaced during a gradual evolution propelled by such factors as increasing education, changes in the social environment of business, the steady separation of ownership from control in large corporate enterprises, the "technique orientation" and conformity that seem to characterize business education, and perhaps the very nature of bureaucracy itself. These factors have caused the risk preferrers of the late nineteenth century to become the risk avoiders of the current era.

[19]Robin Marris, *Economic Theory of "Managerial" Capitalism;* pp. 57–58. Galbraith's description is consistent with Marris's view: "These characteristics [of individualistic entrepreneurial behavior] are not readily reconciled with the requirements of the technostructure. Not indifference but sensitivity to others, not individualism but accommodation to organization, not competition but intimate and continuing cooperation are the prime requirements for group action. ...The assertion of competitive individualism...to the extent that it is still encountered, is ceremonial, traditional or a manifestation of personal vanity and...self delusion" (Galbraith, *The New Industrial State*, at 92–93).

[20]See, for example, Kenneth E. Boulding, *A Reconstruction of Economics* (New York: Wiley, 1950); Richard M. Cyert and James G. March, *A Behavioral Theory of the Firm* (Englewood Cliffs, N.J.: Prentice–Hall, 1963), pp. 118–119; Herbert A. Simon, "Theories of Decision-Making in Economics and Behavioral Science," *American Economic Review* 49 (June 1959): 253.

[21]J. R. Hicks, "Annual Survey of Economic Theory: The Theory of Monopoly," *Econometrica* 3 (January 1935): 1, 8.

[22]William H. Whyte, Jr., *The Organization Man* (New York: Simon and Schuster, 1956), pp. 18–22.

[23]Antony Jay, *Management and Machiavelli* (New York: Holt, Rinehart, and Winston, 1967), esp. pp. 189–198.

The implications of this attitudinal change for antitrust policy are clear. Policy designers should be highly sensitive to this change in risk attitude, realizing that a risk averse management is more likely to be deterred by high financial penalties than by a high probability of detection and conviction with accompanying penalties that are not so severe. Thus, the deterrent benefits of a policy of increased fines far outweigh the deterrent benefits of expending additional enforcement resources.

Potential Objections to Raising Fines

Even given the relative deterrent benefits of increasing fines as opposed to increasing enforcement efforts, potential objections to a fine–oriented system still remain. First, it could be argued that judges and juries would be substantially less likely to convict a violator if such a conviction demanded a significantly higher fine. If so, an increased fine, even if enforcement efforts remained constant, would result in a decrease in the proportion of antitrust violators who are convicted. The decrease, the argument would assert, would result in the reduction of moral inhibitions against engaging in anticompetitive behavior. As a consequence, antitrust violations would increase, even if management is risk averse and therefore initially inclined to avoid any flirtation with violation because of the increased penalties. This objection to a system based on higher fines rests on the belief that the moral, educative force of law is critical in influencing behavior and that to the extent that punishment occurs less frequently, the law's moral force is weakened.[24] Punishment, it is argued, greatly reinforces society's condemnation of inappropriate behavior. Hence high fines that are seldom imposed would lead in the long run to more, rather than less, monopolistic behavior because the moral inhibitions against such behavior would be weakened.

However convincing this objection to a fine–oriented system appears at first glance, on closer examination it has two critical weaknesses. First, it is far from inevitable that statutory provisions for higher fines, even if mandatory, would impel judges and juries to punish fewer antitrust violators. Legislation that increased fines while eliminating private damage suits, for example, would clearly show that Congress intended the fine increase to be comprehensively implemented; this demonstrated intent could be expected to influence judges and juries. These individuals would probably have a greater tendency to fine antitrust violations when assured that private treble damage actions would not follow. Furthermore, judges and perhaps juries could be expected to recognize that, with relatively fewer investigative resources devoted to punishing anticompetitive behavior, fines would carry a greater deterrent burden.

Second, even if one ignores the real possibility that the increased moral inhibitions accompanying heightened financial penalties may in themselves

---

[24]See, for example, Johs Andenaes, "General Prevention—Illusion or Reality?" *Journal of Criminal Law, Criminology, and Police Science* 43 (May–June 1952): 176.

compensate for the moral inhibitions lost by a decrease in the frequency of enforcement, the moral force argument is not persuasive. It assumes that the decision to engage in unlawful behavior is made largely on the basis of an individual's personal moral code. It is more likely, however, that in the area of antitrust deterrence, the attitude of managers toward risk is far more important than any of their moral attitudes, and that antitrust policy will be more effective in deterring illegal behavior if it takes more account of the former than the latter. In consequence, a fine–oriented system would produce less, rather than more, monopolistic behavior. Until attitudes of business management toward risk change, there is no reason to expect that these risk averse managers would ever return to the monopolistic behavior once prevalent in society. Surely the moral inhibitions against such behavior—and perhaps against all illegal behavior—would be reinforced, rather than weakened.

A second potential objection to an increase in fines is that other less tangible disadvantages might accompany it. For example, such an increase might augment the sense of inequity fostered by a system that penalized some but not all violators. The equity in an after–the–fact sense (ex post equity), which is involved whenever some violators of a law are punished and others allowed to go free, decreases as the potential punishment increases. However, to achieve complete ex post equity in antitrust enforcement would entail the apprehension and punishment of all lawbreakers, an employment of resources that would clearly be too costly from the point of view of economic efficiency. At some point a balance must be struck. The crucial question is: how much is society willing to give up to achieve ex post equity?

The answer to this question should be at least partially determined by the amount of equity in the before–the–fact sense (ex ante equity)[25] that exists in the system under examination. Whatever the ex post equity in a fine–oriented system, the ex ante equity in such a system is potentially close to perfect. Each risk preferrer who cold–bloodedly decides to violate the law and enter a cartel could be made to have the same probability of being caught as anyone else. In terms of the government's enforcement efforts, each individual violator could have an equal chance of actually paying the fine. So long as the chances of being detected are equalized at the start under a clear set of rules, perfect ex ante equity can prevail. The existence of this almost perfect ex ante equity, combined with the high costs of achieving additional ex post equity, seems to indicate that a high fine system would not unduly disturb most persons' sense of justice.

Other drawbacks of an increase in fines may, however, be more significant. First, it may be that a high fine, if it represents a sum far in excess of the amount of damage done by a given antitrust violation, will also infringe on

---

[25]The distinction between ex ante and ex post equity is that of Mark V. Pauly and Thomas D. Willett. See Pauly and Willett, "Two Concepts of Equity and Their Implications for Public Policy," *Social Science Quarterly* 53 (June 1972): 8.

most persons' sense of justice. Furthermore, extremely high fines could cause the collapse of businesses that have at least the potential of making substantial contributions to the national economy.

Both of these considerations, however, rather than demanding that fines not be raised at all, simply indicate that there is some ceiling above which they should not go. As applied to many American businesses, the current fine structure certainly does not exceed that ceiling. The Sherman Act's maximum $1 million fine would be only an annoyance for many large firms. Nevertheless, the fact that there is a level of fines beyond which marginal costs begin to be greater than marginal benefits should be kept in mind in designing a specific proposal for a fine–oriented system.

The Fine: A Suggested Approach

It should be clear from this discussion that an absolute monetary exaction should not be set by statute for every antitrust violator. An absolute fine level that might be an enormous deterrent for small firms might not deter larger firms from anticompetitive activity. The ideal fine should be large enough in the case of each individual firm to make its management unlikely to violate the antitrust laws, but it should not be so large as to cause a violator to go out of business or to offend the American sense of equity. Thus one must think in terms of fines based on proportions rather than on absolute amounts. The determination and application of these proportions should result in a fine that would "hurt" each firm just enough to deter a risk averse manager.

Four possible measures of a firm's "ability to pay" come to mind. In the case of the first standard, managerial salaries, fines would be assessed against the managers themselves. If the other three measures—sales, assets, and profits—were used, the fines would be assessed against the violating firms.

Levying fines on managers themselves would not be without advantages. While economists are no longer particularly prone to emphasize the separation of ownership and control in large corporations, some managers' actions may still be insulated from stockholder control and reprisals. These managers may not be as much deterred by a potential fine on their companies' sales, assets, or profits as by the prospect of losing a percentage of their own salaries. Consequently, there is a great temptation to fine directly the businessman engaged in the illegal activity. If accomplished this sort of fine would seem not only to effectuate solid deterrence but also to constitute an equitable incidence of the fine. A manager willfully engaging in anticompetitive behavior should not be able to use a corporate shield to escape punishment.

Two factors, however, militate against levying a proportional fine upon managerial salaries. First, as noted in chapter 3, the task of clearly identifying those responsible for anticompetitive behavior, especially in large corporations, might be excessively difficult;[26] managers would be encouraged to develop very subtle methods of concealing the origins of anticompetitive behavior so that responsibility for the behavior could not be traced to them. A fine based on salaries could thus fall on those not responsible for the illegal activity. Indeed, judges, unsure that imposed fines would fall upon the real violators, might be reluctant to impose fines high enough actually to deter. As in the case of the imprisonment penalty, convictions might be even fewer if such fines were mandatory.

Second, the gains to be had from anticompetitive behavior are frequently so large relative to the salaries of the managers involved that boards of directors would find it tempting to arrange for hidden side payments as "bribes" to management to engage in violations of the antitrust laws. With potentially huge rewards to be gained from anticompetitive action, even a 100 percent fine on salaries would constitute a small amount relative to the potential monopoly gains to the firm. The existence of such potential "gains from trade" would clearly invite the development of means to circumvent the fine structure. Thus, although in an abstract sense levying fines on managers' salaries would unquestionably be an effective deterrent, practical problems of implementation would seem to dictate that the use of such a standard be rejected.

The other three standards impose fines on the violating firms themselves. The sales figure standard has the advantage of being the least susceptible to illegal manipulation. This fact may have led a recent study group to recommend that violations of the Sherman Act be punished by fines equal to a percentage of the violator's sales.[27] However, the benefits of using a sales standard are more than offset by the disproportionately heavy impact that a fine on sales would have upon some firms. Firms with low profits/sales ratios would be hurt far more than those with high profits/sales ratios. In fact, a percentage fine in the range of 1 to 5 percent of sales, which could cause a retailing firm with a high inventory turnover to go out of business, might be easily endured by many manufacturing firms. The deterrent value, equity, and destructive potential of a fine based on sales, then, would fluctuate so widely with the character of the violating firm that the sales standard should be rejected.

---

[26]Reflecting on his hearings on the electrical equipment cartel of the late 1950s, Senator Estes Kefauver wrote: "[I]t has been found that many times, top corporate executives 'wink' at criminal antitrust violations going on right under their noses. Rather than assure that the antitrust laws were being obeyed by their subordinates, such executives take great pains to make certain they have no 'knowledge' of any illegal activities." Press release of Senator Estes Kefauver, July 13, 1961, quoted in "Increasing Community Control over Corporate Crime—A Problem in the Law of Sanctions," *Yale Law Journal* 71 (December 1961): 280, 303 n. 71. See also pp. 297, 302.

[27]Green, *The Closed Enterprise System*, p. 175. The basic proposal of this Nader study group was a fine ranging from 1 percent to 10 percent of the violating firm's sales (during the time of the violation) for the first offense and 5 percent to 10 percent of sales for a second violation within a five-year period.

Basing the fine on assets would produce the same problem of widely varying impacts. Upon conviction for identical offenses, firms with low profit/assets ratios would in effect pay greater fines than firms with high ratios. Fines more than adequate to deter anticompetitive behavior in manufacturing firms (in which there is large investment in durable capital) might not dissuade the management of retailing or other merchandising enterprises with relatively few assets. In addition, the fact that varying depreciation methods in different industries exert a significant effect on the asset figure further reduces its usefulness as a peg upon which to hang the fine structure.[28]

A firm's profits constitute a far more desirable standard for the imposition of fines than either sales or assets. The profit standard would go further than either of the other two toward providing a constant impact, regardless of the sales–assets structures of the firms that are potential violators. Specifically, we suggest that antitrust violations be penalized by a mandatory fine of 25 percent of the firm's pretax profits for every year of anticompetitive activity.[29] Government tax returns would provide a very convenient measure by which to determine the relevant profit figure.

The 25 percent figure is not to be taken as either an estimate of the firm's profits attributable to its antitrust violation or an estimate of the misallocative damage done to society by the firm's anticompetitive activity.[30] Rather than being concerned with compensation, our proposal is directed toward deterrence. The 25 percent figure is not sacrosanct, but it does represent our judgment of a penalty that would deter in an evenhanded fashion. Even a management relatively isolated from its firm's owners would feel the impact from a fine of this magnitude. The experience of lower stock prices, greater difficulties in attracting funds, and an increased probability of a takeover bid would be unpleasant consequences of such a fine. The figure of 25 percent would, on the other hand, not seem so high as to cause violators to go out of business, nor so onerous as to offend most persons' sense of equity. If experience with this percentage finds the antitrust authorities still uncovering frequent violations, Congress could increase it until anticompetitive behavior became rare.

---

[28]Moreover, during a time of inflation, a fine based on assets might impose greater hardships on new firms than on old ones since the older firms are more likely to have their assets undervalued.

[29]Under current antitrust doctrine, the penalty of the fine is used only in criminal cases. Since we are also proposing the use of fines as a deterrent to what have been considered civil violations (such as illegal tying arrangements), we see no need to retain the civil–criminal distinction and would prefer that all antitrust cases be civil ones. Discussions with lawyers have persuaded us that if all antitrust cases were criminal, convictions for heretofore civil violations (such as tying) would be difficult to obtain because the criminal conviction has such an odious connotation. The imposition of fines in civil cases is not unusual—it is a common penalty, for example, for federal tax violations. On the importance of stressing the civil nature of antitrust, see the illuminating discussion by Victor Kramer, "Comment, Criminal Prosecutions For Violations of the Sherman Act: In Search of a Policy," *Georgetown Law Journal* 48 (Spring 1960): 530–542.

[30]Chapter 8 shows that the present state of economic knowledge does not enable these estimations to be made with confidence.

There are, of course, some difficulties in basing the fine on a percentage of company profits. Economists have long noted the inability of current accounting practices to reflect costs rationally and consistently; the vagaries of cost accounting are necessarily reflected in the profit residual. Two problem result. First, a fine on profits may have some disproportionate effects due to different accounting practices among firms and across industries. Second, the malleability of cost figures, coupled with a potential fine on profits, gives management added incentive to hide profits. For example, a firm may have opportunities to engage in activities providing attractive tax shelters. If there were a 25 percent fine on profits, such tax shelters would benefit a firm not only by providing tax savings but also by assuring lower antitrust fines.[31] However, insofar as these problems are deemed substantial, they could be addressed by devising regulations that would use income tax profit figures not as a final base from which to compute antitrust penalties but rather as a starting point for computations.[32]

This recommendation might seem to impose an inappropriately heavy burden on multidivision firms, because the proposed fine is based on a given firm's aggregate profits even though a particular antitrust violation might have been perpetrated by only one of the company's divisions. But determining the corporate profit levels attributable only to the product line where the antitrust violation has occurred could be made extremely difficult through the use of accounting practices that obscured the source of the firm's profits. Moreover, huge multidivision firms, with many sources of profit, would probably not be "hurt" or deterred by the threat of losing a portion of profits in only one division. Furthermore, imposing even relatively frequent but relatively low fines on the profits of single divisions of conglomerates would have particularly little deterrent effect if, as concluded earlier, management is generally risk averse, and if the size and diversity of the enterprise makes the incidence of such fines more or less statistically predictable.

A final difficulty with a proportional standard is that it seems to preclude making adjustments at the margin. A firm engaging in collusive behavior in only one of its divisions, it might be argued, could lose its incentive to be honest in the economic activities of its other divisions when the penalty for violations of the antitrust laws in only one product line would be a fine that took a specific proportion of all profits made in all product lines. This objection might suggest the appropriateness of a progressive fine. After all, a progressive fine would give a potential violator less incentive to try to maximize the amount of profits from illegal corporate activity. Further reflection indicates, however, that

---

[31]This problem should not be overemphasized. It is unlikely that our proposal would cause corporations to engage in much more tax–sheltered activity. Already existing inducements to minimize taxable income have probably exhausted concealment options.

[32]Incremental concealment of profits could if necessary be made less appealing by adjusting the profit figure for antitrust penalty purposes so as to take into account returns that are otherwise hidden through sheltering devices. Firms would then be fined on the basis of an adjusted profit figure.

even with a proportional fine incentives exist to reduce the amount of profits earned from willfully violating the antitrust laws. The expected value of the fine goes up *pari passu* with increasing amounts of illegal activity, since the more any firm engages in such behavior, the more likely are the prospects of its detection and conviction. The situation facing the firm's management is analogous to that faced by a person at a cocktail party who must decide whether to chance driving home under the influence of alcohol. Since the fine for drunk driving is a flat amount regardless of the number of miles driven while intoxicated, it might at first appear that the individual would make the same decision regardless of the number of miles that would have to be driven to reach home. But clearly that is wrong. The probability of detection, and therefore the expected value of the fine, is greater the further the distance to be driven. So adjustments at the margin are made even under a flat rate fine.

The benefits of determining antitrust fines by a profit standard, then, outweigh the costs of using that standard. Considerations of efficiency, ease of administration, and equity together compel the judgment that the profit standard is the most desirable of the four options that have been analyzed here.

Given the general risk aversion of American management, it is more efficient to deter antitrust violations by heavy reliance on financial penalties. In advocating reliance on a single penalty instead of a host of weapons and in recommending the elimination of private damage suits, a mechanism that has been called the "strongest pillar of antitrust,"[33] we are not, we stress, calling for a weakening of the antitrust laws. On the contrary, we are convinced that more discouragement of anticompetitive behavior is needed. But economic analysis involves considering both the benefits and the costs of using the available antitrust material. Thus we do not follow the altogether too common tendency of antitrust literature to simply recommend more of everything—more fines, longer jail terms, bigger government enforcement budgets, enlarged rules of standing, easier access to the courts—with little discussion of the relative efficiencies and costs of these alternatives.

---

[33]L. Loevinger, "Private Action—The Strongest Pillar of Antitrust," *Antitrust Bulletin* 3 (March–April 1958): 167.

List of Contributors

Henry Carter Adams was professor of economics, University of Michigan.

Dominick T. Armentano is professor of economics, Hartford University.

Elizabeth E. Bailey is Hower Professor of Public Policy and Management at the Wharton School, University of Pennsylvania.

Joe S. Bain was professor of economics at University of California, Berkeley.

William Baumol is professor of economics at Princeton and New York Universities.

Robert H. Bork is professor of law, George Mason University.

William Breit is professor of economics, Trinity University, San Antonio, Texas.

Yale Brozen is professor of economics, Graduate School of Business, University of Chicago.

John Bates Clark was professor of economics at Columbia University.

Harold Demsetz is professor of economics, University of California at Los Angeles.

Henry Sturgis Dennison was Director and Deputy Chairman of the Federal Reserve Bank of Boston.

Kenneth Elzinga is professor of economics, University of Virginia.

Joan E. Greenwood is Vice President at Charles River Associates.

Richard H. Fink is Vice President of Governmental Affairs, Koch Industries.

Franklin M. Fisher is professor of economics, Massachusetts Institute of Technology.

John Kenneth Galbraith is professor of economics, Harvard University

Robert Liefman, a prominent German authority on trusts, was professor at the University of Freiburg.

Edward S. Mason is retired professor of economics, Harvard University.

John J. McGowan was Vice President of Charles River Associates, Boston.

Janusz A. Ordover is professor of economics, New York University.

G. B. Richardson is Warden of Keble College, Oxford University, England.

Joseph Schumpeter was professor of economics, Harvard University.

Robert D. Tollison is professor of economics, George Mason University.

Oliver E. Williamson is a professor in the Department of Business Administration and the School of Law at the University of California, Berkeley.

Allyn A. Young was professor of economics, Harvard University.

Index